Social World of Ancient Israel,
1250–587 BCE

Social World
of Ancient Israel
1250–587 BCE

Victor H. Matthews
Don C. Benjamin

HENDRICKSON
PUBLISHERS

Copyright © 1993 by Hendrickson Publishers, Inc.
P.O. Box 3473
Peabody, Massachusetts 01961–3473
All rights reserved
Printed in the United States of America

ISBN 1-56563-948-0

First printing, softcover edition—April 2005

Excerpts on pages 20, 25, 49, 76, 77, 78, 95, 104, 112, 150, 164, 177, 193, 203, 21‹
230, 231, 233 and 245 were taken from V. H. Matthews and D. C. Benjamin, *Ol*
Testament Parallels: Laws and Stories from the Ancient Near East. Copyright (
1991. New York/Mahwah, N.J.: Paulist Press. Used with permission.

Library of Congress Cataloging-in-Publication Data

Matthews, Victor Harold.
     Social World of ancient Israel, 1250–587 BCE / Victor H. Matthews
and Don C. Benjamin
          p.   cm.
     Includes bibliographical references and indexes.
     ISBN 0-913573-89-2
     1. Sociology, Biblical.   2. Jews—Civilization—to 70 A.D.
3. Palestine—Social life and customs—to 70 A.D.   I. Benjamin,
Don C.   II. Title
DS112.M333   1993
306'.0933—dc20   93-34183
                                                                    CIP

For James C. Moyer and Bernice Warren
whose encouragement made this work possible
and
For Dominique DeMenil
whose grant gave Don such generous time to write

Table of Contents

Preface

S*ocial World of Ancient Israel, 1250–587* BCE is a se-
lective, not an exhaustive study of ancient Israel. Although the world of the
Bible comprised at least four different worlds: early Israel (1250–1000 BCE),
the monarchy (1000–587 BCE), the exile (587–537 BCE), and the post-exile
(547–333 BCE), *Social World of Ancient Israel, 1250–587* BCE deals with only two
of these worlds: early Israel (Part I) and the monarchy (Part II). And we
have selected only representative social institutions from these two worlds,
principally those which are most important for understanding the world of
the Bible and those which are most often misunderstood by readers of the
Bible today. Finally, our readings of the biblical texts are meant only to
highlight the way in which a particular social institution functions, not to
provide a complete exegesis. We attempt to show the reader what the social
sciences can do for the interpretation of a text, not to summarize what all
the other methods of interpretation have done for it.

Villages and states were actually a complex of many similar, but distinct
social institutions. To make it easier to understand these similarities and
distinctions, each major part of this volume selects institutions from five
comparable areas of daily life: politics, economics, diplomacy, law, and
education. These five categories, it is hoped, will remind the reader of the
communal character of the biblical world. But to better explain this communal world to a modern audience which understands and appreciates
individuals better than institutions, we have reconstructed one or more
functions of each institution as if they were typical individuals in the world
of the Bible. Therefore, we explain the communal institution of politics with
chapters entitled "The Father" and "The Mother."

Politics is an institution for distributing power to protect and provide for
the village or state. It is the structure developed by a society designed to
match both its ecological constraints and opportunities as well as to maxi-
mize the abilities of households to contribute to the overall success of their
community. In the villages of early Israel, power was distributed to the
households administered by a father (chapter 1) and a mother (chapter 2).

Anthropology of Villages and States

Politics is the power of a father, mother, monarch, or virgin to protect and provide for a village or state.

Economics is the power of a farmer, herder, midwife, priest, or slave to work the land and bear children.

Diplomacy is the power of a host, chief, legal guardian, or prophet to make war or to trade with strangers.

Law is the power of an elder, widow, or lawgiver to solve problems between neighbors.

Education is the power of the wise, the fool, and the storyteller to hand on culture to the next generation.

When Israel was centralized into a state, power was distributed to a monarch (chapter 12). A married and marriageable woman or virgin (chapter 13) in the royal household was a living symbol of the state to be provided for and protected by the monarch.

Economics is power over the land and children of the village or state. It is the power to farm, herd, and bear children. The villages of early Israel used economics to determine how its springs, wells, cisterns, fields, and vineyards were to be preserved, exploited, and shared by various households. The farmer (chapter 3) was responsible for agriculture, and the herder (chapter 4) for the production and care of domestic animals. The mother and the midwife (chapter 5) were responsible for bearing and rearing children. Like the economics of the village, the economics of the state were also concerned with land and children. Taxation and slavery were two important economic institutions which developed the natural and human resources of the state. The priest (chapter 14) collected sacrifices or taxes from the land, and the slave (chapter 15) provided the state with laborers or children.

Diplomacy is the power to deal with the stranger. It is the power to trade and make war. Diplomacy develops external or foreign policies. Trade is the non-violent distribution of people and goods by means of negotiations and covenant. War is the violent distribution of people and goods by means of combat and covenant. The architect of village diplomacy in the world of the Bible was the host (chapter 6). In ordinary circumstances, villages used the host to determine whether strangers were friends or enemies. And they used the chief (chapter 7) and the legal guardian (chapter 8) to deal with extraordinary threats to their ability to work the land and bear children. In a state, the monarch conducted war and trade with foreigners. The prophet monitored the trade and war policies of the monarch (chapter 16).

Law is the power to solve problems between neighbors. The legal system which helped villages in the Mediterranean world solve their internal problems was a code of honor and shame. Villages used the elder (chapter 9) and the widow (chapter 10) to help maintain public order and resolve conflicts. The state used the lawgiver (chapter 17).

Education is the power to hand on culture to subsequent generations. On the one hand, households with similar traditions made up a clan or educational community. A clan or sib used labels to hand on values. Labels were the reactions of the clan to the performance of its households. Labels of honor like "wise" (chapter 11) rewarded a successful household for its performance, while labels of shame like "fool" punished a household which was failing. The state, on the other hand, used the storyteller (chapter 18) to preserve and hand on its traditions which in ancient Israel resulted in the development of the Bible which we have today.

Each chapter begins with an anthropology and ends with an ethnography. The anthropology describes how a social institution like hospitality or prophecy functioned in the ancient Near East. We want this part of the chapter to be clear enough so that after just one reading the reader understands the nature of the institution. It is vital to remember that the social institutions which we reconstruct are typical, not definitive. They are intended to give our readers a sense of what the biblical world was trying to accomplish and how it used a particular institution to achieve that goal. Further study will allow readers to refine, correct, and even challenge our proposals. The ethnography reads one or more biblical texts whose interpretation is enriched by understanding the world which it reflects. We want this part of the chapter to help our readers realize that knowing something about the cultural anthropology of the biblical world makes a difference in the way we read the Bible.

Unless otherwise indicated, we quote the Bible from the *New Revised Standard Version* (NRSV). These quotations point to places in the Bible where, in our opinion, the social institution we have reconstructed can be observed in operation. In some cases the translation in the NRSV is not as accurate from a social scientific perspective as we would like. Nonetheless, we decided not to alter it to support our reconstructions, but instead, to allow our readers to see how differently modern people would translate and read familiar biblical texts if they were better acquainted with the world of the Bible from which they come.

Like *Old Testament Parallels: Laws and Stories from the Ancient Near East* (Paulist Press, 1991), with which we began our writing collaboration, *Social World of Ancient Israel* also wants to make the advances of scholarship in biblical and ancient Near Eastern studies accessible to a wider audience. Both of us are avid undergraduate teachers, one at a public, the other at a private university. Like everyone who teaches or takes an introductory course to the Bible, we too are overwhelmed by more and more topics and texts to teach and to study, and yet we find ourselves with less and less time to do so. Therefore, we have tried to write a book which will be easy to understand and easy to use.

Writing *Social World of Ancient Israel* inevitably made us more conscientious observers of the world in which we live, and the institution of the Scholar, the Teacher, or the Writer to which we belong. Were we to describe the anthropology of our own craft, it would certainly include a description of the thoughtful attention which our colleagues have given to this book during its writing. As expectations for teaching faculty continue to increase, so does our appreciation for the men and women who have made time to search for a draft of one of these chapters on a cluttered desk, read it, and then use their own training and experience to evaluate it for us. Each has immeasurably improved the quality of the work we have tried to do here, and we are grateful to them all. Among those who gave us their time and sent us their assessments are David C. Hopkins (Wesley Theological Seminary, Washington, D.C.), Rabbi Samuel E. Karff (Congregation Beth Israel, Houston, Tex.); Thomas W. Overholt (University of Wisconsin, Stevens Point); Frank J. Glassy, M.D. (Sacramento, Calif.); Michael M. J. Fischer (Rice University, Houston, Tex.); John W. Baker (Rice University, Houston, Tex.), James W. Flanagan (Case Western Reserve University, Cleveland, Ohio), and Patrick H. Alexander, our editor and friend at Hendrickson Publishers.

Victor H. Matthews, Southwest Missouri State University
Don C. Benjamin, Rice University

Introduction: Anthropology and the Bible

The Bible reflects an exotic and fascinating world. Although the world of the Bible is now extinct, the Bible itself remains. And virtually everyone who knows anything about it soon begins to wonder what people in the Bible were really like. *The Social World of Ancient Israel* is a guide for such inquirers, whether they are full-time college students, candidates for congregational ministry, or adult learners. Like every anthropology, *The Social World of Ancient Israel* introduces the people of one time and culture to the people of another. It is a book for those who want to understand biblical people better, so that they can better understand the Bible which they hear, or read, or study, or pray, or according to which they live.

The world in which the Bible developed was dramatically different from the world in which we read the Bible. There are many ways to describe the differences. The world of the Bible, for example, is ancient; our world is modern. It is an Eastern world; ours is Western. The world of the Bible is virtually changeless; our world is ever changing. It is agricultural; ours is industrial. Biblical people think of their goods and resources as limited. We consider ours renewable. They think of themselves as households; we think of ourselves as individuals. In their world old age is a blessing; in our world it is a burden. Their favorite genre of literature is story; ours is history. And perhaps most difficult of all for us to understand, in the world of the Bible there is no separation between religion and daily life or between church and state.

**Sex and Family in the Bible and the
Middle East (Patai 1959:13–14)**

We of the Western world, born and bred in the big cities . . .
find it increasingly difficult to identify ourselves with the characters of the Bible, to recognize the common element in their
lives and in ours, and to apply to our own situation solutions
found by them when they grappled with problems of their
world. . . . In fact, in the majority of cases our behavior, both
the expected and the actual, is the exact opposite of that of
the Biblical characters in analogous situations. Thus, much that
is contained in the Bible—the main source and fountainhead of
our religion—has become in our eyes a mere collection of genre
pictures describing a strange and remote world with which we
have little if anything in common.

These differences are not accidental or superficial. They profoundly influence
the way we live. The values of the world of the Bible are not right and the
values of our world wrong; they are simply different from one another.

An Ancient, Not a Modern World

The world of the Bible is 3,000 years older than our world, and the years
significantly affect our ability to understand it accurately. Even when we
can recall an event, the passage of time blurs the context. Just sorting
through old photos or reading old newspapers reveals how time separates
us even from experiences in which we took part. We stare at a snapshot
and wonder where we were, what we were doing, whether we were happy
or sad. We scan old headlines and find many of them are almost meaningless. We do not know why we took the picture, or why a reporter wrote that
article.

Several calendars have been designed to measure and describe the time
between our worlds. Today, there is a common calendar used for scheduling
business and political events. There are also calendars dating religious and
cultural events. And there are academic calendars which mark developments in a particular art or science. According to the common calendar,
we live in the twentieth century of the Common Era; according to the
Christian calendar we live in the twentieth century AD. Biblical people, on
the other hand, lived in the twelve centuries before the Common Era or in
the twelfth century BC. According to one academic calendar, we live in the
Industrial or the Space Age, while biblical people lived in the Bronze or the
Iron Age.

The common calendar is almost identical to the Christian calendar introduced by Pope Gregory XIII in 1582. In the Christian or Gregorian calendar

the year one—there is no year zero—celebrates the birth of Jesus Christ, and hence is called 1 AD, an abbreviation for the Latin phrase "anno Domini" meaning "in the year of the Lord." Dates before 1 AD in the Christian calendar carry the suffix BC abbreviating the English phrase "before Christ." In the common calendar, the year one marks the beginning of the era common to Jews, Christians, and Muslims, and hence is called 1 CE. Dates before 1 CE carry the suffix BCE. The numbers for the years are exactly the same in both calendars.

Before 1900, anthropologists and archaeologists designed an academic calendar with periods named for the raw materials which humans used to make tools and weapons. Scientists now think the Earth was formed some four and one-half billion years ago and that the first humans probably appeared in Africa about two and one-half million years ago. Since these first humans used stone or flint to make weapons and tools, the archaeological calendar labels the period beginning in 2,500,000 BCE the "Stone Age." The "Bronze Age" begins about 3,000 BCE and the "Iron Age" about 1250 BCE. Although research now shows that the names of the periods in this calendar no longer correspond to the actual dates when humans began to use a particular raw material, they are still used to mark significant thresholds in human development.

An Eastern, Not a Western World

Our world developed from the western Mediterranean cultures of Greece and Rome. The Bible developed in the eastern Mediterranean cultures of Mesopotamia, Syria-Palestine, Asia Minor, and Egypt. Many ways of thinking and doing things which we take for granted did not even exist in the ancient Near East.

For example, philosophical thinking about abstract concepts like goodness and truth and beauty—or even history and religion—are peculiarly Western. In eastern Mediterranean cultures thinking was a graphic, not an abstract process (Breasted 1986:7–8). There are not even words in eastern Mediterranean languages for many of the concepts introduced by Greek philosophy into Western culture.

Likewise, Westerners reason or work out problems in a linear fashion like balancing one playing card on the other. Linear logic or problem-solving was unknown in the ancient Near East. In the world of the Bible, humans reason in a circular pattern like rolling up a ball of yarn or a garden hose. Consequently, discussions in the biblical world like those in the book of Job appear illogical to Westerners. Even though the text says "Job responded," his responses seldom mention the arguments of his dialogue partners. Only when the discussion is complete is it possible to see that the question has been adequately covered.

Eastern people never thought about the world as having been created from nothing (Westermann 1984:98–100; 109–10). Nothing, like other abstract concepts, never appears in their vocabulary (Kramer 1956:71–96). For biblical people, the Creator was not a magician who made something from nothing, but an administrator who organized the cosmos out of chaos. In the beginning there was not a vacuum, but a flood. Creation was a question of management. The Creator knew where everything was supposed to go, and how to put it in place.

A Changeless, Not a Changing World

Our world promotes change, while the Bible endorses stability. In the world of the Bible, change was a threat and a danger. Today change drives our economy, dictates our tastes, and shapes our lives. Today no one really wants to wear old clothes, drive old cars, or espouse old ideas.

**Audit of the Order of Nature
(Eccl 1:4–10)**

A generation goes,
  A generation comes,
  But the earth remains forever.
The sun rises,
  And the sun goes down
  And hurries to . . . where it rises.
The wind blows to the south,
  And goes around to the north.
Round and round goes the wind,
  And on its circuits the wind returns.
All streams run to the sea,
  But the sea is not full.
To the place where the streams flow,
  There they continue to flow. . . .

What has been is what will be. . . .

An Agricultural, Not an Industrial World

Our world today is an industrial world. The foundational metaphors in our world are images drawn from production, which controls and exploits nature. When it is dark we turn on lights. When we want to get up we set an alarm clock. The world of the Bible is agricultural. In an agricultural world human life is synchronized with nature. Work ceases when daylight disappears, and people sleep until it is light again. Farming and herding become the foundational metaphors or basic analogies which people use to understand their daily life (Eilberg-Schwartz 1990:115–40). Agricultural metaphors abound in the Bible. It describes the herder as a draft animal (Hos 10:11), the farmer as an olive tree (Jer 11:16), the childbearer as a vine (Ps 128:3), and the newborn as first fruits (Gen 49:3). It describes Israel's enemies as predators (Isa 5:29) and Yahweh as a shepherd (Ps 23). In an agricultural world, every human challenge can be met by carefully studying the world of plants and animals. God, parents, siblings, friends, sex partners, enemies, and even birth and death are all evaluated by carefully observing nature. The life cycles of plants and animals create an archive of metaphors which farmers and herders use to understand and interpret their relationships. And the world of plants and animals not only mirrors or parallels the human world, but also serves as a model for what the human world should be.

**Land Grant
(Deut 1:6–8)**

The Lord, our God, said to us at Horeb, "You have stayed long enough at this mountain. Leave here and go to the hill country of the Amorites and to all the surrounding regions, the land of the Canaanites in the Arabah, the mountains, the foothills, the Negeb and the seacoast; to Lebanon, and as far as the Great River. I have given that land over to you. Go now and occupy the land I swore to your fathers, Abraham, Isaac and Jacob, I would give to them and to their descendants" (NAB).

A Limited, Not a Renewable World

Today, we consider our resources unlimited or renewable. We are consumers. Biblical people, however, considered their goods and resources to be limited. They were conservationists. They rationed everything because they believed goods were irreplaceable (Malina 1986:87–89). Goods can be redivided, but no new resources can be discovered. For example, there were no new or uninhabited lands where a landless people could migrate without disturbing anyone else. All the land in the world already belonged to someone. If Hebrews without land were ever to have land, they had to take someone else's land. Everything in the world of the Bible already belonged to someone. For anyone to receive, someone had to give. For anyone to win, someone had to lose.

A Communal, Not an Individual World

Today we census our population by counting individual adults. The Bible, in contrast, counted households. Today, a single individual can earn an adequate living, marry, parent, buy, sell, pay taxes, and vote. In the world of the Bible an individual could not survive. An individual was not socially, economically, or politically viable. An individual could not make a living, marry, parent, buy, or sell. The world of the Bible was dyadic, or group-oriented, which means that only members of a household, a village, and a tribe could survive (Malina 1986:18–20). An individual without a household, a village, or a tribe was a convict sentenced to death.

Census
(Num 1:1–20)

The Lord spoke to Moses in the wilderness of Sinai. . . . "Take a census of the . . . Israelites, in their clans, by ancestral houses according to the number of names, every male individually; from twenty years old and upward, everyone in Israel able to go to war. . . ."

Moses and Aaron . . . assembled the whole congregation together. They registered themselves in their clans, by their ancestral houses, according to the number of names from twenty years old and upward, individually, as the Lord commanded. . . .

The descendants of Reuben, Israel's firstborn, their lineage, in their clans, by their ancestral houses, according to the number of names, individually, every male from twenty years old and upward, everyone of the tribe of Reuben were forty-six thousand five hundred.

A World Where Aging, Not Youth, Is a Blessing

Our world idolizes youth and considers old age a burden. Today, the elderly are retired, not sought out for their knowledge and wisdom and experience. The world of the Bible venerates age as an award for experience and an emblem of wisdom. The old are wise; the young are foolish (Blank 1962). The old are teachers; the young are learners (Prov 7:24; 8:32–6; Job 12:12). The old know that without discipline there is failure; the young are easily tempted to think success comes without sacrifice. The young are warriors who have the strength to fight and to die (Num 1:3); but only the old have the wisdom to counsel, to govern, and to prophesy so that the people might live in peace (Jer 1:6; 1 Kgs 3:7; Prov 20:29).

A World of Story, Not History

Common questions asked today about the Bible are: "Did it really happen?" or "Is the Bible history, or just a story?" For modern Westerners, histories are the objective or uninterpreted presentations of the military, political, economic, or cultural events of a nation. This kind of history first became popular in the eighteenth and nineteenth centuries with the rise of Western democracies. Previously, the highly interpreted accounts of a nation were commonly labeled "propaganda." If people were going to be responsible for choosing their own governments, they wanted to form their own interpretations of events, not have them explained by their rulers. We still pride ourselves in being individuals because we have a strong commitment to make up our own minds. We want news or history. We do not want people delivering us editorials, haranguing us with propaganda, or telling us stories. Just give us the facts and we will decide what they mean on our own. Since we place such a premium on the genre of history, we assume that a writing as important as the Bible must be history.

For the people of the biblical world, history as we understand it was almost meaningless. For them, uninterpreted facts were of no help at all in understanding who they were. Consequently, the two most common genres in the Bible are story and law, not history. But biblical stories and laws are not lies or propaganda. Storytellers in the world of the Bible did not just make up the Bible, but they did explain what was going on around them in colorful and artistic language, which we lovers of history must patiently learn to understand and appreciate. History is the genre of "what happened?" Story is the genre of "what does it mean?" One does not exclude the other, but they are different. The historian is a scientist; the storyteller is an artist. Both make only limited observations of all that occurs in their worlds.

A World of Established Religions, Not Religious Pluralism

Culture, society, and religion were coextensive in the biblical world. There was no atheism and there was no separation of church and state. These are modern legal fictions whose role in contemporary Western and industrial cultures is certainly important, but played a minor role in the world of the Bible. Culture, society, and religion are terms which refer to a traditional complex of social institutions governed by law and handed on from one generation to the next by tradition. They include all the reactions, habits, techniques, ideas, values, and behaviors which humans learn and teach. Culture, society, and religion are specifically and exclusively human products (Kroeber 1948:7–8). Humans are unique in being able to speak, to create symbols, to abstract, and to generalize. No other creatures can transcend time and influence other generations with these faculties by handing on their learning, knowledge, and accomplishments.

Religion pervaded every activity of daily life in the world of the Bible (Breasted 1986:4). It was never limited to a single day or a prayer before eating or sleeping. Biblical people used religion to explain and to manage their natural surroundings. Every hour of the day had its religious significance, every season of the year had its sacred feast days, and the ordinary and extraordinary chores of every household were celebrated with ritual. The religion of the ancient world inspired its culture, and handed it on from one generation to the next. Every art and science was sacred, and had a different purpose and a different motivation from the art and science of today. In the biblical world the arts and sciences were a profession of faith. Consequently, there is no single chapter in *Social World of Ancient Israel* on the religion of ancient Israel because every chapter about its world is a chapter about its religion.

Anthropology: A Definition

Despite all the differences between the world in which the Bible developed, and the world in which we use the Bible today, there is still a common humanity and a common search for a fully human life which draws these two worlds together. In both worlds there are people searching for their proper place with one another, with nature, and with God.

Anthropology is a social science which can open many doors between today's world in which the Bible is read and yesterday's world in which the Bible developed. By observation, not by laboratory experiment, anthropology seeks to understand the principles that govern human physical and cultural development (Beals and Hoijer 1971:5). Anthropologists ask: "What kind of creatures are human? What kinds of humans are there? How did humans evolve? How were they distributed over the earth? How are human communities organized? How do their social institutions work? What kinds of arts and sciences do humans use? And how do necessity, reason, and luck influence human development?" (Montagu 1974:23). One of the most important questions in anthropology concerns how the physical constitution of humans and their cultural characteristics are related. What is the relationship between nature and nurture (Kroeber 1948:2; Beals and Hoijer 1971:3)?

Because so many human physical developments were stimulated by cultural evolution, physical anthropology and cultural anthropology are interdependent. For example, hunting, a cultural development, stimulated such human physical developments as upright posture which freed the hands for toolmaking and led to the expansion of the brain. And human hunters developed improved functional traits like the ability to solve problems (Montagu 1974:xii). During the nineteenth century, scholars like Charles Darwin and Carveth Read worked to understand the extent to which anatomy and culture depend on one another.

Although anthropology is related to a wide range of other social sciences, it principally studies the behavior and material culture of humans as a group, as do history, political science, economics, sociology, and geography, rather than the human individual as psychology does. Sociology is the area of anthropology which studies how cultures organize themselves (Kroeber

1948:7–10). Although, originally, sociology studied only existing cultures, today it is equally interested in ancient and extinct cultures (Kroeber 1948: 12; Gottwald 1979).

History of Anthropology

Today, anthropology does not assume evolution or progress, although such assumptions were once common (Kroeber 1948:6). And the relationship of one culture to another is predetermined not by chronology or by its relationship to twentieth-century Western, industrial culture. Earlier human cultures and the practices of cultures which differ from those in twentieth-century, Western, industrial culture are not, because of that fact, primitive or savage (Douglas 1966:23–24; pace Tylor 1891).

In antiquity, there was an interest in the world of the Bible even before the Bible was canonized in the shape we have it today (Kohler 1957:11–12). Ancient geographers, for example, noted that the Mount of Olives "lies before Jerusalem on the east" (Zech 14:14), and ancient anthropologists explained that "the one who is now called a prophet was formerly called a seer" (1 Sam 9:9).

Likewise, Herodotus, who lived between 484–425 BCE, has often been called the first anthropologist (Montagu 1974:21–47). His supporters point out that more than half of the nine volumes in his History study the peoples known to the Greeks under the same basic categories used in anthropology today (Kroeber 1948:13). He describes the kinship, marriage, economics, technology, and religion of the peoples whom he encounters (Bereman 1971:33). However, Herodotus' critics disqualify him from the honor of being the first anthropologist because of his ethnocentrism. He judged every other culture on the basis of Greek culture and concluded that all other cultures were barbaric (Rowe 1965:2; Hoebel 1972:56).

During the Renaissance, a concern for the social world of ancient Israel also appears in the interpretive tradition. For example, Cornelius Bertramus published a book on the relationship of religion and government in biblical Israel (1574); Cavolus Sigonius wrote a study of biblical politics (1583); Martinus Geier composed a work on biblical ritual (1656). Johannes Henricus Ursinus concentrated his research on the trees of the Bible (1663), and Hadrianus Relandus wrote a book on the monuments of antiquity in Palestine (1716).

During the nineteenth century W. Robertson Smith (1889) introduced anthropology into his study of the Bible by comparing the culture of ancient Israel with the culture of bedouin Arabs. But it was during the twentieth century that the groundbreaking work of Hermann Gunkel on biblical folklore (1917) and of Alfred Bertholet (1919), Johannes Pedersen (1920), and Gustaf Dalman (1928–39), on the culture of biblical Israel, pioneered the use of anthropology in biblical interpretation. Slowly it became apparent that while naming and dating the principal persons, places, and events may be appropriate for understanding written literature, these are less critical when working with oral tradition. Oral tradition avoids naming names and accepts a timelessness that blurs dates. Interpreting oral tradition requires an understanding of the social institution (German: *Sitz im Leben*) in which these traditions developed and were told. Social institutions use oral traditions to educate and to motivate people in the essentials of survival. It is as important to study Israel's social institutions to understand its traditions as it is to study Israel's traditions to understand its social institutions.

But despite these breakthroughs few biblical scholars immediately began using anthropology to interpret the Bible (Rowley 1952). There was the work of Albrecht Alt on the early forms of Israelite tradition and state development (1925, 1929, 1930), of Roland de Vaux, who attempted a reconstruction of the life and institutions of ancient Israel (1958), and of Martin Noth, who examined Israel's tribal system (1960). Nonetheless, anthropologists continued to include ancient Israel in their research (Lewis 1971; Kapelrud 1967; Eliade 1964; Evans-Pritchard 1964). One such classic study was *Ancient Judaism*, published in 1920 by the German sociologist Max Weber; another was *Myth, Legend and Custom in the Old Testament* by Theodor Gaster, who pursued Gunkel's interests in folklore (1950, 1969). But by the end of the twentieth-century, biblical scholars were applying the work of anthropologists to virtually every area of daily life in the world of the Bible. Some of the most vital work being done by anthropologists today has great significance for understanding the Bible and its world. Every chapter of *Social World of Ancient Israel* cites their works, which are collected together in the bibliography at the end of the book.

The Savage in Judaism
(Eilberg-Schwartz 1990:239–40)

Jews have frequently been presented as a "People of the Book." But it would be equally appropriate to describe them as a "People of the Body." The former description emphasizes the life of the mind and the importance of learning within the tradition. But at the same time it diverts attention from the fact that those books, which were of such obsessive interest, were deeply concerned about the body and other equally mundane matters. The anthropology of Judaism thus allows Judaism to be embodied even if its God is not.

Culture is always a delicate blend of story and daily living, of mythos and ethos. Mythos is the story a people tell. Ethos is the way a people live. Biblical scholars study one, anthropologists the other. It is impossible to understand any culture, ancient or modern, without studying both. Stories make sense only in the light of the social institutions where they develop, and social institutions are intelligible only when they are interpreted in stories. Biblical people preserved their cultural identity not simply by repeating their stories, but by developing social institutions which reflected their values. Throughout every period of biblical history—early Israel, the monarchy, the exile and the post exile—mythos and ethos together helped the biblical people maintain their identity. To divorce mythos and ethos—to study only the Bible without its social world—incorrectly assumes that ideas alone, disconnected from material and social reality, have the power to transform individuals and society (Elliott 1986:76–77). They do not. If we are to continue to study the Bible of ancient Israel profitably, we must better understand the world from which it comes.

PART I

Ancient Israel as Villages

The two most important social institutions in the Mediterranean world were the village and the state. Both appear in the Bible. Early Israel was a village culture, and the monarchy was a city culture or state. Villages use a decentralized political system to feed and protect their people; states use a centralized system.

The first Hebrew villages appeared in the hills or highlands of Judah, west of the Jordan River and north of Jerusalem. Archaeological surveys suggest that their initial growth took place around 1250 BCE (I. Finkelstein 1989:53–59; Zertal 1986; Kochavi 1972). No dates for the ancient world are absolutely accurate, but some are more accurate than others. Three prominent wars help date the appearance of these Hebrew villages.

The Appearance of Hebrew Villages

Egypt and the Hittites (1286 BCE)

The first war took place around 1286 BCE. Pharaoh Ramses II of Egypt and Hattusilis III, the Great King of the Hittites in today's central Turkey, battled at Kadesh on the Orontes River in today's Syria. For more than one hundred years, Egypt and Hatti had wrestled for control of Syria-Palestine. The conflict drained the resources of both super powers. Following this famous but inconclusive battle at Kadesh a treaty was signed.

In the early 1900s archaeologists recovered both Egyptian and Hittite versions of the treaty. In the Egyptian version, Ramses II elaborates his role in negotiating the treaty. He had one copy carved in hieroglyphics on the walls of the Temple of Amon in Karnak and another on the walls of the Ramesseum, his funeral chapel in the Valley of the Kings. Both are located near today's Luxor in central Egypt. The Hittite edition is a more sober legal document written on clay tablets in Akkadian cuneiform, which was the diplomatic language of the ancient Near East. Archaeologists recovered the tablets from the archives of Hattusas, the Hittite capital.

The treaty of Ramses II and Hattusilis III was a remarkable political and military accomplishment. It was motivated both by Egypt's and Hatti's need for economic recovery and the increasing military threat of the Sea Peoples migrating across the islands of today's Greece and into the eastern Mediterranean. The treaty ended the war and liberated the people of Syria-Palestine from both Egyptian and Hittite domination. Peace ensued for virtually the next fifty years. But the withdrawal of the Egyptians and the Hittites from Syria-Palestine was not an unqualified blessing for its indigenous peoples. Population, for example, dropped dramatically. Cities and towns collapsed, trade caravans vanished, and the Late Bronze period (1500–1250 BCE) came to an end (Coote and Whitelam 1987:122, 129). By 1250 BCE perhaps sixty percent of the people of Syria-Palestine had died from starvation due to crop failures, which followed subtle changes in climate and the exhaustion of natural resources. Famine led inevitably to the outbreak of regional wars and endemic diseases aggravated by shifting populations. These disasters were not isolated and sporadic but ongoing. Some of Egypt and Hatti's former villagers and slaves in Syria-Palestine took advantage of their freedom and tried to insure their households against an uncertain future by migrating into the hills where they reestablished abandoned villages or founded new ones of their own. Among these refugees were the ancestors of biblical Israel.

Egypt in Syria-Palestine (1224–1214 BCE)

The second war took place during the reign of Pharaoh Merenptah (or Merneptah; 1224–1214 BCE), who commissioned his scribes to prepare a hymn of victory celebrating his triumph over the Libyans in the fifth year of his reign. They used a stele originally inscribed by Amenhotep III (1398–1361 BCE). In 1896, excavators recovered this granite column, which is almost seven and one-half feet high and three and one-quarter feet wide, from Merenptah's funeral chapel at Thebes. It is now in the Egyptian Museum in Cairo. The end of this hymn includes an excerpt from his annals recording similar victories over Asiatic peoples in Syria-Palestine. The stele contains the only mention of Israel yet discovered from the Egypt of this period. As a result, it has been used to argue that the Israelite group which Merenptah encounters in Syria-Palestine before 1200 BCE was founded by the Hebrews who must have fled Egypt before 1250 BCE.

Sea Peoples' Invasion of Egypt (1194–1163 BCE)

The third war took place between 1194 and 1163 BCE. The outside walls of Medinet Habu, which is the funeral chapel of Ramses III in the Valley of the

Kings in Egypt, celebrate Egypt's war with the Sea Peoples. Following their invasion of Egypt, some of the Sea Peoples settled along the coast of Syria-Palestine to become the Philistines of the Bible. The arrival of the Sea Peoples after 1200 BCE was a major influence in the centralization of the Hebrew villages by David to form a state after 1000 BCE.

Therefore, based on current archaeological dates for the war between Egypt and the Hittites (1286 BCE), Egypt's wars in Syria-Palestine (1224–1214 BCE), and the war between Egypt and the Sea Peoples (1194–1163 BCE), many scholars now date the appearance of ancient Israel to 1250 BCE, after the end of the Late Bronze period and before peoples like the Philistines and Israel in Syria-Palestine began to affect seriously the foreign policies of Egypt.

Establishment of Hebrew Villages

Some of the stories in the books of Joshua and Judges describe the arrival of these settlers as a conquest, but other stories portray their arrival as part of a mass migration from or as a revolt against the cities on the plains along the Mediterranean coast (Isserlin 1983:85-93). Throughout Syria-Palestine's history, herders migrated from the Sinai and other regions to settle there (Strange 1987:18). But it seems unlikely that all these villages were founded by Hebrews who invaded Syria-Palestine like the Sea Peoples (Albright 1966), or by migrants who infiltrated unoccupied areas (Alt 1925; Noth 1960) or by revolutionaries who overthrew the states of Syria-Palestine (Mendenhall 1973; Gottwald 1979). The settlement picture is too complex to credit any one of these groups exclusively.

Furthermore, archaeological evidence that these Hebrews were outsiders or invaders is questionable. The material remains in their villages are neither foreign nor military. And nothing in the ruins of these villages points to the Hebrews as warriors who invaded Canaan or revolutionaries who overthrew it. These villagers were farmers and herders from civilization centers in the foothills and on the plains of Syria-Palestine, not nomads from the desert (de Geus 1976:159; Ahlstrom 1984:171). The economy of these villagers was agricultural, not military. They left almost no weapons for excavators to discover. They built few walled towns or monumental buildings. Giloh, south of Jerusalem, is a major exception. They came from inside, not outside, Syria-Palestine. The writing, language, material culture, and religious traditions of the Hebrews who resettled or founded these villages link them to the Canaanite culture found throughout Syria-Palestine (M. Smith 1990:1–40). However, given the disintegration in the previously heavily populated areas of the coastal plain and the foothills, these villages were not simply colonies founded by the cities of the plain (Frick 1989:90). These pioneers did not wage war, they survived war. What these

early villagers had in common was that they were social survivors who fled
the famine, plague, and war which brought the Bronze Age to an end
(Stiebing 1989). These Hebrews were segments of the population who for
environmental or economic reasons removed themselves from the urban
centers of Canaan and settled into a politically less complex society in the
hills along the Jordan (Chaney 1983:51; Lenski and Lenski 1978:229). They
left a centralized state culture and created a decentralized village culture
(Salzman 1980:4). There was no stigma to be attached to their decision. It
was simply a sign of the adaptability and flexibility inherent within the
world of the Bible at the end of the Late Bronze period.

Nonbiblical literature from the period suggests that these villages may
have originally been no more than camps from which bandits (Akkadian:
ḫāpiru) raided caravans on their way to and from Damascus (Judg 11:4–11;
Coote and Whitelam 1987:131; Soggin 1981:207). After the battle of Kadesh,
it was impossible for Egypt, Mycenae, and Hatti to protect the trade lanes
along which their ships and caravans traveled. As a result, the goods upon
which these bandits preyed soon disappeared. This made it necessary for
the bandits to agree to cease hostilities and cooperate with one another in
order to meet the environmental and economic challenges of life in a
marginal region, now cut off completely (Coote and Whitelam 1987:132).

Hebrew villages were politically quite simple and egalitarian societies
(Chaney 1983:51; Lenski and Lenski 1978:229). Archaeologists have identified more than three hundred village sites in the hills which date from the
Iron I period (1250–1000 BCE). Ninety percent were new foundations (Hopkins 1987:178–91; Callaway 1983:53). For example, in one sample of 136
villages, 97 did not exist before 1250 BCE (Stager 1985:2–3; Hopkins 1985:139).
Similar villages appear east of the Jordan, which the Bible calls Gilead
(Mazar 1990:337). The villages were small and scattered. Most were only
one-acre parcels of land. There were some 50–300 inhabitants per village.
For example, Ai was a modest 2.75-acre village founded about 1220 BCE on
the site of a 27.5 acre city destroyed at the end of the Early Bronze period
(3000–2000 BCE). The nearest village was Khirbet Raddana, four miles west
(Callaway 1983:43).

The archaeological record shows the Hebrews were remarkably successful
at maximizing their labor and spreading their risks (Hopkins 1985:225, 256;
Mendenhall 1976b:143–44; Gottwald 1979:257–84; Wilson 1983:63; Lemche
1988:90–99). The number of villages without walls and other defenses increased rapidly. Between 1000 and 800 BCE their population expanded to
80,000, and more than 100 new villages were founded in the hills of
Samaria, Galilee to the north, and the Beersheba basin to the south (Dar
1986:2; Kochavi 1972:154–55; Stager 1985:3). Every household shared in the
labor intensive work of terracing, planting, and processing the grain and
fruit. More and more agriculturally marginal land was turned into productive farms and vineyards. What was not consumed was stored in huge

buildings like those at Raddana, Shiloh, and Tel Masos as a check against famine (Hopkins 1985:169–70).

Early Hebrew villages farmed a combination of wheat and barley, depending on the quality of the soil, temperature, and rainfall. Villagers also produced and processed flax to make linen (Josh 2:6). They cared for fig and olive trees and skillfully managed grape vines on terraced hillside plots. They cleared new areas of their scrub forest and cultivated the land, using wooden or iron blades (Aharoni 1967:219; Hopkins 1985:223).

A significant influence on the social structure of early Israel was where its pioneers chose to live. They fled from the coast with its trade routes, commercial centers, and farms where no one was safe to pioneer villages in the hills just north of Jerusalem. Here the land was safe, but it was barren and rugged and demanding, all of which would affect the society which developed there and the roles which men and women would play in it. Here in the hills there would be no surplus to fuel the economy as there had been in the cities below. The surplus economies of the Bronze Age were built by monarchs, soldiers, and slaves. Monarchs provided a centralized government for the great cities, soldiers controlled its population and expanded its borders, and slaves produced goods for trade. It was an efficient but brutal system. Taxation, slavery, and war painfully affected the lives of all but a minority of the people who lived in these states. When great wars of commerce and conquest brought down the international trade empires of Mycennae, Hatti, and Egypt about 1250 BCE, survivors in Syria-Palestine had neither the resources nor the desire to rebuild the social system which had enslaved them. Therefore, the economy of early Israel was not a surplus or slave economy, but a subsistence economy. There would be no monarchs, no soldiers, no slaves, no taxes, and no war. It was a demanding and idealistic society. Nonetheless, it lasted almost 250 years.

1

The Father

$\mathbf{T}$he basic community in the Bible was the extended family or household headed by a father (בית אב, *bêt 'āb*, בית, *bayit*). The household was made up of as many sets of childbearing adults and their dependents (גבר, *geber*) as was necessary for the entire group to feed and protect itself (Stager 1985:22; de Geus 1976:133–35; Gottwald 1979: 285–92; Lemche 1985:245; Netting, Wilk, and Arnould 1984; Yanagisako 1979; Hopkins 1985). Occasionally, the Bible refers to the basic community in early Israel as the household of a mother (בית אמה, *bêt 'immâh*; Gen 24:28; Ruth 1:8; Cant 3:4; 8:2), especially in texts dealing with sexuality, marriage, and strong female protagonists (Levine 1992:80).

In the Bedouin household today (Arabic: *khamseh*), there are five generations. The household tree begins with the father of the household and all his brothers or his father's sons, to which are added the two preceding generations and the two following generations. The preceding generations include his father and uncles or his father's brothers and his grandfather and great-uncles or his grandfather's brothers. The two following generations include his sons and his grandsons (Patai 1959:125). The book of Leviticus (Lev 18:6–18), however, omits the grandfather and his brothers from the household (Wolff 1974:166; Elliger 1966:239). It constructs the household with only four generations: the father of the household and his brothers; his father and his uncles; his sons and his grandsons.

Kinship and Covenant

The household was part of a remarkably sophisticated system for distributing power. Like many traditional societies, the society of the Bible describes Israel's political system as kinship. Patterns of kinship in the Bible are preserved in genealogies (Edelman 1991:179–201; Johnson 1969:3–36; Wilson 1975:169–89; Wilson 1977:195–205; Smith 1903:1–19; J. Finkelstein

1966:95–118; Malamat 1968:163–73; Malamat 1973:126–36; Wilson 1979c:11–22). Genealogies describe not only blood relationships, but also economic relationships, social status, financial worth, and the power which a household can exercise in the community as a whole (Barth 1973b:6; Bloch 1973:77; Sahlins 1968: 10–11; Wolff 1966:8; Malina 1981:25–93). To understand a genealogy it is necessary to understand what particular social system it reflects and the language which it uses (Steinberg 1989:44; Rendsburg 1990:203).

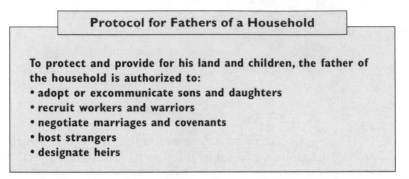

Protocol for Fathers of a Household

To protect and provide for his land and children, the father of the household is authorized to:
• adopt or excommunicate sons and daughters
• recruit workers and warriors
• negotiate marriages and covenants
• host strangers
• designate heirs

Neither covenant nor blood kinship ever completely replaced one another (Fox 1967:13). Even when villages distributed power from parents to children and between brothers and sisters, this kinship was ratified by covenant. No blood relationship was taken for granted. And although members of households, clans, villages, and tribes in early Israel may have been physically related, the critical requirement for membership was not kinship, but covenant (Meyers 1988:127). The Hebrews were not just households with the same biological parents, but households with the same sociological experience and a shared legal commitment to one another. To be a Hebrew was to have passed from slavery to freedom; some through the waters of the Red Sea (Exod 5—18), some through the waters of the river Jordan (Josh 1—5), and some through the waters of the wadi Kishon (Judg 4—5).

The interaction between kinship and covenant creates differences between the meanings of terms like "father," "mother," "son," "daughter," "brother," "sister," "uncle," or "nephew" in the Bible, and the way we use these titles in everyday speech. In the Bible, their connotations are often more legal than biological (Steinmetz 1991:13; Oden 1983; Donaldson 1981). They identify a variety of people besides blood relatives (Bright 1981:98–100). The father of a household was not just someone who sired, but someone who fed and protected (Hanson 1989:75–84). "Son" (בֵּן, bēn), "slave" (עבד, 'ebed) and "brother" (אח, 'āḥ) in the Bible are often technical terms for covenant partners, people related to one another, not necessarily by blood, but by covenant (Josh 14:8; Num 14:24; Benjamin 1983:215; McCarthy 1978:222, 279n, 288).

In the books of Samuel–Kings, Ahaz, monarch of Judah, acknowledges his treaty with Tiglath-Pileser III, ruler of Assyria, by saying: "I am your servant and your son" (2 Kgs 16:7). The book of Amos indicts Tyre for betraying "the covenant of brotherhood" (Amos 1:9) or its covenant partners. The convention of using family titles outside the family was common throughout the ancient Near East (Meyers 1988:127–28; Wilson 1985:302). In Babylon, master craftsmen were called "fathers" and their apprentices were called "sons" (CH 188–89; Driver and Miles 1960: vol. 1:392–95). In Nuzi, an important Mesopotamian city around 1500 BCE located in northern Iraq today, master herders and scribes were fathers and their apprentices were sons (Wilhelm 1970:8–11).

The clan, the village, and the tribe were the three most crucial forms of kinship and covenant into which a household could enter to protect and enrich its land and children. Households with similar traditions formed a sib or clan (מִשְׁפָּחָה, mišpāḥâh). It was the clan which told ancestor stories like those of Jacob, Leah, and Rachel in the book of Genesis (Gen 25:20—37:2) and those of David's rise to power in the books of Samuel–Kings (1 Sam 13:1—2 Sam 1:27). The clan was primarily an educational community, but it also played a strategic role in inheritance (Pedersen 1926:46–60). It handed on unique skills from one generation to the next in stories that celebrate the ancestors who first taught the clan how to survive. Clan skills were always matched to particular natural resources. For example, clans allowed only skilled herders to inherit livestock and only skilled brewers to inherit beer vats.

Clans sharing the same natural resources formed a lineage or village (כֹּפֶר, kōper; 1 Sam 6:18). The village determined how its springs, wells, cisterns, fields, and vineyards were to be preserved, exploited, and shared by various clans (Josh 13—19; Bohannan and Bohannan 1968:13–24). It also provided for some specialization in the labor which each clan contributed.

Villages insured themselves against war and natural disasters like famine, epidemic, and other catastrophes by creating a phratry, chiefdom, or tribe (שֵׁבֶט, šēbeṭ; אֶלֶף, 'elep). Tribes spread the risk faced by the several hundred adults who made up a village to the thousands who made up a tribe (Sahlins 1968:16; Sahlins 1967:96; Fried 1967:14). When a village became unable to feed itself, the tribe provided a legal guardian (יָבָם, yābām; Latin: levir); when it became unable to protect itself, the tribe provided a judge (שֹׁפֵט, šōpēṭ) or chief (נָשִׂיא, nāśî').

Life and Death

The father exercised the power of life and death in the household. But the authority of the father was not absolute. For example, he did not have the power of life and death over his grandsons, his brothers, his father, his grandfathers, or his uncles. His primary responsibility was for his wives and their sons and daughters. Likewise, the father was not a despot. He was "to be fruitful and multiply, and fill the earth and subdue it" (Gen 1:28). In Hebrew, "subdue" (כבשׁ, *kābaš*) and "have dominion" (רדה, *rādâh*) certainly can imply a use of force (Num 32:22–29; Josh 18:1; 2 Sam 8:11; Esth 7:8; Isa 14:2), but fathers were not expected to be ruthless (Wolff 1974:163–64).

When the father exercised his authority to determine how the household would farm and herd, he was the image of the Creator feeding and protecting (Gen 1:26; 9:6; Ps 8; Wolff 1974:159–61; Benjamin 1992). The tradition identifying the father with the Creator was widespread in the world of the Bible. For example, Egypt celebrated its pharaoh as the image of the Creator. Both Ramses II's hymn to Ra as father (1290–1224 BCE) and his relief in the Nahr el-kelb, between Beruit and Byblos in today's Lebanon, describe the authority of Ramses as the father of Egypt and of Syria-Palestine as if he were Ra the Creator (Pritchard *ANET* 1969: 335).

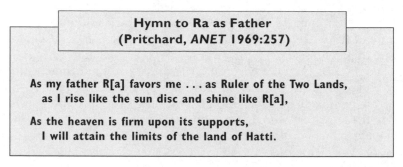

**Hymn to Ra as Father
(Pritchard, *ANET* 1969:257)**

As my father R[a] favors me . . . as Ruler of the Two Lands,
as I rise like the sun disc and shine like R[a],

As the heaven is firm upon its supports,
I will attain the limits of the land of Hatti.

But despite their use of the image of the Creator tradition to describe the father of a household, the Hebrews carefully distinguished the power of the father from the power of Yahweh over the children and the land. Fathers covered their genitals during worship (Exod 28:42), and removed their sandals upon entering a sanctuary (Exod 3:5). Genitals symbolized power over children and sandals denoted power over land. No signs of reproductive ability or land ownership were displayed before Yahweh.

The father exercised his power over life and death by adopting sons and daughters into his household and resolving conflicts between them; recruiting workers and warriors; negotiating marriages and covenants; hosting strangers and designating heirs. These were public or common powers which determined how the resources of the household were to be invested in the village, the clan, the tribe, and eventually in the state.

Adoptions

At the time a child was born, the father had to decide whether or not to adopt it into the household (Patai 1959:135; Qur'an 16:58–59). In the world of the Bible, life began not with a viable birth, but only with adoption. Regardless of the status of the newborn at the moment of delivery, without adoption it was considered stillborn. If the father did not adopt the child, the midwife took it from the birthing room and left it in an open field to declare it eligible for adoption by another household (Ezek 16:3–5; Stager and Wolff 1984:50; Patai 1959:127).

Legal Disputes

Birth was not the only occasion on which the father exercised his power of life and death over his sons and daughters. The commandment "honor your father and mother" (Exod 20:12) expects the members of a household to fulfill concrete political expectations, not simply to react to the whims of its father in blind obedience or with vague devotion and deference (Lemert 1967:6; Pitt-Rivers 1977:117). Sons honored their father and mother by a willingness to farm, to herd, and to bear children for the household. When a son failed to honor his father and mother, it was the father who had the authority to judge the case.

Any son who cursed (קלל, qālal) or refused to support the household financially (Exod 21:17) or who physically assaulted the mother and father of the household could be sentenced to death (Exod 21:15). An assault against one member of the household by another was also a failure to honor its father and mother. Fathers determined restitution for bodily harm done to the sons of their households on the basis of work days lost (Exod 21:18–19). Since maiming the assailant would only extend the damage inflicted on the household by depriving it of two workers, restitution benefited the household of the assailant as well as the victim.

Restitution for bodily harm done to women was calculated on their ability to bear children following the assault. If a member of a household who is involved in a fight caused a woman to miscarry, the father of her household was to determine the fine which must be approved by the village assembly (Exod 21:22–24). The fetus was already the property of the household, which might be permanently damaged by losing this unborn life.

And whenever one member of the household killed another, the father of the victim's household was responsible for prosecuting the case. Sometimes fathers prosecuted murders by designating a legal guardian (Num 35:19; גאל, gōʾēl) to execute the killer, but generally they shared their power to prosecute with the fathers of the other households in their village assembly.

In the world of the Bible, killing was a legal tort which required compensation, rather than a crime which required punishment. If the killer was from the same household as the victim, the offense was fratricide; if the killer came from another household it was murder.

The village assembly punished murder according to the norms of reciprocity which required that a life be given for a life. But even when an assembly sentenced a murderer to death, it executed its sentence in more than one way. For example, the assembly could impose the death sentence on the actual murderers, but it could also execute any other member of the household in their place. Likewise, the assembly could also allow the killer's

---

Story of the Heavens and the Earth
(Gen 1:26–28)

Then God said,

"Let us make humankind in our image,
   according to our likeness;
. . . let them have dominion over the fish of the sea,
   and over the birds of the air,
   and over the cattle,
   and over all the wild animals of the earth,
   and over every creeping thing . . . upon the earth."

So God created humankind in his image,
   in the image of God he created them;
   male and female he created them.

God blessed them,
   and God said to them,

"Be fruitful and multiply,
   and fill the earth and subdue it;
And have dominion over the fish of the sea
   and over the birds of the air
   and over every living thing . . . upon the earth."

---

household to pay compensation to the victim's household (Pitt-Rivers 1977: 119). The assembly imposed a death sentence when it determined that a swift execution of justice would best restore the balance of power in the village (Exod 21:12). It permitted compensation when it decided that the taking of one life should not deprive the village of another (Exod 21:13–14). Compensation spared the life of the killer by transferring the killer's contribution in land and children to the household of the victim. In Africa, village assemblies often commute the death sentence to paying a fine of livestock, or providing the victim's household with a human being physically comparable to the victim, or with a woman who will bear a child for the victim's household (Schapera 1985:31).

Work and War

The labor of every worker was also the property of the household. The father determined if and when and how his household would participate in the efforts of the village to feed and protect itself. He enjoyed the authority over its resources and he was held responsible for determining the extent to which workers from his household could be committed to work on village projects in both peacetime and in war.

Marriage and Covenant

There were certainly sexual relationships in the ancient Near East which reflected the deep personal and emotional love of one person for another. There was romance in the world of the Bible, just as there is romance in every other world. The Bible describes romance not only between unmarried men and women (Cant 5:10–16; 8:1–4), but also between husbands and wives (Gen 24:67; 29:16–20; Judg 14:3; 1 Sam 1:5; 18:20; 25:44; 2 Sam 3:15; 11:27), and between husbands and concubines (Exod 21:7–11).

But not every reference to romance in the Bible refers to affairs of the heart. For example, the "wife of your youth" (Prov 5:18–20) and the "good wife" (Prov 31:10–31) in Proverbs refer to the wise woman who teaches the student discipline, not to a woman with whom the learner is in love. Likewise, the "loose woman" (Prov 5:2–5) is a fool who teaches the student that success can be achieved without discipline, not a woman with whom the learner is having an affair (Camp 1985:79–149).

But in the world of the Bible, sexual relationships were more than romantic, they were political and economical as well. Sexual relationships held societies like early Israel together (Levi-Strauss 1969; Janeway 1980:4–20). Marriage was a delicately negotiated covenant sealing a significant political or economic contract (Pitt-Rivers 1977:160; Levinson and Halpern 1980: 508). It was designed to bring together two households that were willing to exchange substantial goods and services with each other over a significant period of time (Gen 24:3–4; 34:21; Exod 2:21; 1 Sam 25:43). Marriage was more a matter of business than of pleasure.

Consequently, men and women themselves rarely chose their own sexual partners. It was the father of the household who was responsible for safeguarding the status of the men and women in his household and then deciding which were eligible to marry. The legal eligibility of marriageable men or women within the household was determined by codes of sexuality and gender roles (Peristiany 1965:9; Gilmore 1987:3–4; Giovannini 1987:67). And the legal eligibility of the men for marriage was determined by different criteria than the legal eligibility of women. Virginity (בתולים, *b^etûlîm*; Arabic: *ird*) was the technical term for the legal eligibility of a woman to enter a marriage, and chastity was the technical term for the legal compliance of a woman with the terms of her marriage covenant (Zeid 1966:247; Schneider 1971:20–21). Chastity described a woman's ability to bear children and contribute to the work needs of her household (Gilmore 1987:4).

The father was responsible for the virginity or legal eligibility of the women in his household for marriage, and for the chastity or legal compliance of the women with the terms of their marriage covenants (Pitt-Rivers

1977:78; Davis 1973:160; Gilmore 1987:8). Few responsibilities of a household were more important (Deut 22:13–21). Fathers carried out this responsibility by restricting the movements and associations of women in the village (Pitt-Rivers 1977:165; Giovannini 1987:69).

Any man who attacked a marriageable or married woman was sentenced to death. Both the Code of Hammurabi and the book of Deuteronomy extend the same protection to the betrothed woman as they do to the married woman (Frymer-Kensky 1989:93–95). The Code of Hammurabi, article 130 (Matthews and Benjamin 1991b:64) sentences to death any man who rapes a betrothed woman. The book of Deuteronomy (Deut 22:23–27) determines the sentence on the basis of where the crime takes place (Benjamin 1983:23–27; Matthews 1987:32). If it occurs in the village where the woman could cry for help, then both she and the man are executed. If the crime takes place in the fields outside the village where no one could hear a cry for help, then only the man is executed.

Any father who negotiated a marriage for a woman in his household who was not a virgin, that is, who was legally ineligible to marry, forfeited his land and children (Frymer-Kensky 1989:93). Likewise, any father who failed to see that a woman in his household remained chaste or fulfilled the terms of her marriage covenant also lost the patrimony which her marriage was intended to increase and multiply.

Marriage was not a single event, but a drawn-out process of negotiations (Gen 24:52–54). Each stage furthered the alliance between the two households and spelled out their contract in more exact terms. Thus, contained within the legal action of betrothal was the final choice of partners and the agreement on bride price (מהר, mōhar) and dowry (זבד, zēḇeḏ). There were some exceptions to this rule, in which a socially unattached male arranged his own marriage with the household of the bride (Gen 29:16–30), but they were rare (Gottlieb 1989:63).

To tender a proposal of marriage or covenant (Mal 2:14), the father of the household of the groom sent an expensive gift to the father of the household of the bride (Gen 34:12; Exod 22:16; Deut 22:29; 1 Sam 18:25). The father of the bride accepted the proposal by allowing the groom to take the bride (לקח, lāqaḥ) to his household (Deut 20:7; 28:30; Exod 21:10). The marriage covenant was ratified when the groom spread his cloak over the bride (Ruth 3:9) and conferred on her either the title "wife" (אשה, 'iššâh) or "concubine" (פלגש, pilegeš; Exod 21:7–11). The words "prostitute," "mistress," or "concubine" in English translations of the Bible do not always refer to a woman who lives with and has intercourse with a man to whom she is not legally married or to a woman who engages in promiscuous sexual intercourse for pay. In Hebrew, the terms are not always degrading, but often simply distinguish secondary wives from the primary wife who is the mother of the household (1 Kgs 11:1–8).

When the marriage was concluded, an exchange of property took place (Goody and Tambiah 1973b:61–67). An elaborate legal framework was de-

> **Annals of Solomon**
> **(I Kgs I:1–3)**
>
> King Solomon loved many foreign women along with the daugh-
> ter of Pharaoh: Moabite, Ammonite, Edomite, Sidonian, and Hitt-
> ite women. . . . Among his wives were seven hundred princesses
> and three hundred concubines.

veloped to administer these items to provide a circulating pool of resources (Goody and Tambiah 1973a:5), used to arrange future family marriages, and in the event of the husband's death, to provide for the financial support of the widow (Hiebert 1989:131–37). For one year following the marriage, the couple was freed from their obligations to the village (Deut 24:5).

In some villages, households were exogamous and required the father to choose marriage partners from different villages (Fox 1967:53; Hanson 1989:75–84; Malina 1981:25–93; Cronk 1990). Exogamous marriages are typical of economically aggressive and expanding societies. They are de-signed to expand ties and increase their property rights and holdings, as well as their political power and influence (Murphy and Kasdan 1968:199). They are financially a high risk, high return investment. If the marriage succeeds, both households enjoy significant economic returns. If it fails, the financial loss is substantial.

But in the villages of early Israel, most households were endogamous and required their fathers to choose marriage partners from the same village (Patai 1959:19–20; Levi-Strauss 1969:45). Marriage partners had to come from households which had an existing economic relationship with one another. But even in exogamous households not every man and woman were eligible marriage partners. For instance, Leviticus (Lev 18:6–18) directs fathers not to arrange a marriage between a man and his widowed mother, his father's wife, his sister or half-sister, his granddaughter, his paternal or maternal aunt, his daughter-in-law, or his sister-in-law. These women were taboo: they were inappropriate choices as marriage or sexual partners.

Taboos involve a variety of socioeconomic factors (Pitt-Rivers 1977:162–63). Sometimes a taboo is economically based. No marriage is possible between members of two radically different economic classes since that would be an unfair advantage to the poorer and an unwise business deci-sion for the wealthier household. Some taboos are socially based. Within a rigidly stratified society, some social classes are considered inferior to others and therefore marriages between them would strain the social fabric of that society. Cultures having members of more than one ethnic group, for example, often generate taboos against miscegenation or intermarriage.

Endogamous marriages are financially conservative. They strengthen an already existing and proven relationship between two households. The financial risks are small and, in general, so are the financial rewards. Endogamous marriages are designed to keep property within the village (Barth 1954:170–71; Holy 1989:12). They are typical of farmers and herders in subsistence societies whose material resources are scarce.

The most common endogamous marriage combined the households of two brothers (Murdock 1965:260–83; Fox 1967:188–207; Oden 1983:198; Donaldson 1981:84; Holy 1989:21; Cresswell 1976:101). Therefore, the bride and the groom were cousins, not necessarily blood relatives, but at least legal relatives. The words "uncle" or "father's brother," in many kinship systems, referred to a covenant or business partner, not necessarily a sibling. In the world of the Bible, the relationship between a man and his uncle was as important as the relationship between a man and his father (Oden 1983:197; McCarter 1988:14–15). The uncle's son had a legal right to marry his parallel cousin (Murphy and Kasdan 1968:186; Musil 1928:137–140; Cohen 1965:71–75, 121). In fact, very often when Genesis describes marriage (Gen 24; 27:46—28:2), it describes cross-cousin marriage. For example, Nahor marries his cousin to establish a bond with his uncle (Gen 11:29). And, if Rebekah is Nahor's daughter (Gen 24:48; 29:5) rather than Bethuel's (Gen 24:15, 24), then Isaac marries his uncle's brother's daughter (Von Rad 1972:157; Oden 1983:194).

After they were married, the couple generally lived with the father of the groom until he chose an heir. The household was not only patriarchal, it was patrilocal (Meyers 1988:38). For instance, Rebekah joins the household of Abraham after her betrothal and marriage to Isaac (Gen 24:58–67), and the sons of Micah live within his household (Judg 17:5). Joining the young couple with the household of the groom had both social and economic advantages. Their children supplied the household with its future farmers and herders. And the resources of the household could be shared with the newlyweds without having to divide them so that they would have enough land and animals to start a household of their own. The household of the groom also became a school perpetuating its clan ethos, by developing in the couple a sense of common ancestry and kinship obligation. Even today in Arab cultures, architecture points to the practice of providing space for the newly married couple. Steel rods extend skyward from the roof of nearly every house in anticipation of the marriage of the son, who will be expected to move into a room these rods will support when the time comes.

A few cultures in the Mediterranean world were matrilocal. In these cases, the households expected their men to enter the households of their brides, rather than for their women to enter the household of their grooms (Akkadian: erēbu; Gottlieb 1989:117, 130–32). A possible example of this may be found in Jacob's living with Laban for over twenty years, along with his wives and children (Gen 29—30). The arrangement, however, may simply have been one of necessity. Jacob had no choice since he could not return home until he was strong enough to compete with his brother Esau, and in any case he was obligated to pay the bride price for his wives through his labor service.

Inheritance

The concept of inheritance formed an integral part of marriage customs, especially with regard to the ability of the father to hand on his goods and property. He had to decide which of his sons would inherit and which would not. Ancient Israel was patrilineal (Meyers 1988:20–37) and authorized the father to hand on the possessions of the household to another male from his side of the family. Therefore, he generally handed on control of the members and material resources of the household to his own son. But the father could also designate an heir who was his own daughter (Num 36:2–12; Josh 17:3–6; Sakenfeld 1988:39), or who was not his natural child (Gen 15:2; Paul 1979–80:175–76).

The Father in the Stories of Jacob, Leah, and Rachel (Gen 25:20—37:2)

The stories of Jacob, Leah, and Rachel (Gen 25:20—37:2) offer a particularly good window through which to see the way in which a father in the world of the Bible combined inheritance and achievement to help his household survive in a hostile world. Israel remembered its fathers as survivors who compensated for their lack of power by an ability to manipulate the power of others. Jacob or Israel was the favorite father of Middle (2200–1550 BCE) or Late (1550–1250 BCE) Bronze Age clans whose stories appear in the Bible and whose social setting may be reflected in documents from Mesopotamia and Egypt. The geographical settings in the stories roughly define the territory of these early Hebrew villagers in the hills north of Jerusalem. For example, Jacob's rivals live along the frontiers north of Jerusalem and on both sides of the Jordan. Esau lives in Edom along the south, Laban in Aram along the north, and Shechem along the west. And Jacob's encounters with God take place at the sanctuaries of Jabbok and Bethel (Gen 28:10–22).

The clans who told the stories of Jacob, Leah, and Rachel were always threatened by rivalry from within and invasion from without. Similarly, Jacob is portrayed as a father always embroiled in protracted negotiations with Esau, his brother; with Laban, his uncle; with Levi and Simeon, his sons; and even with Yahweh, his god. These clans wanted to remember Jacob not as a trouble-maker, but as a survivor.

Hebrew villagers lived on the margins of their social world. Like all marginalized people, they admired the clever who improved themselves at the expense of the establishment. Cleverness was the wisdom of the powerless. Like Anubis in the story of Anubis and Bata from Egypt, Jacob could have worked for Esau (Matthews and Benjamin 1991b:41–45). But Jacob became the father of his household by tricking Esau into granting him Isaac's inheritance. The Bible regularly celebrates the father who inherits his household by achievement, rather than by birth. Younger sons like Jacob and Solomon often supplant older sons like Esau and Adonijah to become fathers of households or monarchs of states (1 Kgs 1:15–46). Jacob tricks Esau into selling him his birthright (Gen 25:19–34), Isaac into designating him as his heir (Gen 27:1–45), Laban into selling him his sheep (Gen 30:25–43) and his land (Gen 31:1—32:3), and even Yahweh into letting him cross the Jabbok (Gen 32:23–33). Jacob was not an outlaw, but he knew how to work the system to his own advantage (Matthews and Mims 1985).

Jacob lays claim to his own household in the way he deals with both his father Esau and his uncle Laban. He marries Leah and Rachel, who were sisters and the daughters of his uncle (Oden 1983:194–97). This double cross-cousin marriage establishes a bond between him and his uncle twice as strong as that between an ordinary nephew and his uncle.

Although Laban tries to exercise his responsibility to punish Jacob by pursuing him to recover the statues that were titles to the land of the household (תְּרָפִים, $t^{e}r\bar{a}p\hat{\imath}m$), he fails. Cuneiform tablets from Nuzi now document Jacob's legal sophistication by showing that birthrights could be bought and sold; oral wills, even when conferred on the wrong beneficiary, were irrevocable; citizens without natural heirs like Laban could adopt an heir like Jacob (Gen 29:1–30); and title to property belonged to whomever could produce the statues of a household's gods (Gen 31:19–35).

Jacob, Leah, and Rachel not only manipulate society, but also use nature to their advantage as well. Rachel uses a mandrake plant to conceive a child (Gen 30:14–22). Mandrakes are only one plant the clever use to help the childless conceive. And Jacob builds a breeding corral from multicolored poles so that his sheep will conceive multicolored lambs. Traditional societies have a wonderful inventory of techniques like this for priming nature to imitate human behavior.

Nonetheless, the Bible is quite balanced in its assessment of cleverness, which is, at best, only a temporary challenge to the establishment. The clever are fugitives at risk. Jacob is always on the run, a wanderer (Deut 26:5–10). Esau (Gen 27:30–45), Isaac (Gen 27:46—28:9), and Laban (Gen 31:1–24) all exile Jacob when they discover their losses. When Jacob offers Simeon, and then Benjamin, as collateral for grain (Patai 1959:128), his actions are consistent with his authority as the father to negotiate loans insured by the land and children of the household (Exod 21:7). But the Jacob who outwits Isaac is eventually outwitted by Simeon and Levi (Gen 34:1–31) and Joseph (Gen 47:27—48:22).

The Bible does not celebrate cleverness in order to teach that it is permissible to lie, cheat, and steal to get ahead, or even to say that it is all right for the father of a household, but not for ordinary people. In the Bible cleverness celebrates the tenacity with which the powerless (עֲנָוִים, *ʿᵃnāwîm*) survive, and it honors Yahweh for helping the poor rather than supporting the powerful (Gen 49:24; Ps 132:3–5; Isa 1:24; 49:26; 60:16).

The Father in the Story of Jephthah and his Daughter (Judg 11:1–40)

The anthropology of the father also makes it easier to understand the story of Jephthah and his daughter (Judg 11:1-40). Jephthah is a father who offers his daughter as a human sacrifice in thanksgiving to Yahweh for delivering his household from its enemies. Audiences today can seldom understand his actions as anything other than child abuse and murder. But there is more. The story does not celebrate Jephthah as a killer. It remembers him as a father who paid a terrible price for carrying out his responsibility for deciding to what extent his household would participate in the defense of his village and for appointing an heir who would inherit his household.

Jephthah, just as Jacob, combines birth and achievement to become the father of his household. His birth mother is not the mother of the household, but a harlot, concubine, or prostitute (Judg 11:1). Consequently, Gilead, who is the father of the household, may or may not designate Jephthah as his heir. Even when the son of a slave is adopted by the father, he still holds only a secondary position within the protocol of inheritance to the son born to the mother of the household (Richter 1966:496). In fact, Jephthah's hopes to become the heir are quickly dashed when his father has other sons by his wife (Judg 11:2).

When it is time for Gilead to designate an heir, the sons of the mother of the household try to disqualify Jephthah: "You shall not inherit in our father's house; for you are the son of another woman" (Judg 11:2). The same motif appears when Joseph's brothers try to prevent him from becoming Jacob's heir (Gen 37:19–20), when Sarah tries to prevent Ishmael from becoming Abraham's heir (Gen 21:9–12), and when Laban's sons try to prevent Jacob from becoming the heir (Gen 31:1–2). In none of these cases does the father initiate the process of designating an heir. Abraham only acts when Sarah confronts him about Isaac's rights, and it is Jacob's awareness of the angry words of Laban which leads him to depart from that household, ironically and unknowingly with the statues which entitle him to the very land of which he thinks he has been deprived. Similarly, it is not Gilead, but his sons, who drive out Jephthah and force him to become a man without a household (Akkadian: *ḫāpiru*).

The issue of Jephthah's membership in his father's household is brought up again when the Ammonites invade the land of Gilead and the same sons who drove him into exile now want Jephthah to become the chief who will deliver them from their enemies. Jephthah reminds the sons of Gilead: "Did you not hate me, and drive me out of my father's house" (Judg 11:7)? Then he negotiates with them for his reinstatement in the household. He will serve as their chief, on the condition that, if he defeats the Ammonites, they will designate him heir. The covenant they make with Jephthah is contingent on his success against the Ammonites and is comparable to the covenant made between the divine assembly and Marduk in the Enuma Elish story (Matthews and Benjamin 1991b:10). Despite the fact that Jephthah regains his position within the household of Gilead, he is ultimately unable to pass on his inheritance and the household passes back to his brothers. This is due to the vow he makes prior to his battle with the Ammonites.

As the father of a household, Jephthah has the right to make oaths which affect the land and children of the household. He does this when he vows

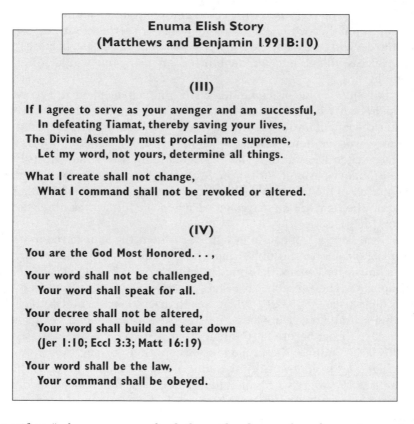

Enuma Elish Story
(Matthews and Benjamin 1991B:10)

(III)

If I agree to serve as your avenger and am successful,
  In defeating Tiamat, thereby saving your lives,
The Divine Assembly must proclaim me supreme,
  Let my word, not yours, determine all things.

What I create shall not change,
  What I command shall not be revoked or altered.

(IV)

You are the God Most Honored. . . ,

Your word shall not be challenged,
  Your word shall speak for all.

Your decree shall not be altered,
  Your word shall build and tear down
  (Jer 1:10; Eccl 3:3; Matt 16:19)

Your word shall be the law,
  Your command shall be obeyed.

to sacrifice "whoever comes forth from the doors of my house to meet me, when I return victorious from the Ammonites" (Judg 11:30–31). His vow is part of the ritual of holy war. A sacrifice of this magnitude is part of the high stakes game Jephthah is playing. He has been restored to the position of father by reason of merit and achievement as a chief. In order to keep his position, he must be willing to sacrifice everything to obtain his goals. Saul does virtually the same thing when he sacrifices his team of oxen prior to rallying his forces against the Ammonites (1 Sam 11:7). He also nearly falls into the same trap as Jephthah by making a vow prior to his battle with the Philistines (1 Sam 14:37–45). His son Jonathan is nearly sacrificed to maintain Saul's honor, but the people ransom him, perhaps by providing a substitute sacrifice, but certainly by depriving Saul of a portion of his authority and honor (1 Sam 14:45).

The first person to greet Jephthah is his daughter, who is celebrating his victory by playing a tambourine and dancing (Exod 15:20; 1 Sam 18:6). The narrator identifies her with the legal formula: she is Jephthah's "only child; besides her he had neither son nor daughter" (Judg 11:34). Jephthah's role as father is dependent on this single child, whom he must now sacrifice in order to keep his vow. Since his daughter is his only child, her death will leave his household without an heir. The same motif appears in Greek and Roman traditions like the *Iliad* of Homer, where Agamemnon nearly sacrifices his daughter Iphigenia to the god Artemis (Soggin 1981:216).

When Jephthah realizes the implications of his oath, he has second thoughts, but his daughter is very certain of her obligations. She knows that the honor of the household must be maintained at any cost and thus she insists that her father fulfill his vow (Judg 11:36). Her request magnifies the significance of what Jephthah is giving up by delivering the household of Gilead from the Ammonites (2 Sam 13:18–19). It also suggests the general acceptability of human sacrifice in this area of Israel (Soggin 1981:217). The daughter of Jephthah, like the daughters of Lot (Gen 19:30–38), is not a tragic or pathetic figure. She is a heroic figure who shares in her father's selflessness. But unlike the daughters of Lot, she is not silent in the story. Her words reinforce her actions, and she decides to lay down her life for her household. Jephthah's willingness to allow his daughter these two months to "wander on the mountains and bewail my virginity" (Judg 11:37–38) functions almost as a marriage contract in which his consent is necessary before she may give up her virginity for the good of the household.

Finally, the four-day ritual of lament by the "daughters of Israel" is not over the premature death of the daughter of Jephthah. It laments her inability to fulfill her role as mother. Jephthah, in making his vow, only partially serves his household. He protects its land, but he does not provide for an heir to inherit that land.

2

The Mother

The most important adults in every household in the world of the Bible were the father (אב, 'āḇ) and the mother (אם, אמי, 'ēm, 'immî). All cultures expect women to contribute differently to their households than men, and the roles of men and women vary greatly from one culture to another (Friedl 1975; Ardener 1975; Kelly 1984). Except for childbearing and nursing, virtually no other roles are assigned exclusively to women (Brown 1970:1073). There has never been a completely egalitarian society in which gender played no role (Rosaldo 1974:17; Ortner 1974: 57–71), and there has never been a completely matriarchal society in which all power and authority were delegated to women (Meyers 1988:30). Amazon women exist in the *Odyssey* of Homer, but nowhere else in the Mediterranean world.

Protocol for Mothers of a Household

To protect and provide for their land and children, mothers of households:
- **bear children and arrange for other wives to bear children**
- **manage the household by supervising domestic production, rationing and preparing food, processing and storing beer, grain, vegetables**
- **teach clan traditions**
- **mediate domestic conflicts**
- **designate heirs**

The Bible itself grants women much more access to the administrative, judicial, and economic systems than many of today's generalizations about women and the Bible acknowledge. The status of women in early Israel may be no model for the reconstruction of contemporary society on more inclusive principles, but neither is it a unilateral endorsement for the subordination of women. And the world of the Bible may not be feminist, but neither is it completely male oriented. It may not be liberated, but it is liberating.

The world of the Bible was a "patriarchy." The word refers to particular kinds of social systems. Theoretically at least, patriarchy is not sexism, which is a form of prejudice and oppression based on the faulty assumption that women are biologically inferior to men (Meyers 1988:24–27; Rogers 1975). Sexism misuses power to deprive women of autonomy (Bird 1974). It exists in societies of all kinds, but not because they are patriarchal. And patriarchy is not simply another word for the economic system of capitalism in contrast to socialism or communism. There are a variety of patriarchal societies, but they all have two characteristics in common. They are all "patrilocal," which means that a woman lives in the household of her husband. And they are all "patrilinear," which means that the heir of the household must be a natural or adopted son of the father.

The basic resources in every society are land and children. In both villages and states, status is determined by how authority over land and children is delegated (Selvidge 1984:619–23; Meyers 1983:573; Goody 1972). The ability to determine how a community uses its resources or the ability to exploit a community's resources is power. The approval of the community to use power is authority. It may seem logical that those who have the power to cultivate land and children ought to have the authority to determine when and how to use their power. But neither the power to control a community's resources nor the power to exploit them implies the authority to do so. Power does not guarantee authority.

Those who have the power to cultivate land and bear children often lack the authority to determine when and how to use it. And those who exercise authority over the land and children often have no practical knowledge of how to farm, herd, or rear. But sometimes, those without authority manage to exercise power. For example, the father of the household in the Bible has the authority to select an heir, but the mother, in fact, often exercises that power (Gen 27:1–17). Some societies retain only the appearance of male dominance by allowing the father of the household to retain authority in a particular area of public life, while actually expecting the mother to exercise the power on behalf of the household (Meyers 1988:42–45; Rogers 1975, 1978).

The mother of a household in the Bible had significant power and authority over decision-making and problem-solving for both land and children. Patriarchy in ancient Israel was based not on the subordination and exploitation of women, but rather on the efforts of all the men and women in its household to survive. The father was authorized to make communal decisions for the household. He oversaw the public use of its land and children. Whenever the households in a village worked together on common projects, it was the father who decided to what extent his own household would participate.

> ### "The Sage in Family and Tribe"
> ### (Fontaine 1990:156)
>
> . . . a status or position is "a location in the social structure de-
> fined by expectations for performance by an incumbent"; and a
> role is the "organized set of behaviors that belongs to an iden-
> tifiable position." Both status and role may be ascribed (by
> means of age, sex, and kinship) or achieved (occupation, mar-
> riage), formalized or non-formalized, public or private. Role ex-
> pectations, then, are the "rights and privileges, the duties and
> obligations, of any occupant of a social position (status) in rela-
> tion to a person occupying other positions in the social struc-
> ture," with a particular "role set" of a status referring to the
> entire set of complementary roles associated with the position
> in question.

Although the power and authority of the mother of the household were
distinct from the power and authority of the father of the household, they
were not necessarily inferior to his. Hebrew villagers did not systematically
empower every male and subordinate every female (Rosaldo 1974:19; Meyers 1988:34). Not every man became the father of a household. And, in some
cases, the status of the mother of a household was equal to or greater than
the status of many men in the village (Meyers 1983:570; Emmerson 1989:
377). Homemaking and childbearing were by no means inferior or unre-
warding roles. They were responsibilities, not restrictions. And even when
the status of women was inferior in one area of village life, such as the
priesthood, it does not necessarily follow that the status of women in
ancient Israel as a whole was inferior (Meyers 1988:37; Frymer-Kensky
1985:6–7). In fact, the legal injunction throughout the biblical text is to
honor both parents (Exod 20:12; 2 Sam 19:37; Prov 15:20; 30:17; Emmerson
1989:385).

A Mother's Role in the Village

The Mother as Childbearer

In most villages herding and farming involved both men and women
(Meyers 1988:574). Women often helped manage herds, clear new fields,
construct terraces, harvest, thresh, and winnow the fields, orchards, and
vineyards (Meyers 1988:146; de Vaux 1961:39). They also planted, hoed,
weeded, and picked household gardens. However, the primary responsibility
for farming and herding was delegated to men, especially during their

wives' pregnancy and in cases where their greater physical strength was required. The primary and gender specific responsibility for childbearing belonged to women. The mother of the household was authorized not only to bear sons and daughters for her household, but also to see that all the other women in her household regularly bore sons and daughters as well. The midwife assisted the mother of the household in arranging for them to have children, and to care for them during their pregnancy.

The Mother as Manager

One important role of the mother that was not gender specific was her responsibility as the manager of the household (Camp 1985:79–148). Early Israel believed that only in a subsistence economy could its households really understand Yahweh as Lord, which meant that Yahweh was the sole protector and provider in Israel. Hebrew villages assigned major responsibilities for the creation and maintenance of this subsistence economy to the mother of the household (Meyers 1988:139–64). Therefore, she directed the manufacture of soap, pottery, baskets, cloth, and tools. But more importantly, she determined how much food was to be consumed and how much was to be stored as beer, parched grain, and dried vegetables (Meyers 1988:147). To assure that everyone in the household was fed and that the food lasted until the next ration was distributed, her authority over the goods and produce assigned to her household by the village was absolute (Goody 1982:40–70; Whyte 1978; Adams 1972:6). In the world of ancient Israel, a man's home was his wife's castle. She had the domestic authority which he did not.

This dynamic is clearly seen in the Sufferer and the Soul from Egypt, a dispute over suicide that dates between 2050 and 1800 BCE. It includes a parable which compares the domestic authority of the mother of a household to the authority of the divine assembly over human life. The sufferer in the dispute wants to commit suicide and end his life of pain and failure. The soul tells him the parable to argue that it is as foolish for him to

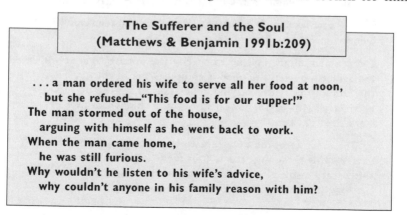

**The Sufferer and the Soul
(Matthews & Benjamin 1991b:209)**

...a man ordered his wife to serve all her food at noon,
   but she refused—"This food is for our supper!"
The man stormed out of the house,
   arguing with himself as he went back to work.
When the man came home,
   he was still furious.
Why wouldn't he listen to his wife's advice,
   why couldn't anyone in his family reason with him?

challenge the authority of the divine assembly over his life as it would be for a father to challenge the authority of a mother of the household over the food she distributes. The sufferer has no more right to take his life into his own hands than the father has a right to take more food into his hands than the mother of the household rations out to him.

The mother also rationed the olive oil which was burned in small clay lamps. These were lighted just before dark, not so much to allow the household to work at night as to protect it from intruders. The mother had to determine the precise moment when it was dark enough for the household to be in danger before lighting the lamps. Lighting the lamps too soon or too late both left the household vulnerable to thieves. A mother who lighted her lamps too soon would have them burn out in the darkness before dawn (Prov 31:18). A mother who lighted her lamps too late left her household in the darkness following sunset.

Anubis in the story of Anubis and Bata from Egypt (ca. 1225 BCE) knows that something is seriously wrong when his wife "did not trim, nor light the lamps when it got dark" (Matthews and Benjamin 1991b:44). And the Parable of the Ten Virgins in the Gospel of Matthew (Matt 25:1–13) compares the responsibility of the mother to ration oil for the lamps of her household with the responsibility of the followers of Jesus to prepare their households

> ### Lighting the Sabbath Candles
> ### (Klein 1979:55–57)
>
> **When all work is brought to a standstill, the candles are lit. Just as creation began with the word, "Let there be light!" so does the celebration of creation begin with the kindling of lights. It is the woman who ushers in the joy and set ups the most exquisite symbol, light, to dominate the atmosphere of the home. . . .**
>
> **It is a mitzvah to light candles on the eve of the Sabbath, before sunset, at home in the room where the meal is taken. . . .**
>
> **. . . The candles should be lit not later than eighteen minutes before sunset.**
>
> **The problem of attempting to specify the precise time at which the Sabbath begins and ends is complex. One of the causes of this complexity is the varying definitions of . . . the period between . . . the astronomical sunset and the appearance of stars. . . .**
>
> **. . . The most accepted determination is . . . about eighteen minutes. By this reckoning, the sign of night is the appearance of three stars in the sky . . . they must be of medium size . . . and . . . together and not scattered about the sky.**

for his return. Today, it is still the responsibility of mothers in observant Jewish households to determine the precise time to light the Sabbath candles (Klein 1979:55-8; Cohen 1992; b. *Shab* 31b; Maimonides, Hil. Shabbat 5:3).

The Mother as Teacher

The mother was not only the childbearer and the manager of the household, she was also the teacher of its women and children (Fontaine 1990: 161). Once boys became young men (נערים, n^e'*ārîm*) and could participate in the communal labor of the village, the father of the household became responsible for their education. But even when girls became young women (בתולת, b^e*ṯûlōṯ*) and could conceive a child, they continued to be educated by the mother.

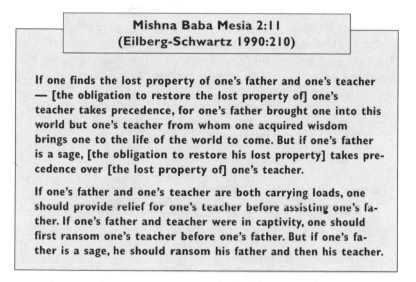

Mishna Baba Mesia 2:11
(Eilberg-Schwartz 1990:210)

If one finds the lost property of one's father and one's teacher — [the obligation to restore the lost property of] one's teacher takes precedence, for one's father brought one into this world but one's teacher from whom one acquired wisdom brings one to the life of the world to come. But if one's father is a sage, [the obligation to restore his lost property] takes precedence over [the lost property of] one's teacher.

If one's father and one's teacher are both carrying loads, one should provide relief for one's teacher before assisting one's father. If one's father and teacher were in captivity, one should first ransom one's teacher before one's father. But if one's father is a sage, he should ransom his father and then his teacher.

Teaching and childbearing were comparable if not identical roles (Amsler 1979:112–16; Camp 1985:81–82; Eilberg-Schwartz 1990:229–34). The book of Proverbs honors the mother of the household not as a childbearer, but, almost exclusively, as a teacher (Prov 1:8; 6:20; 23:22–25; 31:1–9). Teachings in the Mishna (200 CE) and the Talmud (400 CE) of Judaism continued to emphasize the connection between childbearing and teaching found in the Bible (m. *Baba Mesia* 2:11).

To a certain extent, the role of the mother as a teacher was an understandable development of the bond which forms between any mother and the child she carries and nurses (Fontaine 1990:161). Such close physical contact in traditional societies lasted not simply during the months of pregnancy, but for as long as four years after birth, during which children were nursed (1 Sam 1:22–23). But the role of the mother as teacher was not simply a development of her physical closeness to the children for whom she cared. Not every childbearer was the mother of a household, not every woman who was physically close to her children during pregnancy and nursing became their teacher.

The mother of the household taught children how to walk, how to talk, how to dress themselves, and how to feed themselves (Hos 11:1–4). And she taught them how to help with gardening, herding, cooking, weaving, and making pottery. The mother in early Israel also taught her children how to read and write so that they could make lists and keep records. The cuneiform languages of Mesopotamia and the hieroglyphics of Egypt were so complex that literacy demanded a lifetime of formal schooling. Hebrew, on the other hand, was a simple language system with only twenty-two signs which could be learned at home by anyone (Meyers 1988:152–54; Kraeling and Adams 1960:94–123).

The general education which the mother provided her children included not only these practical skills, but other kinds of wisdom as well (Camp 1981:29). It was the mother who taught children their role and the roles of everyone else in the household and the village. The book of Proverbs preserves many of her teachings on how to acquire honor and how to repair or remove shame (Prov 1:7–19).

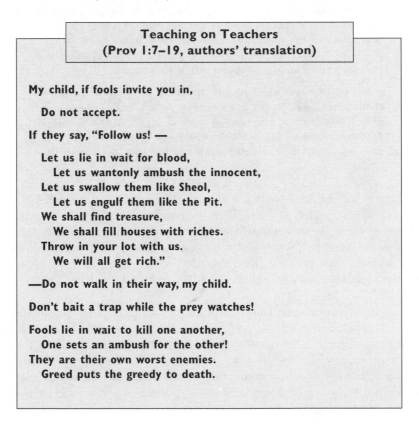

Teaching on Teachers
(Prov 1:7–19, authors' translation)

My child, if fools invite you in,

  Do not accept.

If they say, "Follow us! —

  Let us lie in wait for blood,
    Let us wantonly ambush the innocent,
  Let us swallow them like Sheol,
    Let us engulf them like the Pit.
  We shall find treasure,
    We shall fill houses with riches.
  Throw in your lot with us.
    We will all get rich."

—Do not walk in their way, my child.

Don't bait a trap while the prey watches!

Fools lie in wait to kill one another,
  One sets an ambush for the other!
They are their own worst enemies.
  Greed puts the greedy to death.

Finally, the mother was the children's storyteller. In words and rituals, she was the first to hand on the traditions of the Hebrews as slaves-set-free. Each time the mother of the household taught a child to dress, she explained the meaning of the clothing. Each time she showed children how to wash their hands and comb their hair, she told them how washing and combing set them apart. She explained to the children who helped her why the foods they ate at harvest times were different from those the household enjoyed everyday, why certain plants and animals were prepared and others were not, why some foods were consumed and others were shared. Washing, dressing, combing, gardening, herding, cooking, weaving, and making pottery were not simply skills to be learned; they were rituals which enacted the traditions that distinguished one people from another.

The Mother as Mediator

The mother of the household also attempted to defuse conflicts and broker out-of-court settlements between members of her household before they reached the village assembly. This role of mediator may, to some extent, have developed from the institution of patrilocality, in which a woman left the household of her parents to live in the household of her husband (Gen 24:54–61). The experience of having lived in two households may have enhanced her reputation as an informed, yet creative mediator (Fontaine 1990:158–63). Although she was an outsider in the household of her husband, her intimate knowledge of traditions of both her father's and her husband's respective households allowed her to arbitrate disputes more impartially than would other family members (Leach 1976:74–75). In the world of the Bible, the mother often mediated disputes involving the appointment of an heir, as did both Rebekah (Gen 27:5–17, 42–46) and Bathsheba (1 Kgs 1:11–31). While these women were not entirely impartial, their judgment was more reasonable than that of the male heads of household.

The Mother as Priest

In the religions of Canaan and Mesopotamia, there is inferential evidence that some women were hierodules or priests with whom pilgrims had sexual intercourse. Ritual intercourse for the father of the household was a prayer that his own wives and his own land would be fertile (Wolff 1979:14; Hooks 1985:65–151; Barstad 1984:22–29; Bird 1989:76). In general, however, women priests did not bear children, which is the reason for the popular identification of them as prostitutes. Their function was sexual but its significance was more than erotic.

Few, if any, women in early Israel became priests (Meyers 1978:91–103). The prohibition of women priests was not so much a factor of sexism among the Hebrews as it was part of their overall effort to distinguish their subsistence village culture from the surplus cultures of the states around them.

...men priests were an institution of surplus cultures built on slavery. Consequently, early Israel prohibited women priests, just as it prohibited a monarchy, a standing army, and slavery. The Hebrews did not object only to women becoming priests, but to any social institution connected with a surplus economy.

Every culture consciously takes its priests out of production as a way of demonstrating total dependence on God. Early Israel needed every available adult to clear the land and build their new society. As a result, there were very few priests, male or female, in early Israel. And because there were more adult males in the population of early Israel than adult females (Meyers 1978:98), it was easier to exempt males from production to become priests than to exempt females. Likewise, early Israel needed every available woman to bear children, and since women priests did not bear children, Hebrew women did not become priests.

Although in 1000 BCE David transformed Israel into a state, he was careful to maintain at least the appearances of the values on which the villages of early Israel were founded. Therefore, the priesthood in the state of ancient Israel remained male. Later legislation, based on the demand for ritual purity as the essential condition for sacred service, may have been used to justify an all-male priesthood (Lev 21; Ezek 44:15–27). Women who were menstruating or pregnant were excluded from service based on the discharge of blood or birth fluids (Emmerson 1989:379; Hayter 1987:70; Buckley 1988:189). However, this did not exclude them from cultic celebration or from ministering at the door of the tent of meeting (Exod 38:8; Ps 68:26; Childs 1974:636).

The Mother as Israel

The mother of a household enjoyed such a distinct status in the world of ancient Israel that she became a symbol of Israel itself. Semitic peoples were unique in the ancient Near East in referring to prominent cities as mothers and the villages within their spheres of influence as daughters (Josh 15:45–47; Judg 1:12). Not only Israel, but Babylon and Ugarit (near the Mediterranean coast in Syria) referred to their cities as mothers (Babylonian: *ummatum*; Ugaritic: *'umt*; Malamat 1979:527–36). And Phoenician coins depicted cities as women with the title "lady" or "godmother" who, like some cities in the Bible, had the same names as their divine husbands (Josh 9:10; 15:9).

Consequently, when Deuteronomy (Deut 4:41—26:19) and other legal codes in the Bible refer to women and deal with women's issues, they are seldom interested simply in regulating physical relationships between men and women. The vocabulary dealing with women and with sexuality is concerned far more with property than with gender and sexual contact. It is concerned with more sweeping issues of social justice and the equitable distribution of goods and services by maintaining a strong subsistence economy (Benjamin 1983:12–18). For traditional societies, social justice, and not sexual conduct, is the basis of morality. Consequently, teachings dealing with virginity, marriage, divorce, infidelity, adultery, promiscuity, and rape are concerned not only with the sexual relationships of individuals or couples, but also with the social and economic relationships between the households in the village as a whole (Gordis 1974:241–64; Meyers 1988:123–24; Porter 1967).

When a woman married, for example, her marriage ratified an important political and economic covenant between her household and the household of her husband (Fontaine 1990:162; Lerner 1986:67–68). The precise economic significance of a particular sexual relationship was indicated in the various titles which households bestowed on women. The rendering of these titles in English today carry almost no economic connotations, and, in some cases, carry unnecessarily negative moral overtones. Among the most common titles for women in the Bible are "harlot" (זונה, *zônâh*; Josh 2:1), "concubine" (פלגש, *pilegeš*; 2 Sam 15:16; 16:20–23), "wife" (אשה, *'iššâh*; Gen 12:5), "virgin" (בתולה, *bᵉtûlâh*, Deut 22:19; עלמה, *'almâ*), Isa 7:14), "princess" (שרה, *śārâh*; 1 Kgs 11:3), or "queen" (מלכה, *malkâh*; 1 Kgs 10:1). Each title is not so much an indication of the ethical behavior of a particular woman, but rather of the economic status of the relationship between her household and the household of her husband.

The Mother in the Stories of Hagar and Sarah (Gen 16:1–16; 21:1–21)

The stories of Hagar and Sarah in Genesis (Gen 16:1–16; 21:1–21) are ancestor stories about mothers of households which have been artfully combined with elements of creation stories. Both stories of Hagar and Sarah open with a crisis modeled on the sterility affidavit with which a creation story begins. The affirmation that "Sarai, Abram's wife, bore him no children" (Gen 16:1) and the sterility affidavit that "the earth was a formless void and darkness covered the face of the deep, while a wind . . . swept over the face of the waters" (Gen 1:2) certify there is no life (Trible 1984:10). And like a creation story, both stories end when Yahweh makes a covenant with the newborn child and endows it with land and children of its own. The words "now you shall conceive and shall bear a son" in the first story of Hagar and Sarah (Gen 16:11) are comparable to the words "be fruitful and multiply" in the story of the Heavens and the Earth (Gen 1:28). The central episodes of the stories of Hagar and Sarah, however, preserve the authentic character of the ancestor story, which is quite different from the cosmogony which makes up the main section of a creation story.

The traits of a biblical ancestor story appear in the folk stories of many other cultures (Thompson 1955:58; Olrik 1965:129–41). It has a plot with a crisis which disturbs the peace and proceeds beyond the climax to the peace-restoring denouement. The plot is never abrupt. It never begins with the most important part of the action and never ends abruptly. There is a leisurely introduction or crisis episode, and then the ancestor story always proceeds beyond the climax to a point of rest or stability in the denouement episode.

An ancestor story has only three main characters, but only two at a time may appear together. Even if there are more characters, only two of them act simultaneously. Because it limits each episode to two characters, the folk story is a perfect script for puppeteers who can operate only one puppet with each hand at a time (Thompson 1977:460–61). To include more than three characters, ancestor stories often use two minor characters in one role. Sometimes these minor characters cooperate, sometimes they compete, but they are still equivalent to only a single character.

The plot in an ancestor story is always simple or one-dimensional; it is never complex. One story is told at a time (Coats 1973:389–90). Description is also handled as simply as possible. Similar things are described as nearly alike as possible, and no attempt is made to secure variety. But most importantly, the characters in an ancestor story are always simple or polarized. Polarized characters are one-dimensional. Only such qualities as directly affect the story are mentioned; no hint is given that the persons in the story have any life outside the story.

Ancestor stories delight in repetition, not only to give the story suspense but also to fill it out. Repetition in the Bible is usually threefold, though sometimes it may be fourfold (Judg 16:15–17). Tellers make generous use of irony. Hence, the weakest or worst character often turns out to be the most successful. The youngest is often the heir, the weakest is often the victor.

Clans tell ancestor stories to celebrate a father or mother whose particular virtue saved the community from extinction. In these stories, tellers celebrate this single virtue; they do not intend to establish a universal system of values. The virtue is never trivial. It is a virtue which makes the difference between life and death, not just for a single household or village but for the entire clan. The ancestor story inspires households to identify with their ancestors, thus giving them a sense of their roots.

Perfection discourages imitation, and therefore, ancestor characters are always flawed, giving them a very human, very imitable quality. Their flaws or limitations put them within reach of the present generation and encourage the present generation to imitate their resourcefulness in dealing with crisis. Ancestor stories provide households with companions in crisis and, to some extent, are also apologies, explaining why some households survive when others in the village are destroyed.

The stories of Hagar and Sarah celebrate Hagar as a mother whose perseverance allowed her to found a household. The two stories are not chronological, they are parallels of the same story. As they are told in the Bible today, these stories have been integrated into the stories of Abraham and Sarah. But neither Abraham nor Sarah is their protagonist. Neither Abraham nor Sarah reach a goal or undergo a change in the course of the story. The Abraham character is indecisive throughout, and his actions only ratify the actions of either Sarah or Hagar. Abraham is Sarah's helper. Neither does the Sarah character reach a goal; she only tries to block Hagar (Trible 1984:10). She is the antagonist. The protagonist in these stories is Hagar. She sets out at the beginning of the story to obtain land and children, and she accomplishes her goal.

If, like Sarah, the mother of a household was unable to have children due to infertility, she provided her husband with a surrogate who would bear sons and daughters for him (Seibert 1974:15). A mother was not shamed by designating a surrogate, which was a legal remedy developed precisely to protect her honor (*pace* Trible 1984:11). The mother of the household, not the father, designated the surrogate. She selected her from slaves who were already members of the household, and once a surrogate had a child, she could not be dismissed from the household (Gen 30:3–9).

Infertility was not the only circumstance in which the mother of a household designated a surrogate. The Code of Hammurabi from Babylon permits a woman who is a priest to designate a priest of lower rank or one of her own slaves as a surrogate (*CH* 144–46; Seibert 1974:16–19). And at Sumer, women who were *naditu* priests took a vow not to have children so that their inheritance would remain intact. If they chose to marry, their husband could take a second wife to serve as a surrogate childbearer (Harris 1964: 108, n. 14). Their children were entitled to inherit only from their husband's household, not from the household of the *naditu*, whose property reverted in most instances to her brothers (Harris 1975:364–67).

The Bible does not make it clear whether Sarah is a priest who has made a vow not to bear children, or is a woman who is physically unable to do so (Teubal 1984). But since she is infertile, she designates a surrogate who will bear a child which she and Abraham can adopt. "Sarai . . . gave [Hagar] to Abram . . . as a wife" (Gen 16:3, NRSV) or "to be his concubine" (NAB).

Although Hagar initially accepts Sarah's covenant to bear her a child, she later reneges. She understands the kicking of the child in her womb as a declaration of independence. The movements of an unborn were significant in the world of the Bible (Gen 25:22–23). For example, Elizabeth in the Gospel of Luke (Luke 1:44) understands the movement of her child as a dance with which it welcomes the coming of Mary into the village, just as David danced to welcome the coming of the ark of the covenant into the city of Jerusalem (2 Sam 6:14–16).

Hagar's response to the child's movement is generally rendered: "she looked with contempt upon her mistress" (Gen 16:4). But before this reading in the Hebrew text became standard, Hagar's words may have been a hymn rather than an insult: "I am going to give birth to a wild ass of a man."

| **Hymn to Yahweh as Midwife** |
| **(Gen 21:6)** |

Abraham was a hundred years old when his son Isaac was born to him. Sarah then said,

"God has brought laughter for me;
  everyone who hears will laugh with me. . . .
Who would . . . have said . . . Sarah would nurse children?
Yet I have borne [Abraham] a son in his old age."

Mothers regularly celebrate the birth of their children with a hymn like those now preserved in the words of the angel of the Lord to Hagar in the desert (Gen 16:12). The Hebrew word commonly translated "to look on with contempt" (קלל, qālal) also has the meaning "to jettison" or "unload" (1 Kgs 12:10; Jonah 1:5). Since the story describes Ishmael as a wild animal, it would be consistent for his mother to describe Ishmael's birth as if she were "dropping" (קלל, qālal) a calf or foal. Her words do not shame Ishmael. They celebrate the strength and vigor which he began to exhibit even in the womb. Furthermore, the Hebrew word commonly translated as "mistress" (גבירה, gᵉḇîrâh) and used in reference to Sarah (Gen 16:4), can also mean "warrior" (גבור, gibbôr; 1 Sam 17:51).

Sarah, however, taunts Hagar and turns the words of her surrogate's hymn against her in the same way that Elijah turns the words of the prophets of Baʿal against them (1 Kgs 18:17–26, 29). Hagar sings: "I am going to give birth to a wild ass of a man" (Gen 16:4); Sarah taunts: "she looked with contempt on her mistress" (Gen 16:5). Then Sarah asks for and receives Abraham's approval to mediate the conflict between her and Hagar by submitting Hagar to an ordeal in the desert.

There are legal precedents for Sarah's reaction to Hagar (Seibert 1974:73–85). As Abraham reminds Sarah, the mother of the household has the legal authority to punish any woman who fails to honor her father and mother: "your slave-girl is in your power; do to her as you please" (Gen 16:6). Rubbing salt into a woman's gums, for example, is one punishment permitted by the Code of Ur-Nammu (Pritchard 1969 ANET:525; Seibert 1974:16). The Code of Hammurabi permits a mother to demote a slave or sell her (CH 147; Seibert 1974:16). However, if the woman was a surrogate who had actually borne a child for the father of the household she could not be sold (CH 146; Leach 1976:74–75). Furthermore, after the death of the father, a surrogate and her children were emancipated, and her child could even become the father's heir (Seibert 1974:16–17; CH 170–71).

Sarah does "deal harshly with" or punish Hagar before sending her into the desert to let Yahweh decide whether she or Hagar is to be the mother of the household (Gen 16:6). In one story of Hagar and Sarah, it is clear that

Hagar runs away. Sarah is not selling her away from the household (Gen 16:6). However, in another, when Sarah demands that Abraham "drive out that slave and her son" (Gen 21:10), she may be clearly violating Hagar's legal rights to remain in the household once she has conceived or given birth to a child. But it is more likely that by driving Hagar out, Sarah is subjecting her to an ordeal (Gen 21:10; Num 5).

The ordeal is a judicial institution. It resolves conflicts between households which could not be resolved by the elders in a village assembly and reestablishes harmony (שלום, šālôm) within the village. Crimes which carried the death penalty, such as adultery and jealously (Num 5:11–31), required the plaintiff's charge be supported by the testimony of two eyewitnesses. Without these eyewitnesses the plaintiff had no recourse to the village assembly. The village assembly could not function when there were no witnesses (Benjamin 1983:198–210, 297–98). Since harmony in the village was essential for the prosperity of its economy, the ordeal was intended to help break a stalemate and to allow the village to render a decision between the households.

In the ordeal the defendant is exposed to a strenuous, life-threatening experience (Frymer 1976). If she survives, then the divine assembly has cleared her of the charges made against her and the honor of her household is reaffirmed. If she does not, then her household is shamed. An ordeal was a legally constructed "day of judgment" (Deut 32:34–36; Job 21:30; Ps 18:7 MT [ET v. 6]; 32:6). According to one protocol, defendants were thrown into the river as they cried out for deliverance (McCarter 1973:403–12). If they survived they were innocent; if they drowned they were guilty and their property was confiscated (Job 21:17; CH 2). Exercising this legal option, Elijah the prophet submits the prophets of Ba'al to an ordeal by water in the River Kishon (1 Kgs 18:40; Benjamin 1992:19–28).

In the stories of Hagar and Sarah, Sarah subjects Hagar to an ordeal by thirst in the Negeb desert. The desert is not a place of punishment in these stories as it is in the stories of Adam and Eve and the stories of Cain and Abel in Genesis. Here the desert is a place of judgment. Hagar appeals to Yahweh and the divine assembly for a judgment against Sarah by taking Ishmael into the desert in Genesis, just as Moses appeals to Yahweh and the divine assembly for a judgment against Pharaoh by leading the Hebrews into the desert in Exodus. Hagar places Ishmael before the sacred tree, and it is Hagar, not Ishmael, who cries out to Yahweh for justice (Trible 1984: 24–25; 1985:234–35; Ps 18:7 MT [ET v. 6]; 69:15–16 MT [ET vv. 16–17]; Jonah 2:3). Clear legal characteristics also appear in Yahweh's words to Hagar: "Hagar, maid of Sarai, where have you come from and where are you going" (Gen 16:8)? Yahweh summons or subpoenas Hagar with the same formula used to subpoena the people primeval in the stories of Adam and Eve (Gen 3:9). And legal language continues as Hagar serves as her own defense attorney: "I am running away from my mistress, Sarai" (Gen 16:8); and Yahweh announces the verdict and sentence imposed by the divine

assembly: "go back to your mistress and submit to her abusive treatment"
(Gen 16:9).

The verdict of the divine assembly should not be understood as an endorsement of physical abuse. It is a covenant similar to that in the stories
of Adam and Eve (Gen 3:14–19) and the stories of Abraham and Sarah (Gen
12:2–3). In fact, Yahweh's words to Hagar (Gen 16:10–12) are virtually

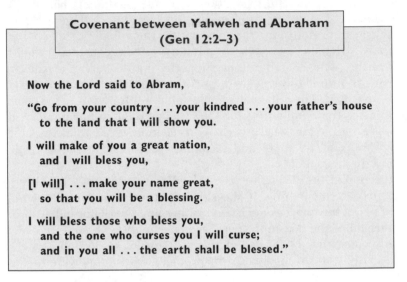

**Covenant between Yahweh and Abraham
(Gen 12:2–3)**

Now the Lord said to Abram,

"Go from your country . . . your kindred . . . your father's house
    to the land that I will show you.

I will make of you a great nation,
    and I will bless you,

[I will] . . . make your name great,
    so that you will be a blessing.

I will bless those who bless you,
    and the one who curses you I will curse;
    and in you all . . . the earth shall be blessed."

identical to Yahweh's words to Abraham (Gen 12:2–3). First, Yahweh endows Hagar with children and land. Yahweh gives her both a son and the
oasis of Beer-lahai-roi in the Negeb. She is no longer a slave, but free.
Second, Yahweh tutors Hagar in the consequences of her fertility. The
intention of the verdict of the divine assembly is not to punish Hagar and
her descendants but to persuade them that the blessings of fertility are
worth the abuse or labor. Fertility demands labor, and labor distinguishes
human fertility from divine fertility (Von Rad 1962:142–43). For humans,
the ecstasy of giving life to another human being in birth, or to the earth
through farming, demands the agony of labor. As in the stories of Adam
and Eve, Yahweh here in the stories of Hagar and Sarah (Gen 16:9) is more
a midwife than a judge (Benjamin 1989:115–20; Benjamin 1993). The midwife does not impose labor pain upon a mother as a sentence for conceiving
a child, she interprets that pain. Thus, the stories of Hagar and Sarah
assume that the ability to create, which Hagar has acquired, cannot be
exercised without labor. Hagar must bear children, manage resources,
educate women and children, and mediate disputes. She must be the mother
of a household.

3

The Farmer

The economy of the biblical world was dedicated to the two basic resources of land and children (Gen 12:1–8), which it was committed to develop (Gen 1:26–28). Possession of land and children distinguished free households from their slaves and residents of a village from the exiles who lived with them. The free and the resident had land and children; the slave and the exile did not.

The Bible seldom explains farming, but simply assumes the audience understands it so well that no additional details are needed. And there are few, if any, stories in the Bible which provide explanations for developments in the technology of farming. Farmers are simply portrayed as using the tools necessary for life in the hill country. Plowing, planting, threshing, and winnowing form a part of their everyday life. For instance, the stories of Gideon in Judges (Judg 6:11) refer to a threshing floor and wine press at Ophrah, but tellers do not describe them because there was a threshing floor to process grain and a wine press to squeeze grapes in or near every village.

Environment

The economics of farming involved environment, demography, and technology. Environment was the land which villagers farmed. Demography was the villagers who farmed it. And technology included the tools and skills with which farmers worked.

The panhandle of Syria-Palestine, which the Bible calls "Canaan" and then "Israel," makes up less than 60 miles of land mass, west to east (between the 34th and 36th meridians of longitude) and 350 miles, north to south, between the 31st and 33d parallels of latitude. Nonetheless, there are six clearly defined geographical and climatic zones. Moving from west to east, the first zone encountered is a coastal plain along the shore of the

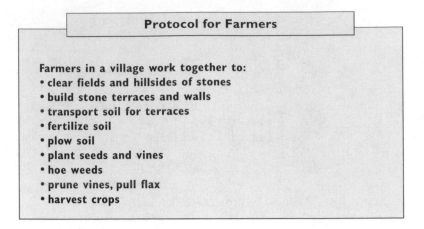

Protocol for Farmers

Farmers in a village work together to:
• clear fields and hillsides of stones
• build stone terraces and walls
• transport soil for terraces
• fertilize soil
• plow soil
• plant seeds and vines
• hoe weeds
• prune vines, pull flax
• harvest crops

Mediterranean. The plains are separated by foothills (שפלה, *š^epēlâh*) from the hills west of the Jordan River or Cisjordan. These hills make up the second zone. The third zone is the valley (ערבה, *ʿªrābâh*) created by the Jordan River and the Dead Sea. The fourth is the hills or plateaus east of the Jordan River or Transjordan. To the south, the fifth zone, the coastal plain with its foothills and the hill country are separated from the sixth zone, the deep-desert in the Sinai by a fragile near-desert region (נגב, *negeb*) which provides the last year-round springs or wells large enough to support permanent settlements.

Throughout Syria-Palestine there are only two seasons, wet and dry. Moist winds blowing west to east create the wet season. Hot dry winds (Arabic: *sirocco, khamsin*) blowing from east to west create the dry season. The plains cause temperature changes in the winds blowing west to east off the Mediterranean Sea which create the rain (Aharoni 1967:8–9).

The range of what each village planted or the animals they herded was determined by the physical environment of their settlement site. There were many different kinds of local geography with which farmers had to contend. There was desert to the east, highlands to the north and south, slopes and foothills to the west (I. Finkelstein 1988a:119–39). For instance, the Hebrew villages farthest north of Jerusalem lived on land marked by outcroppings of limestone and poor soil. Each village, by necessity, adapted its farming techniques to match the potential of its environmental conditions with existing technology.

A standard harvest in the hills produced ten to fifteen times the grain which was needed to plant it. Positive changes in the quality of the land, the number of farmers available, and the way in which they worked could increase the standard harvest, yet there was always a greater risk that negative changes could destroy the economy of the village and its households altogether (Hopkins 1987:178–91). Fields which produced as little as a ten to fifteenfold harvest in good years typically failed altogether in three years out of ten.

Month in Gregorian Calendar	Weather	Agriculture	Season
January	rain	harvest	winter
February	rain	harvest	winter
March	rain	harvest	winter
April	sirocco	fallow	summer
May	sirocco	fallow	summer
June	sirocco	fallow	summer
July	sirocco	fallow	summer
August	sirocco	fallow	summer
September	sirocco	fallow	summer
October	rain	planting	winter
November	rain	planting	winter
December	rain	planting	winter

Seasons in Ancient Israel

Demographics

To get the most from the labor available in the village farmers used a variety of techniques. They managed their time, pooled their resources, and had as many children as possible. Farmers staggered sowing by planting a single crop in several stages over a period of time. Although it would be impossible for them to care for a single large crop at one time, the same number of farmers could handle the same size crop one section at a time. Planting in stages also provided some insurance against losing an entire crop when the planting and harvesting rains were off-cycle.

Farmers also planted a variety of cereals with tree, vine, fruit, and nut crops. The technique had two effects. Like staggering the sowing of a single crop, varying the kinds of crops planted allowed farmers to spread out their work. Trees and vines did not require attention at the same time as grains. Planting more than one crop also restricted the damage done by plant disease. Since the disease or drought which affected one crop did not always affect others, planting a variety of crops prevented the loss of an entire harvest. Even when one particular crop failed completely there was still a chance that others would survive.

The Gezer Almanac from around 925 BCE preserves a typical farm schedule in the world of the Bible. It matches each month with a particular chore. It has the same number of parts as the year, and, like the agricultural cycle, it arranges the parts in a planting-cultivating-harvesting pattern. The almanac graphically demonstrates the diversified agricultural picture of the hill country. Staggered planting protected against environmental disasters

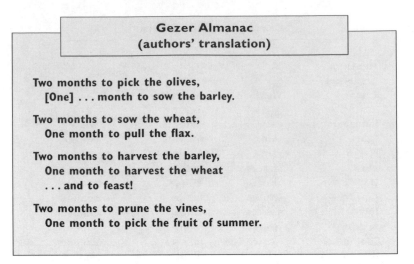

Gezer Almanac
(authors' translation)

Two months to pick the olives,
  [One] . . . month to sow the barley.

Two months to sow the wheat,
  One month to pull the flax.

Two months to harvest the barley,
  One month to harvest the wheat
  . . . and to feast!

Two months to prune the vines,
  One month to pick the fruit of summer.

such as drought (Hopkins 1985:215–17). The use of both wheat, a slowly maturing grain, and barley, which matures quickly in poor or salty soil, provides successive harvests and allows farmers time to harvest one crop and process it before the next one ripens (Turkowski 1969:105). Finally, grapes and figs can be harvested at the end of the summer without interfering with major grain harvests. In a region where the labor supply seldom met labor needs, spacing of major farming events would have been absolutely necessary. For Deuteronomy, one of the blessings of the land is that it will grow barley, grapes, figs, pomegranates, olives, and honey, making crop mixing possible (Deut 8:7–8).

Farmers in the villages in early Israel also worked long hours and full weeks. The values of hard work and the six-day work week find strong endorsement in Genesis (Meyers 1988:47–71). The stories of Adam and Eve (Gen 2:4b—4:2), for example, teach the value of hard work. The story of

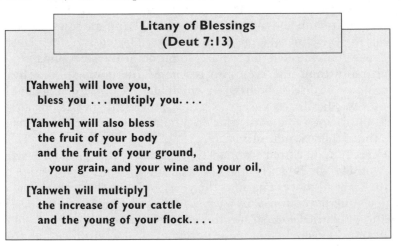

Litany of Blessings
(Deut 7:13)

[Yahweh] will love you,
  bless you . . . multiply you. . . .

[Yahweh] will also bless
  the fruit of your body
  and the fruit of your ground,
    your grain, and your wine and your oil,

[Yahweh will multiply]
  the increase of your cattle
  and the young of your flock. . . .

the Heavens and the Earth (Gen 1:1—2:4a) teaches the importance of a six-day work week.

By living together in pillared houses, farmers pooled their labor (Callaway 1983:44). Together they cleared land, terraced fields, planted, cultivated, and harvested crops (Hopkins 1985:266–70; Borowski 1987:163–65). Pillared houses excavated to date reveal a variety of different patterns to meet space and environmental needs. After 1250 BCE, pillared houses appear in villages throughout Syria-Palestine (Mazar 1990:343). They were designed to meet the same three basic needs: living and working space, space for livestock, and storage space for grain, animal fodder, and products such as wool (Seeden and Kaddour 1984:497).

The pillared house was a simple rectangle divided lengthwise into three areas by a row of roof-supporting pillars on one side and a solid wall on the other (Miller 1977:252–62; Weippert 1971:135; Dar 1986:2; Martin 1989:107; Mazar 1990:334; Hopkins 1985:144–47). The row of pillars was nearer to one long wall, creating an area about four and one-half feet wide on the narrow side and about ten feet wide on the other. Some houses had an additional room across the back of the basic rectangle which was entered through a door off the main section of the house. Beams six to eight inches in diameter were set into notches in the solid outer wall of the house and stretched to the pillars and inside wall. They supported a roof which was six feet above the floor. The roof itself was made up of slats coated with a layer of white clay (Arabic: *huwwar*).

Based on the size of the cisterns at Raddana, which held 23.2–28.3 cubic yards of water, 8 to 10 adults using 2.6 cubic yards of water per year, could live in one pillared house (Callaway 1983:50; 1984:61). Each would have about 12 square yards of living space (Callaway 1983:50). There was no furniture. People sat cross-legged on the packed clay and stone floor or on a stone ledge along the base of the inside wall of the house. Flat stones were used for stools. Everyone slept on the floor. Several households shared a common outdoor courtyard kitchen. Bread was baked on a pottery bowl inverted over the coals (Hos 7:8).

Hebrew villagers wore a loincloth and a tunic. Everyone also had a cloak which doubled as a blanket. Hence there were no closets in a pillared house. Few villagers bathed or regularly washed their clothes, so there were no rooms for washing or bathing. They relieved themselves in the fields which they farmed (1 Kgs 18:27; Ezek 16:5).

Some farmers also herded. They herded sheep, goats, and cattle for their milk, meat, and wool, and as a hedge against a bad harvest and the incursions of their neighbors (Judg 6:4; LaBianca 1979:229; Sherratt 1981). Herding was often carried out by children who did not deprive the village of needed field labor (1 Sam 16:11). At Giloh, south of Jerusalem, there are large corrals fenced by stone walls attached to some of the pillared houses, whose presence suggests a fairly large-scale herding operation, with safe haven given to the animals in the village at night (Mazar 1990:340).

From time to time, farmers also raided passing caravans transporting goods between Syria and Egypt, or they served as transit agents, taxing goods which passed through their territory. In some cases, farmers served as trading partners, especially in metals which were acquired as imports and shaped into tools (Callaway 1983:53). They also turned their own pottery, wove linen from flax, and fashioned tools of wood, flint, and bronze. By combining farming with herding, raiding, trading, and manufacturing, farmers distributed their labor more evenly and insured themselves against facing the dry season without having produced any food at all (Chaney 1983:61).

Another major strategy which farmers used to improve their labor force was to increase the absolute number of workers by having more children. Women in Hebrew villages not only produced by working in the gardens and homes, but reproduced by bearing children. Nonetheless, the population of the Hebrew villages in the hills between 1250–1000 BCE continued to suffer a fifty percent infant mortality rate. With every woman carrying four pregnancies to term, less than two newborns survived. But this strategy of increasing the size of the household also meant there were more mouths to feed. Therefore, increasing the number of workers, by itself, did not create a higher standard of living (Hopkins 1987:189).

Technology

Farmers in the hills made extensive use of the time-tested tools and techniques to clear, plow, water, and fertilize their farms and improve their harvest. Efficient clearing and plowing of the land in the hills were essential to its cultivation. The clearing and planting techniques used by the Hebrews had been used since 10,000 BCE when at first Stone and then Bronze Age peoples set fires to flush game, and farmers used slash and burn techniques to clear the hills of maquis brush and terebinth oak (Hopkins 1987: 180, 222). Crops were planted around stumps in the cleared terra rossa soil.

There is little paleobotanical evidence in excavations today that dense forests ever existed in the hills (*pace* Borowski 1987:15). The word commonly translated "forest" (יַעַר, *ya'ar*) simply means wild, untilled land covered with year-round vegetation. The Bible uses the word to describe a wide variety of overgrown land. It can mean cedar forests, open woodlands, thickets, or scattered shrubs (Callaway 1983:48). The pine trees, terebinth oak, and maquis brush which covered the mountains in Lebanon as well as the hills in Judah in prehistoric times had been heavily utilized for firewood, cleared for farming, and cut for building materials by 1250 BCE when the first Hebrew villages were settled in the hill country (Zohary 1982:43, 59). Consequently, it was not iron axe heads and plow blades alone which served as a catalyst for the settlement of the hill country (Hopkins 1985:221; Gottwald 1979:655).

> ### Land Grant
> ### (Josh 17:14–15)
>
> **The tribe of Joseph spoke to Joshua, saying,**
>
> **"Why have you given me one lot and one portion as an inheritance, since we are a numerous people, whom all along the Lord has blessed?"**
>
> **And Joshua said to them.**
>
> **"If you are a numerous people, go up to the forest, and clear ground there for yourselves in the land of the Perizzites and the Rephaim, since the hill country of Ephraim is too narrow for you."**

Metallurgical evidence from excavations shows that iron working did not appear suddenly throughout Syria-Palestine, but spread gradually and haphazardly. The artifacts which archaeologists are recovering from sites now indicate that iron plow points and axe heads were not widely used there until Israel became a state about 1000 BCE (McNutt 1990:128, 144, 202). In the stories of Elisha, for example, iron axeheads are still considered as precious possessions; a farmer who loses a borrowed axe and becomes visibly upset at the loss of this valuable implement (2 Kgs 6:4–7).

Nonetheless, Hebrew farmers supplemented their Stone and Bronze Age techniques with some important new dry-farming techniques like terraces and cisterns to increase agricultural production and make life in the hills more possible (Hopkins 1985:162, 186–87, 200–202). Farmland in the hills was never irrigated, but Hebrew farmers did construct terraces to manage the available water supply (Borowski 1987:163–64). The terraces (מדרגות, שרמות, maḏrēgôṯ, śᵉḏēmôṯ) not only converted sloping hillsides into workable farm plots and prevented erosion, but also caught and preserved rain water (Borowski 1987:17). Terraces slow the runoff and allow the moisture to seep deep into the soil where it evaporates more slowly. Terracing was limited until after Israel became a state in 1000 BCE, because the cost in time and labor to build and maintain them was prohibitive (Borowski 1987:16–17; Edelstein and Gibson 1982; Stager 1982).

There are only two seasons each year when it rained in the hills. It rained just before the planting season, and it rained just before the harvesting season. This rainfall was critical to farming. It had to rain at the end of the long hot summer to soften the soil enough for farmers to plow and plant. And it had to rain near the end of the growing season to bring the crops to reach full fruit. To prevent crop failure, these rains had to come at the right time and in the right quantity. Three years in ten, however, the quantity

---

Land Grant
(Deut 11:8–12)

Keep, then this entire commandment that I am commanding you today, so that you may have strength to go in and occupy the land that you are crossing over to occupy, and so that you may live long in the land that the LORD swore to your ancestors to give them and to their descendants, a land flowing with milk and honey.

For the land that you are about to enter to occupy is not like the land of Egypt, from which you have come, where you sow your seed and irrigate by foot like a vegetable garden.

But the land that you are crossing over to occupy is a land of hills and valleys, watered by rain from the sky, a land that the LORD your God looks after. The eyes of the LORD your God are always on it, from the beginning of the year to the end of the year.

---

or timing of the rain varied enough to damage crops. Either there was not enough rain to plant or there was too much rain after the crops were planted.

Most of the Hebrew villages did not have a nearby spring to provide a continuous flow of water to drink. Generally villagers had to travel to reach a fresh or living water source. Khirbet Rabud, for example, is almost two miles south of the nearest spring. And Hesban is one and one-half miles from the nearest springs (LaBianca 1979:2; Hopkins 1985:162). Consequently, cisterns for storing rainwater were an important technology for conserving water. They provided a water source independent of the natural springs in the valleys, which had held earlier villages hostage to such vulnerable locations.

The cistern was not the unique invention of the Hebrews who settled in the hills. Early cisterns were cut into water-tight bedrock. At both Ai and Raddana, for example, cisterns were cut into the impervious rock underneath and adjacent to each new house. They were hewed out of the rock when the houses were constructed. But it was the technology of cutting into porous rock and plastering cisterns with slake lime which was most important to Hebrew farmers. The rock on most of the hilltops in the area north of Jerusalem consists of thick layers of Senonian chalk interspersed with thinner layers of Lower Cenomanian limestone. Farmers cut their cisterns into the chalk layers, which have a self-sealing quality when wet. The thin layers of hard limestone most often were at the bottom of the cisterns. These cisterns were bell-shaped with narrow openings at the top. One cistern at Ai was even connected with two others located under the adjacent house. The three cisterns operated together as a filtration trap system (Callaway 1983:49). As the water stood in each cistern, impurities settled out of the water and collected at the bottom. When it flowed out of one cistern and into the other, impurities which had not settled out were trapped in rock filters.

In the hills, there was little or no bottom land, only shallow soil. Planting a field season after season mined or used up soil nutrients. The only fertilizer used by Hebrew farmers was human excrement and manure dropped by grazing herds. Farmers compensated by fallowing (Lev 25:2–3). They planted a field one year, but used it as pasture the next. After they harvested a crop, they would plow the land, but would not replant it at the beginning of the next season. The process helped destroy weeds, conserve moisture, and somewhat offset the destructive effects of soil mining.

Farmers always stored a portion of every harvest as insurance against a short-fall in the produce of the upcoming season. To protect these reserves they dug pit silos (Hopkins 1985:149; Ibrahim 1978:124). And they manu-factured collared rim jars (Greek: πίθοι) uniquely shaped for storage (Mazar 1990:345–48). This stored grain was reinvested in population growth (Men-denhall 1976a:157).

Farming the hills demanded adaptations based on the economic and social reaction of the Hebrews to their new physical and cultural environment. Consequently, farming, more than any other challenge, created a new people from the Hebrew villagers who settled there after 1250 BCE (Butzer 1982:290; Frick 1985:193). To meet the demands of peak labor periods, and to fill the times between with maintenance of facilities and less intensive work periods like the grape harvest, both men and women farmed (Freeman 1970:178). The lives of these village farmers, while hard, contained both a healthy respect for the environment and an appreciation for its bounty (Judg 21:19). But even with the concerted efforts of the entire village, no single village could have coped in every instance with their local en-vironmental constraints or the labor needs of their fields without the help of other villages (Sahlins 1968:77; Hopkins 1985:256–57). Consequently, villages shared the risk and responsibility of farming a marginal agricul-tural region by forming tribes. The continued reliance of the villages upon the tribe eventually built permanent political networks which contributed to the formation of a state. Their village culture grew in size and organiza-tion to the point where the Hebrews began to compete economically and militarily with their neighbors in the cities to the west. By 1000 BCE, the tightly knit relationships forged by risk spreading and cooperation drew the farmers together politically and forged the networks necessary for the formation of a state.

A Hymn to Yahweh as a Farmer (Isa 5:1–7)

Although often subtle, many of the sophisticated techniques early He-brews developed to cope with the land they farmed appear in the laws and stories of the Bible (Jer 31:39; Ezek 38:20; Hab 3:17). A Hymn to Yahweh as a Farmer in Isaiah (Isa 5:1–7), which is retold in the Gospel of Mark as the Parable of the Tenants (Mark 12:1–9), is a good example. A Hymn to Yahweh as a Farmer is an oracle of judgment or a verdict of the divine assembly in the trial of Jotham, who was the monarch of Judah between 742 and 735 BCE (Niehr 1986:99–104).

Verdicts of the divine assembly promulgated by the prophets were always intended for monarchs, even though not every one was delivered directly to the royal court itself (Lang 1983a:63). After 850 BCE, when Assyria began its conquest of Syria-Palestine, Assyrian diplomats often challenged a local ruler's authority by negotiating directly with the local population instead of negotiating with rulers themselves (2 Kgs 18:13–37). During the same period, prophets like Isaiah began to employ the same technique by announcing their verdicts to the people rather than to the monarchs. Consequently, Isaiah promulgated the Hymn to Yahweh as a Farmer in Jerusalem during the festival celebrating the grape harvest (Kaiser 1972:59–60; Oswalt 1986:154; Willis 1977:362).

The Hymn to Yahweh assumes that Yahweh has appeared before the divine assembly on behalf of Judah's farmers to sue Jotham, the king who owns the vineyards. The hymn contains an indictment presenting the

---

Annals of Hezekiah
(2 Kgs 18:13–37)

The king of Assyria sent the Tartan, the Rab-saris, and the Rabshakeh. . . . They went up and came to Jerusalem.

Then Eliakim son of Hilkiah, and Shebnah, and Joah said to the Rabshakeh,

"Please speak to your servants in the Aramaic language, for we understand it; do not speak to us in the language of Judah within the hearing of the people who are on the wall."

But the Rabshakeh said to them,

"Has my master sent me to speak these words to your master, [King Hezekiah], and to you, and not to the people sitting on the wall . . . ?"

. . . Then the Rabshakeh stood and called out in a loud voice in the language of Judah,

"Hear the word of the great king, the king of Assyria! . . . Do not let Hezekiah deceive you, for he will not be able to deliver you out of my hand. . . . "

charges Yahweh filed and a sentence prescribing the punishment that the divine assembly imposes on the monarch.

The indictment uses some of the same sexual language which appears throughout the Song of Solomon (Junker 1959:264). It describes Yahweh as a farmer or lover (יָדִיד, *yādîd*) whose vineyard or beloved (דוֹד, *dôd*) ignores him (Cant 2:15; 4:16; 6:1; 8:12). This language is a development from the significant liturgical role of women at harvest time. For example, at Shiloh women play music, dance, and sing in the vineyards to celebrate the end of the grape harvest (Judg 21:16–24). Consequently, the words "let me sing for my beloved my love-song," with which the Hymn to Yahweh begins, imitate those regularly intoned by a woman celebrating the grape harvest and would have been addressed by her to the vineyard owner (Isa 5:1; Ackerman 1992:163).

Sexual imagery does not always shift the focus of a text from economics and social justice to romance and unrequited love. Semitic vocabulary for having sexual intercourse, learning, eating, farming, fighting, and sacrificing often overlaps (Gilg I:iv:16ff.; Cant 5:1; 6:11–12; 7:11–12). The play on words with which the hymn closes defines the love with which it opens as judgment and justice. Yahweh looks for judgment (מִשְׁפָּט, *mišpāṭ*) and justice (צְדָקָה, *ṣᵉdāqâh*), but finds only oppression (מִשְׂפָּה, *miśpâh*) and cries for help (צְעָקָה, *ṣᵉʿāqâh*).

There are actually two women in the Hymn to Yahweh as a Farmer: the woman who sings and the vineyard. In the hymn itself the divine assembly sentences this second woman, or the vineyard, but economically it is the monarchy of Judah who suffers the loss. Just as the names of cities who are women and their divine husbands are often interchangeable in the ancient Near East (Josh 9:10; 15:9), here the vineyard, personified as a woman, and the monarch who owns it are interchanged.

The indictment in the hymn describes each of the painstaking steps which farmers take to farm the land of Judah: clearing the ground, turning the soil, planting and pruning the vines, protecting the vineyard from predators, grazing animals, and raiders, and finally processing the grapes into wine (Yee 1981:33–34; Willis 1977:356–58). Yahweh cites each step to the divine assembly to add credibility to the charges that despite all this hard work which the farmers do for the monarch, they starve.

Vineyards were labor intensive to install and to maintain. Unlike fields for grain, which only required plowing, farmers had to carve vineyards (כֶּרֶם, *kerem*) into rugged hillsides which did not lend themselves to cultivation (Luria 1985–86:289–92). Their deforested and often overgrazed slopes were badly eroded by wind and rain. The construction of terraces required clearing of stones from the area, building retaining walls, and transporting new topsoil from elsewhere. Only after the hillside terracing was completed could the farmer plow the soil. Installations as difficult to build and maintain as terraces should have become prized possessions whose produce would bring prosperity to the farmers of Judah for generations (1 Kgs

21:2–3). But despite all the hard work of the farmers, Jotham and the other monarchs of Judah took everything for trade.

When planting a new vineyard, it was necessary to obtain choice cuttings from proven vines (Latin: *vitis vinifera*). The farmer in the hymn plants fine purple grapes (שֹׂרֵק, *śōrēq*; Akkadian: *saraqu‘*). The cuttings have potential, based on earlier harvests. They were not only prized for food, but also for the shade provided by intertwining branches (1 Kgs 4:25; Ps 80:11 MT [ET v. 10]). Although they were not a wood that could be used for building materials, the trunks of these vines became synonymous with strength and fertility (Ezek 15:2–5; 19:11). In the world of the Bible, grape vines were not staked, but were allowed to trail along the ground (Dalman 1928: 1.69; Borowski 1987:102–14).

To protect the vineyard the farmer built a hedge or wall with the rocks cleared from the hillside (Oswalt 1986:153). The wall protected the vines from grazing or wild animals, or uncaring travelers who would consume fruit which they did not work to produce (Ps 80:13 MT [ET v. 12]; Cant 2:15). It also marked off the vineyard from others in the village. The wall was complimented by a tower where a child would have been stationed to watch for flocks of birds, for predators, and for raiders (Isa 5:2).

Before vines began to produce, years of labor were required. Only when the vines reached maturity did they produce grapes of their own. In order to mature properly vines had to be pruned annually (Lev 25:4; John 15:2). The ground around the vines had to be hoed to prevent the growth of water-stealing briars, thorns, and other vegetation (Zohary 1982:146). Vines were normally hoed in January and February, and pruned in March (Dalman 1928:1.264). But even with the greatest care given to the vineyard, a successful harvest was never a sure thing. Insects, drought, or war could singly or together rob farmers of their harvest (Deut 28:39; Isa 5:5–6).

The final installation added to the vineyard was a wine press carved out of the bedrock of the hillside (Isa 5:2). In one vat the grapes would be tread into pulp. Their juice drained into another vat where it would be allowed to ferment before being transferred to large storage jars or wine skins (Jer 13:12–14; Matt 9:17). Some wine was consumed by the villagers, but much of the wine produced by the farmers of Judah was collected as taxes by the monarchs (1 Chron 27:27). Ostensibly, the wine collected by the monarchs was used to feed and protect their people. But Yahweh charges that Jotham and the other monarchs of Judah squandered the wine and let the farmers starve. The predators in the hymn who steal the harvest are not animals or travelers but monarchs who turn the hard work of farmers into garbage. Jotham dashed the farmers' hopes (קָוָה, *qāwâh*) and left them with nothing but grapes (בְּאֻשִׁים, *bĕ'ušîm*) rotting on the vine and unfit for use (Jensen 1990:233).

Some prophets promulgate the verdicts of the divine assembly at a site—like the threshing floor, where food is processed for the village or the gate which protects the city—which has some architectural association with the

---

Visions of Neferti
(Matthews & Benjamin 1991b:236–37)

No one cares about the pain in this land, No one sheds a tear for Egypt, no one cries out: "What will be its fate?" [Ezek 9:4] The sun is shrouded, the Sun never shines, The people cannot see, There is no life . . . The canals are dry. . . . Dry land replaces water . . . The south wind defeats the north wind . . . the land is weak. . . . All good things perish.

---

responsibility of the village or the state to feed and protect its households (Matthews 1987:30–31). Therefore, Isaiah promulgates the Hymn to Yahweh as a Farmer at the temple. The temple is not simply where Yahweh dwells, but also where Jotham and the other monarchs of Judah store taxes. During the festival the farmers built the same kind of temporary shelters for their households which they threw up in the vineyards during the harvest itself (Neh 8:13–18). On the first and last day of the eight-day festival, the farmers gathered at the temple to deposit their taxes on the season's harvest. Here Isaiah promulgates to them the verdict imposed on Jotham and all the monarchs of Israel and Judah.

The sentence imposed by the divine assembly is extreme. Land, especially worked land, is precious. To undo physically all the labor which had gone into preparing the terraces, the fences, the tower, and the vines, is very unlike the resource-conscious people of ancient Israel. To cry out against bad weather, a plague of insects, or even an unfruitful vine is one thing, but to both rip out the plants and tear down the vineyard itself is another (Oswalt 1986:154). Only farmers who planned to abandon totally their land and to depart without leaving any evidence of their presence would do such a thing.

The sentence which Isaiah promulgates in the hymn uses the same world-turned-upside-down motif found in the flood stories in Genesis (Gen 7:11–24), the hero stories in Judges, the stories of Balaam from the lands east of the Jordan River, and the Visions of Neferti from Egypt (Lasine 1984; Matthews and Benjamin 1991b:59–61; 235–40). It calls on the farmers of Judah to turn the world of the monarchy upside down. Ironically, it uses the same words which the women sang in the vineyard when the harvest began, celebrating the fertility of Judah under Jotham. In this instance, however, they function to announce its total destruction at the temple, where the wine from the harvest was finally deposited. Jotham and the other monarchs of Israel and Judah continue to break the covenant with Yahweh and to serve other gods. Despite the labor and care lavished on the land by Yahweh and the farmers of Judah, the monarchs continue to use the wine of Judah to make treaties with foreign nations for food and protection (Williams 1985:463). Three times the hymn repeats that since the honest labor of the farmer did not produce its intended results the vineyard will be destroyed (Williams 1985:459).

By the time Isaiah promulgated the Hymn to Yahweh as a Farmer, the Assyrians, who would destroy the kingdom of Israel in 721 BCE, were already crossing the Euphrates River and campaigning in Syria-Palestine. And the traditions of Isaiah would still be vivid in 587 BCE when the Babylonians tore down the wall of Jerusalem and destroyed the kingdom of Judah. Jotham and his supporters may have readily associated the hymn's vineyard imagery with the northern kingdom of Israel. Perhaps they would have been entertained and somewhat self-justified to hear this verdict against their rival, who was to be destroyed like an unproductive vine. Ultimately, however, their condemnation of Israel actually caused them to convict themselves (Yee 1981:37–40; Williams 1985:462). The farmers who survived the military disasters which destroyed Israel and Judah recalled not only, again and again, sentences like that in the hymn, but those which the books of Jeremiah (Jer 7) and Ezekiel (Ezek 8—10) describe as well. And these survivors would further define the images of the prophets with their own bitter memories of the destruction and abandonment inflicted on the vineyards of Israel and Judah by their conquerors.

The destruction of the vineyard will bring the old world of the monarchy to an end. The terraces will be allowed to fall, resulting in the erosion of the soil so laboriously carried up the hillside. The wall will be breached and predators, both animal and human, will be allowed to ravage the vines. What remains will not be permitted to grow again. Instead, without cultivation and pruning, the weeds will strangle the vines and ultimately take over the vineyard, returning it to its previous unworked condition. Finally, the rains will be withheld. With every trace of the farmer's work destroyed, things will become, once again, as they are described in the beginning of the stories of Adam and Eve from Genesis. The farmer whose work integrated Israel and Judah into the cosmic life-cycle will be gone. The land will be without life. Without good farmland, no farmer could survive; without good farmers, no farmland would exist. With the Hymn to Yahweh as a

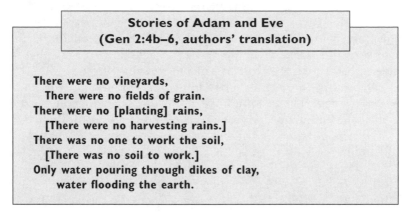

**Stories of Adam and Eve
(Gen 2:4b–6, authors' translation)**

There were no vineyards,
  There were no fields of grain.
There were no [planting] rains,
  [There were no harvesting rains.]
There was no one to work the soil,
  [There was no soil to work.]
Only water pouring through dikes of clay,
  water flooding the earth.

Farmer, Isaiah reminds the farmers of Judah that the promises which Yahweh made to Abraham and Sarah in Genesis (Gen 12:1–3), and which farmers in Deuteronomy (Deut 26:5–11) remembered at every harvest, were not to be fulfilled while monarchs ruled their land (Knierim 1981:84, 98–99). Thus, the prophet challenges them to clear the land and bring this old world to an end so that a new world can begin. It was a task for which they were well suited.

4

The Herder

$\mathbf{B}$y the 1980s anthropologists had studied more than 1200 different cultures (Murdock 1981). Each culture had unique characteristics. Herding cultures, for example, were distinguished by their land and climate (Barth 1961; Zeid 1966), their animals, the politics of the region in which they worked, and the labor needs of the herding group (Rubel 1969; Irons 1974; Galaty and Johnson 1990:3). Each of these factors affected the herders' ability to hire workers, secure pasture and water, ward off predators, breed stock, shear wool, milk, slaughter, buy, and sell. But the characteristic making the greatest impact on social structure was whether the herders were nomadic or semi-nomadic (Khazanov 1984:19–25).

Nomadic herders operated within a specialized system and had no permanent relationship with any particular villages. They were economically self-sufficient, although they supplemented their diet through trade, tribute, or exchange (Murdock 1981:99; Galaty and Johnson 1990:2). Today nomadic herders, who do no farming at all, live in a very few regions, like northern Russia, Mongolia, Afghanistan, Turkestan, Uzbekistan, Kazakhstan, Saudi Arabia, and the Sahara (Bar-Yosef and Khazanov 1992:2). Some nomadic herders settled down and became villagers. To do so, they migrated from the marginal regions, which ecologically could only support herding, to regions which could support some kind of mixed economy including farming (Khazanov 1984:200). Such a move placed economic pressures on nomadic herders to change the mix of their herds to include more sheep and goats as they became more settled (LaBianca 1990:38). These animals bred more often and thus increased the household's capital so they could more effectively compete with the villages in their region. Nomads became villagers when economic factors demanded it, when the environment began to deteriorate, or when their military superiority in a area declined (Barth 1973a; Rowton 1977; Bates and Rassam 1983). However, there was generally nothing to prevent movement back and forth between sedentary and nomadic existence (Khazanov 1984:199–200; Yedid 1984:29; LaBianca 1990:38–43).

Herders as Neighbors

Semi-nomadic herders, on the other hand, were an integral part of village life, and were not economically independent. Villages which integrated farming and herding were economically dimorphic. Farmers developed one way of exploiting the plant and animal resources of the village, and herders developed another (Sherratt 1981; Salzman 1971). Herders in dimorphic villages could not survive without farmers, and farmers could not survive without herders. They were mutually dependent or symbiotic (Barth 1962: 345). For farmers, herd animals were capital on the hoof, producers of milk, meat, and wool, and a hedge against famine (Gen 12:10). For herders, farms were a source of grazing land, fodder, fresh water, and carbohydrates (Bar-Yosef and Khazanov 1992:5). Some semi-nomadic herders worked part-time, some full-time.

Part-time Herders. Part-time herders were much like family farmers in North America today. They farmed during certain seasons when every member of the household was in the fields planting, tending, harvesting, or processing produce. They herded during others when everyone was totally involved with breeding, shearing, and slaughtering livestock (Awad 1959; Bailey 1969). Part-time herders were self-employed; they owned their own stock. And part-time herders were local; they seldom stayed away from their villages for any length of time. During the rainy seasons they grazed their animals close to the village, and during the dry season they fed them with fodder from village silos (Khazanov 1984:24).

Full-time Herders. In villages where farming and herding were specialized, the majority of the population led a sedentary life and was occupied with agriculture. Village livestock was maintained all year round on pastures, sometimes quite far from the settlement, and tended by full-time herders (Khazanov 1984:20–22; Bonte 1977:177).

Transhumance describes one method of full-time herding that was designed to preserve pasture land while at the same time provide sufficient fodder for the herds. The term "transhumanance" was originally applied to seasonal migration of herds in the area of northern Spain and the Pyrenees region in France, and thus its use to describe the world of the Bible is not always accurate (Sorre 1950). However, if transhumance is defined simply as the movement of herds by a few villagers from one grazing area to another at a different altitude, reflecting the changing of the seasons, then it can also apply to the world of the Bible (Parkes 1987:639; Bates and Rassam 1983:110–12; Balikci 1990:307).

Eventually a system of restraints was established to guard grazing areas from becoming exhausted (Arabic: *hima'*). Sheep and goats could devastate pastures in marginal ecologic regions with close cropping of vegetation. Within this system, certain areas were either prohibited for grazing by sheep

and goats or were open only during times of drought or following the
harvest. This allowed for fuller use of these areas by cattle, donkeys, or other
livestock, as well as hunting and beekeeping (Shoup 1990:196).

But even when herders camped away from the village for days or weeks
at a time, they were still working together with the farmers who remained
in the village. The herders and farmers were still part of one economic
system (Murdock 1981:99). Thus, herding complemented farming. Whether
herders were a resident part of a village population, or moved herds from
one pasture to another, they supplemented rather than competed with the
economy of the village (Alon and Levy 1983:107; Chang 1986:102).

Herders as Strangers

Full-time herders were not restricted to the grazing and water resources
of their immediate area. They were more flexible than part-time herders in
managing their livestock (Salzman 1971; Spooner 1973). Sheep were capable
of traveling only two or three days without water (Mitchell 1971:70; Khazanov 1984:55; LaBianca 1990:37). This period could be lengthened to ten
days if the vegetation was fresh and green (Beaumont et al. 1976:154). In
any case, herders had to have a clear knowledge of the water resources of
a region, just as they did of all of its geographical features. This information
was passed on from one generation to the next along with other herding
skills (Bailey 1984:48–49; Spooner 1973:17).

But in their search for water and pasture, herders often left the security
of their own land for the lands of strangers. Consequently, although herders
did not compete with the farmers in their own villages, they competed with
both the farmers and the herders of other villages. To survive, herders were
cautious in dealing with the foreigners whose lands they traversed. Only
herders who were masters of diplomacy could successfully negotiate with
strangers for access to their limited grazing land and water resources
(Pastner 1971:286; Musil 1928:359).

Herders in strange lands compensated for their lack of power by an ability
to manipulate the power of others. Like all marginalized people, they admired the clever who improved themselves at the expense of the local
farmers and herders. Foreign herders were not outlaws, but they knew how
to work the system to their own advantage. They were always embroiled in
one kind of conflict or another. Their rights were never secure and had to
be defended continually.

Herders as Covenant Partners

Likewise, although farmers and herders from the same village worked
cooperatively or symbiotically with one another, they considered herders
from other villages to be spies or tricksters. These herders were foreigners
who preyed on their land and water (Matthews 1986). Local villagers tried

to restrict the freedom of movement of foreign herders for their own security (Rowton 1974). If foreign herders passed unchallenged through their land, important military information might be transmitted to an enemy, or scarce natural resources might be exhausted, depriving local herders of their livelihood (Gen 26:19–22; Exod 17:8–13). In addition, foreign herders might engage in raiding or other unsanctioned activities which would drain the local economy and force the local villagers to expend time and effort in order to bring them under control or drive them from the area.

To change the foreign herders from enemies to friends some local farmers and herders cut covenants with them (Gen 21:22–34; 26:26–33). Such covenants were common and enabled the local villages to keep some measure of control over the movement of the foreign herders (Bates 1974; Swidler 1973; Mohammed 1973). Local farmers and herders typically invested in covenants sealed with endogamous marriages. Foreign herders typically entered exogamous covenants with local farmers and herders (Exod 2:16–22). In return for pasture and water, foreign herders provided their covenant partners with various services.

Once fields were harvested, for example, villages contracted foreign herders to graze their animals on the stubble (Hopkins 1985:255; *ARM* 2.99; 14.22). The arrangement provided the animals with rich fodder from the fields in exchange for the dung which the animals dropped on the fields as they grazed (Koster and Koster 1976). A verdict promulgated in Jeremiah alludes to this method of fertilizing fields when it describes the sentence which the divine assembly imposed on Judah as bodies lying like dung on the ground (Jer 8:2; 9:22; 16:4)

Villages wishing to increase the number of animals they owned also contracted with foreign herders to tend them. The root of the relationship between these villages and the herders was economic. The villages needed

Protocol for Owners and Herders

owners
- provide a herd of about thirty-eight animals (two-thirds sheep, one-third goats, two breed males) and silage or pasture near village during dry season,
- in return for minimum eighty percent birthrate after a maximum fifteen percent loss of adult sheep and a fourteen percent loss of goats to disease and predators

herders
- feed the herd (near the village during dry season; away during the wet season) and protect, breed, shear and slaughter the herd,
- in return for a flat fee or a commission after repaying owner for any advances and/or losses due to negligence

the herders to care for their animals; the herders needed the villages for a livelihood, fodder, rations for their household, and loans of grain. Both the local villages and the foreign herders profited from the herders' success. Livestock owners not only provided animals, but also pasture or fodder for them during the months of the year when they were grazed or fed near the village (Morrison 1983:157).

Larsa was a Middle Bronze period city which prospered between 2030 and 1763 BCE in southern Mesopotamia. It was located near Ash Shatrah in modern Iraq. Ash Shatrah is on the Euphrates River about two-hundred miles south of Baghdad. Archaeologists there have recovered a number of contracts between livestock owners and their herders.

The herders in the contracts from Larsa are clearly not slaves, but free citizens with full legal rights. For example, they are identified by a patronymic, which is a last name or title, such as "son of Wantiya." They are paid for their work, and they settle disputes with their employers before the village or city assembly (Morrison 1981:261; Wilhelm 1978:209).

The herders' skills are not simply the talents of a gifted individual but the corporate resources of a household. In Larsa, herding was hereditary, and in a number of cases households of herders worked for the same livestock owner year after year (Morrison 1981:262; Oppenheim 1939:2).

Larsa's bookkeepers noted that livestock owners negotiated to pay their herders either a flat fee or a commission as payment for their services. A herder's fee for one season might be a certain number of young stock or a weight of wool, dairy products, clothing, or grain. Commissions, on the other hand, were generally figured in one of two ways. At Larsa, owners expected eighty percent of their ewes to bear lambs, and they planned to lose fifteen percent of a herd to predators or disease. Consequently, some owners paid their herders with all the lambs over the projected eighty percent increase or with any animals which survived the projected fifteen percent loss (Morrison 1983:157).

Owners and herders cut covenants once a year. During a roundup (Akkadian: *buqūnu*) or sheep shearing (גֵּז, *gōzēz*; Gen 38:12), one herding season was concluded and another begun. Owners and herders counted livestock, sheared wool, and settled accounts according to the terms of the covenant which they cut with one another the previous year. Then they negotiated a new covenant for the herding season ahead (Morrison 1981: 268). The contract between the owner and the herder identified not only the breed animals consigned to the herder but also the basis on which the yield of the herd was calculated (Morrison 1981:271).

Nuzi is a Late Bronze period city (1500–1250 BCE) where archaeologists have also recovered herding contracts. Nuzi (Arabic: *Yorghan Tepe*) today is near Kirkuk, Iraq about one-hundred fifty miles north of Baghdad. At Nuzi, contracts indicate that the livestock roundup took place in May (Morrison 1981:268–69). From November through April its herders grazed their sheep near the city. From May through October they grazed them in foreign pastures.

At Nuzi, a standard herd included some thirty-eight animals. Ninety percent of a herd would be adult animals. Seventy-eight percent were ewes, serviced by a single ram. The number was not arbitrary, but economic. With thirty-eight animals, more or less, herders at Nuzi maximized breeding, production of wool and goat hair, dairy products, and meat. The number also allowed the herd to sustain losses and still recover its standard strength while in the field (Morrison 1981:276).

Sheep in the ancient Near East were expected to live seven to ten years. Ewes gestate lambs for about five months. Herders who bred in May expected their ewes to drop their lambs in October or November (Morrison 1981:276). Herders would slaughter animals who were between eighteen and thirty months old, although animals only twelve months old were also slaughtered as a delicacy.

There were about two sheep for every goat in the flock (Morrison 1981: 274–75). Goats were mixed with sheep because goats browse and sheep do not. Goats eat only the leaves of the grass, leaving the stem and roots intact, and thus allowing the pasture to recover. Sheep consume the entire plant, thus totally destroying the pasture in a single season. Nonetheless the sheep will follow the browsing goats and thus not overgraze and destroy a pasture (Morrison 1981:273, n. 125). Goats are also hardier than sheep, and they are not as susceptible to disease and deprivation. Furthermore, they are better climbers than sheep and thus have access to additional pasture areas (LaBianca 1990:37). At Nuzi, owners projected a fifteen percent loss of sheep during a season, but only a fourteen percent loss for goats. Thus, during difficult seasons or in harsh climates like the Negeb, herders increased the ratio of goats to sheep in order to maintain the stability of the herd as a whole (Morrison 1981:174, n. 127).

Besides finding copies of the contracts between owners and herders, archaeologists have also recovered promissory notes (Akkadian: *muddû*) recording herders' commitments to repay the owner for any animals lost because of negligence (Morrison 1983:156). On the one hand, herders were not responsible for animals lost due to an "act of God" (Akkadian: *lipit ilim*), and they might be excused from repaying the loss if the livestock were killed by another animal or if the herder could show that he had not been negligent. The hides of the lost animals were produced as evidence (*HSS* 15.196 *me-du-ti*, read as *mituti*, *pace CAD* M/2:3, 5; *HSS* 16.260; 16.432; Morrison 1981:271). Human negligence, on the other hand, cost the households of contract herders dearly. For example, at Larsa a sheep cost 1.33 shekels of silver, approximately the average ration of grain which the household of a herder consumed in three months, or about three months' salary (Morrison 1981:267).

Besides villages which contracted with foreign herders to manage their sheep, there were also villages which simply assigned foreign herders specific grazing zones and water rights in return for leaving the local economy intact (Bates 1971). Neither strategy was completely successful (*ARM* 3.38;

6.30; 14.121). Villages continually struggled to negotiate with foreign herders. As a result, relations between the villagers and foreign herders were
often strained at best (Amiran and Ben-Arieh 1963:162; I. Finkelstein 1984:
201–202). Foreign herders considered themselves exploited by local villagers, and villagers never felt secure with foreign herders in the region
(Matthews 1981a; Salzman 1979). Herders regarded villagers with suspicion,
and villagers considered herders as spies and tricksters.

Again and again, the Bible describes the ancestors of ancient Israel as
foreign herders contracted by local villages to manage their livestock (Gen
13:5–12; 21:25–34; 26:17–33; 29:1–10; 37:12–17). Herding held the households
of early Israel together and provided them with a livelihood and a sense of
group purpose (Tapper 1979:49). Like all traditional people, the ancestors of
ancient Israel treated land and animals in the same way they cared for
themselves. Herding, like farming and gardening, structured the social life
of early Israel (Lakoff and Johnson 1980). Daily chores like cooking, eating,
and sexual intercourse reflected their world view (Levi-Strauss 1966; Douglas 1973).

The Herder in the Book of Genesis

Abram and Sarai (Gen 11:9—13:1)

In a story of Abram and Sarai in Genesis famine forces them to leave their
villages in Canaan and work as contract herders in Egypt. Pharaoh as the
livestock owner and Abram as the contract herder negotiate competitively
to get the best possible terms from their covenant. Ostensibly, Pharaoh
dominates the covenant by negotiating an exogamous marriage with the
household of Abram. By the time the story ends, however, it is Abram the
herder who has actually received the best terms when Pharaoh offers
Abram's household a generous settlement to leave Egypt and return home
where the story began.

The story celebrates Abram and Sarai as ancestors who used their ability
to negotiate well even with the Pharaoh of Egypt. The household of Abram
has neither the land nor the children to compete equally with Pharaoh, but
Abram compensates by being clever, Sarai by being attractive. Tellers never
consider whether Abram is also a liar and Sarai the victim of a chauvinist
husband and an employer who sexually harasses her. Their story celebrates
Abram and Sarai for a single virtue and takes for granted that even Israel's
ancestors were not perfect.

A Covenant between Abram and Lot (Gen 13:2—14:24)

In a covenant between Abram and Lot in Genesis (Gen 13:2—14:24), two herders resolve a common herd management problem: too many animals and not enough pasturage. The issue here is the application of proper herd management techniques and the solution is one adopted by any good manager—division of the flocks and splitting off of a portion of the household to graze another area while the main body remained with Abram (Gen 13:8–9). This strategy, known to anthropologists as "tribal fluidity," prevents internal friction as well as overgrazing and unnecessary loss of animals (Swidler 1972). It promotes the creation of a new, fully independent household related by covenant to the original household (Spooner 1973:41; Khazanov 1984:168).

There is no reason to assume that, after the households of Abram and Lot separate, Lot eventually stops herding and starts caravaning salt from the Dead Sea valley (Bates 1974; Potts 1983:209–210; Deatrick 1962:42). Such a radical change is unlikely, although a mixture of the two activities is possible given the degree of tribal fluidity inherent in the world of the Bible between foreign herders and villagers (Adams 1981). Even though the stories of Lot and his daughters (Gen 19:1–38) place them in the city of Sodom, the dynamics of the stories and the anthropology of herding would suggest they are still foreign herders with whom Sodom has cut a covenant. In fact, the city assembly addresses Lot as a foreign, contract herder (גר, gēr). They may well be confronting him for violating the stipulations of his covenant which prohibit interfering with the internal affairs of the city by offering hospitality to strangers (Gen 19:4).

A Covenant between Abraham and Abimelech (Gen 21:22–34)

In a covenant between Abraham and Abimelech in Genesis (Gen 21:22–34), a foreign herder makes a covenant with a local ruler to use wells dug in his land. By making a covenant, in this case sealed by the payment of seven ewe lambs, Abraham also lays a legal claim to the well he has dug, and this claim will be recognized by Abimelech. He will not have to keep coming back to Abimelech every time a dispute arises. Reciprocally, it will restrict Abraham's use of other wells, thereby forestalling additional tensions between foreign herders and those from Gerar's own villages (Matthews 1986).

The Story of Isaac and Rebekah (Gen 26:1–34)

Traditions with Isaac as the main character are all retellings of stories about other ancestors. A story of Isaac and Rebekah in Genesis (Gen 26:1–11) retells the story of Abram and Sarai in Egypt (Gen 12:9—13:1) and the story of Abraham and Sarah at Gerar (Gen 20:1–18). The covenant between Isaac and Abimelech (Gen 26:12–33) reenacts the covenant between Abraham and Abimelech (Gen 21:22–34). The Isaac tradition never speaks for itself. Isaac is a phantom, seen only through the stories of Sarah, Abraham, Rebekah, Esau, and Jacob, in which he appears without definition or development.

Since Abram tricked the Pharaoh into increasing his herds, Isaac tricks Abimelech. And Isaac negotiates a covenant for water rights with Abimelech just as Abraham had done. Both covenants resolve conflicts between local inhabitants and contract herders in a region with limited water and pasture.

The wells originally dug by Abraham were filled in by local herders no longer willing to share water and grazing with foreign herders (Cornelius 1984; ARM 4.24). The growing hostility between Isaac and the people of Gerar may reflect either worsening ecological conditions or a genuine fear that the foreign herders would take complete political control of Gerar and of all its resources (Khazanov 1984:104–5).

The names of both the reopened wells and of the new wells reflect the stipulations established by the covenant. Some wells are designated for the exclusive use of foreign herders, some are shared, some remain in dispute. The names of the wells not only codify the terms of the covenant, they inform herders precisely who is entitled to water and who is not (Matthews 1986).

The Stories of Jacob, Leah, and Rachel (Gen 25:20—37:2)

The stories of Jacob, Leah, and Rachel in Genesis (Gen 25:20—37:2) are wonderful examples of how indigenous and foreign herders deal with one another. In one story, Jacob leaves Beersheba, the village of his brother Esau, for Haran, the city of his uncle Laban. Beersheba is approximately fifty miles south of Jerusalem. It is one in a series of ancient human settlements where the last year-round sources of water can be found before entering the deep desert of Sinai. Haran (Arabic: *Sultan Tepe*) is an equally ancient human settlement located twenty-five miles south of Urfa or Edessa, near the border between Turkey and Syria today.

Jacob has two reasons for making this epic journey of more than five hundred miles. First, with his mother's help, Jacob had founded his household by tricking Esau and Isaac into giving him Esau's inheritance (Gen 27:5–29). To prevent Esau from taking revenge, Jacob travels to Haran and out of harm's way (Gen 27:41–45). Second, Jacob wants to expand his potential assets by covenant and marriage with the household of his uncle Laban.

Jacob enters Haran as a foreign herder and tries to negotiate with the local herders for water. When Abraham wanted to expand his household by covenant and marriage to the household of his brother Nahor, his herders also entered Aram Naharaim as foreigners. The household of Nahor was anxious to negotiate with them for water. Nahor's daughter Rebekah, who would later become Jacob's mother, immediately drew water for Abraham's herders and their animals (Gen 24:15–27). In contrast, Haran's herders are so deadlocked in their own disputes over the use of their well that they cannot even water their own herds, much less negotiate with foreign herders like Jacob to water his (Musil 1928:359). Laban's daughter Rachel arrives at the well just like Rebekah, but unlike Rebekah she cannot draw water for her own herd or those of Jacob (Gen 29:1–8).

The stalemate which Jacob finds in Haran is parallel to the one which Moses finds in Midian in Exodus (Exod 2:15–22). Unless the dispute can be resolved, neither the animals nor the herders will survive. Both Moses and Jacob break through the impasse by taking the well by force, and then offering to cut a covenant with one of the local households. Moses contracts with the household of Jethro, whose daughter he marries, and Jacob contracts with Laban whose daughters he marries (Gen 29:15–20).

The covenant which the household of Jacob negotiates with the household of Laban is similar to covenants between livestock owners and herders recovered from Nuzi (Morrison 1983:157; HSS 9:64) and Babylon (J. Finkelstein 1968). Like most herders, Jacob agrees to work for a commission rather than a fixed wage (Evans 1963; Postgate 1975). The terms of these covenants are reviewed and revised by the owners and the herders every year when they shear (Gen 31:19; 38:13; 2 Sam 13:23) and breed their animals (Gen 30:32–42).

The previously existing kinship between Jacob and Laban makes Jacob more likely to expect favorable terms from his uncle (Gellner 1977:2). But the relationship between Jacob and Laban quickly changes when Laban's household produces sons (Gen 31:1) and Jacob is perceived as an economic and social rival to their inheritance. Under these constraints, Jacob accepts the reality of the situation and voluntarily leaves Haran and returns to Canaan—not, however, before tricking Laban into expanding the household of Jacob far more than he had ever intended.

A Covenant between Jacob and Shechem (Gen 33:18—34:31)

The covenant between Abraham and Hebron in Genesis (Gen 23:1–20) deeds Abraham, as a foreign herder, the cave of Machpelah and the right to bury Sarah there. A covenant between Jacob and Shechem (Gen 33:18—34:31) grants Jacob similar land rights and a permit to build an altar to El, the God of Israel, in the land of Shechem. Two important dynamics take place in this covenant. First, the fathers of Shechem and of Jacob attempt to cut a covenant with one another. Second, Shechem and Jacob's sons compete with their fathers for control of their own households, and seek to dominate the other's household. Ultimately, the sons break away and resolve the issue with violence rather than negotiations.

A crisis erupts when a prince or son of Shechem rapes Jacob's daughter, Dinah (Gen 34:2). The assault threatens to destroy the covenant between the two households, because the rape indicates the household of Shechem's intention to take over the household of Jacob. Initially the two fathers agree to resolve the dispute by allowing Dinah and the prince to marry, since a marriage between her and the prince would ratify, rather than destroy their covenant. The ceremonies ratifying the covenant begin with the circumcision of the warriors of Shechem. Before they are completed, however, Simeon and Levi lead the warriors of Jacob in a surprise attack on Shechem and destroy it. This restores the honor of the household and provides additional assets in the form of herds and slaves (Gen 34:27–29), but it destroys the opportunity for a long-term economic relationship with Shechem.

The Stories of Joseph (Gen 37:2b—50:26)

In the stories of Joseph in Genesis (Gen 37:2–36), the household of Jacob contracts with one city after another to graze its herds on their harvested fields. Joseph runs messages for Jacob to his brothers who are with the herds some distance from the village of Jacob in Hebron. Joseph delivers the itinerary which Jacob schedules, and reports back to Jacob on the quality of his brothers' work for the cities with whom Jacob contracts. This follows standard procedure among herders since the father of the household had to remain informed about the movements of his herds, especially those in distant pastures, in order to make correct decisions (Salzman 1971).

As a matter of course, Jacob sends most of his sons north from Hebron with the flocks to seek better pastures in the hill country. But the brothers leave Shechem, with whom their father has a covenant, to graze the herds at Dothan. When they fail to send back word of their movements for some time, Joseph is sent in search of them (Gen 37:12–14). Joseph first looks for his brothers in a harvested field (שָׂדֶה, śāḏeh) near Shechem. This was no accident since it would be just the sort of seasonal grazing area used by foreign herders (Bates 1972; Hopkins 1985:247). It was also a place where word of the herders' movements could be gathered from local farmers, who were preparing their fields for the next season's planting (Gen 37:15–17).

Tellers develop two levels of competition in the plot for this story of Joseph. When the story opens, Joseph and his brothers are challenging Jacob's authority as father of the household to designate his "beloved son" (Gen 37:3–4) or heir. Because Jacob gives Joseph a special garment—"a coat of many colors" (KJV) or "a long robe with sleeves" (NRSV)—it is easy to assume that Joseph is Jacob's unannounced choice (Schneider 1987:409). But Joseph challenges his father to make the appointment official by recounting dreams which lay his claim to the household on divine authority.

Joseph and his brothers not only compete with Jacob for control of the household, they also compete with one another. Joseph taunts his brothers with the same kind of dreams with which he challenges Jacob, flaunts the garment which Jacob has given him, and reports all their violations of

Jacob's covenants (Gen 37:5–8). The brothers retaliate by ostracizing Joseph and then contriving his death.

The crisis is further complicated when the brothers move the herd from Shechem to Dothan without Jacob's permission. Jacob contracts them to graze Shechem's fields until he notifies them through Joseph where they are to go next. Whether or not they fulfill the terms of Jacob's covenant with Shechem, whether they contract with Dothan on their own or move the herd without a contract, and whether or not they plan to turn the income over to the household, the brothers' actions challenge Jacob's authority as the father of the household just as Simeon and Levi usurp Jacob's authority by attacking Shechem (Gen 34:25–31).

At the heart of the dissension among the brothers, however, is jealousy over Joseph's usurping a high place within the household. Reuben, Jacob's oldest son and likely heir, does demonstrate a desire to maintain peace within the household in his plan to save Joseph (Gen 37:21). It is only after Joseph is gone, however, that the brothers can unite to serve the good of the household. Dissension does not surface again until the famine drives them to Egypt to purchase food and to deal with the disguised Joseph (Gen 42:1–5). Judah once again raises the question of Jacob's leadership by refusing to return to Egypt (Gen 43:3–5) unless Benjamin is given permission to accompany them. His argument is based on the survival of the entire household, and once Jacob overcomes his personal grief, his response is as crafty as ever. He sends the brothers along with gifts to bribe Pharaoh's official (Gen 43:11–14).

Herder Stories in Psalms and Ezekiel

The Herder in a Hymn to Yahweh (Ps 23)

In most interpretations, the Hymn to Yahweh as a Shepherd in Psalms (Ps 23) is assumed to be a fable which portrays the household of Jacob as a herd animal celebrating the virtues of Yahweh as its shepherd (Kraus 1988:306; Weiser 1962:228). A better reading of the hymn results when the speaker is identified, not as a herd animal, but rather as a livestock owner. The owner celebrates Yahweh as a herder who faithfully carries out his covenant. The identification of Israel as a local villager and Yahweh as a contract herder is more strongly supported by the literary and anthropological traditions of the biblical world, and it brings a number of important connotations to the interpretation of the psalm (Ps 80:1).

Fable is a literary technique. It casts non-human characters like plants and animals as humans (van Wyk 1981:89–95; De Waard 1989:362–70). The technique not only gives animals human qualities, but develops the plot line as a quarrel or dispute between the protagonist and the antagonist as well (van Wyck 1981:90). Finally, ancient Near Eastern fables regularly employ satire to ridicule the antagonist.

Although fables were very popular in Egypt and Mesopotamia, only a few appear in the Bible. For example, the Fable of Jotham (Judg 9:8–15) casts the Hebrews as trees in search of a ruler. Their candidates for monarch are an olive tree, a fig tree, a grape vine, and a thorn bush (Deut 8:8). The fable is a satirical portrayal of monarchs as being as useless as thorn bushes. No tree with any socially redeeming value, like the olive, the fig, or the grape, would consider becoming a monarch.

Therefore, the fable technique is simply too rare in the Bible—and virtually unparalleled in the Psalms—to assume that it appears in the hymn. Furthermore, the corroborating literary characteristics of quarrel and satire are completely missing in the hymn. For the Hymn of Yahweh as a Shepherd to employ the fable technique, it would be necessary for the sheep that speaks to be arguing with Yahweh its shepherd about who is of more value.

Contracts or covenants were important socioeconomic institutions in the world of the Bible that regularly describe Israel's relationship with Yahweh as a covenant. Although most studies of covenant theology focus on covenants between monarchs, the covenant between a local village and foreign herders would be a more likely model for biblical traditions prior to the establishment of a state by David and Solomon in 1000 BCE. Neither the Bible nor the anthropology of herding, however, ever refer to the relationship between the animals and the herder as a covenant.

All cultures develop ways of describing the relationship between their rulers and the divine assembly. In Egypt the Pharaohs carry titles that clearly indicate they are regarded as divine. The rulers of Mesopotamia, while not explicitly honored as divine, are regarded either as the servants of the divine assembly or as the spouse of a member of the divine assembly. But even when the Bible uses ritual language common to the tradition of divine monarchy, it never considers the monarchs of Israel and Judah to be divine. In fact, the prophets of ancient Israel regularly indict the monarchs of Israel and Judah for acting like Yahweh. For the prophets, Yahweh alone was entitled to feed and protect Israel. Prophets considered the covenants which the monarchs of Israel and Judah cut with foreign countries for trade and military aid to be heretical. They clearly violated the covenant which Israel had with Yahweh. Although the monarchs saw the treaties as a logical responsibility of their role as stewards, the prophets considered them to be acts of idolatry.

The identification of Israel or its monarch as a livestock owner and Yahweh as a herder would also provide some insight into the way the Bible understands the ancient Near Eastern tradition of divine monarchy. If Israel or its monarch are considered livestock owners and Yahweh is considered a shepherd who manages Israel's livestock, then there is no question that the rulers of Israel are not divine. On the contrary, Israel is served by a good shepherd who not only faithfully fulfills all the stipulations of the herding

> ### Teachings of Jotham
> ### (Judg 9:8–15)
>
> The trees once went out to
>   anoint a king over themselves,
> So they said to the olive tree,
>   "Reign over us."
>
> The olive tree answered them,
>
> "Shall I stop producing my rich oil
>   by which gods and mortals are honored,
>   and go to sway over the trees?"
>
> Then the trees said to the fig tree,
>   "You come and reign over us."
>
> But the fig tree answered them,
>
> "Shall I stop producing my sweetness
>   and my delicious fruit,
>   and go to sway over the trees?"
>
> Then the trees said to the vine,
>   "You come and reign over us."
>
> But the vine said to them,
>
> "Shall I stop producing my wine
>   that cheers gods and mortals,
>   and go to sway over the trees?"
>
> So all the trees said to the bramble,
>   "You come and reign over us."
>
> And the bramble said to the trees,
>
> "If in good faith you are anointing me king over you,
>   then come and take refuge in my shade;
>
> but if not, let fire come out of the bramble
>   and devour the cedars of Lebanon."

contract, but season after season returns the herd with fewer losses and more births than when it left the village.

The Hymn to Yahweh as a Shepherd catalogs with wonderful accuracy the same responsibilities delegated to the herders of Nuzi and Mari. Yahweh is a faithful herder: "goodness and love unfailing" (Ps 23:6). Yahweh is not a hired hand who flees at the first sign of trouble, but will remain with the sheep (John 10:12; Johnson 1983:261). Israel as a local livestock owner celebrates Yahweh as a contract herder for his skill in grazing the hungry animals: "he renews life within me" (Ps 23:3; Johnson 1983:256–58), and for his knowing the best routes from the village to pasture and water: "in the right path" (Ps 23:3; Johnson 1983:258). Both lines of the hymn celebrate Yahweh for knowing how to feed the hungry (Ps 23:1–3).

The hymn also celebrates Yahweh for knowing how to protect the animals from harm (Ps 23:3–4). The good herder is responsible, which is the technical meaning of the phrase "for his name's sake" (Ps 23:3). Unlike Abel, whom Cain accuses of getting lost and therefore not being worthy of the name "shepherd," Yahweh does not wander off and is therefore worthy of the name "shepherd" (Gen 4:9–10; Johnson 1983:259–60).

The "valley dark as death" through which Yahweh leads the animals is full of shadows and in every shadow there is the potential for death. It is not simply a metaphor for death, but describes the actual dangers which can lead to the loss of herd animals (Kraus 1988:307; Johnson 1983:260).

As long as Yahweh is the herder the sheep are safe: "I shall dwell in the house of the Lord my whole life long" (Ps 23:6). The sense here is that because Yahweh will always feed and protect them, the herd will survive. The "house of the Lord" is not the temple, but the household of Yahweh. The herds of this household are safe because they are cared for by the good shepherd (Johnson 1983:261–71).

The Herder in a Trial of the Monarchs of Israel (Ezek 34:1–16)

There is remarkable similarity in tone and language between the Hymn to Yahweh as a Shepherd and a Trial of the Monarchs of Israel from Ezekiel (Ezek 34:1–16). Like herders, rulers were responsible for feeding and protecting. Consequently, "shepherd" was a common title for monarchs in the biblical world (Kraus 1988:306–7). Good shepherds were monarchs whose people thrived while they reigned; bad shepherds were monarchs who exploited their people. The prophet indicts the monarchs and their priests for failing to fulfill their responsibilities as herders, basing his accusation on a similar statement in Jeremiah 23:1–2 (Allen 1990:161).

Ezekiel charges the monarchs of Israel and Judah with feeding themselves instead of their sheep. They use the products of the herd—its fat, wool, and meat—but do not care for the animals. They do not nurse the weak animals, tend the sick or look for strays. Instead, they abuse all the animals. As a result, the animals are scattered and predators devour them.

Consequently, Yahweh as the owner of the animals will herd them himself. With a good shepherd the animals will enjoy good grazing near the villages and on the mountains far away. They will drink from fresh springs. And when they are weak, sick, or lost, Yahweh will look out for them, tend their wounds, seek them out, and bring them back. Herding was not only important economically as a way of life, it was also Israel's way of understanding Yahweh.

5

The Midwife

In the world of the Bible, birth (מולדת, *môledet*; Greek: γένεσις) was an ordinary part of human life. Villages gave midwives the clinical and legal authority both to negotiate the precoital covenant, and to provide the mother with prenatal, labor, delivery, and postpartum care (Richardson and Guttmacher 1967:3–4; Baab 1962:440). The clinical services of midwives were limited to women, but their legal services were offered to men as well. Clinical or medical institutions and legal or religious institutions today still share in the arrangements for birth. Both obstetricians and pastors offer prenatal instructions. Both rabbis and physicians perform circumcisions. And before resuming sexual intercourse, some women still follow the six-week check-up with their physicians by going to be churched or blessed by their pastors.

Trades and skills were carefully guarded secrets in antiquity (Frick 1971: 379–87; Frick 1976; Eliade 1964). There were no handbooks on how to be a potter, a metalworker, or a midwife. Masters revealed their skills to candidates during deliberately long periods of apprenticeship. Procedures were subdivided into lessons which by themselves were meaningless. Only when candidates completed the entire internship did all the lessons fit together and make sense.

The protocol for midwives was a rite of passage which contained a separation terminating the candidates' relationships with their communities, and a transition marking the separated as taboo, holy, impure, or unclean. They were free agents without community. The rite concluded with an incorporation joining the separated to new communities (van Gennep 1960: 52–53). The care which midwives provided during labor and delivery, for example, separated the newborn from its birth mother. During the moments when it was unwashed, not anointed, unclothed, and unclaimed the newborn was in transition. Once it was claimed or adopted, midwives incorporated it into the household whose father and mother spoke up for it.

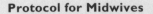

Protocol for Midwives

before the birth, midwives

- negotiate covenants with divine assembly, wife, childbearer
- monitor menstruation of childbearer
- supervise nutrition of childbearer
- prepare room for intercourse
- certify pregnancy of childbearer
- respond to midterm traumas like miscarriages, abortions

during the birth, midwives

- sterilize room for birth
- ease labor pain with birth chair, music, massage
- initiate respiration
- cut umbilical cord
- negotiate covenant with household for name of newborn
- bathe, anoint, clothe, nurse newborn
- respond to labor-delivery traumas like breech births

after the birth, midwives

- dispose of umbilical cord
- supervise care of childbearer, newborn
- respond to traumas like still births, crib deaths

Prenatal Care

When the father of a household decided to have a child, he began negotiations with the divine assembly. The divine and the human attorneys who helped him were midwives (Matthews and Benjamin 1991b:87–88). They helped him not only in obtaining permission to have a child, but also in specifying the woman who would bear the child, when they would have intercourse, who would adopt the child, and who would nurse it. In many households only one wife conceived, bore, adopted, and nursed its sons and daughters, but in some, each function was performed by a different woman. Therefore, a child could be conceived and carried by one woman, adopted by another, and nursed by yet another. Clinically, midwives were responsible for seeing that any woman who was going to give birth or care for a child was physically prepared to fulfill her role (Delaney 1988:264, n.3). They were also responsible for seeing that these women were legally designated and financially compensated.

Menstruation (Latin: *menses*) played a key role in the preparation of the childbearer. By observing when a woman between puberty and menopause discharged a bloody fluid from her nonimpregnated uterus through the vagina, midwives determined the appropriate time for the couple to have sexual intercourse (Jensen et al. 1977:733). Intercourse during menstruation was strictly prohibited (Lev 15:19–24; Delaney 1988:89; Buckley and Gottlieb 1988:19–20). Midwives monitored menstrual flow to prevent contamination which would require purification rituals.

Before a woman had intercourse, midwives monitored the nutrition of their mothers-to-be and prescribed special foods or aphrodisiacs considered to increase fertility. For example, the mandrake, which is a Mediterranean herb with egg-shaped leaves, white or purple flowers, and a large forked root (Latin: *mandragora officinarum*), was used by midwives as an aphrodisiac in ancient Israel (Cant 7:13; Gen 30:14–20). Aphrodisiacs were often shaped like or smelled like the reproductive organs they were expected to stimulate.

Both the room where the child was conceived and the room where the child was to be born were under the supervision of midwives. When the day for sexual intercourse arrived, midwives prepared the room where the couple would meet. All unauthorized inhabitants, whether human or divine, were expelled. Any members of the divine assembly who might prevent fertility and conception were exorcised with music which the midwives played or chanted.

Once the room had been cleaned, the midwives assembled all the people and things necessary to conceive a healthy and viable child. They summoned all the members of the divine assembly required for fertility and conception, and arranged whatever furniture and food would be needed.

Midwives certified that the mother was indeed pregnant following sexual intercourse. Their declaration was based on examinations which took place following the days of intercourse and at various intervals during pregnancy. The first confirmation of fertilization was the bleeding caused by the rupture of the woman's hymen during intercourse. Midwives inspected the bed clothes for blood stains and then presented them to the woman's parents as evidence (Deut 22:15). Second, midwives noted any changes in the woman's menstrual cycle to determine if she was pregnant. Third, midwives palpated or massaged the uterus of their women. The fourth and definitive sign of fertilization was the movement or kick of the fetus in the uterus (Gen 16:4; Luke 1:44).

Midwives continued using massage to examine the development and position of the fetus throughout pregnancy. The physical contact between the midwife and the unborn child not only created an enduring bond between her and the child, but also provided a safeguard against any dislocation which might endanger the mother and child. Fetal trauma and any other maternal discomforts were also treated with massage. The fetus not only grew accustomed to the touch of its midwife, but responded to her gentle hands as well.

Labor and Delivery Care

The preparations for the birth room were comparable to those for the marriage room. In some cultures, midwives constructed a special hut for each delivery. After the child was born and the mother returned to her own house, the birth hut was burned. When the delivery took place in the mother's own house, however, midwives prepared it by expelling anyone not authorized to be present for birth. Generally, no men, children, or unmarried women were permitted to attend a birth. Midwives also checked for the presence of any members of the divine assembly who were not welcome at birth, exorcised them with music and prevented their return by caulking any openings in the room and carefully sweeping the dirt floor or scattering flour on it so that no intruder could enter undetected. Pioneer mothers in the American West used similar tactics to protect their families from rattlesnakes. They removed all the shrubs and grass from around their houses which were built off the ground on pilings of brick or stones. Every day, they swept the dirt smooth so that any snake which crawled up into the cool shade under the house would leave a clear trail to its hiding place.

Midwives used birthing stools, music, and massage to control pain (Donegan 1978:141-63; Jordan 1983). Nothing was done to violate the modesty of a mother. Midwives asked no probing questions about anatomical symptoms, did not perform pelvic examinations and did not undress the mother during labor (Jordan 1983).

In traditional cultures virtually all mothers deliver kneeling, squatting, sitting, or standing. Paleolithic (9000 BCE) rock drawings from Europe and a Neolithic (6000–4000 BCE) clay figurine from Catal Hüyük, a sister city to Jericho in today's Turkey, show steatopygous or large hipped women birthing children in squatting positions (Towler and Bramall 1986:1–5; Anati 1987: 125). One of the most important items in the repertoire of midwives was a birthing stool, used to support the mother's weight and position her hips for delivery.

The Cuna in Panama use hammocks during labor (Severin 1973:124). The mother sits over a hole in the hammock through which the midwife delivers her baby. Among the indigenous people of colonial Mexico, an expectant mother announced her pregnancy by wrapping a long black sash around her waist. During pregnancy it helped support her uterus, and during labor, the midwife tied the sash over a beam in the hut to create a sling to support the mother's hips. On the American frontier, midwives used a variety of items including a wooden milking stool as a birthing stool (Wertz and Wertz 1977:13–14).

A physician of Louis XIV (1638–1715) may have been the first to have mothers lay down on their backs during labor (Towler and Bramall 1986:8). This horizontal position makes the work of the physician easier, but the labor of the mother more difficult. Nonetheless, it became popular throughout the courts of Europe and is still a standard medical practice. Some physicians and midwives today, however, now allow mothers to sit or squat during labor (Donegan 1978:19). Birthing chairs are beginning to appear again in delivery rooms in the United States in response to the increasing demand of healthy mothers who intended to deliver their babies without drugs and in an upright position (Roberts and Van Lier 1984:33–41). In design these twentieth-century birthing stools are much like the chairs used by dentists or by surgeons in out-patient clinics.

In the ancient Near East, the birthing stool was simply two rocks or bricks pushed close enough together to support the mother's hips (Thompson 1986:267). These rocks were as characteristic of midwives in the world of the Bible as the saws used for amputations were of doctors on the American frontier. And just as frontier surgeons were nicknamed "sawbones," biblical midwives may have been called "the rock" (Deut 32:1–43).

Just as the midwives used music to prepare the rooms in which intercourse and birth would take place, they also used music during labor and delivery. The rhythm or melody was as important as the words. Midwives, however, were not simply entertainers or even the nymphs of Greece and Rome who dwelt in the mountains, forest, trees, or waters, and were represented by beautiful young women at their shrines (*pace* Gray 1982:96). Music in the ancient Near East was a sympathetic or imitative magic which was a source of great power (Meyers 1991:24–25). The rhythm of the voice or the drum set a healthy pace for respiration and heartbeat, and tuned the parents and their child to the rhythm of the universe with which they were joined during these creative moments.

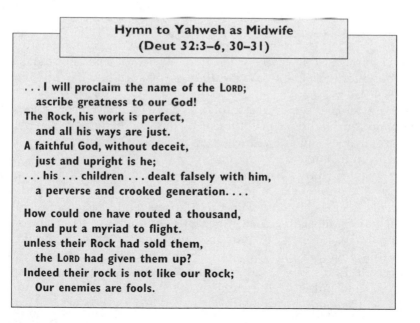

Hymn to Yahweh as Midwife
(Deut 32:3–6, 30–31)

. . . I will proclaim the name of the LORD;
   ascribe greatness to our God!
The Rock, his work is perfect,
   and all his ways are just.
A faithful God, without deceit,
   just and upright is he;
. . . his . . . children . . . dealt falsely with him,
   a perverse and crooked generation. . . .

How could one have routed a thousand,
   and put a myriad to flight.
unless their Rock had sold them,
   the LORD had given them up?
Indeed their rock is not like our Rock;
   Our enemies are fools.

When the mother pushes the fetus from her uterus (Jensen 1977:732), it is normally the head of the fetus facing down which first descends into the pelvis. The midwife had to recognize and respond to abnormal presentations when the fetus presented face up, or buttocks or shoulders first (Jensen 1977:736). Today about three percent of all fetuses breech during delivery.

During pregnancy, circulation in the fetus is made possible by the ductus arteriosus, an anatomic shunt between the pulmonary artery and the aorta (Jensen et al. 1977:727). To establish normal circulation in the newborn today, the child is held with its head lowered 10 to 15 degrees to allow any amniotic fluid, mucus, or blood to drain from its mouth and nose. Then the obstetrician or nurse uses a small bulb syringe to suction its mouth and then its nose (Jensen et al. 1977:325).

To clear the newborn's airway in traditional societies, however, midwives set newborns down firmly on the ground (Severin 1973:124). The Cuna splashed the newborn in a stream or a water-filled canoe (Severin 1973:124). Clinically, the technique closed a valve in the shunt so that the newborn can begin to breathe. It also jolted them out of primary apnea, which sometimes arrests their respiration. Apnea is the cessation of breathing for more than ten seconds (Jensen et al. 1977:724). Legally, however, the procedure affirmed the bond between the child and its Mother Earth (Dieterich 1905:1–21, 34, 39). By placing the newborn on the ground and then removing it, midwives reenacted with Mother Earth the parturition she had just completed with the human mother. Earthing affirmed the widespread belief that before entering the womb of its human mother, newborns gestated in the soil, rocks, trees, plants, flowers, rivers, and springs (Ps 139:15; Wis 7:1–6; McKenzie 1907:253–82). For traditional cultures in Germany (Dieterich 1905:57), Australia (van Gennep 1974:xxxi–lxvii), Africa (Burton 1961: 115), and Japan (Batchelor 1892:235), the soil was the primary mother of all humans (van Gennep 1960:52). Mourners repeated the earthing with which midwives aspirated newborns when they placed the bodies of the dead on the ground for burial: "there is for all one entrance into life, and one way out" (Wis 7:3–6).

Once the fetus was delivered, midwives cut its umbilical cord and tied off the stump. During pregnancy, the cord connects the fetus to the placenta with two arteries and one vein encased in a tissue, in order to provide the fetus with nutrition and respiration.

After delivery, the midwife held up the child, inviting its adoption. The first cry of a newborn as it inflates its lungs and begins to breathe was considered a legal petition to join the household and become a member of the village. To adopt the child, a parent would answer its primal scream with a hymn or joyful cry inviting the household to praise the Creator and accept this child (Job 3:7). The parent would officially declare "a . . . child is conceived" (Job 3:3) or "I have produced a man with the help of the Lord" (Gen 4:1), and introduce the child to the household officially using and explaining its name for the first time (Gen 21:6–7). In the story of Atrahasis,

Nintu-Mami celebrates the successful delivery of her first creatures by singing: "You commanded me a task—I have completed it" (Matthews and Benjamin 1991b:19). Eve celebrates the successful birth of Cain and Abel with a similar hymn: "I have gotten a man with the help of the Lord" (Gen 4:1). Just as Nintu-Mami calls her newborn: "Alive," Eve calls her first twin "Cain," which means "dominant" or "strong as iron" (קין, qayin). She names her second child "Abel," which means "recessive" or "fragile as a breath of air" (הבל, hebel; Eccl 1:14). Some hymns in the book of Psalms may be patterned on the word art sung by midwives and their mothers at the birth of a child.

If the birth mother was a wife, she could adopt her own child. If the birth mother was a surrogate, however, then another woman would adopt it. If no one adopted it, the midwife left it, just as it came from the womb, in an open field where it could be adopted by another household (Stager and Wolff 1984:50). In the world of the Bible, life began, not with the physical process of birth, but rather with the legal process of adoption. The midwife acknowledged the adoption with the words: "the child is a boy/girl" (Job 3:3).

Once a parent had spoken for the child, midwives rinsed off the placenta with a saltwater solution in order to clean and sterilize the child. Then they gently massaged its body with oil to protect it from drying and cracking. Washing the afterbirth from a newborn conferred legal standing on it. A child which had been washed and cleaned was no longer eligible for adoption, because it already belonged to a household.

Midwives further defined the identity of a the child by clothing it. The receiving blanket was not simply a practical necessity, but a uniform which identified the child as a member in good standing entitled to all the rights and privileges of the household. The Mbuti of Australia strengthen the bond between the newborn and its earth mother by swaddling it in a carefully prepared bark blanket (Severin 1973:85–87).

Finally, midwives placed the newborn in the nursing position on the lap of its mother who fed it herself or handed it to her nurse. Again the Mbuti further strengthen the bond between the newborn and its earth mother by nursing it with catch water from the pulp of trees before offering it the breast milk of a human mother (Severin 1973:85–87).

When the stump of the umbilical cord fell off in four to ten days, midwives carefully disposed of it (Jensen et al. 1977). The umbilical cord and its stump were intimately associated with the fate of the child. So midwives treated them the way they wished the newborn to be treated in later life. Every precaution was taken to keep the cord and stump from being eaten by an animal who was considered to be the totem of any member of the divine assembly who could do the newborn harm (Jakobson 1950:1149). Among the Swahili, for example, the cord is placed around the child's neck and then later buried where the child was born so that the child will always be welcome in the house of its parents. Sometimes the umbilical stump is saved and used as a medicine. Illness is suffered by those who lose their way in life; vaccinating them with a potion made from their umbilical cord reorients them by reenacting their birth, and thus relieves the illness.

With the child safely born and legally adopted, midwives continued to serve as pediatricians, teaching childbearers how to care for themselves and childrearers how to care for their children (Gruber 1989:80; Habicht et al. 1985:213). Mothers sought their advice on ordinary matters like birth control. Breast-feeding was common and would have provided a natural spacing of the children since it was believed that a woman who was breast-feeding several times a day was less likely to ovulate or conceive. Female infants would be weaned in eighteen months; male infants in thirty, in order for the mother to resume ovulating (1 Sam 1:21–24; Granqvist 1947:108; Gruber 1989:68).

Mothers also looked to their midwives for support in extraordinary crises like stillbirth or crib death. Birth and death mirrored each other in traditional societies. Midwives and mourners assisted at each threshold. High infant mortality rates and the need to provide an adequate labor supply would have required multiple births for each couple. Even with this as the norm and an average of 4 births per couple, the average number of children surviving to adulthood during this period was only 2 (Hopkins 1985:156; Angel 1972:94–95).

The Midwife in the Bible and Its Parallels

For ancient Israel and early Christianity, God is neither male nor female, and yet like both male and female (Mollenkott 1983:1–35). Among its rich archive of metaphors for the Creator, the Bible regularly portrays Yahweh as a mother (Latin: *dea mater*), as a midwife (Latin: *dea obstetrix*), and as a nurse (Latin: *dea nutrix*). As a mother Yahweh carries a child in her womb (Acts 17:26–28), labors to give birth (Deut 32:18; Job 38:28–29; Isa 42:14; John 1:12; Rom 8:22), teaches her child to walk (Hos 11:3–4), and wipes tears from its eyes (Isa 66:13–14; Rev 21:4). As a midwife Yahweh delivers a newborn (Job 38:8; Isa 66:9), clothes it (Gen 3:21; Job 10:10–12; 38:8–9), and places it in its mother's arms (Ps 22:9–10). As a nurse, Yahweh cradles her child (Hos 11:3–4; Isa 46:3–4), nurses it (Ps 34:9; Isa 49:15; Hos 11:4; 2 Esd 1:28–29; John 7:37–38; 1 Pet 2:2–3), and weans it (Ps 131:1–2; Wis 16:20–21).

In the world view of traditional societies, the cosmos is recreated at the beginning of each day, and after the end of each time (Kay 1982:vii, 1). Each new day and each new world is like a child, skillfully delivered by a midwife. Likewise, the creation of the people primeval, the formation of the state, the education of the young, the formation of Christian churches, the burial of the dead, the resurrection, child sacrifice, and the desecration of cemeteries during war are all procedures modeled on the services of midwives. The book of Wisdom preserves a good example of the identification of childbirth with human creation. The Wise Woman declares: "I also am mortal, like all humans, a descendant of the first-formed child of earth" (Wis 7:1). It also compares the relationship between the midwife and birth mother, as well as between the nurse and the child, to the relationship between teacher and student. The teacher tutors a learner just as a midwife delivers a child, and the teacher advises the adult just as a nurse rears a child. The work of the midwife is also a model for the work of the monarch on New Year's day, which commemorates the birth of the state. The monarch gives birth to the nation using the same procedures with which the midwife delivers a child. At the inauguration of every royal administration, the monarch draws the state out of chaos into cosmic order. Even a general understanding of the protocol for midwives in the world of the Bible brings out dimensions of texts which are often ignored or misunderstood.

The role of the midwife in negotiating covenants for the father of the household with the divine assembly, with the wife, and with the childbearer appears in the story of the Two Shrewd Midwives in Exodus (Exod 1:12–22). Here two midwives (מְיַלְּדֹת, $m^eyalle\underline{d}et$) inform Pharaoh that their negotiations with his Hebrew childbearers to control the slave population have failed. "The Hebrew women . . . are vigorous and give birth before the midwife comes to them" (Exod 1:19).

Another midwife appears as an attorney in a text from Mari, a thriving city during 2500–1765 BCE on the border between modern Syria and Iraq. Queen Dam-hurasi, in her official capacity as the supervisor of the palace, reports to King Zimri-Lim (1779–1745 BCE) on a midwife (Batto 1974:21–22). Like the midwives in Exodus, this midwife has challenged the authority of the monarch. In the world of the Bible, even absolute monarchs are dependent upon the services of midwives, who could effectively use their legal authority for or against them, to carry out their policies over life and death. Even the Creator needed a midwife. In both the Enuma Elish and Atrahasis stories from Mesopotamia, the Creator must retain the services of a midwife before beginning to fashion the people primeval (Matthews and Benjamin 1991b:7–27, 153–56). The malpractice of the midwife at Mari was not simply bad medicine, it was treason. Queen Dam-hurasi, however, assures King Zimri-Lim that she will be punished.

The role of the midwife in monitoring the menstruation of the childbearer appears in the stories of Yerah and Nikkal-Ningal from Mesopotamia. Here, seven midwives calculate the date for the wedding of Yerah and Nikkal-Ningal by charting the moon's cycle from new to full (Gray 1982:89–91). The confluence of the moon's cycle with menstruation made it a centerpiece in the work of the midwife. Such ancient observations eventually divided the lunar cycle into four weeks of seven days, which influenced the choice of seven as the necessary number of midwives in this story. Similarly in the story of Atrahasis, Nintu-Mami bathes Enki the Creator, first when the new moon appears, then seven days later, and finally fourteen days later when

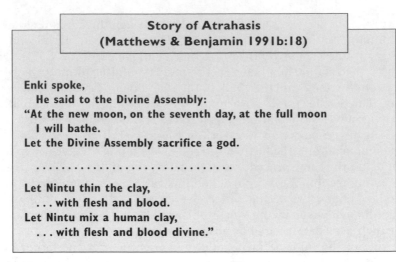

Story of Atrahasis
(Matthews & Benjamin 1991b:18)

Enki spoke,
  He said to the Divine Assembly:
"At the new moon, on the seventh day, at the full moon
  I will bathe.
Let the Divine Assembly sacrifice a god.

. . . .

Let Nintu thin the clay,
  . . . with flesh and blood.
Let Nintu mix a human clay,
  . . . with flesh and blood divine."

the full moon appears, as if this godfather were menstruating in preparation for creating.

The Hymn to the Aton from Egypt praises the Creator as a midwife with an entire range of legal and clinical skills. Aton negotiates the marriage contract between the man and the woman, massages the fetus in the womb and resolves midterm crises. But among the most interesting is its description of Aton as a midwife who supervises the nutrition of a mother during pregnancy or "nurses the hungry infant in the womb" (Matthews and Benjamin 1991b:155).

The story of Aqhat from Ugarit preserves a good example of midwives sterilizing the room in which sexual intercourse will take place (Matthews and Benjamin 1991b:85–94). This story refers to midwives as "wise women" (Ugaritic: *katirātu*). Danil, who will become the father of Aqhat, is a ruler of Ugarit, a powerful port city from 2000 to 1250 BCE on the Mediterranean coast of today's Syria. El authorizes Danil to have a child. Then Danil contracts with midwives to chant any threatening members of the divine assembly from the room where he and his wife Danitiya will have intercourse, and to prepare the special foods which will enhance their fertility.

In the Atrahasis story, the midwife Nintu-Mami not only prepares the room for intercourse, but also participates in the ritual of love-making by which the people primeval are conceived. Tellers describe her work as if she were a potter shaping a vessel. The godfather, Ea-Enki, works the mixture of clay and blood, while Nintu-Mami sings. Once it is thoroughly kneaded, she cuts off fourteen pieces, shaping seven as males, seven as females. She beats a drum while the figures gestate.

Describing love-making as if it were pottery-making is not the only euphemism for sexual intercourse which appears in creation stories. They also describe intercourse as rain falling. Both the stories of Ba'al and Anat from Ugarit and Isaiah (Isa 26:16–19: *pace* Kaiser 1974) compare semen to rain

---

Hymn to Yahweh as Midwife
(Wis 7:1–6)

I also am mortal, like everyone else,
  a descendant of the first-formed child of earth;
and in the womb of a mother I was molded into flesh,
  within the period of ten months, compacted with blood,
from the seed of a man
  and the pleasure of marriage.

And when I was born, I began to breathe the common air,
  and fell upon the kindred earth;
my first sound was a cry, as is true of all.
  I was nursed with care in swaddling cloths.
For no king has had a different beginning of existence;
  there is for all one entrance into life, and one way out.

(נפל, *nāpal*; Mattingly 1985). Rain and semen are the "dew of light" (אורת
טל, *ṭal 'ôrōṯ*) which allow seeds to blossom into plants, fetuses to grow into
infants, and interestingly enough, the bodies of the dead to rise from their
graves. The dead, like seeds, are buried in the soil. And just as the rain
moistens seeds which germinate and sprout, the world of the Bible expects
the rain to bring the dead back to life as well.

Hymn to the Aton
(Matthews & Benjamin 1991b:155)

O Lord, our Lord,
  how majestic is your name,
You join a woman and a man
You form the fetus in its mother's womb,
  You soothe the crying child unborn,
You nurse the hungry infant in the womb,
  You breathe into its nostrils the breath of life,
You open the newborn's mouth on the day of its birth
  You meet every human need....

While most English translations of Psalms describe Yahweh as a tailor
who "knits . . . [the fetus] in . . . [its] mother's womb," it is more likely that
Yahweh here is being described as a midwife massaging the uterus of her
mother to certify that she is pregnant and to keep the fetus in position for
birth (Ps 139:1–24). Midwives know the children they deliver from the day
they take physical shape in the womb, and so, the singers proclaim, does
Yahweh.

Story of Aqhat
(Matthews & Benjamin 1991b:87–88)

Danil went home,
  Danil entered his palace.
The midwives arrived,
  The singers . . . ,
  The chanters . . .
Then,
Danil the powerful,
  Danil the hero,
  Danil the protégé of the god Harnam . . .
Roasted an ox for the midwives,
  Threw a feast for the midwives.
Wined the midwives,
  Dined the singers,
  . . . the chanters. . . .
. . . . . .
Then, on the seventh day,
The midwives left his house,
  The singers . . . ,
  The chanters. . . .

Again it is the Hymn to Aton which describes Egypt's Creator as a midwife who responds to midterm traumas and "soothes the crying child unborn" (Matthews and Benjamin 1991b:155). With gentle hands and a soothing voice, midwives massage and calm mothers in crisis. With no less intimate and personal attention, Aton reaches out to those who suffer and eases their pain. The Atrahasis story best describes a midwife sterilizing the room in which birth will take place when pregnancy comes to term. Here Nintu-

Hymn to Yahweh as Midwife
(Isa 26:16–19, authors' translation)

In childbirth, we sent for you, Yahweh,
  In labor, we cried out when you told us to cry out,
At the moment of birth, we pushed and cried out,
  As you instructed us, Yahweh.
We conceived, labored and gave birth to a mortal child.
  But we cannot conceive and birth a savior. . . .
But you can make the dead live and corpses rise;
  Awake those who lie in the dust and make them sing.
For your dew is a dew of light
  And the land of shades gives birth.

Mami puts on her cap and apron to exorcise all the members of the divine assembly who are not welcome at the birth. Once they have gone, she dusts the floor with flour, so that the foot prints of even an invisible intruder will immediately appear. Only once she has secured the room is it safe for labor and delivery to begin.

The Atrahasis story continues its description of her preparations by explaining how she constructs the birthing stool which will support and position the hips of the birth mother during labor. Before opening the womb and delivering the newborn, she lays down a brick, just as the midwives in Exodus set up two rocks (העבנים, ha'abnāyim). This ability to help a mother deal successfully with labor pain is what distinguishes authentic midwives from impostors. For example, the story of the Shrewd Midwives satirizes the Pharaoh of Egypt as someone gullible enough to believe that "Hebrew women are not like the Egyptian women, for they are vigorous and are delivered before the midwife comes to them" (Exod 1:19). The storyteller's audience knows, even if Pharaoh does not, that there is no such thing as painless childbirth. A Pharaoh who is ignorant of the fundamentals of labor is not a giver of life.

By contrast, the book of Isaiah identifies Yahweh as a true midwife who is Judah's companion in labor (Isa 26:16–18). Most traditions of interpretation understand the words "distress" (צרה, ṣārâh) and "pain" (עצב, 'eṣeb; Gen 3:16) in this lament as a punishment inflicted by Yahweh on Judah (Kaiser 1974:213). If the same words, however, are translated "labor pains," then the lament is reminding its audience that salvation and resurrection from the dead are like childbirth. Only Yahweh can give birth, raise the dead to life, and bring the soil to life.

The book of Psalms also describes Yahweh as the midwife who aspirates newborns and protects them from crib death (Ps 8:1–10 MT [ET vv. 1–9]). Some of the same imagery appears in the book of Wisdom (Wis 7:1–6), where Yahweh delivers the Wise Woman and then sets her down firmly on the ground until she begins to breathe (Wis 7:3).

In Genesis, Rachel dies during a breech birth, but not before the midwife negotiates a covenant with the household to adopt her newborn (Gen 35:16–20). Rachel's midwife announces the decision of the household with the formula: "Fear not; for now you will have another son." The words are particularly significant for understanding how strong the connection between the work of the midwife and the work of Yahweh. In the Bible, humans speak the formula: "Fear not" only fifteen times, whereas, Yahweh uses them more than sixty times. Yet a human midwife may speak to her mother with the words of Yahweh.

Rachel ratifies the adoption by naming her child: "labor baby" (בֶּן אוֹנִי, ben 'ônî), which Jacob later changes to: "my baby" (בְּנִימִין, binyāmîn). If it was customary for the birth mother or adopting mother to name the newborn, then it is unusual for the adopting father to rename it, thus changing the death bed request of the child's mother. It may be that only when a mother died did the father name the infant, or that Jacob considers Rachel's name for the child unsuitable, or that Rachel's death orphans the child, and Jacob signifies his adoption of the child by giving it a new name (Exod 7:14—10:29; Josh 5:13—6:27; Isa 26:10—27:13).

The legal responsibilities of the midwife to negotiate with a household for a name for the newborn also appear in Job (Job 3:1–26). Job pleads with his midwife to take back the name she negotiated for him, so that he can escape the suffering which his life has brought. Whereas Yahweh as the midwife in the story of the Heavens and the Earth prays: "let there be light" (Gen 1:3), Job petitions his midwife to pray: "let that day be darkness" (1 Kgs 19:4; Job 3:5; Jer 20:14–18; Ezek 16:6–14; Jonah 4:3–8; Sir 23:14).

The Parable of the Good Parent in Ezekiel (Ezek 16:2–5) preserves the most complete list of a midwife's postpartum services in the Bible. It expects a midwife to cut and tie off the umbilical cord, to rinse the placenta off the newborn, to sterilize the newborn with a saltwater solution, and then wrap it in a receiving blanket. But because no one in this parable adopts the child, the midwife takes the newborn from the birthing room and leaves it covered with afterbirth in an open field. The field to which the midwife takes the newborn is like the "valley . . . which is neither plowed nor sown" (Deut 21:4) to which Deuteronomy directs citizens faced with an unsolved murder. Both sites are uncivilized. Here human jurisdiction ends. In this field, the midwife transfers the newborn from human jurisdiction to the jurisdiction of the divine assembly over which Yahweh presides. By placing it here in the same condition in which it left the womb, the household waives its own right to adopt the child, and declares that it is eligible for another to claim.

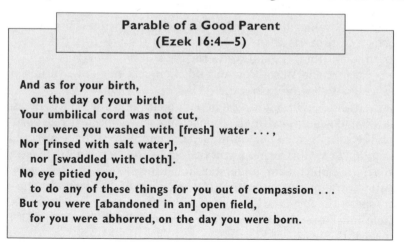

Parable of a Good Parent
(Ezek 16:4—5)

And as for your birth,
  on the day of your birth
Your umbilical cord was not cut,
  nor were you washed with [fresh] water . . . ,
Nor [rinsed with salt water],
  nor [swaddled with cloth].
No eye pitied you,
  to do any of these things for you out of compassion . . .
But you were [abandoned in an] open field,
  for you were abhorred, on the day you were born.

A lament in Isaiah compares Yahweh's on-going concern for Israel with the enduring bond between pregnant or nursing mother and her infant: "can a woman forget her nursing child, that she should have no compassion on the child of her womb" (Isa 49:14–20)? The same motif appears in the

Letter to the Thessalonians which describes Paul founding the Christian community with the same gentleness as a nurse feeding a newborn: "while we were among you we were as gentle as any nursing mother fondling her little ones" (1 Thess 2:1–8).

In Genesis, Tamar survives a compound presentation and delivers twins (Gen 38:27–30) when her midwife responds to the breech birth during labor and delivery. The midwife performs both obstetrical and legal functions for Tamar. Obstetrically, she determines that Tamar is carrying twins (Gen 38:27) and helps her survive the trauma (Towler and Bramall 1986:6–20). Legally, she also identifies the first born by banding its wrist with a red cord.

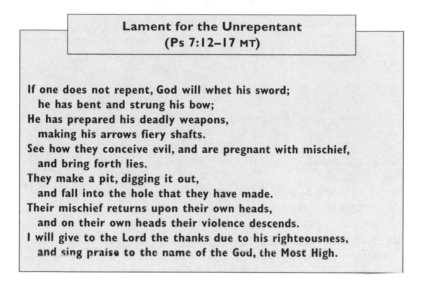

Lament for the Unrepentant
(Ps 7:12–17 MT)

If one does not repent, God will whet his sword;
　he has bent and strung his bow;
He has prepared his deadly weapons,
　making his arrows fiery shafts.
See how they conceive evil, and are pregnant with mischief,
　and bring forth lies.
They make a pit, digging it out,
　and fall into the hole that they have made.
Their mischief returns upon their own heads,
　and on their own heads their violence descends.
I will give to the Lord the thanks due to his righteousness,
　and sing praise to the name of the God, the Most High.

For Psalms (Ps 7:12–17 MT [ET vv. 11–16]), facing a post partum trauma without a midwife is like undertaking a task without the approval and assistance of Yahweh. Both are doomed to fail. A woman who conceives without the help of a midwife, will carry her child to term and go into labor, but her fetus will not be viable. She will suffer post partum trauma, and without a midwife her newborn will die. Translations often obscure the obstetrical metaphors by translating the expression for an unassisted birth simply as "evil," the phrase for labor as "mischief," and the image for post partum trauma as "lies."

Throughout the world of the Bible midwives were as highly regarded as they are in most traditional societies. But midwives were important in ancient Israel not only to the parents they helped conceive, birth, and rear children, but also to the whole community which learned from their work how to understand God. Israel's gratitude to these women remains enshrined in the powerful metaphors of birth and birthing with which it described the Creator and creation.

6

The Host and the Stranger

Travel provided a natural stimulus to the development of a protocol for the host and the stranger. If water, food, and shelter were not offered, travelers in the ancient Near East could not have survived. Hospitality created a code of reciprocity which obligated the fathers of households to treat travelers properly, so that when they themselves traveled they would be properly treated. But hospitality in the world of the Bible was more than simply an amenity for travelers. It was a village's most important form of foreign policy. Villages used hospitality to determine whether strangers were friends or enemies; whether or not they would improve the distribution of resources, labor, and goods, prevent war, and keep the peace (Herzfeld 1987:77). No community could tolerate strangers for long. When strangers approached, they threatened the inhabitants of a place. Hospitality neutralized the threat which strangers posed by temporarily adopting them into the community.

There were regions between zones of hospitality without any host at all. In these uninhabited zones, travelers were truly on their own and subject to the dangers of the road—climate, wild animals, and bandits. But around every village there was a specific geographical area within which hosts had the responsibility of offering hospitality. This zone of hospitality had boundaries.

Similar geographical zones appear in laws concerning unsolved homicides and cities of asylum (Deut 19:1–13; 21:1–9). Deuteronomy (Deut 21:1–9) describes how the responsibility for prosecuting a murderer is transferred from the city assembly in whose jurisdiction the body was found to the divine assembly. The transfer takes place at the city limits where there is no controlled water supply, no cleared land, and no tame animals. The members of the city assembly, who are responsible for trying the case, wash

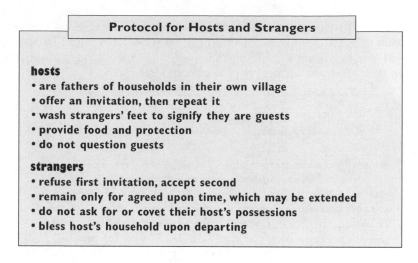

Protocol for Hosts and Strangers

hosts
- are fathers of households in their own village
- offer an invitation, then repeat it
- wash strangers' feet to signify they are guests
- provide food and protection
- do not question guests

strangers
- refuse first invitation, accept second
- remain only for agreed upon time, which may be extended
- do not ask for or covet their host's possessions
- bless host's household upon departing

their hands and swear, as they break the neck of a heifer, that they lack the testimony necessary to prosecute. If they are guilty of perjury, they will be executed like the heifer. Once this procedure rules out the possibility of a conspiracy, jurisdiction is transferred to the divine assembly, which becomes responsible for prosecuting the case (Benjamin 1983:297–98)

Deuteronomy (Deut 19:1–13) also describes the right of a citizen accused of a crime to a change of venue and the extradition of criminals. Originally provision was made for just three cities to which a trial could be moved, but as the geographical size of the community expanded three more were added. This suggests that a specific grid was laid over the land, mapping out the regions and providing changes of venue within reach of most population centers—a set of geographical zones to prevent the death of someone who did not deserve to die (Deut 21:6).

Villages also used hospitality to acknowledge their status on the land as guests of their divine patron. As hosts they did for others what their divine patron was doing for them. The Hebrews understood themselves as strangers, not landowners (Deut 26:5–11; Ps 39:12). They did not own the land, Yahweh did (Lev 25:23). As the divine landowner, Yahweh fed and protected the Hebrews as guests (Ps 104; Isa 25:6–8; Joel 3:18; Amos 9:13–15). Israel's commitment to hospitality was celebrated each year during the Feast of Booths or Sukkot. Sukkot took place for a week at the end of the grape and fruit harvest. During the celebration, households built huts (סכה, *sukkōt*) where they hosted a variety of strangers—slaves, Levites, orphans, and widows (Deut 16:13–17).

Father of a Household in His Own Village

Only fathers of households could extend invitations of hospitality. It was the responsibility of the father of the household to provide for and protect

d; therefore, he also served as host and extended the initial
f hospitality. In Genesis, Abraham (Gen 18:2–3) and Laban (Gen
invite strangers to share the comforts of their homes and thereby
.heir status as strangers (Pitt-Rivers 1968:23).

> ### Teaching on Hospitality
> ### (Deut 16:13–15)
>
> You shall keep the festival of booths for seven days, when you
> have gathered in the produce from your threshing floor and
> your wine press. Rejoice during your festival, you and your sons
> and your daughters, your male and female slaves, as well as the
> Levites, the strangers, the orphans, and the widows resident in
> your towns. Seven days you shall keep the festival for the LORD
> your God at the place that the LORD will choose; for the LORD
> your God will bless you in all your produce and in all your
> undertakings, and you shall surely celebrate.

Wives and daughters could invite strangers into their homes only with
the permission of the father of the household. Although Rebekah in Genesis,
Ruth in the book of Ruth, and Bathsheba in Samuel–Kings exercise the
authority characteristic of the head of a household, technically, it is not
their own authority but the authority of Isaac, Boaz, and David which they
are using (Gen 27:5–17; Ruth 3:1–4; 1 Kgs 1:15–21). Tamar in Genesis and
the daughters of Zelophehad in Numbers are similar (Gen 38; Num 27:1–11).
Although only men had legal standing and could serve as the head of a
household, the daughters of Zelophehad legally petition to serve as the head
of the household after their father's death. Technically, they are acting on
his authority, not their own.

Some strangers who remained within the community were classified as
sojourners or resident aliens (גר, gēr; Deut 24:17–18). They were protected
by the village, and they had the right to come and go freely, but they could
not legally invite strangers into the village (Deut 24:17–18; Spina 1983:321).
The right of granting hospitality is reserved for citizens. When a resident
alien like Lot in Genesis (Gen 19:2) or a sojourner like the old man from
Ephraim in Judges (Judg 19:20) tries to offer strangers hospitality, both are
challenged by the citizens of the place.

Refusal

Strangers could refuse the first invitation (Gen 19:2; Judg 19:9–10). Regardless of the reasons which strangers offer for declining an invitation of
hospitality, such as not wishing to delay their journey, protocol may have
demanded the first invitation be turned down. This first refusal signaled that

the strangers did not intend to threaten or impose upon those through whose territories they passed. Traditional people often decline offers of privilege or power. For example, Moses, Isaiah, and Jeremiah all initially decline Yahweh's call, which is then promptly repeated and accepted (Exod 3:11; Isa 6:5; Jer 1:6). Strangers who refused repeated invitations, however, offended the honor of their hosts.

From Strangers to Guests

Strangers who accepted invitations were promoted to the status of guests when their host washed their feet. In the world of the Bible, people would bathe their entire body, as well as simply wash their face, hands, or feet (Gen 43:31; Ruth 3:3; 2 Sam 12:20; 1 Kgs 5:10; Cant 5:3; Ezek 23:40). To some extent bathing and washing were understood as part of personal hygiene. Feet get dusty, so it was customary to provide water for guests to wash their own feet. But to a greater extent bathing and washing signified a change in social status. Hosts washed the feet of strangers to signify that they were now completely in the care and under the protection of their household.

Provide and Protect

Households had to provide the best available for their guests. It was typical for hosts to make a modest offer of a cup of water, a bit of food, and a simple night's shelter when offering hospitality to strangers. The simplicity of the invitation, however, did not preclude more being given. This action by the host of first offering little and then providing even more than initially offered served two functions. First, it prevented the guest from feeling the necessity to decline an overly generous offer, one which the host obviously could not afford (Cole 1975:67). Secondly, it allowed the host to fulfill his role by bringing out the best he had to offer to his guest (Pitt-Rivers 1968:28). Both parties were then honored by this act of generosity and no hint of rivalry could spoil the moment. Regardless of the actual wealth of the household, an elaborate invitation would be considered bragging and immodest. In any case the household would make every effort to insure the guest's comfort, including in one instance the killing of a calf from the herd, which would have involved a real financial sacrifice (Gen 18:7). Once hospitality was offered, a household also had a sacred duty to protect its guests from harm (Zeid 1966:252). Failure to carry out this duty brought shame upon the entire household (Black-Michaud 1975:139–40).

Length of Stay

Strangers could remain guests only for a specified length of time, which was usually set at the time of the invitation. The time limit was determined both by the desire of the guests to reach their destination and the need of the host not to be impoverished by guests who stayed too long. Generally an invitation involved a short visit. No example in the Bible exceeds four days, and this was an extended stay (Judg 19:4–9). Most travelers wished to be refreshed, not detained. For strategic and political reasons, a host could delay guests, but not permanently detain them (*ARM* 14.97:5–14; 6.19:17–22; 2.133:20–25). Keeping a guest beyond a set period was an act of war (Gen 18:5; 19:2; 24:31, 54; Judg 19:5, 20; El-Barghuthi 1924).

In Mesopotamia, many strangers were messengers (Akkadian: *mār šipri*), responsible for communications and negotiations between one monarch and the other. Several kinds of messengers appear in the archives of Mari. Ṣuhāru messengers were runners who carried letters from one ruler to another (*ARM* 12.131; 2.21:15–22) usually announcing the arrival of an important official or a foreign army. Ṣa sikkim messengers served as proxies for their monarchs. They carried letters of introduction (Akkadian: *wûrtum*) outlining the royal prerogatives which they enjoyed. These could include authorization to draft treaties (*ARM* 2.77). Hosts throughout Mari's kingdom lavished messengers with food, clothing, and slaves (*ARM* 12.747; 2.76:5–19, 34–38; 23.43). They also provided them with bodyguards and escorts (*ARM* 6.14:22–28; 14.117:5–15; 2.73:4–15), both to protect them from harm while they were in the country (*ARM* 14.58:5–15; 6.20:6–13; 2.123; 14.127:5–17) and to prevent them from spying (*ARM* 2.41:3′–4′). Records carefully note all the messengers who came and went (*ARM* 6.14 and 17; 6.15:6–15; 6.23; 14.125:4–9, 21–23).

No Questions, No Requests

Hosts could not ask questions which pried into the affairs of a guest, although guests could volunteer information (Fares 1932:95). And guests could not ask for anything, or even show undue interest in the host's food or possessions by staring at them. By asking or staring, guests usurped the right of the household to offer everything they needed. By asking for something, guests implied that their hosts were selfish or slow in providing for their needs. To ask for anything broke both ritual protocol and custom by reversing the roles of guest and host (Pitt-Rivers 1968:27).

Blessing Upon Departure

Strangers who successfully completed their probation as guests were presented to the village as friends. Strangers who failed were executed or expelled as enemies (Pitt-Rivers 1968:21–22). Strangers who became friends blessed the households in which they had been guests by becoming their allies. In ancestor stories, guests often announce the blessing with which the covenant between them and their hosts conclude. In Genesis, the guests of Abraham and Sarah announce that before the first anniversary of their covenant with one another, their hosts will have a child (Gen 18:1–15). Since hosts bestowed the blessings of life on their guests, guests always blessed their hosts with gifts of life as well. The gifts of guests were always living or life-giving. They always promised that the land and children of the household in which they were guests would become fertile.

The Host and the Stranger in the Story of Jael and Sisera (Judg 4:17–22)

Understanding the protocol of hospitality is critical to understanding the story of Jael and Sisera in Judges (Judg 4:17–22). Only by understanding how hospitality works in the world of the Bible is it possible to understand that Jael is not a host who betrays her guest, but a hero who defends her household against an intruder.

As the story opens, Heber sets up camp with Jael and the rest of his household beneath "the oak in Zaanannim which is near Kedesh" (Judg 4:11). Storytellers use both the name "Kedesh" and the presence of a sacred oak to identify the site as a sanctuary where the household of Heber and all who take refuge there will be out of harm's way during the impending battle between Sisera and Barak. Sisera is the military commander of the king of Hazor; Barak, the chief of the Israelites.

After the warriors of Hazor have been routed, Sisera seeks asylum at the sanctuary of Kedesh under the sacred tree. It is the sanctuary, not the camp of Heber, which offers Sisera protection (*pace* Soggin 1981:67; Halpern 1988: 85). When he finds the household of Heber at the sanctuary, however, Sisera tries to take control of it (Judg 4:17; Gilmore 1987:4). If Sisera were merely seeking hospitality he would have approached the tent of Heber, not that of his wife, Jael. A wife may share the tent of her husband, but a man with more than one wife was expected to provide each with a tent (Ahmed 1973:79). The story assumes Jael has a tent to herself.

Sisera does not approach Jael the way Abraham's slave approaches Rebekah in Genesis (Gen 24:17) or the way Jesus approaches the Samaritan woman in the Gospel of John (John 4:6–9). Both Abraham's slave and Jesus approach a woman at a well, not at her tent. The story of Jael and Sisera assumes that Sisera approaches Jael's tent unnoticed by the rest of the household. The expression (ברגליו, *bᵉraglāyw*) translated "on foot" in English (Judg 4:17) can also mean "secretly" as it does here. There are always warriors in camp to protect the women and animals (Pehrson 1966:85). For example, in the stories of Joseph in Genesis, Jacob remains in camp while his sons take the herds out to pasture (Gen 34:5). Thus, whether Heber was present or not, warriors would have been within the camp to protect Jael.

> ## Story of Abraham and Sarah
> ## (Gen 18:1–10)
>
> ... as [Abraham] sat at the entrance of his tent in the heat of the day[, he] looked up and saw three men standing near him. When he saw them, he ran from the tent entrance to meet them, and bowed down to the ground.
>
> He said, "My lord, if I find favor with you, do not pass by your servant. Let a little water be brought, and wash your feet, and rest yourselves under the tree. Let me bring a little bread, that you may refresh yourselves, and after that you may pass on— since you have come to your servant."
>
> So they said, "Do as you have said."
>
> And Abraham hastened into the tent to Sarah, and said, "Make ready quickly three measures of choice flour, knead it, and make cakes."
>
> Abraham ran to the herd, and took a calf, tender and good, and gave it to the servant, who hastened to prepare it. Then he took curds and milk and the calf that he had prepared, and set it before them; and he stood by them under the tree while they ate.
>
> They said to him, "Where is your wife Sarah?"
>
> And he said, "There, in the tent."
>
> Then one said, "I will surely return to you in due season, and your wife Sarah shall have a son."

Unlike Dinah in the stories of Jacob, Leah, and Rachel in Genesis, who "went out to visit the women of the land" (Gen 34:1–2) where her body-guards could not protect her, Jael does not leave the protection of the camp when she "comes out to meet Sisera" (Judg 4:17). On the contrary, Jael confronts the intruder who has eluded her bodyguards and is trespassing. Jael's actions here are similar to those of Jezebel in the annals of Ahab in Samuel–Kings, who confronts Jehu when he eludes her bodyguards and trespasses into the palace (2 Kgs 9:31).

Sisera's actions threaten Jael physically and legally usurp Heber's rights (Zeid 1966:253; Van Nieuwenhuijze 1971:701). To exert his claim to the household of Heber, Sisera must have sexual intercourse with Jael. His assault constitutes a legal bid to take over Heber's household. In the stories of David's rise to power in Samuel–Kings, David uses the same strategy when he has intercourse with Bathsheba to exert his claim to the household of Uriah (2 Sam 11:1–17). And in the stories of David's successor, Amnon

---

Annals of Ahab
(2 Kgs 9:29–33)

When Jehu came to Jezreel, Jezebel heard of it; she painted her eyes, and adorned her head, and looked out of the window. As Jehu entered the gate, she said, "Is it peace, Zimri, murderer of your master?"

He looked up to the window and said, "Who is on my side? Who?"

Two or three eunuchs looked out at him. He said, "Throw her down."

So they threw her down; some of her blood spattered on the wall and on the horses, which trampled on her.

---

has intercourse with Tamar to exert his claim to the household of Absalom (2 Sam 13:1–22), and Absalom has intercourse with ten diplomatic wives to exert his claim to the household of David (2 Sam 16:15–22). Every action and reaction in the story of Jael pivots on Sisera's plan to rape her (Zakovitch 1981:370–71).

The story of Jael heightens the literary tension of the plot of the story of Deborah which precedes it. Suddenly, the audience realizes that it does not know whether the protagonist in these stories is Deborah or Jael (Amit 1987:89). And they have no idea how the story will end (Murray 1979:182). Until this point the audience has been led to assume that "the Lord will sell Sisera into the hand of [the] woman Deborah" (Judg 4:9), but now there are two women—Deborah and Jael. Not only is it uncertain whether Deborah or Jael is the main character in the story, it is also uncertain whether Jael is playing the role of a hero or a host. The protocol of hospitality and other literary parallels to this story in the Bible provide some important clues for understanding the often misunderstood development of Jael's character.

Even in biblical times, Jael's opening words to Sisera—"Turn aside, my lord, turn aside to me; have no fear" (Judg 4:18)—raised questions about her role in the story. Are they an invitation on behalf of Heber or even Jael herself? Is Jael lying to Sisera? Is she trying to be ironic? The words appear only in the story of Jael and Sisera (Judg 4:18). In the stories of Deborah, Jael says nothing at all to Sisera (Judg 5:24–27). In fact, there is no reference at all in the stories of Deborah to this opening episode in the story of Jael (Judg 4:18). This discrepancy has been explained by arguing that the telling of the stories of Deborah omitted Jael's words to avoid portraying a woman as a host (Bal 1988:62), or that the story of Jael added her words to explain why Sisera was laying under the rug in Jael's tent (Halpern 1988:83).

But Jael's words to Sisera are not an invitation on behalf of Heber. Jael does not invite Sisera to come over to her the way Boaz invites his neighbors to sit with him in the gate in Ruth (Ruth 4:1). Nor does Jael invite Sisera to be her guest the way Lot invites the two strangers to his household for the night (Gen 19:2). First of all, both storytellers and audiences knew that only male heads of households had the right to offer hospitality (Van Nieuwenhuijze 1971:287). Second, while the words "Turn aside, my lord, turn aside to me" (Judg 4:18) can be used to offer hospitality, the words "have no fear" (Judg 4:18) cannot. Customarily only Yahweh uses this formula to address candidates like Abraham (Gen 15:1) and Gideon (Judg 6:23), who are being dispatched on divine missions.

And Jael's words are not her personal invitation to negotiate a treaty with Sisera and overthrow Heber. There is nothing in the story which suggests that Jael's words are part of a free political act against her husband (*pace* Bal 1988:60). Jael does not consider Sisera an ally the way Abigail considers David an ally in her revolution against her husband Nabal in the stories of David's rise to power in Samuel–Kings (1 Sam 25:2–43).

Likewise, Jael's words are not an outright lie. There is nothing in the story to suggest that Jael and the household of Heber are double agents working for their own advantage with both Israel and Hazor (*pace* Halpern 1988:86). Lies need credibility, but there is no reason in the story for Sisera or the audience to believe her. Once Sisera's chariots have been routed, the "peace between Jabin the king of Hazor and the house of Heber the Kenite" (Judg 4:17) is abrogated. He has been shamed by the loss in battle, and his flight. He has lost his former status and is reduced to the role of a refugee (Bal 1988:120). Hazor can no longer protect and provide for the household of Heber; consequently the household of Heber is no longer obligated to support Hazor. Heber and Jael are no longer Sisera's allies. If anything, they are the war trophies of Barak, whom they are obligated to support (Halpern 1988:86; Soggin 1981:77). Consequently, Jael is not treacherous. She cannot be placed in the same league with the men of Judah who turned Samson over to the Philistines in Judges (Judg 15:10–13), or with the people of Keilah who informed Saul of David's whereabouts in the stories of Saul in Samuel–Kings (1 Sam 23:12).

And finally, Jael's words are not ironic. Irony needs subtlety, but there is no misunderstanding her words. In contrast, Sisera's words to Jael (Judg 4:19–20) and the words between the queen mother and her counselors (Judg 5:29–30) are brimming with the subtlety and misunderstanding irony requires. There would be no irony in a woman offering a warrior something to eat and drink. There is no shame in accepting something offered by a woman. Rebekah does not shame the slave of Abraham by offering him water (Gen 24:17–20) and Abigail does not shame David by offering him food (1 Sam 25:18–35).

Jael's words are a protest against Sisera, who is planning to rape her and thus lay claim to the household of Heber. They are a final warning, advising Sisera to change his decision or face the consequences. Jael's words here serve the same purpose as the words of Tamar to Amnon in the stories of David's successor (2 Sam 13:12–13). She warns him to leave her alone (Lam 4:15), to give up his plan to attack her and the household of Heber (2 Kgs 10:29; Prov 13:14; Isa 11:13), and to disappear before he is discovered by her bodyguards. Like Deborah, Jael is a liminal woman, who acts heroically when men fail to fulfill their responsibilities (Murray 1979:178, 183; Webb 1987:135; Amit 1987:93). Both go above and beyond the call of duty as mothers of their households. Both risk their own lives to save their house-

---

Stories of David's Successor
(2 Sam 13:12–13)

No, my brother, do not force me; for such a thing is not done in Israel; do not do anything so vile! As for me, where could I carry my shame? And as for you, you would be as one of the scoundrels in Israel. Now therefore, I beg you, speak to the king; for he will not withhold me from you.

---

holds. When Barak fails to defend Israel against Hazor, Deborah acts. When Heber fails to defend his household, Jael acts. Jael is not a host, but like Deborah she is a hero who delivers her household from slavery.

Jael's warning plays on the word "turn" (סור, *sûr*). She gives Sisera one last chance to turn away from or abandon his plan (Judg 9:29; 1 Kgs 16:13; 2 Kgs 17:18). But Sisera ignores her protest and turns or pushes her out of his way. Jael says "Turn aside from your plan." Instead, Sisera "turns her aside" and invades her tent.

Once Jael's opening words to Sisera are read as a protest rather than as an invitation the significance of her actions which follow becomes clearer. Jael never designates Sisera as her guest. On the contrary, she declares war on him as her enemy. And Sisera never regards Jael as his host. Throughout the story he treats her with disdain. He never speaks to her as an equal, much less as the woman on whom his life depends. Such blatant disdain for Jael identifies Sisera as typical of the arrogant who make alliances with groups and states they consider inferior in order to survive (Soggin 1981:77). His underestimation of Jael in particular could be another ironic factor utilized by the narrator. By forcing his way into Jael's tent Sisera does not merit the protection accorded a guest. He shames Heber by approaching Jael's tent uninvited and in complete disregard for her protest. Sisera is not in an agitated mental state after the failed battle; he is clear thinking and calculating, and he plans to use Jael to aid his escape. This action, freely taken, marks him as a danger which must be dealt with by any means at hand.

If Sisera had entered Jael's tent as a guest she would have washed his feet (Gen 18:4; 19:2; 24:32; Judg 19:21). Jael does not omit washing Sisera's feet because such a leisurely and relaxing task was inappropriate in the middle of Barak's and Deborah's hot pursuit of Sisera. The omission of the foot washing ritual clearly indicates that Sisera has not been granted true guest status. Although most translations say Jael "covered him with a rug" (Judg 4:18), there is no precedent in this gesture connected with hospitality. It is more likely that "she closed the curtain of the tent (שׂמיכה, $s^e m\bar{\imath}k\hat{a}h$) behind him" (Soggin 1981:67; Bal 1988:122). After Sisera barges past her into the tent Jael neither runs nor screams for help. She coolly and decisively steps into the tent behind Sisera and draws the curtain across the entryway. She confronts the enemy of her household alone.

Sisera is undaunted by Jael's courage. Mistakenly, he assumes he is safe and that the household of Heber is now in his power. In reality, it is precisely at this moment that the great warrior, stained with mud and sweat, has fallen into the power of a woman. Deborah's prophecy that "the Lord will sell Sisera into the hand of a woman" (Judg 4:9) has been fulfilled.

Unwilling to believe that he is in any danger, Sisera orders Jael to wait on him like a slave by bringing him a drink and guarding the door. If Sisera were Jael's guest he could not ask her for anything. In contrast, when Abraham's slave asks Rebekah, "give me a little water to drink from your jar" (Gen 24:17), he is not a guest addressing his host. By requesting a drink he is seeking access to a natural resource of the village (Matthews 1986:121). The well functions as communal property and thus any member of the village may be approached for access to the water. Rebekah's response to Abraham's slave in giving him a drink and watering his camels is not the offering or granting of hospitality, only the extension of temporary water rights. The fact that the slave's test to find Isaac a proper bride included the provision that the woman would also water his camels (Gen 24:14) suggests that Rebekah's generous action was an unexpected one, thus not part of any ritual expectation or obligation.

Skillfully manipulating Sisera's false sense of security, Jael responds by treating him like a child: she "opens a skin of milk and gives him a drink" (Judg 4:19). Jael fills Sisera's order for the simple necessity of water with the luxury of fermented goat's milk. Upgrades are part of the protocol of hospitality, but only on the part of the host. Hosts fulfill their responsibility to provide the best possible food for their guests by offering something simple, and then upgrading it. Abraham offers his guests "a morsel of bread" (Gen 18:4–5), and then upgrades it to three measures of fine meal made into cakes, a calf, curds, and milk (Gen 18:6–8). Nonetheless, since it is Sisera who orders the water, Jael's response has nothing to do with fulfilling the obligation of a host to provide the best for guests. Jael would have had to offer a little water and then upgrade it to milk. When Jael gives Sisera milk to drink she repeats the challenge she issued by drawing the curtain of her tent and courageously takes another step to trap and kill him (Cundall 1968:95). Her offer is not a gesture of a host, but the strategy of a hunter. Milk is an aphrodisiac with which a husband and wife toast their marriage contract (Bal 1988:62–63). Milk is also a soporific whose lactic acid soothes away the anxieties which prevent sleep (Boling 1975:98). Tellers exploit both associations. Sisera drinks the milk to prepare for sex while Jael serves the milk to prepare him for death.

Jael stalks Sisera the way Judith stalks Holofernes in Judith (Judith 12—13) and Pughat stalks Yatpan in the story of Aqhat from Ugarit (*CTA* 19.205–221). With threatening deliberation, Jael closes in on her prey. She closes the curtain to her tent, she serves him milk, and finally she tucks him into bed. Jael's act of covering Sisera before (Judg 4:18) and after (Judg 4:19) serving him a drink frames the episode. Like Jael, both Judith and Pughat serve their enemy drink, and both provide an alluring and beguiling picture to further cloud their victim's mind. Each woman hunts and kills her enemy to set their households free (Hendel 1987:90–94; Gaster 1969:260). What the men of their households—Barak, Danil, Heber, Uzziah—could not do, these women accomplished on their own.

Hosts regularly guard the door to protect their guests. Rahab in the Battle of Jericho stories in Joshua, for example, guards the door to protect her two guests (Josh 2:4–6). Likewise, the slave woman at En Rogel does the same for Jonathan and Ahimaaz in the stories of Saul in Samuel–Kings (2 Sam 17:17–21). But a guest can never order a host to stand guard. Sisera's order does not remind Jael of her responsibility as a host but dramatizes his helplessness as a fallen warrior. The same audience who first met Sisera as commander of the nine hundred chariots of Hazor (Judg 4:2–3) now listens to him crying out to the woman caring for him like a child afraid of the dark (Bal 1988:92). He is alone and helpless, and yet he continues to command Jael as if she were a soldier in his now vanquished army.

Sisera's helplessness is further played out in the words which he orders Jael to pass on to those who approach her tent. "If anyone comes and asks you, Is there a man in this woman's tent? Say, No!" Tellers have carefully chosen a word (אִישׁ, 'îš) which can mean both "anyone" and "a man" so that this once-great warrior can now unwittingly admit that he is no longer a man (Judg 4:20; Bal 1988:123). Sisera orders Jael to lie, but she can use his exact words and tell the truth, which the audience already knows (Webb 1987:135).

The milk, plus his own exhaustion, seal his fate as he falls into a deep sleep. Similarly, Samson sleeps in Delilah's lap in Judges (Judg 16:14, 19); Yatpan passes out in a drunken stupor before Pughat in the story of Aqhat (*CTA* 19.213–224). In each story the hero is a woman who first puts her enemy to sleep and then to death. Her enemy is totally unaware of his impending death. He thinks he is making himself helpless to taunt the woman who confronts him as helpless (Williams 1982:74; Soggin 1981:78).

Jael fetches the hammer and a peg which she uses to pitch her tent. The same skills and strength which she uses to erect her home Jael uses to defend it. She drives the peg through Sisera's skull with the same speed with which she normally sinks it into the ground. Jael's weapons are not only available, they are familiar. But the weapons of Jael are symbolic as well as functional. It is characteristic of the hero stories in Judges that their protagonists wield unorthodox weapons. Ehud is armed with a two-edged sword (Judg 3:16), Shamgar with an ox goad (Judg 3:31), Samson with a jawbone (Judg 15:15). The motif characterizes them as farmers and herders, not professional warriors. Nonetheless, they skillfully wield the tools of their peace-time trades to free their households from well-armed invaders. Jael's homespun weapons mark her as an authentic deliverer.

The hammer and the peg are also strong sexual symbols. The male who violated the door of her tent is penetrated by the woman he threatened. Sisera's sentence is designed to fit his crime. His attack on the household of Heber does not need to be consummated with Jael (*pace* Brenner 1985:119–20); from a legal point of view, Sisera is guilty of rape the moment he passes through the door of her tent. The door is a common sexual symbol as love songs from both Egypt (Papyrus Harris 500) and the Song of Solomon (Cant 5:4) from ancient Israel indicate.

From a literary point of view it is unlikely that storytellers wanted their audiences to think that Sisera succeeds in having sexual intercourse with Jael. Their story turns on the characterization of Sisera who is crazed, but impotent. Sisera "falls between her legs" (Judg 5:27), as much a failure against Jael (Bal 1988:120) as he had been against Deborah (Judg 4:15). On neither field does he mount a successful assault. Sisera is a dead man from the moment he appears in the story. He tries to bring shame upon Barak and Heber and instead suffers the shame of death at a woman's hand (Judg 9:53). His death is not only inevitable, but expected and justified.

Like Deborah who leads Barak to Sisera on the battlefield (Judg 4:14–16), Jael now leads Barak to Sisera on the floor of her tent. The episode frames the two stories and draws them to a close. This final episode in the story of Jael (Judg 4:22) creates a frame with the opening episode (Judg 4:18) around the story (Bal 1988:92). In both, Jael "came out to meet" a stranger. The fabric of the narrative is thus woven together resuming the story of the aftermath of the battle and providing a sense of déjà vu in which once again a man approaches a woman at the door of her tent.

The protocol of the host and the stranger is a key to the interpretation of this story of Jael. It clearly shows that Jael does not misuse hospitality to lure Sisera to his death. On the contrary, it is Sisera who violates hospitality, bringing shame on himself and his household. Each of Jael's actions is carefully chosen to reflect both the gentle nurture of a mother tending her young and the fearless courage of a mother defending them. In this way, the story consciously acknowledges both qualities in honoring Deborah and Jael as "mothers in Israel" (Judg 5:7; Williams 1982:73). Each woman is a

---

Egyptian Love Songs
(Matthews & Benjamin 1991b:230)

My lover is the lady of a great house,
  Whose entrance is right in the middle!

Both doors are left wide open,
  The bolt is unfastened.

And my lover is furious!

If she hired me as her doorman,
  At least when I made her angry,

I would get to hear her voice,
  Even as I tremble like a child.

---

mother of a household honored as a chief for delivering their household when it is left in harm's way. Mothers in Israel were selfless not only in birthing and rearing their children but in protecting them from harm. In stark contrast, the mother of Sisera pines selfishly for the child who will feed and protect her (Judg 5:28–30; Bal 1988:64). The irony with which this mother speaks is exquisite. She rationalizes Sisera's delay by assuming her warrior son is busy handling the two women he has won in a single day (Judg 5:30). Meanwhile, the audience knows that just the reverse is true; it is Sisera who has fallen into the hands of two women in a single day. In her fantasy Sisera's mother sees her loving son arriving with a bolt of fabric dyed in royal purple for her (Judg 5:30). But the audience knows her son will soon arrive shrouded in the carpet he has dyed with his blood.

For ancient Israel, Deborah and Jael were deemed "blessed among women" (Judg 5:24). The title is superlative in no small way because Israel confers it on two women equal in honor to Othniel, Ehud, Gideon, Jepthah, Samson, Saul, Jonathan, and David in Judges and Samuel–Kings (Gilmore 1987:9; Blok 1981:429). Deborah and Jael were "friends of Yahweh" (Judg 5:31) who set their households free.

7

The Chief

There were no police or standing armies in villages. In early Israel, soldiers were not only an expense which the village could not afford, but a threat to its balance of power. Nonetheless villages were subject to attack. To offset this risk, villages allied themselves with one another to form a tribe which provided them with temporary military assistance whenever their land or population was threatened. The Bible does not report the exact order of events or the precise political climate which contributed to the transition from villages to tribes in Israel (Coote and Whitelam 1987:143; Lemche 1988:122), but anthropology can enrich the outline which the Bible preserves. The contours of any particular tribe varied in response to the nature of the external crisis with which it was confronted (Earle 1989:87; 1991:10) and the internal opposition which it faced (Johnson and Earle 1987:313–14; Renfrew 1982:3–6). Hence, more than one model can be reconstructed (Frick 1985:71–97; Service 1975:304; Harris 1979:92; Renfrew 1972:73), and not all the components of the protocol for commissioning a chief appear in every hero story in the Bible (Gottwald 1979: 322–27).

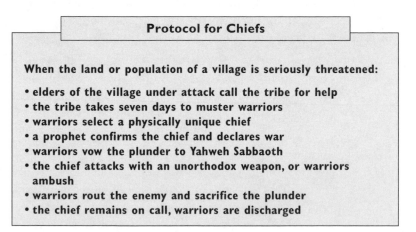

Protocol for Chiefs

When the land or population of a village is seriously threatened:

- elders of the village under attack call the tribe for help
- the tribe takes seven days to muster warriors
- warriors select a physically unique chief
- a prophet confirms the chief and declares war
- warriors vow the plunder to Yahweh Sabbaoth
- the chief attacks with an unorthodox weapon, or warriors ambush
- warriors rout the enemy and sacrifice the plunder
- the chief remains on call, warriors are discharged

Threat to Land and Children

Any serious threat to the land or population of a village could set the protocol for commissioning a judge (שֹׁפֵט, šōpēṭ) or chief (נָשִׂיא, nāśî') in motion. Ultimately the threat was military (Judg 19:1; 1 Sam 11), even when it originated as an economic (1 Sam 13:19–21) or diplomatic crisis (1 Sam 8:4–5; 11:12–15). A threat was serious when the village could no longer survive on its own and its elders could no longer adequately feed and protect the households of the village.

Faced with a serious threat, the elders of the politically smaller and more democratic village moved to allow it to be indefinitely absorbed into a larger and more totalitarian social system called a "tribe." A tribe was primarily an army or people at war. It centralized its power in fewer leaders, required more land to operate, demanded more able-bodied adults, and consumed more natural resources than a village (Earle 1989:84; 1987:279; Carneiro 1981:37–38, 45). The tribe did not farm, herd, or bear children. The members of a tribe were not farmers, herders, or childbearers, they were warriors and quartermasters. A village reclaims land; a tribe conquers it. A village bears children; a tribe takes prisoners of war. A village solves problems through consensus at the gate court; a tribe uses the police power of martial law. A tribe was an effective, but violent social structure. Some tribes developed into states, others did not (Earle 1987:280; 1977:213; Friedman and Rowlands 1977:201–276).

Call to Arms

The elders of a village under attack began the process of transferring it to the tribe by issuing a call for help to the other villages with which it was allied by covenant. If these villages decided the threat to the village under attack also placed them in harms way, they too agreed to transfer their political and economic power to the tribe.

Villages had seven days to make their decision. Practically, the villages needed time to circulate the call to arms and for their elders to weigh its merits and the resources of their villages to respond. Symbolically, however, seven also indicates that the process of discernment involves not just the human community, but Yahweh and the divine assembly as well. In the world of the Bible, seven was a cosmic number. The moon passes through four seven-day weeks before repeating its cycle. The universe houses seven heavenly bodies: the sun, the moon, and the five planets visible to the unaided eye. Consequently, it was assumed that Yahweh and the divine assembly created in cycles of seven. Hence, the protocol for appointing a chief involved suspending human work for seven days to give Yahweh and the divine assembly time to work. Joshua and his warriors wait seven days before attacking Jericho in Joshua (Josh 6:1–16), and Saul waits seven days before attacking the Philistines in Samuel–Kings (1 Sam 13:8).

Raising Up a Chief

Villages signified their decision to transfer their political and economic power to the tribe by mustering warriors. At the end of the waiting period the warriors who assembled selected a chief. The unique physical appearance of a warrior was a significant element in the designation of a chief. "The spirit of the Lord" physically distinguished the chief from the other warriors. In Judges, Ehud is left-handed (Judg 3:15); in the stories of David's rise to power in Samuel–Kings David is "ruddy, and had beautiful eyes, and was handsome" (1 Sam 16:12). When the selection was made, a prophet (נביא, nābî') confirmed the candidate and declared war (1 Sam 13:8–12). It was the prophet who certified that the deliberations of Yahweh and the divine assembly were complete, that a chief had been legally selected, and that war had been declared (Eslinger 1985:477, n. 6).

The Bible often combines the roles of the prophet and the chief in the way it describes the Levites in early Israel. Sometimes, like a chief, the Levite provides a village with the strategy and tactics necessary to defend against aggression. And, sometimes like a prophet, the Levite confirms the candidate whom the warriors selected as chief and declares war by retelling the Exodus stories. This reminds the villagers that if Yahweh could deliver the Hebrews from Egypt, the most vicious slaveholder in the ancient world, then certainly Yahweh could deliver the Hebrews in the hills from Egypt's governors in Canaan (Gottwald 1979:496).

Numbers (Num 1:44) makes a peacetime application of Israel's ancient wartime institution of appointing a chief. The figures in Numbers are not so much a civil census as a military roll-call used in drafting warriors to defend villages under attack. Each tribe is mustered by a chief (נשיא, nāśî'), who reports the count to Moses and Aaron who, as prophets, are responsible for declaring war (Pedersen 1926:34).

Prisoners and Plunder

Before going into battle, warriors in the world of the Bible vowed all or a portion of their anticipated prisoners and plunder to Yahweh Sabbaoth (חרם, ḥērem). The execution of prisoners of war and the destruction of all their property seems today to be both barbaric and wasteful. In traditional cultures like ancient Israel, however, this aspect of what scholars have strangely enough called "holy war" may have actually served as a deterrent to violence and waste (Schwally 1901). Prisoners and plunder were an economic surplus shared by warriors. A significant portion of the budget of ancient states, in fact, came from prisoners and plunder taken in wars. States were supported by the taxes they collected and the wars they declared. Tribes, on the other hand, set limits on the profits of war by vowing before the battle to retain only a certain portion of the proceeds. The rest of the prisoners and plunder were executed or burned, not as a sadistic act

> ## Stories of David's Rise to Power
> ## (1 Sam 30:18–20, 23–31)
>
> **David recovered all that the Amalekites had taken. . . . David
> also captured all the flocks and herds, which were driven ahead
> of the other cattle; people said, "This is David's spoil. . . ."**
>
> **But David said, "You shall not do so . . . with what the Lord has
> given us; he has preserved us and handed over to us the raiding
> party that attacked us. . . . For the share of the one who goes
> down into the battle shall be the same as the share of the one
> who stays by the baggage; they shall share alike. . . ."**
>
> **When David came to Ziklag, he sent part of the spoil to his
> friends, the elders of Judah, saying, "Here is a present for you
> from the spoil of the enemies of the Lord": it was for those in
> Bethel, in Ramoth of the Negeb . . . all the places where David
> and his men had roamed.**

of revenge but to transfer them to the divine assembly. If villages could not
profit substantially by war, they would hopefully resort to it only as a last
choice, and not use it, as states did, as a regular source of public funding.
Likewise, life in any condition is considered preferable to death today. In
traditional cultures, however, life as a slave was not necessarily preferable
to death in battle or as a sacrifice following the battle (Beavis 1992:37–54).

But in early Israel not all plunder and prisoners of war were sacrificed.
Some chiefs channeled them back to the villages. Redistribution was not
just a policy of taking from the rich and giving to the poor. The formula
which a chief used for redistribution corresponds to the level of support
which the villages had provided the tribe (Service 1962:144; Renfrew 1976:
171–73). In some cases the wealth which was redistributed was originally
taken in taxes or tribute from the same villages to whom it was returned
(Carneiro 1981:63; Peebles and Kus 1977:421; Adams 1984:91). The stories
of David's rise to power demonstrate the use of redistribution quite well
(1 Sam 22—23; 27—30).

Duel and Ambush

The tactics of a tribe seldom employed full-scale maneuvers. Most often,
either the chief single-handedly attacked with an unorthodox weapon or
ambushed the unsuspecting enemy with only a portion of the tribe's warriors. Only then did all the warriors join in the rout. Attacking at less than
full strength had both practical and ritual significance. Practically, tribes
seldom mustered a sufficient number of warriors who were adequately
armed to operate like the army of a state. The chief, therefore, had to

compensate for this lack of strength with better strategy. Ritually, a chief down-sized an attack to emphasize that the victory belonged not to the tribe, but to its divine patron with whom the warriors fought only as auxiliaries (Von Rad 1991:44–46). In ancient Israel, the main attack was always carried out by Yahweh and the heavenly host (צבאות, $s^e b\bar{a}'\hat{o}\underline{t}$).

Stories of David's Rise to Power
(2 Sam 5:22–25)

. . . the Philistines came up, and were spread out in the valley of Rephaim. When David inquired of the Lord, he said, "You shall not go up; go around to their rear, and come upon them opposite the balsam trees. When you hear the sound of marching in the tops of the balsam trees, then be on the alert; for then the Lord has gone out before you to strike down the army of the Philistines." David did just as the Lord had commanded him; and he struck down the Philistines from Geba all the way to Gezer.

Disarmament and Military Preparedness

After the enemy had been destroyed, the chief remained on call, but warriors returned to their villages. Initially, the "raising up" or "anointing" of a chief like Saul (1 Sam 9:15—11:15) or David (1 Sam 16:1–13; 17:31–58; 18:7) only streamlined the distribution of power exercised by the elders. In times of relative stability, commissioning a chief interrupted but did not replace the distribution of power which made day-to-day life possible in the villages. However, during times of widespread instability, power was permanently redistributed to the chief. Although theoretically the elders only delegated their power to the chief temporarily, chiefs could and did use various strategies to permanently consolidate the elders' power in themselves (1 Sam 11:5–15; 13:5–9; 14:16–24; 15:4–9).

No strategy, however, could make a chief omnipotent (Earle 1989:85). When, in Judges, Abimelech attempts to become ruler of Shechem, he uses two strategies. First, he promises its people more effective leadership: "Which is better for you, that all seventy of the sons of Jerubba'al rule over you, or that one rule over you?" (Judg 9:2). Second, he appeals to the loyalty of the household of his mother in Shechem. Abimelech is modestly successful. For three years, the city gives him the power to hire mercenary troops. But soon Abimelech faces the threat of another chief taking his place (Judg 9:26–41). Abimelech survives this challenge by slaying a city's entire population and sowing its ruins with salt (Judg 9:42–45). However, the expenditure of time and effort invested in maintaining his rule is too singularly directed toward force. Ultimately, he is killed in battle at Thebez (Judg 9:50–55) and his tribe is dissolved.

Even chiefs as powerful as Saul and David were subject to the counter-balance created by the elders (1 Sam 10:27; 11:12; 13:10–15; 14:24–46). Regardless of how long a tribe existed, it was always possible that the villages could revolt to demand a new tribe and a new chief, to demand even greater centralization and form a state, or to demand less centralization and a return to the village system (1 Kgs 12:3–4). Nonetheless, statistically the state more often than any other system is the one which replaces the tribe. The expansion and collapse of the tribe carries within it the seeds for the development of states. Regional organization was established through alliance, force, and economic contacts as tribes were formed (1 Sam 13:2–4). The competitive nature of neighboring chiefs, circumscription, and the tenuous system of succession in tribes all contributed to their dissolution. Consolidation of tribes into larger political units with bureaucratic levels of rule and centralized control over production and distribution was made easier by both the strengths and the weaknesses of tribes (Carneiro 1978:208; Earle 1987:281).

One strategy for continuing a chief in power was storytelling. Stories were performed as part of regularly celebrated rituals endorsing the chief as a divinely chosen deliverer of the people (Kristiansen 1982:245). The stories of Gideon in Judges, for example, celebrate his destruction of the altar to Ba'al and the tree of Asherah by conferring the title *Jerubba'al* on this villager "who fought against Ba'al" (Judg 6:25–32). The story elevates Gideon the elder to the status of Gideon the chief.

The stories of Saul in Samuel–Kings (1 Sam 11:12–15; 14:47–52) argue that the success of Saul in preserving Israel from its enemies is an endorsement by Yahweh entitling him to remain in power. The stories introduce him at first only as a temporary chief, but he uses his skills as a military leader (1 Sam 11), his anointing by Samuel (1 Sam 10:1), and his election by lot under Yahweh's supervision (1 Sam 10:17–27) to consolidate his power (Lemche 1988:121). Saul's actual control over the affairs of the villages, whose loyalties were divided, was fairly minimal (Judg 6:12–18). Still, Saul's tribe created a central identity for Israel, based on his role as a permanent military commander (Vikander-Edelman 1986:9, 31; Hauer 1986:6–7).

The Chief in a Story of Saul from Jabesh-Gilead (1 Sam 11:1–15)

The story of Saul from Jabesh-Gilead in Samuel–Kings (1 Sam 11:1–15) is a fascinating demonstration of the anthropology of a tribe. Saul is chosen chief because the people of Jabesh-Gilead need more rapid decision-making than the elders can supply. To deal with Rabath-Ammon they need more centralized leadership and greater cooperation with other villages in the region. The fragile nature of the tribe is demonstrated as Saul the chief and Samuel the prophet confront one another.

Gilead is a region 25 miles wide and 100 miles long between the Jordan River and today's city of Amman. Amman was once Rabath-Ammon, the great city of the Ammonites. Northern Gilead ran from the Jabbok River (Arabic: *Nahr es Zarqa*) near Amman, 50 miles north to the Yarmuk River (Arabic: *Wadi el Yarmuk*). Southern Gilead ran from the Jabbok to the Arnon River (Arabic: *Wadi el Mujib*) some 50 miles south. On this great plateau of land there were timber forests, grain fields, and grazing lands. Through it ran the Royal Highway (Arabic: *Tariq es Sultani*). Caravans moved goods along this ancient trade lane connecting the Gulf of Aqaba and Damascus. Less than 25 miles north and west of Rabath-Ammon in northern Gilead the Wadi Yabis joins the Jordan Valley. Here stood Jabesh-Gilead (Arabic: *Tell Abu Kharaz*) where they told a story of Saul, the chief who delivered them from Nahash, king of Rabath-Ammon.

A longer version of this story of Saul, recovered by archaeologists from 1947 to 1967 to the library of Qumran on the west coast of the Dead Sea, describes in greater detail than the Bible just how the war between Rabath-Ammon and Jabesh-Gilead began (Cross 1985:16–35; Rofe 1982:129–33). The longer version also makes it clearer that the maneuvers of Nahash were part of a sophisticated strategy threatening the land and children of Israel, and not simply unprovoked acts of mayhem.

The Ammonites enjoyed the same monopoly on transit trade along the Royal Highway east of the Jordan as the Philistines enjoyed along the Coastal Highway to the west. Both profited greatly from guarding the

---

Stories of Saul
(4QSam[a], I Sam 11:1–3, authors' translation)

When Nahash, king of Rabath-Ammon, conquered the tribes of Gad and Reuben, he gouged out the right eyes of their warriors. When he had conquered all Israel, Nahash gouged out the right eye of every Israelite warrior east of the Jordan, except for seven detachments which escaped to Jabesh-Gilead.

About a month later Nahash laid siege to Jabesh-Gilead. The elders of the city sued for peace. "Make a treaty with us and we shall become your slaves." But Nahash issued an ultimatum. "If I make a treaty with you, you must gouge out the right eyes of the Israelite warriors in your city, so that I may shame all Israel." The elders of Jabesh-Gilead agreed to consider his terms. "Give us seven days to send messengers throughout all Israel. If there is no one to deliver us, we shall surrender them to you."

caravans, feeding, watering, and restocking their animals, bedding and boarding their caravaneers. Between 1250 and 1000 BCE, raiders from some Israelite villages both east and west of the Jordan regularly plundered caravans to supplement their income from herding and farming (Judg 5:6–7; Rowton 1967:382; Chaney 1983). Raids cost both the Philistines and the Ammonites dearly. Both eventually mounted campaigns against Israelite villages suspected of harboring raiders.

When the story of Saul opens, Nahash and his soldiers have swept through all the villages of Israel in southern Gilead and halfway through those in northern Gilead as well. Nahash did not want to exterminate the Israelite population, he simply wanted to destroy its ability to raid caravans along his section of the Royal Highway. Gouging out the eyes of Israel's warriors is both a practical and a symbolic tactic which targets the power of Israel's villages over both its land and its children. Tellers emphasize the cruelty of Nahash with a play on words. In Hebrew נחש, naḥaš) can mean either "fortune" (Num 23:23; 24:1) or "serpent" (Gen 3:1; Amos 9:3). Although this king of Rabath-Ammon, no doubt, carried the throne name nahash-tob or "Good Fortune," Israelite storytellers always refer to him as the "Snake" (Cross 1985:26).

As a practical matter, mutilating or decimating prisoners of war discourages any further armed resistance. In the biblical world, decimation and mutilation were standard practices. After defeating Moab in Samuel–Kings David executes every third prisoner of war (2 Sam 8:2). In Judges, Adoni-bezek, king of the Perizzites, cuts off the thumbs and toes of seventy kings he defeated before the warriors of Judah cut off his thumbs and toes (Judg 1:4–7). Without great toes it is difficult for a warrior to balance; without thumbs it is virtually impossible to grasp a weapon. The Philistines blinded Samson (Judg 16:21) and the Babylonians blinded Zedekiah (2 Kgs 25:7; Jer 39:7; 52:11). Blinding both eyes not only destroys a warrior's vision but his usefulness as a farmer or herder as well. Blinding his right eye, on the other hand, severely limits a villager's ability to fight, but it does not deprive a villager of his ability to farm and herd. Without a right eye it is difficult to aim a bow, a spear, or a sling, and without full peripheral vision the warrior becomes an easier target on the field of battle. The wound also clearly identifies those convicted of raiding.

Symbolically, blinding is equivalent to castration. There is a legal and symbolic equivalence between the eyes and the testicles in the world of the Bible. To be blind is to be impotent. Something of this equivalence appears in the Middle Assyrian Code (MAL 8) published by Tiglath-Pileser I (1115–1077 BCE).

Blinding is not the only gesture by which warriors threaten the power of their enemies to have children; to be bald is also to be impotent. Shaving the beard or pubic hair of a warrior or cutting off the tunic below the waist are comparable methods of symbolic castration. Both occur in the Bible. In the stories of David's rise to power, Hanun shaves off half the beards and

---

**Middle Assyrian Code, article 8
(Matthews & Benjamin 1991b:72–73)**

If during a fight with a citizen, a woman ruptures one of his testicles, then the sentence is the amputation of one finger; however, if even after medical treatment, his other testicle also
ruptures, then the sentence is the blinding of both eyes (Deut
25:11–12).

---

cuts off half the tunics of the delegation which David dispatched to the
funeral of Nahash, Hanun's father (2 Sam 10:4). By symbolically castrating
David's messengers, Hanun declares that Israel is impotent in Rabath-
Ammon. Likewise, David symbolically castrates Saul by cutting off a corner
of his cloak while Saul is relieving himself in a cave near Ein Gedi. The
gesture declares that Saul is impotent in Israel (1 Sam 24:1–22). In Isaiah,
when Israel and Syria invade Judah, Ahaz sends a call for help to Assyria,
Judah's treaty partner. Isaiah uses this motif to argue that Assyria will
castrate Judah rather than protect it (Isa 7:20).

Although the honor of Rabath-Ammon and the shame of Israel are at
stake in Nahash's decision to cross the Wadi Yabis, there are practical
military considerations as well. For Nahash, caravans crossing through
Ammonite territory would be safe only when every warrior in Israel had
been neutralized. Allowing any able-bodied warriors to remain east of the
Jordan leaves caravans on the Royal Highway at risk. Therefore, Nahash
crosses the Wadi Yabis and lays siege to Jabesh-Gilead.

**Trial of Ahaz
(Isa 7:20)**

On that day the Lord will shave with a razor hired beyond the
River—with the king of Assyria—the head and the hair of the
feet, and it will take off the beard as well.

To avoid a battle, the elders of Jabesh-Gilead offer to negotiate a covenant
with Nahash. Nahash agrees, but points out that as his covenant partner,
they must extradite all the warriors of Israel who are his enemies. In
Samuel–Kings, Joab imposes the same terms on Abel of Beth-maacah where
Sheba and his warriors seek asylum (2 Sam 20:20–21). The terms are standard in covenants throughout the ancient Near East and appear, for example,
in the Treaty of Ramses II and Hattusilis III promulgated after the battle at
Kadesh in 1280 BCE.

Before agreeing to become a covenant partner with Rabath-Ammon and to surrender Israel's warriors, the elders of Jabesh-Gilead send out a call to arms to their tribe. Like Goliath in the story of David's rise to power (1 Sam 17:8–9), Nahash does not expect Jabesh-Gilead to be able to field a chief to meet his challenge (1 Sam 17:8–9). While establishing a covenant with Jabesh-Gilead would give him an investment in the village, winning a war against it would give him complete control of all its land and resources (Edelman 1984:205, n. 39). Invaders like Nahash of Rabath-Ammon or Ben-Hadad of Syria in Samuel–Kings (1 Kgs 20:5–7) care little whether their enemies fall by covenant or conquest.

The crisis in this story of Saul not only locks Rabath-Ammon and Jabesh-Gilead in a duel to the death, but also brings Yahweh the divine patron of Israel and Milcom the divine patron of Rabath-Ammon into direct confrontation with one another. If the people of Jabesh-Gilead become a covenant partner of Rabath-Ammon, they become the people of Milcom as well. If Milcom can conquer the people whom Yahweh cannot protect, then Milcom is divine patron and Yahweh is not (Eslinger 1985:362). The response of the tribe to the elders' call to arms will determine the identity of Jabesh-Gilead as either Israelite or Ammonite (Edelman 1984:203–5).

The call to arms from Jabesh-Gilead reaches Gibeah first. The messengers lament or weep for the fate of their city. The Lament for Ur (Matthews and Benjamin 1991b:169–75), the story of Balaam (Matthews and Benjamin 1991b:59–61), and Lamentations reflect the kind of literary genre which the messengers use.

The call comes first to Gibeah because of the covenant relationship between the two villages (Long 1989:223–24; Mohlenbrink 1940–41:57–64; Stoebe 1973:226–27), not because Gibeah is Saul's capital (Vannoy 1978:86–87; Edelman 1984:207). In the final form of the stories of Saul which appear in the Bible today, the story of Saul told at Jabesh-Gilead is introduced by other stories of Saul in which he is anointed as a leader in Israel. This story is the first in which Saul demonstrates his ability to fulfill his commission as a standing chief (Edelman 1984:205–8). Since there was no immediate action taken by Saul after being anointed and chosen by lot, the story of Saul told at Jabesh-Gilead now functions as the labor that confirms his anointing (Long 1989:227–28; Ishida 1977:47).

The reaction of Saul-the-villager to the call to arms from Jabesh-Gilead designates him as Saul-the-chief, commissioned by Yahweh to deliver the people from slavery. The call tests Saul, who proves himself a chief by reacting appropriately to the crisis (Halpern 1981a:124, 138–45). Some stories characterize Saul as ecstatic (1 Sam 10:10b) or depressed (1 Sam 16:14; Gunn 1980:12). In this story, however, the spirit of Yahweh marks Saul as physically huge: "he stood head and shoulders above everyone else" (1 Sam 9:2). By butchering the oxen, Saul demonstrates the great physical strength which distinguishes him from other villagers.

Saul's sacrifice is not only physically extraordinary, it is ritually excep-
tional as well. The covenant between Gibeah and Jabesh-Gilead is not an
ordinary covenant, and Saul is not simply a generic chief (Halpern 1981a:
132–38). Even, in a state as powerful and wealthy as Mari (1800–1750 BCE),
few villages had oxen. Fields were plowed with equipment and oxen loaned
to villages by the state (*ARM* 13.39; 14.80:4–10). Therefore, only significant
covenants were ratified by the slaughter of oxen or bulls (1 Sam 1:24; 6:14;
2 Sam 24:22). Saul's sacrifice emphasizes the totality of the commitment
which Gibeah will make to deliver Jabesh-Gilead. Saul and the other warriors swear that if they do not deliver Jabesh-Gilead from Nahash of Rabath-
Ammon, they wish their own oxen to be quartered just as Saul quartered
his oxen: "whoever does not come out after Saul and Samuel, so shall it be
done to his oxen" (1 Sam 11:7).

Saul sends the pieces with the messengers to rally other villages to the
cause of Jabesh-Gilead. The pieces of raw meat serve as gruesome physical
evidence that Saul and the warriors of Gibeah will spare nothing to fulfill
the covenant of Gibeah with Jabesh-Gilead. A similar example of this form
of military recruiting is found in the order by Zimri-Lim king of Mari
(1779–1745 BCE) that a severed head be carried on a pole as the recruiters
went from city to city (*ARM* 2.48:15–24). The significance of this action was
not lost on the people of Israel since "the dread of the Lord fell upon them"
(1 Sam 11:7b), and they all turned out for battle. Saul's determination, his
claim to call upon the warriors of Israel, and the sign of divine intervention
all point to the success to come (Miller 1974:167–68).

During the seven-day waiting period, warriors from both Gibeon and
Benjamin respond to Saul's call to arms (Schunk 1963:131–38; Blenkinsopp
1972:64; 1974:1–7). The sheer numbers who come further indicates that Saul
is Yahweh's designated chief. It is a sign of chiefdom development when
villages are able to bind themselves to meet a common regional threat (Earle
1991:13–14).

Samuel is mentioned as an ally in Saul's oath (1 Sam 11:7), but his role
before the battle is not described. In the final form of the story, the role of
Samuel the prophet appears to take place only after the battle. The changes
describing the prophet's role which have been made in the final form of the
story give Saul full authority to act on his own initiative, a type of renewal
of his anointing and a recognition of his leadership role already confirmed
by the prophet in previously told stories.

Saul shows his skill as a chief not only in his ability to recruit warriors
but also through his use of military tactics. He rallies the support and
morale of the people of Jabesh-Gilead by sending messengers to tell them
they would be delivered the next day.

Then the elders send a carefully worded message to Nahash: "Tomorrow
we will give ourselves up (נֵצֵא, *nēṣē'*) to you, and you may do to us whatever
seems good to you" (1 Sam 11:10). The message confirms that the full seven
day waiting period will be observed, and gives Saul's warriors enough time

---

**Stories of Saul
(1 Sam 15:3, 8)**

. . . attack Amalek, and utterly destroy all that they have; do
not spare them, but kill both man and woman, child and infant,
ox and sheep, camel and donkey.

. . . Saul defeated the Amalekites, from Havilah as far as Shur,
which is east of Egypt. He took King Agag of the Amalekites
alive, but utterly destroyed all the people with the edge of the
sword.

---

to arrive to lift the siege. But the message also makes a brilliant use of subtle
irony to threaten the city's arrogant opponent.

Throughout their negotiations with Nahash, the elders of Jabesh-Gilead
stress their willingness to "give up." The Hebrew verb which they use, יצא,
yāṣā'), can mean either "surrender" (Gen 38:24; Josh 2:3) or "attack" (Deut
20:1; 1 Sam 29:6; Prov 30:29). Ostensibly, the elders offer to surrender to the
Ammonites and become their vassals. Now they reiterate that offer, but the
double entendre here allows for their intention to attack the Ammonites,
scissoring them between Saul's warriors and the warriors of Jabesh-Gilead
(Hertzberg 1964:93; Eslinger 1985:371; Long 1989:220).

Saul and the elders of Jabesh-Gilead use the double entendre as a psychological tactic to ambush Nahash and his warriors. Nahash may or may not
have been aware that Saul and his warriors were responding to the call for
help that was sent out by the elders of Jabesh-Gilead. But Saul may have
purposefully leaked the news of his coming. By leaking the news of his
approach and by obliquely announcing the exact time of his attack, Saul
demonstrates skillful use of a terror tactic also employed by the kings of
Mari (*ARM* 1.52:6–35; 43:6'–8'; Sasson 1969:41). Nahash personally may
remain too overly confident to be greatly troubled by the news of Saul's
approach or the double meaning in the message which the elders of Jabesh-
Gilead deliver, but his warriors may not be sure whether they are about to
receive a surrender or an attack. The tactic solicits uncertainty as an ally
in Saul's strategy to deliver Jabesh-Gilead. Saul's battle plan is effective,
with a three-pronged attack which protects his own flanks while driving
the Ammonites from the field and scattering the survivors.

In the telling of the story of Saul at Jabesh-Gilead in Samuel–Kings today
there is no mention of the oath which Saul and his warriors took before the
battle, promising to sacrifice all or a portion of their prisoners and plunder
to Yahweh. Likewise, there is no mention of a sacrifice of the prisoners and
plunder after the battle as there is in the story of Saul and the Amalekites
(1 Sam 15:1–9). Saul and his warriors simply "scatter [Nahash and his
warriors] so that no two of them were left together" (1 Sam 11:11). Nahash

is punished according to the law of talion (Latin: *lex talionis*). What he had intended to do to Israel was in fact done to Ammon. Nahash had hoped to eliminate the military effectiveness of the Israelites by separating one eye from the other. In fact, Saul destroys the military effectiveness of the Ammonites by separating one from the other and depriving them of the territory they had claimed for themselves.

Stories of David's Successor (2 Sam 16:5–12)

When . . . David came to Bahurim, . . . a man of the . . . house of Saul came out whose name was Shimei son of Gera; he came out cursing. He threw stones at David and all the servants of King David; . . . Shimei shouted while he cursed. "Out! Out! Murderer! Scoundrel! The Lord has avenged on all of you the blood of the house of Saul, in whose place you have reigned; and the Lord has given the kingdom into the hand of your son Absalom. See, disaster has overtaken you; for you are a man of blood."

Then Abishai . . . said to the king, "Why should this dead dog curse my lord . . . ? Let me go over and take off his head." But the king said, " . . . If he is cursing because the Lord has said to him, 'Curse David,' who then shall say, 'Why have you done so?' . . . My own son seeks my life; how much more now may this Benjaminite! Let him alone, and let him curse; for the Lord has bidden him. It may be that the Lord will look on my distress, and the Lord will repay me with good for this cursing of me today."

After the battle, Saul's supporters want to execute those who want the warriors to be discharged and Saul to retire as a permanent chief. These opponents try to ally Samuel against Saul, since the prophet confirmed Saul's appointment as chief (Ishida 1977:48). But it is Saul who magnanimously grants his opponents a pardon: "no one shall be put to death this day, for today the Lord has brought deliverance to Israel" (1 Sam 11:13). In other words, his actions have been vindicated by Yahweh and are a divine sanction of Saul's leadership. Magnanimity itself is a royal prerogative which further characterizes Saul's ultimate ambition to become a monarch. Monarchs do not allow others to take their opponents' lives because these opponents are perceived as divine messengers (1 Sam 11:12–13). David exercises the same royal prerogative when he refuses to have Shimei executed for opposing his right to the throne (2 Sam 16:5–12).

Samuel refuses to challenge Saul or discharge the warriors. Instead he assembles them at Gilgal, which is a sacred center of early Israel. It is here in Joshua that the Hebrews enter the promised land and it is here that they designate Joshua to lead them (Josh 3—5). Consequently, Samuel goes to Gilgal to reconfirm the covenant which joins the villages into a tribe and to continue Saul as its chief (1 Sam 11: 14–15). The crisis is resolved. Saul is accepted as chief, and the opposing voices, for now, are stilled.

The use of words like "king" and "kingdom" in this story of Saul shows how later tellers considered the deliverance of Jabesh-Gilead a turning point in the career of Saul and in the evolution of Israel from a tribe to a state. For them, Samuel is not simply celebrating Yahweh's deliverance of the people from their enemies but is proclaiming Israel a state and acclaiming Saul a king (Halpern 1981a:130, 134). In their judgment, Saul's victory allowed him to extend his leadership from Benjamin to the hills of Ephraim to the north (Edelman 1984:204), and Samuel's celebration at Gilgal was, in effect, Saul's coronation.

In reality, however, Israel in Saul's time was not yet formally a state. There was still no centralized administrative bureaucracy, no national cultic center and priesthood, and the roles of prophet, priest, and monarch were still not clearly defined. The covenant which united the villages into a tribe was in continual danger of dissolution. Plus, Saul himself was in danger of being supplanted by another chief who was able to marshal more support for his rule (1 Sam 15:28; 16:1; 18:7). Because of this, Saul was Israel's last great chief, David its first real king (Edelman 1984:208).

The stories of Saul, like the one told by the people of Jabesh-Gilead, graphically demonstrate the many crises in which a chief can be selected and the ease with which his tribe can be supplanted or destroyed. The social institution of the chief was not only a practical strategy for protecting the villages in early Israel. It was an important theological statement for emancipated slaves. It was their way of remembering that only Yahweh can feed and protect Israel. For these idealists, states ruled by absolute monarchs and protected by standing armies were houses of slaves whose people had too much confidence in themselves and too little faith in God. For a remarkable period of almost 250 years these Israelite villages maintained their commitment to a society without monarchs, without soldiers, and without slaves. Then they had to choose between accepting a monarch and becoming a state or facing complete annihilation. It was a difficult choice with which Israel was never completely satisfied.

8

The Legal Guardian

In the world of the Bible, households designated their "heir" or "son" or "firstborn" (בֵּן, *bēn*) either by birth or achievement (Talmon 1980: 247; Weber 1952). In this way the social order of the village and the principles of power and authority were perpetuated (Pitt-Rivers 1977:119). Households in the villages of early Israel were patrilineal. Patrilineal households choose heirs only from the father's side; matrilineal households only from the mother's side; cognate households from either side. In matrilineal households it is the mother who owns the land, because it is the mother who bears the children who cares for the land. Members of the household receive their legal identity and economic standing in the village on the basis of the household of their mother, not their father.

Fathers used primogeniture or birth order to designate an heir in order to achieve stability for their households. By designating the first male born as the heir they reduced competition between the other men and women in the household. Inheritance by birth passed first to the sons of the mother

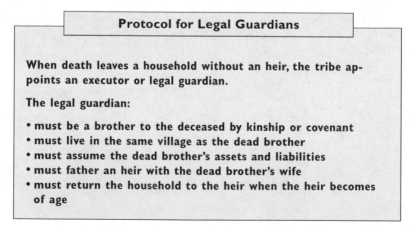

Protocol for Legal Guardians

When death leaves a household without an heir, the tribe appoints an executor or legal guardian.

The legal guardian:

• must be a brother to the deceased by kinship or covenant
• must live in the same village as the dead brother
• must assume the dead brother's assets and liabilities
• must father an heir with the dead brother's wife
• must return the household to the heir when the heir becomes of age

of the household, then to other wives or concubines, and finally to those sons who may have been borne by slaves. According to the custom of primogeniture, the firstborn generally received a double portion of their father's inheritance (*MAL* B:1, Pritchard *ANET* 1969:185; Thompson and Thompson 1968:93–94; Brichto 1973:16). But as is clear from the stories of Isaac and Rebekah in Genesis (Gen 27:1–45), the Code of Hammurabi, and even the *Iliad* of Homer from western Mediterranean culture, primogeniture alone never exclusively determined who became the heir. Regardless of their birth order and the status of their mothers, sons and daughters had no rights other than those granted to them by the father of the household.

Fathers designated heirs on the basis of achievement when they needed to adapt their households to sudden change (Sarbin and Allen 1985). For example, when the first male born could not meet the challenges of protecting and providing for the land and children of the household, a stronger and more competent heir could be designated (McKenzie 1959:523–27). Increases in population, war, and environmental catastrophe all encouraged achievers to take over their households. The ability to designate an heir on the basis of achievement was a basic component for social survival, especially in a fragile or unstable environment like the hills where the first Hebrew villages appeared (Salzman 1980:6; Swidler 1972:69–75).

Households Without an Heir

When the father died without designating an heir, the tribe appointed a legal guardian to look after the household. The tribe could not interfere in the internal affairs of a household unless these two conditions were fulfilled: the father of the household must have died and the household had no son (Deut 25:5). Most English translations render the word for this legal guardian or executor (יבם, *yāḇām*; גאל, *gō'ēl*; Latin: *levir*) as "brother-in-law" or "redeemer." Provisions for the appointment of legal guardians are found throughout the ancient Near East. For example, the Hittite Code, art. 193, which represents a legal tradition in the Empire of Hatti between 1450–1200 BCE, establishes similar provisions for the appointment of a legal guardian (Matthews and Benjamin 1991b:71), as those found in Genesis (Gen 38:1–30), Leviticus (Lev 25:25–38), Deuteronomy (Deut 25:5–10), Ruth (Ruth 3:1—4:22), and Jeremiah (Jer 32:6–44). The social institutions and legal vocabulary in these texts are comparable, but not identical (Sasson 1989:119–36; Benjamin 1983:222–36, 302–5; Rowley 1965:184; Burrows 1940:448; Beattie 1974:256, 266; Thompson and Thompson 1968:97–98; Westbrook 1991 [1977]: 74, 79–80). In some cases, for example, the guardian is delegated to take over only the land of the household, whereas in others he must father an heir with the widow as well. But all of the guardians represent the larger interests of the tribe in ensuring that a leaderless household does not lose the ability to feed and protect its members. To accomplish this end, tribes made use of only some of the components of the following protocol, each of which targets specific needs in the rehabilitation of a household.

Prior Commitment

Deuteronomy stipulates that the guardian must be a brother (Deut 25:5). A brother was not just someone related to the father of the household, but someone who had an existing connection or prior commitment (זיקה, zîqâh) with the household he would assume (Kalmin 1992: vol. 4, 296–97; m. Yebam 3:9; b. Yebam 26a). The title "brother" also indicated that the guardian was someone officially designated by the tribe to take over the household temporarily. He could not be a complete outsider, or simply a strong man acting on his own authority and anxious to expand his resources. By requiring both a prior commitment and an official delegation, the tribe guaranteed that the tribe's involvement in the crippled household would be a friendly and not a hostile takeover. The guardian was to restore the political, economic, and legal status of the household, rather than assimilate it into his own.

> ### Hittite Code, article 193
> ### (Matthews & Benjamin 1991b:71)
>
> **If a married man dies, then his brother must marry the widow; if his brother dies, then his father must marry her; if his father dies, then one of his brother's sons must marry the widow. . . .**

Common Domicile

Deuteronomy also requires that the legal guardian must "dwell . . . together" with the household he is assuming (Deut 25:5). By delegating only someone with the same domicile as the testator to take over responsibility for his household, the tribe prevented the guardian from becoming an absentee landlord. And only a legal guardian from the same village as the intestate household would have the necessary political and economic relationships in place to make it prosper. Finally, a common domicile also guaranteed that the elders of the village could supervise the guardian, thus reducing the possibility of mismanagement.

Protect and Provide for Household

The guardian assumed responsibility for both the land and the children of the household (Sasson 1979:136–40). With the resources of his own household, he was to feed and protect the household for which he was legal guardian. And although its liabilities were generally greater than its assets, he did enjoy the usufruct of the property and people of the household as long as there was no heir. He could keep any profit realized while he was guardian.

Father an Heir

While rebuilding the ability of the household to work its land and tend its herds for which it was responsible to the village, the guardian was also to have intercourse with the widow until she had a son. He did not marry the mother of the household, he simply carried out the physical and economic commitments which her husband had failed to complete before his death (Lev 18:16; 20:21). The guardian was authorized to care for her only until she had an heir, and the household could once again care for its own land and children.

Return Household to its Heir

When the tribe turned a household over to a legal guardian, it expected him to return the household to the control of its heir (Lev 25:25–28). Particularly vibrant households may have been able to recover their independence from a guardian as soon as an heir was born and adopted, thus within a year or two of the death of its father. In such cases the mother of the household would have functioned legally as the trustee for her infant son until he was mature enough to assume the day-to-day responsibilities of running the household himself (Sasson 1989: 139). But more often guardians would have had to administer the households assigned to their care for some years. Thus it was up to the guardian to determine when to turn the household over to the heir.

Since the guardian was given the authority to decide when to grant a household independence, an unscrupulous guardian could deprive a house-

---

Teaching on Legal Guardians
(Lev 25:25–28)

If anyone of your kin falls into difficulty and sells a piece of property, then the next of kin shall come and redeem what the relative has sold. If the person has no one to redeem it, but then prospers and finds sufficient means to do so, the years since its sale shall be computed and the difference shall be refunded to the person to whom it was sold, and the property shall be returned. But if there is not sufficient means to recover it, what was sold shall remain with the purchaser until the year of jubilee; in the jubilee it shall be released, and the property shall be returned.

hold of its income (Gen 38:1–11). In such cases, the wife could take legal action to remove the guardian. For example, she could file a complaint before the elders in the village assembly, who then subpoenaed the guardian and attempted to mediate a settlement. If the guardian remained intransigent, the widow could impeach him by removing his sandal, spitting in his face, and declaring: "This is what is done to the man who does not build up his brother's house" (Deut 25:9). Only in Ruth (Ruth 4:9) does the guardian himself issue a quit claim and refuse to take up his obligation to redeem the land and marry the widow by removing his own sandal (Westbrook 1991 [1977]:83–85; Levine 1992:83).

Sandals (נעלים, na῾ᵃlāyim) are simply leather soles fastened to the feet by thongs drawn between the toes and tied around the wearer's ankles. They were the ordinary footwear in the ancient Near East, but they were also a very symbolic item of clothing, especially in the relationship between the widow and her legal guardian (Leach 1984).

In the world of the Bible, land was purchased not by the acre but rather by the hour. Buyers paid for whatever size triangle of land they could walk off in an hour, a day, a week, or a month (1 Kgs 21:16–17). They surveyed land in triangles, constructed a bench mark with a cairn of fieldstones or an altar at each point of the triangle to serve as a boundary marker. To increase the speed of their surveys, buyers wore sandals. Since they walked off the land in sandals, the sandals became the movable title to that land. And they became the uniform which distinguished a landowner (pace McKenzie 1965). By removing the sandals of her guardian (Deut 25:5–10; Ruth 4:7), a widow removed his authorization to administer the land of her household (Lev 27:10, 33; Job 15:31; 20:18; 28:17; Pope 1965:119). In this gesture the sandal is a land title (Carmichael 1977:324; Gordis 1974:451; Burrows 1940:451).

But in the Bible the sandal is also a symbol of the woman herself, which has been placed on the foot of her guardian (Carmichael 1977:321–36). Therefore, by removing her guardian's sandal the widow was not only removing his authority over her deceased husband's land but also his authority to have intercourse with her until she had a child (Isa 5:8; Mic 2:2; Daube 1947:43–45). Removing the sandal of the legal guardian enacts coitus interruptus, where the sandal is a euphemism for her vagina, the foot of the guardian is a euphemism for his penis (Gaster 1975: vol. 2, 449–50).

The Legal Guardian in the Story of Tamar and Judah (Gen 38:1–30)

The story of Tamar and Judah in Genesis (Gen 38:1–30) revolves around the legal guardian. Will the tribe of Judah fulfill its obligation to support Tamar and provide an heir for her deceased husband Er, who died childless

(Deut 25:5–10; Ruth 4:1–12; *MAL* 30, 33, 43, 45)? Unless it provides her with
a guardian, the household of Er will not be able to hold on to its properties
while maintaining a balanced distribution within the household and attempting steadily to increase its population. The elements of the protocol
for the appointment of the legal guardian and the maintenance of proper
inheritance patterns appear throughout the story. The story begins by
explaining the crisis of premature death which triggers a pattern of obligation within the household of the dead man. What is at stake here is both
the maintenance of his honor, defined as "raising up his name" (שֵׁם, *šēm*),
and the continuity of inheritance; this will insure that the land remains
within the household and will prevent conflict within the household.

The stories of Joseph (Gen 37:1—Exod 1:6), within which the story of
Tamar and Judah is found, are as coherent as a modern short story or novel.
Each episode in the plot depends on those which precede it and prepares
the audience for those that follow. The story of Tamar and Judah (Gen
38:1–30), however, is an exception (von Rad 1961:351). It intrudes into the
stories of Joseph (Gen 37:2—Exod 1:6). Artistically, the story of Tamar and
Judah expands the reference to Judah who saves Joseph's life by selling him
as a slave instead of letting the other brothers murder him (Gen 37:25–36),
and allows Joseph to disappear completely for a time just as he disappeared
from the father and the brothers (von Rad 1961:352). The story of Tamar
and Judah is also inserted here as a reward for Judah for delivering the life
of Joseph and protecting his brothers from murder. In return for delivering
the lives of his brothers, Tamar delivers the household of Judah from
extinction and protects Judah from illegally sentencing her to death. Stories
with an eye for an eye and tooth for a tooth or talion motif were popular
in the ancient Near East.

The story of Tamar and Judah is an ancestor story that celebrates Tamar
for her courage in preserving her household from extinction. Tamar's virtue
is a willingness to become a liminal woman (Latin: *limen*). She acts above
and beyond the call of duty in order to give birth to a child (Niditch
1979:143–49). Tamar, not Judah, is the protagonist in the story. Only Tamar
moves from sterility to fertility, from shame to honor. Although Judah is a
man without a household at the beginning of the story and a man with a
household at the end, it is Tamar, not Judah, who acts to accomplish the
movement.

In some ancestor stories the crisis is allowed to develop through more
than one episode. In each episode the protagonist acts to achieve a goal and
is successfully blocked by the antagonist. For example, in the first episode
of the story of Tamar and Judah, Tamar marries but Judah's son leaves her
childless. Then, in the second episode, the tribe appoints another son as her
guardian but he defrauds her, and Judah himself shuns her (Gen 38:1–11).
In the third episode Tamar successfully conceives a child with Judah himself, but he still does not recognize her as the mother of his heir (Gen

38:12–23). In each episode she acts to preserve her husband's household from extinction and is prevented from doing so.

The storyteller's observation that "Er, Judah's firstborn, was wicked in the sight of the LORD; and the LORD put him to death" (Gen 38:7) seems to portray Yahweh as savage or barbaric. In the world of the Bible, however, the observation carried different connotations. Yahweh was all powerful. Anything which happened, good or bad, happened only because Yahweh decreed it. Yahweh was the cause of everything, a world view called "primary causality." This world view is not the result of ignorance, but of choice. Villagers in early Israel knew that death was the result of accident, widespread disease, or epidemic, but they chose to attribute it to Yahweh. Yahweh was almighty, the master of all life and death. No one died except by the decree of Yahweh. An unexplained or untimely death was always considered a sentence.

Initially, when Judah's son Er dies, there is no question that Onan, Er's brother, should become Tamar's legal guardian. The tribe expected Onan to have a child with Tamar and thus produce an heir for his brother Er (Sasson 1979:132). However, Onan realizes that if Tamar remains childless while he appears to be carrying out his obligations as her guardian, then he and his brother Shelah will divide Judah's inheritance two ways rather than three. Onan is guilty neither of masturbation, nor of uncharitableness (pace von Rad 1961:353), but of social injustice. In Ruth, the "next of kin" declines to accept the responsibility for Ruth "lest I impair my own inheritance" (Ruth 4:6). He is faced with having to provide for the household of Elimelech, a strain on the guardian's household, which may or may not be offset by the usufruct of Elimelech's estate (E. Davies 1981a; 1983:231; Sasson 1989:135–36). Onan, on the other hand, publicly accepts the responsibility and then defrauds Tamar while continuing to enjoy the usufruct of her property.

The result of Onan's calculations is his decision to practice coitus interruptus: "he spilled his semen on the ground" (Gen 38:9). Ostensibly, he fulfills his responsibility as guardian. In fact, he is sentencing Tamar to death as a widow without a husband or a child. He is also denying his deceased brother his right to have his name or inheritance preserved (Westbrook 1991:75–76; E. Davies 1983:233). Tamar cannot charge Onan before the village assembly for his crime because there are no witnesses. Like Job, she has no one to hear her case (Job 31:35). But the very hopelessness of her situation becomes her deliverance. Like all widows, orphans, and strangers, she enjoys the privileges of Yahweh's personal protection (Deut 24:17–22). Unable to be delivered by the village assembly, she is delivered by the divine assembly. For his violation of custom and this dishonorable act against his deceased brother, the storytellers consider the unexplained death of Onan as a divine sentence.

While the death of Onan delivers Tamar from his control it also indicts her as a *femme fatale*, a woman who lures the men who have intercourse with her to their death (Prov 2:16; 6:24). This motif also appears in Tobit, popular among Greek-speaking Jews in Alexandria, Egypt (Tobit 3:7–17). Consequently, like all the innocent who are falsely accused in folk stories worldwide, Tamar becomes a banished woman (Thompson 1977:120–25).

Now Shelah becomes Tamar's guardian. Because of his youth and because of Judah's fear that he will be left without an heir himself, he tells Tamar to wait until Shelah is physically capable of carrying out his duty to his brother. Judah returns Tamar to the household of her parents, which marks her with a label of shame; once a woman has become part of her husband's household her ties and loyalties are then broken with the household of her father (Gen 24:58). To return to her parental household suggests that she is giving up her legal rights (Judg 19:2), casts a legal question of whether her marriage was originally valid (Deut 22:13–21), and lowers her status to that of a childless widow rather than a wife in the process of producing a heir (Hiebert 1989:139, n. 18). By ordering her back to the household of her father Judah deprives Tamar of two important legal rights (Sasson 1989:132–33). First, he treats her as if she is legally a widow (אלמנה, 'almānâh), without a legal guardian when, in fact, she is not. Only widows without legal guardians return to the households of their fathers or mothers (Ruth 1:6–14). Second, by confining her to the household of her father he is depriving her of her freedom of movement, which is certainly the most fascinating and legally the most powerful right of a widow (MAL 33).

Thus Judah deprives Tamar and her deceased husband of the honor due them by endangering the possibility that she will ever produce an heir. This danger is given tangible substance when Judah fails to send Shelah to Tamar when he is of age. Again Tamar has no legal recourse to the village assembly. Technically, Judah is fulfilling the responsibility of his tribe to provide the household of Er with a guardian. In reality, however, he has condemned Tamar to a social and, ultimately, physical death as a childless widow.

Middle Assyrian Code, article 33 (authors' translation)

If the husband of a woman dies while they are still living in the household of his father, she shall live with whichever one of her sons she chooses.

If the widow has no sons of her own, then she shall marry her father-in-law or one of his sons.

If both the husband and his father die, and the widow has no sons, then she becomes a legal widow (Akkadian: almattu; אלמנה), and may live wherever she wishes.

Therefore, Tamar is forced into a manipulative deception that will ultimately fulfill the family's obligation to her husband. Dressed as a sacred
woman, Tamar tricks Judah into fulfilling his responsibility as a legal
guardian and having sexual intercourse with her. The sheep-shearing,
which provided the occasion for Tamar's ploy, was the round-up or rodeo
of ancient Israel (Gen 38:13). At the shearing, the old world of breeding and
grazing came to an end. Milk, cheese, meat, and wool were sold. Debts were
paid. Likewise, at the shearing, the new world of breeding and grazing
began. Contracts for breeding were negotiated.

Stories of Tobit and Sarah
(Tobit 3:7–10, NAB)

On[e] . . . day, at Ecbatana in Media, it so happened that
Raguel's daughter Sarah also had to listen to abuse, from one
of her father's maids. For she had been married to seven husbands, but the wicked demon Asmodeus killed them off before
they could have intercourse with her, as it is prescribed for
wives. So the maid said to her: "You are the one who strangles
your husbands! Look at you! You have already been married
seven times, but you have had no joy with any one of your husbands. Why do you beat us? Because your husbands are dead?
Then why not join them! May we never see a son or daughter
of yours!"

That day she was deeply grieved in spirit. She went in tears to
an upstairs room in her father's house with the intention of
hanging herself.

Judah is not engaging in an act of sexual indiscretion with a prostitute
when he has intercourse with Tamar, he is concluding a covenant or
business contract. In order to finance the breeding and grazing expenses for
the coming year, livestock owners like Judah borrowed from sanctuaries.
Judah approaches Tamar as a sacred woman for a loan and notarizes their
agreement by having sexual intercourse with her. The reproductive ritual
pronounces a blessing of fertility on the coming year.

Tamar is meticulous and efficient in her dealings with Judah. She sets her
commission as a share of the season's herd and collects Judah's staff and
seal as collateral before providing him a loan. Judah on the other hand does
not even recognize that his financial patron is, in fact, his daughter-in-law.
This may, in part, be explained by the veil she wears (Gen 38:14), and her
removal of her widow's garments. Judah had physically and mentally labeled Tamar as his son's widow, and now with business on his mind perhaps
he is unable to make the connection between the woman at Enaim and his
daughter-in-law.

Judah's lack of competence in providing Tamar with a legal guardian is even further displayed in the incompetence with which he negotiates with her for the coming season. Judah recognizes his lack of good business sense when he tries to repay the loan and the sacred woman is gone. His irresponsibility in negotiating and repaying the loan with the woman of Enaim summarizes his irresponsibility to Tamar and the household of Er. Instead of restoring the household, Judah's actions have placed it in greater jeopardy.

The climax of the ancestor story is recognized when the antagonist does not just keep the protagonist from reaching her goal, but attempts to take her life and completely destroy her ability to ever reach her goal. The climax announces that this is the protagonist's last chance when Tamar formally announces her pregnancy and Judah does not recognize her (Gen 38:24–25).

Judah, who has retained his legal control over her despite having sent her back to the household of her father, charges Tamar with adultery and sentences her to be burned to death (Hiebert 1989:129–30). The basis for this sentence is that she has shamed the household of Er by her actions (Bird 1989:77–78).

Story of Tamar and Judah
(Gen 38:24–25, authors' translation)

About three months later Judah was told, "Your daughter-in-law Tamar has played the whore; moreover she is pregnant as a result of whoredom."

And Judah said, "Bring her out, and let her be burned."

As she was being brought out, she sent word to her father-in-law, "It was the owner of these who made me pregnant. . . . [T]hese are [your] signet and . . . cord and . . . staff."

Tamar is able to save her life, however, by producing Judah's staff and seal and proving that he is the father of her twins. Judah's acknowledgment of Tamar's innocence accomplishes two things. First, it fulfills Judah's legal obligation as the guardian of Er's household. Second, it restores Tamar's honor as a wife whose concern for Er's inheritance has driven her to take extraordinary measures to secure that inheritance (Niditch 1979:147).

While there is seldom more than one episode in the climax of an ancestor story, its denouement or conclusion, like its crisis, often has several episodes. Each demonstrates the protagonist taking possession of her goals. In the first episode of the story of Tamar and Judah, Tamar formally sues Judah for recognition and he publicly acknowledges her as the mother of his heir (Gen 38:25–26). In the second, she gives birth to twins. She celebrates their birth with a hymn reflecting their adoption by Judah.

As in the stories of Adam and Eve (Gen 2:21–24; 4:1–2), and the stories of
Lot and his Daughters (Gen 19:30–38), the birth of twins here signifies the
beginning of a new world in which fertility is abundant. For every pregnancy there are two births. As in the stories of Cain and Abel, the twin motif
here reflects the belief of the ancient world that sibling rivalry is the root
of all evil. Onan's refusal to complete his legal obligation had lead to his
death, and yet, ironically, Tamar had produced a heir for both Er and Onan
(Westbrook 1991 [1977]:82).

The protocol for the legal guardian is an interesting example of the
priority of the community over the individual in the world of the Bible
(Campbell 1975:132–33). Although the individual father was dead, his legal
right to land and children remained intact. And even though the individual
guardian had land and children of his own, the household of another
became his responsibility. One individual's life span was extended, another's
was compromised for the good of the household (Abrahams 1973:167).

9

The Elder

The distribution of power in Hebrew villages followed a pattern standard in traditional societies where it was not personal charisma, virtue, or ambition, but the public responsibility of a group to feed and to protect its members. Every political system starts by stratifying or dividing the community into groups with specific tasks and recognized leaders (Adams 1977:388; Bloch 1973:76). Villages in many traditional societies use gift giving to rank their households. The protocol of gift giving controlled both the value of the gift itself and how these gifts were exchanged (Van Baal 1975:50). Reciprocity dictated that only goods or services of equal value could change hands (Radcliffe-Brown 1948:84). Nonetheless, each household had the opportunity to benefit by the exchange (Barth 1981:38). Strategy thus came into play which attempted to determine a favorable outcome for one household while at the same time maintaining parity or dominance over others (Sahlins 1968:9). The actual gifts exchanged in any transaction became politically important depending upon who gave and who received them. Reciprocity shifted from parity to partnership as households recognized that the objects were less important than their social relationships (Feil 1988:105).

Households gave gifts to determine who were their friends and who were their enemies. The fundamental relationship between one household and the other displayed either amity or opposition (Fortes 1969:251). If there was amity, the households were allies or covenant partners who had a common self-interest (Pitt-Rivers 1975:90). Sometimes covenant partners were equals but in most cases one was dominant, or a patron, and the other was subservient or a client. Equals exhibited different attitudes toward each other than did patrons and clients. If there was opposition, the households were enemies whose self-interests were mutually exclusive.

As the divisions between households in a village stabilized, gift giving was replaced by law (Wolf 1966:10–12). Law perpetuated the power of certain households over others. Households whose actions violated the law were shamed while those most closely in tune with the law were honored (Dentler and Erikson 1984:91). While law stabilized a particular division of the village into patrons and clients, it also sowed the seeds of oppression and economic exploitation (Landsberger 1973:29–30). By limiting access to leadership positions and setting policy which did not always meet current needs, law often established a ruling elite who oppressed the people they were appointed to serve (Lees 1979:270). When the level of amity or the societal constraints which made amity desirable were weakened, compensatory services by the elite classes were reduced and tyranny occurred (Pitt-Rivers 1975:96–97; Gottwald 1985:539). To administer the law and control tyranny and oppression early Israel used a village assembly.

Village Assembly

The fathers of the households in the village who were patrons served as its leaders or elders (זקנים, $z^e q \bar{e} n \hat{i} m$; Ruth 4:2; Prov 31:23; Reviv 1989:11). They derived their authority from the confidence placed in them by the villagers who recognized the wealth of experience they held and its value to the community (Seeden and Kaddour 1984:502). The elders served as an assembly upholding the civil rights of the members of the village and protecting the rights of those dwelling there without a household such as the widow, the orphan, and the alien (Weinfeld 1977:81; Bellefontaine 1987: 53; Irons 1971:149).

Government by assembly transcended any one time period in the ancient Near East. Even when great states began to appear, government by assembly remained both an important social ideal and an important social institution in the ancient world. Villages and cities continued to resolve civil and criminal cases by assembly. Similarly, elders continued to function even after more centralized political systems replaced the village in ancient Israel (Salmon 1968:417). Generally, however, as in the case of the seventy elders in Exodus (Exod 24:1) and those present at the dedication of Solomon's Temple (1 Kgs 8:1), elders in a state were overshadowed by other officials (Reviv 1989:9, 21). The elders represented their villages at significant state events, but have little real power to effect change themselves.

In cities, the gates served as court houses where the assembly met (Deut 21:18–21; 22:13–21; 22:23–27). In villages, the assembly convened in the open-air setting of the threshing floors, where grain was processed. There were practical as well as symbolic reasons for using gates and threshing floors as meeting places. The two sides of the main gate which faced one another created bays or areas enclosed on three sides which were used by cities for public meetings and trials. Anyone with a grievance came to the main gate to seek judicial recourse. Plaintiffs initiated proceedings by going to the gate and impaneling a jury of elders to review their course of action (Ruth 4:1–2; 1 Sam 16:4; Jer 26). Standing at the gate when people were on their way to work in the fields outside the walls, the plaintiff shouted: "Justice!" When ten citizens had been impaneled to hear the case, they adjourned to one of the bays in the gate to deliberate. Locating the city's judicial system at the gate not only gave the plaintiff access to a jury pool, but also kept the trial open. Since the deliberations took place in front of the steady flow of people coming and going through the gate, the occasion for bribery and other manipulations of the judicial system were reduced (Exod 23:8; Amos 5:10–12).

Gates and threshing floors also marked the frontiers between the divine plane and the human plane. They were thresholds which separated the cosmos inside the city or village from the chaos beyond. The village assembly was responsible for determining who belonged to the city or village. Members of households accused of anti-social behavior were brought to this frontier between cosmos and chaos to determine if the accused were to be reinstated or exiled. Defendants convicted of the charges leveled against them were consigned to chaos beyond the gate or threshing floor at the outskirts of the city or village.

There were no permanent officials for the assembly. Sometimes members functioned as legislators or judges; at other times, they were prosecutors (Jer 37:1–21; 42:1—43:7), defense attorneys (Jer 7:16–34; 27:1–22; Ezek 14: 12–23; Amos 7:1–9), and witnesses (Gen 23:10, 18). Not every resident could appeal to and serve on the assembly. In the world of the Bible, only certain males were able to marry, own land, appear in a sanctuary, bear arms, and administer justice. In general, women, children, slaves, and resident aliens (גר, gēr) did not enjoy these rights.

Protocol for Elders

When a breakdown in the distribution of power occurred in the villages or cities of ancient Israel, it was resolved by an assembly of elders. Until ten elders came aside to hear the case, the plaintiff:

- stood at threshing floor or city gate,
- at dawn when workers left for fields and pastures,
- and cried out: "Justice!"

Until they reached a consensus acceptable to both the household of the plaintiff and the defendant, an assembly of elders:

- listened to the testimony of witness,
- examined evidence,
- reviewed customary law.

Although plaintiffs could convene an assembly at anytime, the standard time of the day for a meeting was at daybreak. As a practical matter, the greatest number of citizens came and went on their way to work at dawn (Ps 104:22–23). But daybreak was also important because of the connection between the sun and the administration of justice in the ancient world. Ra in Egypt and Shamash in Mesopotamia were both gods of the sun and gods of justice.

City and village assemblies did not have police power to enforce their decisions. Like the litigants in Job, members of the assembly deliberated until they reached a consensus. All of the participants, not just a simple majority, needed to be satisfied enough with the decision to observe it. Assemblies did not simply lack the power to enforce a decision supported by a simple majority. For them, a consensus, voluntarily observed by all the parties involved, was an important safeguard to their understanding that only the power of the divine assembly and not the power of the village assembly or its police was absolute. Furthermore, those who served on the assemblies did not understand themselves as administering a universal code of law, but as advocating the rights of those who came before them. It was not their responsibility to punish those who violated a law, as much as it was to help plaintiffs secure their rights to land and children.

Divine Assembly

Government by assembly was such a cherished ideal in the world of the Bible that Israel used it as a metaphor to talk about Yahweh. If villages submitted all their important decisions to the assembly certainly Yahweh must do the same (Kramer 1956:71–96). A divine assembly appears in the literature of Egypt, Mesopotamia, Syria-Palestine, and ancient Israel (עדה, 'ēḏâh, Ps 82:1; מועד, mô'ēḏ, Isa 14:13; קהל, qāhāl, Ps 89:6 MT [ET v. 7]; סוד, sôḏ, Job 15:8; Jer 23:18). The protocol for meetings of a divine assembly appears in the Enuma Elish story from Babylon and the prophetic literature in the Bible. Following his successful battle with Tiamat in the Enuma Elish story, for example, Marduk convenes a divine assembly to discuss the aftermath of Tiamat's conspiracy and to create the people primeval (Enuma vi 23–43; Jacobsen 1949:156).

The divine assembly was made up of the citizens of the divine plane who were caretakers of the cosmos. These included, among others, the moon, the stars, and the planets. Prophets were regular participants as well (Amos 7—9). To these caretakers fell the responsibility both for the creation of the cosmos and for its maintenance.

Generally, the divine assembly met on a sacred mountain which served as a link between the divine plane, or the heavens, and the human plane, or the earth. Among mountains designated in the Bible and its parallels are Saphon in today's Syria and Babylon in today's Iraq. Many traditions associated with these mountains are used to celebrate biblical sites like

Moriah, Zion, and Bethel. For example, in the story of Jacob's Ladder in Genesis (Gen 28:10–22), the ancestor does not actually see a ladder, but the Esagila, the ziggurat or great stepped-platform which the members of the divine assembly used to enter and leave Babylon. The Babylonians constructed ziggurats as liturgical mountains for the divine assembly. The Book of Genesis (Gen 11:1–9) satirizes the same ziggurat as the Tower of Babel. The story of Jacob's Ladder confers the status of the Gate of God (Akkadian: *bab il(im)* in Mesopotamia on the House of God (בית־אל, *bēt-'ēl*) in Syria-Palestine. Annually the divine assembly convened to renew covenants during elaborate liturgies at sanctuaries atop these sacred mountains.

On special occasions, the divine assembly would also meet at the threshing floor. In Samuel–Kings (1 Kgs 22:1–40), the monarchs and prophets of Israel and Judah meet on the threshing floor at the city gate to discern whether or not the divine assembly has authorized them to go to war against Aram. In this instance, the prophet Micaiah's vision of the divine assembly supersedes and corrects that of the 400 court prophets of Ahab and Jehoshaphat. The cognitive dissonance which results highlights the difficulties of interpreting the decisions of the divine assembly when political considerations intervene (Isa 7:3–25; Jer 28).

Pantheon, Angels, and Trinity

Today the divine assembly of the ancient Near East is often compared with the Greek pantheon or the Christian understanding of angels and the Trinity. To a certain extent these comparisons can be helpful, but at the same time they often distort the significance of the divine assembly.

The Greek pantheon in the *Iliad* and the *Odyssey* of Homer reflects the world view of western Mediterranean cultures. Until 333 BCE when Alexander the Great conquered the ancient Near East, this world view was quite different from that in eastern Mediterranean cultures like ancient Israel. The members of both the pantheon and the assembly are divine, and both are involved with human affairs. However, the sexual and political exploits of the pantheon are not at all characteristic of the more sober undertakings of the divine assembly.

Angels are heavenly helper figures in religious thinking today and certain members of the divine assembly do help humans from time to time. But angels are subordinate members of the heavenly community, whereas the members of the divine assembly have the primary responsibility for both the heavens and the earth.

The Christian Trinity is, like the assembly, a divine community. But the doctrine of the Trinity is a meticulously worded teaching, which reflects an agonizing struggle between 100 and 300 CE to reconcile Christian preaching with Greek philosophy. The divine assembly, on the other hand, is a product neither of Christian preaching nor Greek ways of thinking. It reflects the efforts of eastern Mediterranean cultures from 3000 BCE onward to understand the world in which they lived.

Monotheism and the Divine Assembly

Thinking of Yahweh as a member of a divine assembly was not primitive, ignorant, or heretical. In some ways the tradition of a divine assembly offered the Hebrews advantages which the doctrine of monotheism in Judaism, Christianity, and Islam today does not. For example, understanding Yahweh as a member of a divine assembly emphasized the importance which Israel and all traditional people place on community. Monotheism, on the other hand, may unnecessarily contribute to an unhealthy understanding of God as the ultimate private person, living in splendid isolation. Likewise, talking about Yahweh as a member of a divine assembly allowed Israel to develop a wider variety of meditations on divine characteristics. Monotheism often limits our understanding of God to being powerful. And finally, from the point of view of learning about God, the human mind must subdivide in order to understand. Strict monotheism can frustrate the human ability to know God better.

The Elder in a Teaching on Breach of
Covenant (Deut 22:13–21)

A teaching on breach of covenant in Deuteronomy (Deut 22:13–21) demonstrates one of the many roles of the elder as a member of the village assembly. The judicial system in both villages and cities governed by assembly developed a literary genre called "teachings" or "legal instructions." Assemblies use legal instructions to accomplish several things, but especially to introduce the households in a village to their public responsibilities in a subsistence economy. Each household is taught an elaborate process of arbitration to maintain its own independence and to prevent its disputes with other households from endangering the village as a whole. The arbitration takes place in an assembly which meets at the threshing floor of a village or at the gate of a city.

Legal instructions are made up of citations from codes of law and commentaries. The citations may be direct or paraphrased. The commentaries contain definitions of technical terms (Deut 25:5), explanations of legal procedures (Deut 19:4–13), examples of testimony (Deut 21:7–8), specifications (Deut 13:14), and parenesis, which offers motivations for carrying out the requirements of the law (Deut 6:10–19). The integrity of the village or city rests on the willingness of its citizens to support the legal system and to settle disputes through arbitration rather than force or violence (Deut

5:17–20). By acknowledging their need for one another through this style of legal justice, they guarantee the solidarity of the community.

Today the teaching on breach of covenant (Deut 22:13–21) can seem both barbaric and sexist. But a more careful social-scientific reading uncovers a social world which is both socially sensitive and legally sophisticated. Not even the conditions under which an execution may be carried out reflect the use of brute force. The rights and responsibilities of each household affected by the incident and the indictment are safeguarded.

The litigants in the teaching are two households whose covenant with one another has been ratified by marriage. The man or husband represents one household, the woman or wife—with her father and mother—represent another. The elders must investigate, evaluate, and rule on the merit of the case and prevent the dispute from damaging the ability of the entire village to feed and protect all its households. The question before the elders is not simply slander or sexual promiscuity but a breach of covenant which threatens the established distribution of power in the village.

Today, the sexual activity involved in intercourse, rape, marriage, adultery, and divorce is not considered an economic or diplomatic issue. Sexual activity is part of an individual's personal or private life. But in the world of the Bible, sexual activity is more public than private. The significance of sexual activity is its impact on the political stability of the community as a whole. Human fertility and sexual activity are not only an index of the political health of the village, they control it. Certainly there was as much individual tenderness, emotion, and love in sexual activity then as now, but this teaching on breach of covenant reveals more about covenant liability than alienation of affection.

As a literary genre, legal instructions reflect the decentralized character of village life. Law, on the other hand, is the authoritative genre of a state. Teaching is the educational or persuasive genre of a village. It does not give orders, it explains. Here the teaching explains not only what a father and mother can do to defend their household against a husband who attempts to break his covenant, but also what a husband can do to defend his household against a mother and father trying to defraud it. It also offers the other households motivation to preserve the distribution of power in the village.

A marriage is legal only when the man's household pays its bride-price (מהר, *mōhar*) and the woman's household pays its dowry (זבד, *zēbed*) during eight days of wedding celebration which conclude when the man and the woman officially have sexual intercourse as husband and wife for the first time. Each requirement of the protocol must be met before the covenant falls under the jurisdiction of the village elders.

A dowry is the capital which a woman's household invests in the household of her husband (Gen 31:14–15; 1 Kgs 9:16). The dowry transfers the bride's share of her inheritance from the household of her father to the children which she and her husband will have (Goody 1973, 1976; Roth 1989:249;

Schneider 1987:410). At Nuzi, the dowry remained the bride's property in case of divorce, or until the birth of children (Grosz 1983:200–203).

A bride-price is the capital which a man's household invests in a woman's household in order to make a future gain in land and children (Goody and Tambieh 1973:5; Schlegel 1991:720). Like the dowry, the bride-price may be paid in either goods or services (Gen 29:16–22; Schlegel 1991:720). If the bride-price is equal to the dowry, there is economic parity between the households of the bride and the groom. Households will only pay greater bride-prices or dowries when they wish to improve their social status by the marriage (Grosz 1983:205).

The transfer of the dowry and the bride-price is officially witnessed by the elders and other wedding guests. The length of the ceremony reflects the time assigned for the creation of a new world. In the story of the Heavens and the Earth (Gen 1:1—2:4a), Yahweh labors for six days and rests on the seventh. In the wedding ritual, the two parental households labor for seven days, and rest on the eighth day when husband and wife of the newly created household have sexual intercourse.

In a teaching on a breach of covenant from Deuteronomy, the covenant between two households is both official and ratified. The man has married the woman and he has gone in to her. Nonetheless, he takes legal steps to abrogate it. For whatever reason, he dislikes his bride after the marriage has been consummated. So he shames her. On behalf of his household, the husband alleges: "I married this woman; but when I lay with her, I did not find evidence of her virginity" (Deut 22:13). Literally, the social principle involved here is one of honor, that of the household of the bride and that of the husband (Bird 1989:77). The measure of this honor is the evidence of virginity on the part of the bride at the time when the marriage is consummated.

Simple dissatisfaction with one's bride is not a grounds for divorce. Real proof is necessary to abrogate a covenant. The husband seeks to impose a label of shame on his wife's household because she is not fulfilling the stipulations of the covenant which their marriage ratified (Scheff 1990; Retzinger 1991). The mother of a household who did not prepare adequate meals, or who allowed her household to become disorderly, exposed the household of her father to shame (Braithwaite 1991:xiii; Destro 1989:56). Nonetheless, indictments of her cooking and housekeeping were not just reflections on her own character, they charged the household of her father with having misrepresented the goods and services which it was ready to provide. The teaching deals with enforced pre-marital virginity codes, fraud charges, false witness, shared responsibility of child and parents, the role of the elders in the determination of sufficient evidence to warrant a fine or a death penalty, the shared participation of the community in the process of execution, and the identification of places for legal acts to be transacted.

Productive covenants are essential in the ongoing campaign of a village to better use its labor and land. The teaching on breach of covenant is

certainly evidence that some households negotiated non-productive covenants, which, in turn, threatened the village as well as the partners. The
investment which the man's household made in the woman's household is
not producing a return in land and children. The world of the Bible considered mixing the semen of more than one man in the uterus of one woman
and mixing the seed of more than one crop in the same field a contamination which made it impossible for the woman to bear a healthy child and
the field to produce a good harvest (Delaney 1988:83). If the village is going
to survive, the covenant between these two households must be renegoti-
ated or one of the households must be liquidated. The allegation which the
husband files against the household of his wife is not simply sexual promiscuity but fraud. The father and mother of her household misrepresented
not just their daughter's physical condition but all their economic assets
and liabilities. By filing suit the husband hopes to liquidate the assets of his
wife's household and recover at least the bride-price which his household
invested. A centralized state thrives on such aggressive economic takeovers
(2 Sam 11:2–27; 13:1–22), but raids like this soon destroy the delicate balance of power in a decentralized village.

The maneuver of the elders in the teaching on breach of covenant is a
shrewd protocol for physical evidence. The evidence of the young woman's
virginity (בתולים, $b^e t \hat{u} l \hat{\imath} m$; Deut 22:15) is generally assumed to be the blood-
stained clothes which covered the bed on which she and her husband
consummated their marriage (Driver 1895:255; Bergman, Ringgren and
Tsevat 1975:342). The father and mother are to take or impound this
physical evidence, bring it out or place it in evidence, and say or testify that
they have not defrauded their daughter's husband. The evidence demonstrates both the virginity of the daughter as well as the solidity of her
household (Paige 1983:159, 165). The wife is never questioned. The physical
evidence is the sole determinant of guilt or innocence.

Physical evidence plays a significant role in trials today. In the ancient
Near East, on the other hand, judicial proceedings depended almost entirely
on testimony. By far, the majority of cases reconstructed from the Bible rely
only on oral witness. The Bible reflects a very limited use of physical
evidence. Warriors cut off the hands, the heads (Judg 7:25; 2 Sam 4:7–8;
2 Kgs 10:7–8), or the foreskins (1 Sam 18:25–27) of their victims as physical
evidence of their valor. And herders salvaged at least the hooves or the ear
of any animal attacked by a predator as physical evidence they themselves
had not stolen the animal and sold it (Amos 3:12). The physical evidence in
the teaching on breach of covenant is not only unconventional, it also
seems specifically designed to catch the husband by surprise. Similarly, in
the story of Tamar and Judah (Gen 38:1–30), Tamar also tricks Judah out
of his seal, cord, and staff before having intercourse with him. When Judah
subsequently accuses Tamar of adultery she uses this physical evidence to
establish her innocence.

```
┌─────────────────────────────────────────────────────┐
│        ┌───────────────────────────────────┐        │
│        │      Teaching on Testifying        │        │
│        │         (Deut 19:15)               │        │
│        └───────────────────────────────────┘        │
│                                                       │
│   A single witness shall not suffice to convict a     │
│   person of any crime or wrongdoing in connection     │
│   with any offense that may be committed. Only on      │
│   the evidence of two or three witnesses shall a       │
│   charge be sustained.                                 │
│                                                       │
└─────────────────────────────────────────────────────┘
```

There is no law requiring the collection of physical evidence. Otherwise, the husband would have known physical evidence of his wife's virginity existed, and he would not have charged her household with breach of covenant in the first place. The teaching explains how to use physical evidence to prevent the hostile takeover of one household by another (Paige 1983:160). The primary case in the teaching encourages households to collect physical evidence of their daughter's virginity as insurance against future attempts by her husband's household to breach the marriage covenant (Benjamin 1983:227; Giovannini 1987:61). In highly competitive state economies, women were frequently victims of physical and economic violence. The village traditions reflected in the teaching on breach of covenant outlaw the use of brute force and aggression as a means of economic growth.

If the elders find the husband guilty of perjury, they flog him (יסר, *yāsar*; Deut 22:18; Prov 19:18), place his household under an injunction not to divorce her (Exod 21:7–11; Deut 22:19) and award the household of the wife damages (Deut 22:19). Corporal punishment is a standard sentence for false accusations of fraud throughout the ancient Near East. Flogging is the only penalty imposed in Babylonian codes, whereas Assyrian codes impose sentences of both flogging and damages (Pritchard 1969:181; MAL 7, 18).

The disposition is serious, but short of death. Curiously, the elders do not use the legal principle of talion, or reciprocity, to sentence the husband (CH article 196; Exod 21:23–25; Lev 24:19–20). The husband should be stoned to death, because the stoning of his wife is the sentence which would have been imposed on her household if found guilty of fraud. No codes of law in the ancient Near East sentence a husband to death. Although this leniency certainly reflects a judicial system dominated by men, sexism is not the legal principle involved in the sentence. The wife is her household's legal title to the bride-price. If she is executed, her household forfeits all the goods and services which her husband's household turned over during the wedding. If the husband were stoned to death, his household would lose one member, but her household would gain nothing.

If the elders find the parents guilty of fraud they sentence them to witness the execution of their daughter (Deut 22:21). This companion case further emphasizes the importance for the household of a wife to collect physical

> ### Teaching on Perjury
> ### (Deut 19:16–19)
>
> If a malicious witness comes forward to accuse someone of wrongdoing, then both parties to the dispute shall appear before the Lord, before the priests and before the judges who are in office in those days, and the judges shall make a thorough inquiry. If the witness is a false witness, having testified falsely against another, then you shall do to the false witness just as the false witness had meant to do to the other.

evidence of their daughter's virginity. Without the physical evidence to prove otherwise, she is automatically assumed to be guilty and the social purging mechanism comes into play (Phillips 1970:116; Reviv 1989:63). There is no alternative sentencing, no plea bargaining. She is simply taken to the door of her household and stoned to death. The place of her execution signals that the true defendant in the case is the household, not simply the accused woman (Matthews 1987:32). Her household has dishonored itself by covenanting a marriage without acknowledging the fact that the young woman involved was not a virgin. Her execution at the door of her father's house marks this spot and this household as frauds, open to sanction by the community due to breach of covenant.

Both the household of the husband in the primary case and the household of the mother and the father in the companion case in the teaching on breach of covenant are households in a village who would exercise the powers of a monarch. Practically, elders do not possess the power to police rogue households like these. And, theoretically, it would be no more consistent with the distribution of power in a village for the elders to exercise such brute force than it is for these households.

The teaching reflects how carefully covenants distributed power in a village. Elders did not create law or establish precedent. They were administrators of the public trust and of the social covenant which bound the village together. The elders were not dictators. They could not intervene to mediate a dispute unless a covenant, which had been ratified by a legally contracted and fully consummated marriage, was officially contested. Monarchs relied on force to maintain political stability, but elders governed with more subtle maneuvers. Monarchs had the power to legislate, but elders had the responsibility to educate.

10

The Widow

In the villages of early Israel, most women enjoyed the status of a daughter, a wife, or a mother. The daughter (בַּת, *bat*) was entitled to the rights and privileges of her father, the wife (אִשָּׁה, *'iššâh*) to those of her husband, and the mother (אֵם, *'ēm*) to those of her son (Niditch 1979:143–49). These women upheld the honor of their households by their fidelity or sexual behavior and their fertility or ability to bear children. Daughters who had not borne children were expected to remain sexually inactive and to live in the households of their fathers. Wives were expected to bear children and remain sexually active only with their husbands. Mothers were expected to remain sexually inactive after the deaths of their husbands and to live with the heirs to whom they had given birth. One sign of their change of status was the wearing of widow's garments (Gen 38:14, 19). They could not remarry if their husband had died without an heir until they had conceived an heir with their legal guardian (Ruth 4:5). If there was an heir to care for the household, however, a widow could remarry (Baab 1962:842: Safrai 1974:787). But such a marriage would only have been desirable if the widow brought economic assets to her

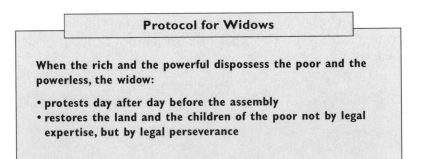

Protocol for Widows

When the rich and the powerful dispossess the poor and the powerless, the widow:

• protests day after day before the assembly
• restores the land and the children of the poor not by legal expertise, but by legal perseverance

new husband, or maintained priestly household ties (1 Sam 25:39–42; Ezek 44:22).

In ancient Israel, daughters who were sexually active outside of marriage, wives who were sexually active with men other than their husbands, or wives who could not bear children even though they were sexually active only with their husbands were shamed (Gen 16:1–4; 2 Kgs 4:14). But curiously, even shamed women had a place within the village. Although they were shamed or dishonored, at least they had social identity as "foolish women" (Prov 7:10–20; 9:13; 30:16; Job 24:21).

But there were women in the villages of Israel who did not belong to any social class. These women were liminal. They had no status. The orphan (יתום, yāṯôm), the prostitute (זנה, zōnâh), and the widow without children (אלמנה, 'almānâh) were all liminal women. The word "liminal" refers to the threshold which everyone crosses to enter and leave the house (Latin: limen). Liminal women were not just out of the house but were without a household. They were legally homeless, without any social, political, or economic status in the village (Sasson 1989:123–24; Cohen 1973:76–77; Turner 1969:94–97). But because they had nothing, they also had nothing to lose. Like the state which was dependent on Yahweh for land and children, the widow could ultimately look to Yahweh for redress of injury or oppression (Deut 1:10, 21; 10:17–18; Ps 146:9; Mal 3:5).

The Bible does not encourage, glorify, or romanticize orphans, prostitutes, or widows. For instance, widows without children or who lose their only child have no hope for the future since they have no one to support them (2 Sam 14:6–7; 1 Kgs 17:17–19; 2 Kgs 4:18 37; Luke 7:12). The book of Leviticus condemns prostitutes, and prohibits priests from marrying liminal women, including widows (Lev 19:29). Although these unconventional women were outside the rules they were precisely the people chosen by Yahweh to perform unexpected and extraordinary tasks within the community (Exod 22:20–24). Yahweh used the orphan, the prostitute, and the widow to work subtle miracles (Hals 1969:16; Campbell 1975:28–29; Scott 1989:187). And that was the key to the power of these women in the world of the Bible. Tamar, the childless widow in Genesis; Rahab, the prostitute in Joshua; Naomi and Ruth, the widows in Ruth; Hadassah in the book of Esther (Esther 2:7); and Judith the widow in the book of Judith are all liminal women who go above and beyond the call of duty to deliver their people. Without any of the resources which villages placed at the disposal of a chief, for example, liminal women risked their lives to recover the land and the children of the clans who told their stories. The widow was the social institution which stood between the exploiters and the exploited in the world of the Bible (Isa 47:8–9; Lam 1:1–2; 5:3; Thurston 1985:280). Since she could suffer no loss she could afford to be uncompromising in her legal perseverance to recover the land and children of the exploited (Benjamin 1990).

Household and Liminal Women	
Women of a Household	**Liminal Women**
The Daughter with a father (בַּת)	**The Orphan** without a father (יָתוֹם)
The Wife with a husband (אִשָּׁה)	**The Prostitute** without a husband (זֹנָה)
The Widow with a son (אֵם)	**The Widow** without a son (אַלְמָנָה)

The Widow in the Dead Sea Scrolls

Near the end of the Second War Between Judah and Rome (132–135 CE), Jews from Ein Gedi took refuge in a cave on the cliffs above the Dead Sea, which archaeologists today call the "Cave of Letters" (Broshi 1984:158–59). These refugees were eventually discovered and killed by the Romans. Among them was a widow named Babatha. When she left Ein Gedi for the Cave of Letters, Babatha brought with her a packet of legal documents. They were transcripts of the actions which she had filed in courts of law between 93 and 132 CE (Yadin 1971:222–53).

Babatha's records were recovered 1960–61 by an Israeli archaeological expedition led by Yigael Yadin. They were written in Greek, Nabataean, and Aramaic. There were twenty-six documents in Greek, which was the official language of the eastern provinces of the Roman empire. Some had been annotated in Aramaic and Nabataean. There were six documents in Nabataean, which was the language of the people of Petra in the southern part

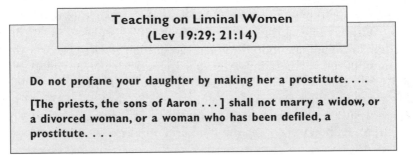

Teaching on Liminal Women
(Lev 19:29; 21:14)

Do not profane your daughter by making her a prostitute. . . .

[The priests, the sons of Aaron . . .] shall not marry a widow, or a divorced woman, or a woman who has been defiled, a prostitute. . . .

of Jordan today. Three documents were written in Aramaic, which was the everyday language spoken by Jews throughout the Roman provinces of Judaea and Syria-Palestine at the beginning of the common era. The widow's files are a unique source from which to reconstruct the everyday life of this region in antiquity, shedding light on such subjects as the legal system, economics, religious observances, geography, agriculture, and linguistics. The archive also reveals much about Babatha's personal history, her family, and its business dealings. But perhaps most of all, Babatha's records are a fascinating testimony to the legal tenacity of a widow before courts of law. Like Tamar and Ruth, Babatha was a persistent widow dedicated to protecting the legal rights of her household.

Babatha was born into a wealthy household in the village of Mahoza near Zoar, south of the Dead Sea. She was married twice. Her first husband was Yeshua. They had one son and named him Yeshua. After the death of her first husband, Babatha remarried. Her second husband was Yehudah, who also died, leaving her a widow for the second time. After the death of Babatha's first husband, the senate of Petra appointed two guardians for her son: Yohanan Egla, who was Jewish, and Abdobdas Illoutha, a Nabataean. This action follows the legal tradition that a widow's care lay in the hands of the heir of the estate or his guardians (Thurston 1985:279). Several of Babatha's records document her legal battle against Egla and Illoutha for control of her deceased husband's land.

For example, on October 12, 125 CE, Babatha filed suit against Yohanan Egla and charged him with failing to pay her child support. Babatha wanted the land held in trust by her son's guardians to be turned over to her and, in return, she would pay her legal guardians a higher rate of interest on it than the guardians could get in the open market.

When the war between Judah and Rome broke out, Babatha moved from Mahoza to live with her relatives in Ein Gedi, which was part of the province

---

**Trial of Yohanan Egla
(Yadin 1971:240–41)**

October 12, 125,

. . . since you did not give . . . to the said orphan . . . as Abdobdas Illoutha has given . . . give me the money against security, my property serving as hypothec, and I shall pay the interest of the money one and a half denarii [per month] in a hundred [as against one per hundred paid by the guardians] in order that thereby my son may be brilliantly [sic!] saved thanks to the most happy times of the governorship of Julius Julianos the governor in whose presence I Babata [sic] summoned you because of the refusal of Ioanes, the afore-written guardian, to pay the aliments.

of Judaea liberated from the Romans by the Jews (Yadin 1971:244). When the war turned against the Jews she left Ein Gedi with the others to hide in the Cave of the Letters.

Like Babatha, widows in the villages of early Israel were never involved in small claims, but always struggled to retain the divine endowments of land and children which distinguished the free from the slave (Exod 21:1–6). These were the endowments which Yahweh conferred on Abraham and Sarah in Genesis (Gen 11:27—12:8) and confirmed by liberating the Hebrews in Exodus (Exod 5:1—18:27). The widow's antagonists were those who deprive ordinary people of their land and children like those described by Deuteronomy (Deut 24:17–22). Her antagonists were the lenders who seized even her clothing as collateral and the growers who locked her out of the fields where she gleaned the food she needed to survive. The widow's resource was not power or property but legal persistence. She knew her rights and how to exercise them (Fensham 1962:135). Like Moses standing before the Pharaoh, the widow stood before the courts again and again to demand that the rich and the powerful "let my people go!"

A Parable of a Persistent Widow
(Ruth 1:1–21)

The book of Ruth tells how two widows raise one household from death to life. It is the story of how Ruth and Naomi become the mothers of the most respected household in Bethlehem into which David, the future monarch of Israel, will be born (Levine 1992:78). Like all truly great stories, images in Ruth are colorful, its plot is punctuated with repetition and laced with foreshadowing (Niditch 1985:451–56). The book combines several parables and ancestor stories. There is the Parable of the Persistent Widow (Ruth 1:1–22), the Parable of the Laborers in the Wheat Field (Ruth 2:1–23), a story of Ruth (Ruth 3:1–18), and a story of Boaz (Ruth 4:1–21). Each had its own tale to tell before it was molded with the others into a single story celebrating David and Solomon as the first monarchs of Israel (Gen 24:1–67; Gen 38:1–30; Gen 36—37; 39—50; 1 Sam 13:1—2 Sam 1:27; 2 Sam 9—20; 1 Kgs 1—2). The Parable of the Persistent Widow with which the book opens highlights the legal perseverance of its main character.

One way to identify a parable is by its opening line. "In the days when the judges ruled," from the Parable of the Persistent Widow in Ruth (Ruth 1:1), is a typical opening line. Everything is generic. There is no specific date, time, or place given, only a broad, universal orientation which is as sweeping and inclusive as possible. Tellers of parables catch audiences in the most ecumenical moments of their lives, moments which they have in common with people of any time and place. The characters, like the opening formula in a parable, are also generic. The Book of Ruth introduces its audiences simply to "a certain man . . . and his wife." Even when tellers give the man and his wife names, the type-casting remains and they name characters for the roles they play (Sasson 1989:17–19). The name "Elimelech" means "El is king," a name only a most observant believer would use. The name "Naomi" means "darling." "Mahlon" means "critical patient" and "Chilion" means "terminal patient." The name "Ruth" means "companion" and Orpah means "deserter."

Parables are folk stories, and like all folk stories they have three main characters. The main character in the Parable of the Persistent Widow is Naomi, the widow who is a fearless advocate for the land and children which Yahweh promised. She is no ordinary widow. To emphasize her extraordinary stature tellers use hyperbole, a rhetorical technique which emphasizes by exaggeration. The antagonists in this parable are Famine, which takes away Naomi's land, Death, which takes away her children, and the Legal Guardian, who refuses to carry out his obligation to Elimelech's household by having a child with Ruth. The final significant character in the parable is Yahweh, who sends the widow Ruth to help (Ruth 1:20–21).

Like Babatha, Naomi perseveres. When famine takes away her land in Judah, Naomi exercises her household's legal right to support by migrating to Moab. Famine in the ancient Near East is difficulty, not crisis. Even in Bethlehem, the breadbasket of Judah, famine was part of life. When there was famine, the hungry in Judah often migrated to Egypt or Moab to obtain food and temporary employment (Gen 37—50). It was never an easy decision to leave their land, but economic exigency could drive them to become immigrants (גרים, gērîm) and to accept the legally weak status that that condition gave them (Sasson 1989:16).

Storytellers portray Naomi as a woman who knows how to cope with the ordinary difficulties of daily life. She is by no means helpless. Rather her

---

Teaching on Harvesting
(Deut 24:17–22)

You shall not deprive a resident alien or an orphan of justice. . . .

When you reap your harvest in your field and forget a sheaf in the field, you shall not go back to get it; it shall be left for the alien, the orphan, and the widow. . . .

When you beat your olive trees, do not strip what is left; it shall be for the alien, the orphan, and the widow.

When you gather the grapes of your vineyard, do not glean what is left; it shall be for the alien, the orphan, and the widow.

condition as a widow seems to have released her socially so that she can become a more dominant force in determining her own fate (Potash 1986:2, 4). When death takes away her children in Moab, she divests herself of her last possessions by emancipating her widowed daughters-in-law before returning to Judah to file suit for her land. She is handicapped by her advanced age which prevents her from directly pressing her rights to an heir by having sexual intercourse with her legal guardian. However, on behalf of the widow Naomi, the widow Ruth initiates legal action by first exercising her right to glean for food (Ruth 2:2). The widows' suit reaches a climax when the widow Ruth sues Boaz for marriage, directing him to "cast his mantle over her" (Ruth 3:9). This gesture has both sexual and legal connotations since it ratifies a covenant which will eventually entitle both Naomi and Ruth to a restoration of their full legal status with land and children (Viberg 1992:141–42).

The virtue of the widow as persevering should not be confused with the vice of nagging (Job 2:9). The important difference between perseverance and nagging can be seen in the Parable of the Persistent Widow from the Gospel of Luke. It is the widow in this parable who knows the law, whereas the judge does not (Luke 18:6). Although it is not often clear in English translations today, the original words with which the parable describes the widow implied legal tenacity, not feminine impatience (Scott 1989:185). The words: "she will end by doing me violence" (Greek: ὑπωπιάζῃ) in the Gospel of Luke (Luke 18:5) are virtually the same as the words: "what I do is discipline my own body" (Greek: ὑπωπιάζω) in the First Letter to the Corinthians (1 Cor 9:27). In neither passage do the Greek words mean "to nag," but rather "to train" or "to coach." In the world of the Bible, the widow is not a nagging woman. She is a teacher, an instructor who perseveres until she trains or coaches the village assembly to apply the law with justice. In fact, the widow in this parable is the only one, human or divine, who is able to teach the village assembly how to carry out its judicial responsibilities and safeguard the land and children of its households (Luke 18:4). Without the widow there would be no justice.

Originally, all parables closed with a question. In place of the normal denouement which, in most other kinds of stories restores the peace which the crisis interrupted, the denouement in the parable simply asks a question. These questions leave the audience to resolve the crisis. The technique is a wonderful teaching tool. Long after the parable has ended and long after the teller has gone, the audience is still pondering the question. The teaching life of a parable is greater than any other form of story.

The Parable of the Persistent Widow in Ruth now closes with the question: "Can this be Naomi?" or "Is this woman Naomi or Mara?" The two words means something like: "Is this woman darling or damned? Is she my people or not my people (Hos 1:9)?" Evidently there was enough similarity in the way the Hebrew words "naomi" and "mara" sounded, either in the dialect in which the parable was told, or in shortened versions of the names, to pull off the pun (Sasson 1989:32–33). Some English translations make the questions sound far too conclusive, and eliminate the ring of uncertainty altogether. The connotation of the question is: "Can this widow persevere until Yahweh helps her?" Naomi is certainly persevering, but tellers want their audiences to wonder whether she is persevering enough.

Many translations also blur the closing questions in the Parable of the Persistent Widow in the Gospel of Luke by rendering them as: "Will he not hasten to the rescue of his elect who cry to him day and night, even if he puts their patience to the test? But when he comes, he will come quickly" (Luke 18:7b–8a). Originally, as in the Parable of the Persistent Widow in Ruth, this parable asked: "How long do you think the judge can hold out? Without a doubt, he will give in quickly, but will the widow persevere until he grants her petition or not?"

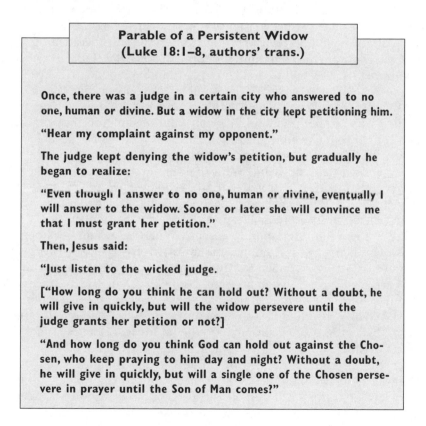

Parable of a Persistent Widow
(Luke 18:1–8, authors' trans.)

Once, there was a judge in a certain city who answered to no one, human or divine. But a widow in the city kept petitioning him.

"Hear my complaint against my opponent."

The judge kept denying the widow's petition, but gradually he began to realize:

"Even though I answer to no one, human or divine, eventually I will answer to the widow. Sooner or later she will convince me that I must grant her petition."

Then, Jesus said:

"Just listen to the wicked judge.

["How long do you think he can hold out? Without a doubt, he will give in quickly, but will the widow persevere until the judge grants her petition or not?]

"And how long do you think God can hold out against the Chosen, who keep praying to him day and night? Without a doubt, he will give in quickly, but will a single one of the Chosen persevere in prayer until the Son of Man comes?"

The Gospel of Luke directs the question to its own audience of early Christian communities. Initially, they expected that Jesus would come back to earth (Greek: παρουσία) only a short time after he ascended. However, time passed and persecutions began, and Jesus did not return. The Gospel of Luke uses the Parable of the Persistent Widow from ancient Israel to teach persecuted Christians to persevere (Scott 1989:176). "Prayer" is the word which the Gospel of Luke uses for perseverance (Rom 12:12; Eph 6:18; 1 Thess 5:17). And widows model this virtue which all Christians will need to survive (Thurston 1985:288). The Gospel continues the characterization of the judge in the parable in order to make it clear that what is true for a lesser character like the judge will certainly be true for God (Luke 18:1–5). The question is not whether God will vindicate the persecuted, but whether the persecuted will persevere until their vindication (Luke 18:6–8). The widow does not know what the judge is thinking or what the judge will do any more than the Christians in Luke's community knew when the parousia would take place. Consequently, the widow may break off petitioning before the judge decides to hear her case, and the Christians may not continue to pray for the parousia. The audiences of the Parable of the Persistent Widow in Ruth were no more certain that Naomi would persevere than the audiences of the Parable of the Persistent Widow in the Gospel were certain that the Christians would persevere through suffering to deliverance.

The widow forces the community to think about what it means to believe. Everyone asks: "How will we hold on to our land and children?" The stories of monarchs say: "By power!" The parables of widows say: "By perseverance!" Parables challenge people with the land and children, which widows lack. In parables about widows, it is not land or children, but persistence which convinces Yahweh to hear their case (Sir 35:1–26). In parables about widows, the violent cannot conquer the land forever. It belongs to the widows whose title is suffering. Yahweh does not march with the armies of monarchs, but travels instead with the widows, the orphans, and the strangers who clog the roads and glean the fields. Violence brings death to the land, perseverance brings life.

Delay is always an invitation to despair. When things do not happen on time human beings worry, doubt, and question. Delay destroys the ability to believe and turns confidence into cynicism. Without results, human beings are paralyzed. Yahweh promises Israel life (Deut 30:15–20), and land and children are the payments which Yahweh makes on this promise (Gen 12:1–8). When Yahweh misses a payment it is easy to begin questioning the value of believing. The same anxiety afflicts Jesus' disciples. When Jesus delays, Christians question. The Parable of the Persistent Widow says to the persecuted: "Cry out!" The measure of faith is not fulfillment, but persistence (Rom 1:10; 12:12; Gal 6:9). Persistence shortens the time of fulfillment not in any absolute sense but in the perception of those who wait. By continuing to tell the story and ask the question, tellers deny the powerful an uncontested claim to the land and its children.

The Parable of the Widow captured the hearts not only of the people on the margins of ancient Israel, but the Jews to whom Jesus preached as well. They fondly remembered him not as a conquering hero claiming colonies for his emperor or riding triumphantly into the cities of his enemies. The lame, the blind, the lepers, the widows, the fishermen, the shepherds, the

---

Teaching on Prayer
(Sir 35:15–19)

. . . the Lord is the judge,
   and with him there is no partiality.
He will not show partiality to the poor;
   but he will listen to the prayer of one who is wronged.
He will not ignore the supplication of the orphan,
   or the widow when she pours out her complaint.
Do not the tears of the widow run down her cheek
   as she cries out against the one who causes them to fall?

---

prostitutes, and the tax collectors who followed Jesus remembered him as a person without status: "Foxes have holes, and birds of the air have nests, but The Son of Man has nowhere to lay his head" (Matt 8:20), who promised that "the meek . . . shall inherit the earth" (Matt 5:5). Those who remembered Jesus in the New Testament, remembered him as someone who not only heard the Parable of the Persistent Widow, but understood it. They remembered Jesus, like they remembered Naomi and Ruth. For them, Jesus was the widow, who day after day cried out against the powerful and who continued to believe that God's promises to the poor would be fulfilled.

11

The Wise and the Fool

Education is the power to influence the next generation. In the world of the Bible, some formal education did take place in schools but most education was informal. By the way they ate their meals, did not get drunk, worked hard, made good friends, sought advice before acting, held their temper, paid their taxes, and imposed fair legal judgments, the wise educated their villages to carry on successfully from one generation to the next. By overeating, drunkenness, laziness, quarreling, selfishness, and perjury, fools endangered their very existence (Crenshaw 1990:205–16).

There were no textbooks to explain why certain ways of doing things were healthy and productive, and others were unhealthy and anti-social. Villagers classified behavior with a word or label (Wikan 1984:636). Labeling was the prevalent means of education and the principal means of dealing with social problems (Misgeld 1978:169; Schur 1971:24–30; Becker 1973:4; Lofland 1969:123; Bott 1971; Brandes 1987:130). Not all labels of honor were of equal value in enhancing the social status (Arabic: *sharaf*) of a household, and not all labels of shame lowered the status of a household to the same degree

---

Protocol for Wise and Fools

"Wise" is a label of honor, and "fool" is a label of shame applied by households as a reaction to the appearance or behavior of the members of another household.

Labels of honor and shame may be accepted or rejected. Accepted labels become permanent. Rejected labels require an effort to acquire a new label based on a change in behavior, appearance, or viewpoint of the village.

> ## "The Sage in Proverbs"
> ## (Crenshaw 1990:215–16)
>
> . . . [the teachers in the Book of Proverbs] possessed
> astonishing confidence in the power of the intellect. By living
> according to the accumulated insights of past generations, indi-
> viduals guaranteed prosperity, long life, honor, and well being.
> For these optimists, the universe seemed to operate in an or-
> derly manner, rewarding virtue and punishing vice. Behind this
> discernible order stood a benevolent creator whose providential
> care brought security to those who practiced "fear of the
> Lord." In their eyes, the wise were righteous and fools were
> wicked; hence to be a sage meant adopting a way of life charac-
> terized by devout conduct. That was by no means all, for these
> aphorisms also describe sages as diligent, self-controlled, mod-
> est, chaste, temperate, and respectful. In other words, the wise
> enabled society to function successfully. Fools disturbed the
> calm, necessitating rigorous measures at the hands of gentler
> people. Sages therefore recognized the reality of evil, but they
> believed in their own ability to cope in the face of adversity.

(Zeid 1966:246). Anthropologists use symbolic interaction theory to study the way villagers apply labels (Blumer 1969:2; Phillips 1964:680). A label may be applied either with words or para-language, which includes gestures, facial expressions, or tone of voice (Sheff and Retzinger 1991:127). Interestingly, labels do not indicate as much about what a household is actually doing or not doing as they do about how the village reacts to it (Goode 1990:60–61; Becker 1973:31).

Life-giving behavior was labeled "wise" or "clean." Destructive or anti-social behavior was "foolish" or "unclean." To be wise or clean was a generic label for honor. To be a fool or unclean was a generic label for shame. Today, the words "honor" and "shame" have little to do with life and death, they are often just old-fashioned ways of saying "reputation." When these words are used at all, honor is only a modest recognition given for achievement, ability, or service. Shame is no more than a word for scolding children.

In the world of the Bible, on the other hand, honor entitled a household to life, shame sentenced it to death (Pitt-Rivers 1965:42; Zeid 1966:245). Honor was the ability of a household to care for its own members and to be prepared to take over a neighboring household decimated by war, drought, or epidemic. "Clean" was the label for the household in good standing, licensed to make a living in the village and entitled to its support. Only the clean were entitled to buy, sell, trade, marry, arrange marriages, serve in assemblies, and send warriors to the tribe. And only the clean were entitled to make wills, appoint heirs, and serve as legal guardians to care for households endangered by death, disease, and war. The key characteristic of the clean was that they were in place and functioning well.

Shame was the inability of a household to fulfill its responsibilities to its own members or its covenant partners. Shame was the loss of land and children. Unclean was the label for households on probation. The unclean were out of line and not functioning properly (Malina and Neyrey 1988:36; Douglas 1966:14–35; Milgrom 1991:780). Consequently, both their contributions to the village and their eligibility for its support were suspended.

Rules of purity and the labels clean and unclean in the world of the Bible had little to do with hygiene (Malina 1981:122–52). They were analogous to credit ratings and distinguished households in good social and economic standing from those who were not. Labels of shame like "fool" and "unclean" downgraded the status (פָּקַד, *pāqad*) of a household, until it demonstrated that it was once again contributing to the village (Cockerham 1981:303; Goode 1975:577; 1990:58; Brandes 1987:126–29; Gove 1980:20; Schur 1974:15). Because reactions were continually modified, shamed households reacted to their label by either attempting to minimize its effect or by attempting to capitalize on its benefits (Link 1987:1490–91). On the one hand, they could appeal their social diagnosis and be re-labeled or cured. On the other hand, they could accept their label and take advantage of their social disability by becoming beggars or risk-takers who had little to lose by their actions (Smith 1980:231–32; Lemert 1972:19–20). The rich who became unclean generally appealed their label, while the poor more often accepted the label and tried to use it their advantage (Nagi 1969:72–73).

A teaching on breach of contract in Deuteronomy (Deut 13:13–19 MT [ET vv. 12–18]) teaches households how to settle landlord-tenant disputes (Benjamin 1983:112–37, 293–94). When one household takes advantage of another by foreclosing on their land and children, it not only steals from its neighbor, but also denies by its actions that land and children were Yahweh's gifts entrusted to Israel. The teaching labels land-grabbers as fools (בְּנֵי־בְלִיַּעַל, *bᵉnê bᵉliyya'al*) for ignoring the generosity of Yahweh who blesses Israel with land and children for whom the Hebrews are supposed to care, not compete.

Likewise, Judges (Judg 7:1—9:57) labels Abimelech and his warriors as fools (אֲנָשִׁים רֵקִים, *'ᵃnāšîm rēqîm*) for their raid on Shechem. After he conquers Shechem the elders change his label from fool to king. During an attack on Thebez, however, Abimelech gets too close to the wall and is mortally wounded by a grinding stone dropped on him by a woman. So Judges remembers him as a fool killed by a woman (Judg 9:54). His label became a classic and was applied to any chief foolish enough to act like Abimelech (2 Sam 11:20–21).

The stories of Saul in Samuel–Kings label the sons of Eli as fools (בְּנֵי־בְלִיַּעַל, *bᵉnê bᵉliyya'al*) because they take more than their share of food (Lev 7:28–36; Deut 18:3; 1 Sam 2:12). The label stands in stark contrast to

Samuel who is wise, and it provides a lingering stigma to the household of Eli (McCarter 1980a:85).

The stories of David's rise to power in Samuel–Kings (1 Sam 25) label one of David's opponents as a fool (איש בליעל, 'îš b^eliyya'al; נבל, nāḇal) whose lack of support for David threatens to destroy his household. However, Abigail, the mother of the household, wisely recognizes David as the new ruler of Israel. She plays on her husband's label in her oath of allegiance to David: "for as his name is, so is he; Nabal is his name, and folly is with him" (1 Sam 25:25). Likewise, when Abner challenges Ishba'al for control of the household of Saul by having sexual intercourse with Rizpah, Ishba'al apparently labeled him a "dog's head" (2 Sam 3:8). The maneuver temporarily blocks Abner's bid for power. Then when Abner challenges Joab for control of the household by returning a daughter of Saul to David, Joab assassinates him at the city gate in Hebron (2 Sam 3:29). David refuses to confirm Joab's bid for power, by permanently barring anyone in the household of Joab from ever again exercising political power in Israel. David labels every warrior in the household of Joab a menstruating woman, a leper, effeminate, a coward, and a beggar (2 Sam 3:29).

The stories of David's successor in Samuel–Kings label David a fool (איש בליעל, 'îš b^eliyya'al) for overthrowing the household of Saul (2 Sam 16:7). Shimei taunts David as he flees from Jerusalem in the face of Absalom's forces (McCarter 1984:373–74). The label is not a personal attack on David's character but an impeachment of him as unworthy to hold the throne. David even accepts the label by ordering his soldiers to leave Shimei unharmed (Anderson 1989:206–7).

Names

The most universal label in the world of the Bible was a name, which provided evidence of the social standing of a person's household. Hebrews, like other ancient Near Eastern people, often carried names which were professions of faith or "theophoric" names. "Samu-el," "Ishma-el," and "Isa-iah" were all theophoric names, which included a shortened form of Yahweh or Elohim like "iah" or "el." The name itself was an abbreviation or summary of the covenant between Yahweh and the household. For instance, the name "Elijah," which means "Yahweh is Lord," was a challenge to Canaanites who did not believe in Yahweh and a pledge of allegiance for the Hebrews who did.

Some theophoric names included "Ba'al" which was also a Semitic title for the Creator. When Saul named his fourth son "Ish-ba'al," he understood it as a label of honor meaning "servant of the Lord" or "son of Yahweh" (1 Chron 8:33; 9:39). The label recalled the adoption formula by which Saul dedicated his child to Yahweh and proclaimed him as heir to his household in Israel. The "son of Yahweh" was "Yahweh's anointed" or "messiah," the most powerful label of honor in ancient Israel. It was an insurance policy in which Yahweh guaranteed that its bearer could not be killed without the wrath of Yahweh falling upon the head of the murderer (McCarter 1980a: 384; 1980b:493; 1 Sam 26:9–23; 2 Sam 1:14–16).

Among some Hebrews, however, "ba'al" referred only to the "other gods," whose worship was prohibited by the Decalogue (Exod 20:2). Consequently, the household of David changed the name of "Ish-ba'al" to "Ish-bosheth." Saul's heir was not "man (i.e., son) of Yahweh," but "son of shame" (2 Sam 3:14–15). David, not Ish-ba'al, was the "son of Yahweh" whose household would lay legal claim to an exclusive dynasty in Israel (Paul 1979–80:178). The name change was not simply a public insult, but a significant legal maneuver by the household of David to justify its takeover of the household of Saul (2 Sam 7:11–16 MT [ET vv. 1–8]; 1 Kgs 8:14–21; Ps 2:6–11; 45:2–9). Similarly, the Pharaoh of Egypt changed the name of Eliakim to Jehoiakim, and the Great King of Babylon changed the name of Mattaniah to Zedekiah, which conferred on them labels of shame (2 Kgs 23:34; 24:17). They were no longer rulers of an independent country but governors of foreign colonies.

Name changes were also an example of humor in the world of the Bible. Tellers were often tendentious and wanted the audience to laugh at someone. By making subtle changes in the spelling or pronunciation of proper names, villagers created funny or bizarre characterizations of a household in order to make hearers laugh at it and thus shame or expel it (Radday 1990:59–97).

Occasionally when the Bible leaves a character without a name it labels that person as powerless or subordinate (Tapp 1989:171), but sometimes the name is replaced by a title. For example, the "wise woman of Tekoa" (2 Sam 14:2) and the "wise woman of Abel" (2 Sam 20:16) are not names but titles equivalent to "elder" (Camp 1981:25). Yahweh changes the names of Abram and Sarai to Abraham and Sarah, both honorable titles (Gen 17:3–16). They have become ancestors of a new people and have taken on a new status (Malina and Neyrey 1988:40).

An official change of labels was accomplished through a rite of passage or a status-altering ritual like the inauguration of a prophet or a monarch (Baltzer 1968:578; Thompson 1980:150, n. 25; Carroll 1986:95; Garfinkel 1956:420–24; Goode 1990:61; Erikson 1962:308). Labels like "monarch" and "prophet" conferred Yahweh's power of attorney on candidates. The ritual followed an identifiable set of steps, during which the candidate stated the old label of his household as a demurer (Deut 18:18; Judg 6:15; Isa 6:5–7), and Yahweh proclaimed the new label (Carroll 1986:101; Holladay 1986:3–27; Reventlow 1963:24–77; Habel 1965:298–301).

In the book of Jeremiah (Jer 1:1–19), Jeremiah states his old label as "only a boy" (Jer 1:6), but Yahweh confers on him the new label: "You are a prophet to the nations" (Jer 1:5). The new title was retroactive to the time Yahweh formed him in the womb (Jer 1:5; Isa 49:1–3; Kitsuse 1962:253; Kramer 1942:14, n.1; Gilula 1967:114). The Enuma Elish story (Enuma iv:7–9) describes the power which the label "God Most Honored" confers on

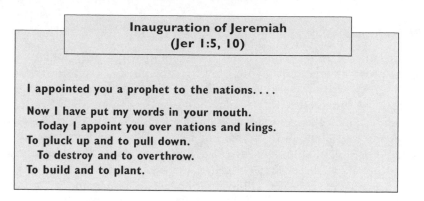

Inauguration of Jeremiah
(Jer 1:5, 10)

I appointed you a prophet to the nations. . . .

Now I have put my words in your mouth.
  Today I appoint you over nations and kings.
To pluck up and to pull down.
  To destroy and to overthrow.
To build and to plant.

Marduk in virtually the same words which Jeremiah explains the label "prophet to the nations."

The final step in the status-altering ritual was investing the candidate with a sign or totem which provided some sense of the candidate's mission and served as a reassurance that the candidate would not be alone (Jer 1:8–19). The totem was a physical or tangible label which entitled the bearer to exercise power (Schneider 1987:412).

Clothing

In the world of the Bible, clothing was not simply an accessory reflecting individual style or personal preference. The style, weave, and color of clothing functioned as a uniform which reflected status (Schneider 1987: 427). Likewise, changing clothes did not simply reflect a practice of good hygiene but a change of labels or status (Schneider 1987:411). Those who changed clothes were preparing to play new roles. In the book of Ruth, Ruth does not bathe, comb her hair, and put on her best clothes simply to appear more physically attractive to Boaz, but to signal to him that she is an official representative of the household of Elimelech and Naomi (Ruth 3:3).

In ancient Mesopotamia, the word "to cover" or "clothe" (Akkadian: *katāmu*) also meant "to exercise power." Therefore, when the monarch put on a cloak, he was taking up the power of a ruler (Waldman 1989:161). In the story of David's rise to power in Samuel–Kings, David has the opportunity to kill Saul, who unknowingly comes into a cave near the oasis of Ein Gedi where David and his warriors are hiding. David's warriors see it as an opportunity to kill Saul (1 Sam 24:4). David, however, does not kill Saul but simply cuts a tassel off his cloak. David is neither teasing Saul nor frustrating his warriors' desire for victory. The tassel represents Saul's authority as ruler (Milgrom 1983:61; Kruger 1988:106; McCarter 1980b:502). David takes Saul's honor and leaves him with shame (Leach 1958; McCarter 1980b: 490–93; Hoffner 1975:50; Waldman 1989:163).

Physical Appearance

Some labels were reactions to the physical integrity—or lack of it—which one or more members of a household might possess (Wright 1990; Blok 1981:432). Integrity was not simply a question of aesthetics but also competence. It was the physical ability of a man or woman to fulfill his or her role in the household. For example, a woman's beauty was not just the color of her hair or the shape of her eyes, but her physical ability to menstruate, engage in sexual intercourse, conceive, bear, and nurse a child. Only when she did not meet these physical criteria was she labeled "barren" (עקרה, 'aqārâh; Schur 1983:66–77). Likewise, the labels "handsome" (יפה, yāpeh), "good-looking" (טוב, tôb), or "ruddy" (אדמוני, 'admônî) often distinguished a chief from the other warriors who mustered for battle (Gen 39:6; 1 Sam 9:2; 16:12; 1 Kgs 1:6). Although some labels which developed from physical appearance were gender specific, they were not explicitly sexist. Men did not possess sole claim to labels of honor, nor were women only subjected to labels of shame. Most gender specific labels developed from the sexual activities unique to males or females (Mernissi 1975; Rosenfield 1982).

Those judged by their appearance as shamed were forced out of the activities of communal life, leaving them less chance to succeed. Although Meriba'al, or Mephibosheth, in the story of David's rise to power in Samuel–Kings (2 Sam 9:6–13; 16:1–4; 19:24–30) has the strongest claim to become the heir of Saul's household, he is crippled, and David inherits the household.

Teaching on Marginalized Men
(Lev 21:17–20)

No one of your offspring throughout their generations who has a blemish may approach to offer the food of his God. For no one who has a blemish shall draw near, one who is blind or lame, or one who has a mutilated face or a limb too long, or one who has a broken foot or a broken hand, or a hunchback or a dwarf, or a man with a blemish in his eyes or an itching disease or scabs or crushed testicles.

Women

Women were physical labels of honor or shame for a household, just like the arms, legs, eyes, feet, and testicles of its men. In the story of David's successor in Samuel–Kings, when Absalom challenges David's title as king of Israel, David orders a strategic retreat from Jerusalem. The maneuver allows David to determine who remains loyal to him (2 Sam 15:13–37). Although David evacuates his capital, he does not surrender it. He leaves the city in the care of the ten women who represent the ten major covenants which make up Israel. They are David's labels of honor who remain as his legal claim to Jerusalem. After Absalom drives David from Jerusalem, he publicly has sexual intercourse with the women in order to claim the power they represent (2 Sam 16:21–22). By this means, Absalom seizes a label of honor and labels David with shame.

The Wise and the Fool in a Teaching on Wills (Deut 21:18–21)

The Bible uses wise or clean and fool or unclean in different ways but the common denominator is always the same. The wise or clean person builds up the life of the village and the fool or unclean person destroys it. The Teaching on Wills in Deuteronomy the mother and father of a household label their heir stubborn, unruly, a drunkard, and a glutton. Again, it is difficult for us to appreciate the significance of these words which we use simply to call people names, or to lament the anti-social behavior of someone we love. In no case do these words represent, for us, criminal behavior punishable by death. In ancient Israel, however, each of these words carries a significant social stigma. The stubborn and unruly son who is a glutton and a drunkard is not simply a petulant child, or even an adult suffering from alcoholism or an eating disorder. He is the heir who is squandering the resources of the household and letting the mother and father of the household slowly starve to death (Luke 15:11–32).

Among the legal rights of full citizens was that of designating or adopting an heir. The heir carried the legal title son (בֵּן, bēn; Deut 21:18) and the testators were called father and mother (Deut 21:18). In several instances in the Bible (Gen 34:2; Judg 9:28; 2 Kgs 16:7), son is the title of a covenant partner, not a word referring to a minor child. In this Teaching on Wills (Deut 21:18) the son means heir. Certainly an heir could be the oldest, natural, male child, but firstborn sons were not the only candidates to become heirs (Gen 15:2).

To bear the label son was an honor. While still alive, fathers and mothers turned their land over to sons, who accepted responsibility for them. Heirs were not only expected to show deference to the elderly; they were responsible for honoring their fathers and mothers by feeding and clothing and sheltering them. Once fathers and mothers probated their wills they were totally dependent on their heirs. The stubborn and rebellious is an heir who is eating and drinking while the father and mother of the household starve. Stubborn and rebellious are labels for breach of contract, not childish petulance (Num 20:10; Ps 97:7–11; Hos 9:15). Since designating an heir was a legal process it could be reversed. This teaching, like the Ur-Nammu Sumerian Code, describes the process.

**Teaching on Wills
(Deut 21:18–21)**

If a man has a stubborn and unruly son who will not listen to his father or mother, and will not obey them even though they chastise him, his father and mother shall have him apprehended and brought out to the elders at the gate of his home city, where they shall say to those city elders, "This son of ours is a stubborn and unruly fellow who will not listen to us; he is a glutton and a drunkard."

Then all his fellow citizens shall stone him to death.

Labels of shame like stubborn and rebellious can only be imposed after due process. The stubborn and rebellious son is brought before the assembly, where the testators identify him as their son and lay out the charges against him. In doing so, they have laid out his case history to support their statements and to convince the elders and the entire village of his guilt (Lemert 1972:22; Bellefontaine 1979).

Once these steps have been taken, the community is responsible for labeling the son as stubborn and rebellious. His actions jeopardize the values which the village considers to be universal and correct. The elders do not even cite the law that parents are to be honored by their children (Exod 20:12). In order to purge this evil from their midst, the legal requirement is death by stoning, an appropriate sentence since it requires every villager to participate while allowing for the legal fiction that his death was not caused by any one person.

**Sumerian Code, article 4
(Matthews & Benjamin 1991b:68–69)**

If a son disowns his father and mother with the oath: "You are not my father; you are not my mother,"

... then he forfeits his right to inherit their property;

... likewise, he can then be sold as an ordinary slave at full market value.

The Wise and the Fool in a Story of
Na'aman and Elisha (2 Kgs 5:1–27)

Until 1871, leprosy was a sinister disease which evoked fear and fascination. When Armauer Hansen of Norway finally isolated and identified the specific bacteria (Latin: *mycobacterium leprae*) which creates the infection, the social stigma which had been applied to the leper began to disappear (Zias 1989:27; Lewis 1987:596; Andersen 1969:15). Eventually, medicine stopped using the term "leprosy" and began referring to the condition as "Hansen's disease." The healthy no longer sentenced the leper to remote colonies like Molokai in Hawaii, and the active persecution of lepers, fueled by a misunderstanding of the biblical world, has basically come to a close.

Strangely enough, Hansen's disease seems to have been virtually unknown in the world of the Bible. There is no hard evidence that leprosy existed in the ancient Near East (Moller-Christensen 1967; Hulse 1975:87–90). The description of leprosy (צרעת, *ṣāra'at*; Greek: λέπρα) in Leviticus (Lev 13:9 23; 14:1–32) is lengthy and full of technical terms, but none of the symptoms are exclusively associated with Hansen's disease. Descriptions of leprosy in the writings of Hippocrates and Polybius are equally inconclusive. Apparently, the disease was introduced into the ancient Near East only after 333 BCE when Alexander returned from India (M. Davies 1988:136).

In the Bible, leprosy refers to a variety of skin disorders known today as psoriasis, eczema, seborrhea, or mycotic infections like ringworm (Wright and Jones 1992:278). These diseases are painful and unsightly, but hardly virulent and disfiguring. Without a doubt certain medical or clinical considerations affected the development of ancient Israel's protocol for dealing with the leper. Even very simple societies carry out forms of medical diagnosis and treatment which are surprisingly sophisticated by today's standards. For example, more than one tradition of folk medicine anticipated today's use of penicillin by prescribing various naturally occurring molds as a poultice for drawing out the infection in a wound (Pilch 1981b:148–49). The reaction of the Bible to the leper, however, is not clinical or medical, it is social (Pilch 1981a:109).

The primary focus of the laws dealing with leprosy in the Bible is on the symbolic character of its symptoms. Lepers break out (Wilkinson 1977:155). The appearance of a rash, flakes, scales, and boils is understood as a physical revolt of the body. These symptoms result when bodily functions are out of place. Leprosy is physical chaos. Consequently, the leper is treated as a living symbol of the disorganization into which society falls when its political and economic institutions fail. Villages consider such disorder aggressively contagious (Milgrom 1992:137; Wright and Jones 1992:279).

The process of discernment which the Bible prescribed for leprosy was neither hasty nor cruel. A patient was labeled a leper only following due process and was entitled to appeal the decision at scheduled intervals. When symptoms first appeared, the afflicted person was taken to a priest for examination of both the primary and secondary features of the disease such as changes in skin or hair color. Priests were agents of social control, responsible for determining any visible deviation from the accepted norm of appearance (Becker 1973:162–63). In the case of leprosy these agents were the sole authorities (Milgrom 1991:772).

Priests used fixed criteria for examination and diagnosis. Once the label leper was applied, the deviant was placed on social and economic probation and distinguished by a change of clothes and mannerisms (Brody 1974:111–12; Levine 1989:82). The leper was restricted in order to prevent the contamination of others. The leper also had to dress in the manner of one in mourning, wearing ragged clothes and uncombed hair. Finally, the leper covered the upper lip with what we might call a surgical mask and cried "Unclean, unclean" (Lev 13:45; Isa 52:11).

There was recourse to examination by the priest after a seven day waiting period during which time the patient could be re-labeled clean (Lev 13:1–17). When a leper had been ascertained to once again be clean, a new rite of passage had to be performed which allowed the leper to re-enter society. The longer lepers were unclean, the longer it took to restore them to full membership in the village (Milgrom 1991:782; Lewis 1987:602–4).

In a story of Na'aman and Elisha from Samuel–Kings (2 Kgs 5:1–27), Na'aman is a high ranking military official (גדול אִישׁ, 'îš gādôl) and an adviser to the monarch of Syria (גּבּוֹר חיל, gibbôr ḥayil). However, the label leper could make even such an influential person virtually powerless (1 Kgs 15:5; Smith 1980:234). The juxtaposition of his former labels of honor with his present label of shame in the story shocks the audience. Na'aman is a mighty one who has fallen. He can no longer command the army and advise the monarch (Cohn 1983:173; Malina and Neyrey 1988:96; Gray 1975:504). In fact, the adviser to the monarch now seeks advice from a slave.

The Hebrew slave tells Na'aman that the prophet Elisha can cure him. So Na'aman the leper goes into voluntary exile, leaving his home in Syria for the land of his enemy (2 Kgs 5:3–5). His leprosy has cost him his titles and his home, but he takes a letter for the monarch of Israel, and gifts for the prophet Elisha.

Na'aman then presents himself and his letter to the monarch asking to be re-labeled. But the monarch finds him still unclean and his letter a threat: "Am I God . . . that this man sends word to me to cure a man of his leprosy? . . . see how he is seeking a quarrel with me" (2 Kgs 5:7). The implication is clear to the monarch of Israel—he has been given an order by a more powerful monarch which he cannot carry out, and which is designed as a provocation for war (Gray 1975:506). For the leper, even the letter of one monarch to another is of no value.

Juxtaposing the monarch's inability to heal with Yahweh's ability to cure Na'aman, it follows naturally in the narrative that Yahweh heals through his prophet Elisha. Elisha intervenes in this matter otherwise only between monarchs (2 Kgs 1:2–4; Nelson 1987:178) and takes the burden off the political agent by ordering the monarch to provide the leper with safe conduct to his home in Samaria (Cohn 1983:176).

Then, Na'aman continues his pilgrimage from the monarch to the prophet Elisha. Again, he presents himself and his gifts to the prophet asking to be re-labeled. The prophet grants his request, but does not accept his gift. This cure, when it comes, is not what Na'aman expected; not a personal audience, no grand invocations of healing spirits, or even a wave of the hand by the prophet. Instead, this great man receives another teaching from the slave of Elisha (נער, na'ar), just as he had from his own slave (נערה קטנה, na'arâh qᵉṭannâh; Cohn 1983:180). In fact, Na'aman never even sees Elisha until after he is cured. He is told to wash seven times in the Jordan River, and is healed, but only after forcibly or voluntarily having relinquished every label of honor he possessed.

The Wise and the Fool in the War
between Israel and Syria (2 Kgs 7:1–20)

In contrast to the well-to-do Na'aman who seeks to remove his label, the four lepers in a story about the War between Israel and Syria in Samuel–Kings (2 Kgs 7:1–20) seek to take advantage of their label (Smith 1980:233). They accept their exclusion and the restrictions which are placed upon them. They have adapted to their label and look for ways to benefit themselves despite or because of it. From their point of view, since nature has physically marked them as unclean, they are free to abandon their responsibility (Safilios-Rothchild 1970:115). Thus these lepers do not appeal their labels; they engage in rule-breaking and live as non-productive members of their society (Malina and Neyrey 1988:37).

The four lepers first appear in the story sitting outside the entrance to the city gate during the siege of Samaria by a Syrian army. The gate area functions throughout this narrative as the focal point of action. The city is besieged and any attack would center on the gate (Yadin 1963:21). The citizens of the besieged city could not exercise their usual right to pass freely back and forth through the gate. And the merchants who sold their wares in the vicinity of the gate were unable to conduct business since grain shipments were cut off (Hobbs 1985:86).

The zone immediately outside the city was available to beggars of various sorts (2 Sam 5:6), where they could accost persons entering and leaving the city. But in this instance, with the city closed and under siege, the lepers have no one from whom to beg. Any cry they made to be admitted into the city would have fallen on deaf ears since the people of the city were also starving, and the lepers had been excluded from the city in the first place.

Therefore, the lepers, lacking their usual means of support, decide to beg from the Syrians. This is such a natural action that it seems to most readers as just common sense. However, their decision also takes into account the fact that as lepers they are marginalized. Without allegiance to Samaria, the lepers are free to desert it and attach themselves to Syria (Jer 38:19). They articulate their liminal status with the legal statement: "if [the Syrians] spare our lives we shall live, and if they kill us we shall but die" (2 Kgs 7:4). There is no hope of a cure here, only relief from hunger. These men have fully accepted the idea that they will always be lepers. Unlike Na'aman they are resigned to their condition, and thus their only option is to use that condition to support themselves.

Unexpectedly they find the Syrian battle camp abandoned. The lepers take full advantage of this remarkable situation to loot the encampment for food and goods, which they hide for later sale. Eventually, however, a sense of their future existence strikes them and they realize that if they fail to inform the Israelites in Samaria of this good fortune they can never again depend upon them for their care. As a result, they return to the city and inform the guards on the wall. The lepers, who had previously abandoned the gate area as a place no longer productive to their survival, now return there to restore its efficacy, and by extension to save the people of the city (Hobbs 1985:86–87). The lepers' message is transmitted through official circles to the monarch. Just as the monarch questioned the sincerity of Na'aman's letter of recommendation, the monarch here questions the truthfulness of the message of the four lepers. He wonders if this is a Syrian tactic to get the Israelites to open the gate, until a slave convinces the monarch to send two scouts with the remaining horses to the Syrian camp (Josh 8:4–17; Yadin 1963:318).

Once the word reaches the monarch that the Syrians have fled, leaving their animals, cloaks, and weapons strewn along their path, things return to normal and the lepers resume begging at the city gate. Ultimately, nothing changes for the lepers in this story. They are not re-labeled, and therefore, still cannot enter the city. But they did not ask for more.

Israel's reaction to the leper does not reflect medical practice or even moral judgment, as much as it reflects a sense of social organization. The desire of ancient societies, as with modern societies, is to establish and maintain certain clearly defined norms of appearance and action. Those who conform as well as those who deviate from these norms must be clearly labeled. Otherwise, social organization will disappear, everyone will be out of place, and human life will become impossible.

PART II

Ancient Israel as a State

In the ancient Near East, the city was fundamentally an economic community. The people in most cities lived together in a single complex of buildings surrounded by a wall. This walled community maintained a successful trade network with smaller, unwalled surrounding villages. Less than half of those who lived in these cities produced enough food for everyone, so trades and arts, such as writing, flourished.

Most cities in the ancient Near East were governed by a single ruler, some, however, by a city assembly. Rulers or monarchs (Akkadian: *hazannu*) managed the land of the city, which they leased to various households to work (Akkadian: *hupsu*). Cities with single rulers had a strong surplus economy, which meant they controlled much more territory and produced more goods than they needed simply for survival. Public worship in these cities regularly celebrated the divine right of their monarchs to govern and educate the rest of the people in their role as obedient servants. The social organization of cities governed by an assembly was similar to the social organization in the villages of early Israel. These cities had a subsistence economy, which meant they controlled little territory and produced very few goods beyond what was needed for survival.

Current archaeological evidence indicates that between 1250 and 1000 BCE, the Hebrew villages in the hills and the Canaanite cities on the plains nearby coexisted peacefully (Zertal 1986). But the villages became victims of what anthropologists call "circumscription." Circumscription occurs when villages or states exhaust their natural resources and are cut off from any further development. What they need for survival is more than they can produce with their present resources (Carneiro 1970:738; 1978:207–8; 1981:64–65). The farms and herds around the Hebrew villages became too small to provide the expanding population with an adequate diet. They were unable to make any more efficient use of their land. And they were unable to expand into the richer valleys and plains because of the superior military power of their Canaanite neighbors (Josh 17:18; Judg 1:19). Typically, when a community is faced with a population explosion, a depletion of its natural resources, and the threat of war, it uses diplomacy to achieve social and political control and take control of external wealth procurement (Earle 1989). In some areas first contact between the Hebrews and their neighbors was amicable. As a consequence, some villages developed a symbiotic relationship with their neighbors on the coastal plain and in upper Galilee (Hauer 1986:9; Stager 1985:5–11; Gnuse 1991:109–17; Stiebing 1989). Hebrew villagers and Canaanite city dwellers peacefully agreed by covenant to exchange certain goods and services with one another.

The more difficult ecological conditions in these newly settled regions required tighter social and political control and a greater specialization of the economy. This necessitated the production of a surplus in these new lands and in the old lands to be used as trade goods to obtain needed products. A greater impetus on the opening of rural roads facilitated the transport of these goods (Dar 1986:142–45; I. Finkelstein 1989:60). Once certain villages became involved in trade with Canaanite cities they enhanced their power and reputation by providing new products and new markets for the villages. Their growing wealth, in turn, purchased support and created an aura of leadership which would eventually become customary for them and their designated representatives (Kipp and Schortman 1989:379). Ultimately, the struggle to maintain or expand the population and the trade connections of the villages led to skirmishes with the Canaanite cities and their caravans. Both trade networks and military activities then provided the opportunity for leaders, such as Saul and David, to rise to positions of greater authority, taking advantage of the increased administrative needs of the allied village populations.

In other areas, however, the friction between the Hebrew villages and outsiders was immediate and violent. Economic growth, population pressures, political threat, and the encroaching Hebrew settlements all contributed to the Philistines' desire to establish firm control over the Hebrews (1 Sam 4:1–11; I. Finkelstein 1985:172–73). There were also continued incursions into Hebrew villages by the Midianites (Judg 6:2–6), land disputes with the Ammonites (Judg 11:4–33), Moabite taxes (Judg 3:12–15), and the raids of the Amalekites (1 Sam 15:2; 30:1–20).

Trickery was a favorite weapon in the Hebrew arsenal. When the villagers of Judah surrendered Samson to the Philistines this may have been a strategy to position him as their own secret weapon in the camp of the enemy (Judg 15:9–17). Continuing clashes with the Philistines reinforced the necessity for a centralized leadership and made it less likely that Saul could disband the tribes and return his power to the elders (Gottwald 1979:415; 1983:31). Eglon of Moab attempted to expand his rule over the Hebrew villages just north of Jerusalem (Judg 3:12–14). He allied himself with the Amalekites and the Ammonites to occupy the City of the Palms at Jericho and use it as a base to collect supplies from the villages of Benjamin nearby. Eglon's warriors took what little the villages would have been able to raise and kept them at a subsistence level, unable to expand their population or fields.

The Midianites and Amalekites raided the farms and vineyards of the Hebrew villages which fought back with ingenious strategies like grinding grain in a wine press to keep the raiders from knowing the grain harvest was completed (Judg 6:11). These deceptions were designed to foil the encroaching people and form the basis of resistance movements led by creative leaders like Gideon.

One unresolved military crisis after the other provided strong support for the idea of strong-man rule, represented by Saul and later David (I. Finkelstein 1989:63). In order to protect their property and their households, the elders were willing to relinquish a portion of their authority. Perhaps they believed it would be a temporary solution. However, the stakes were higher now. No longer could one chief or one group of Hebrew villages defend themselves against the combined forces of their enemies (2 Sam 10:6).

The Hebrews finally broke out of their circumscription early in David's reign and began to occupy, purchase, or conquer new land east, west, and south of their old land in the hills (2 Sam 8; Edelman 1988:257). Portions of these lands, along with those taken from Saul's family on David's accession to the throne, provided the wealth needed to support the palace. Other pieces would have been parceled out to friends (1 Sam 8:14; 22:7–8; 2 Sam 9:7; 14:30; 1 Kgs 2:26; Luria 1969–70:16–18) and supporters of the monarch to strengthen the political network in the country and establish control over the economy of the region (Weinfeld 1970:184–85; Earle 1987:291). In doing this, David followed the pattern set by other ancient Near Eastern monarchs, including his former Philistine patron, Achish of Gath, who had granted him the village of Ziklag (Rainey 1966:31–37; Postgate 1969; Mettinger 1971:84).

No monarch had the legal right to confiscate lands. Thus, in Samuel–Kings, David purchases the threshing floor from Araunah the Jebusite for fifty shekels of silver, and in a later period Omri purchases the hill of Samaria from Shemer as the site of his new capital city (2 Sam 24:21–24; 1 Kgs 16:24). When Ahab and Jezebel make Naboth an offer for his vineyard next to the royal estate, he exercises his right to refuse (1 Kgs 21:1–4; Andersen 1966:45–57). Eventually, Jezebel and Ahab confiscate Naboth's land after he is executed for treason, but Elijah the prophet indicts Ahab both for killing and taking possession (1 Kgs 21:19). While monarchs could legally confiscate the land of a traitor, Ahab and Jezebel's involvement in the murder of Naboth make them subject to the jurisdiction of Yahweh and the Divine Assembly (Ben-Barak 1988:85; Mettinger 1971:82; Matthews 1988b:524–25; 1991:214–15).

Solomon began the integration of the new land acquired by David. From his time on, the monarchs of ancient Israel all constructed monumental orks and fortifications (1 Kgs 9:10–21). Forts were built along outhern border in the Negeb and along its western border at sites ... .pet el-Marjameh (Cohen 1979; I. Finkelstein 1988b:245). Inside the state, monumental gates and casemate walls were installed at Gezer, Hazor, and Megiddo. By the end of Solomon's reign sometime after 925 BCE, the evolution of Israel as villages into Israel as a state became complete.

12

The Monarch

Like the village, the state (ממלכה, *mamlākâh*) in the world of the Bible was a society designed to feed and protect its people. Like the village, it distributed its political, economic, diplomatic, legal, and educational power to various social institutions (Carneiro 1981:69). States form in two ways. When a state evolves without internal or external pressure, sociologists refer to the process as "pristine state formation" (Fried 1967:227–42; Frick 1985:32). When it forms as a reaction to crisis, as it did in ancient Israel, they refer to the process as "secondary state formation."

The Israel which existed as a state from 1000 to 587 BCE was different from the Israel which existed as villages from 1250 to 1000 BCE. Villages were egalitarian and subsistence societies, even though their households were

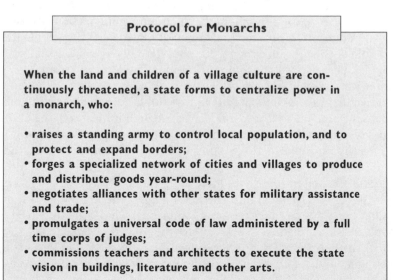

Protocol for Monarchs

When the land and children of a village culture are continuously threatened, a state forms to centralize power in a monarch, who:

- raises a standing army to control local population, and to protect and expand borders;
- forges a specialized network of cities and villages to produce and distribute goods year-round;
- negotiates alliances with other states for military assistance and trade;
- promulgates a universal code of law administered by a full time corps of judges;
- commissions teachers and architects to execute the state vision in buildings, literature and other arts.

not all equal. Some were patrons who exercised power of their own, some were clients who benefited from the power of others. But the power of households in a village was carefully balanced so that the disparity between patrons and clients was slight. Even when its actual jurisdiction was indefinitely ceded to another, no household ever lost its legal right to land and children (Chaney 1983:71). The state, on the other hand, was a totalitarian and surplus society. Its cities and villages were more heterogeneous, and consequently, there was a stark contrast in a state between the rich and the poor (Hopkins 1983:201). Patrons had rights and responsibilities beyond those of their clients and it was their aim to maintain or to widen these differences as a means of protecting their privileges and power (Fried 1978:36).

Nevertheless, the reformation of ancient Israel as a state was not a complete break with the traditions of ancient Israel as villages (pace Noth 1960:165; Bright 1981:187–89). Like the tribe, the state was a centralized or command society (Heilbroner 1962:9–44; Claessen and Skalnik 1978:17–22; Service 1975:16). And like the villages in a tribe, the cities and villages in a state constantly reevaluated the cost of their compliance with its demands. Whenever their losses in self-sufficiency outweighed their gains, they seceded (Haas 1982:168–69).

In some ways the state was a more friendly society than the tribe, because it restored some benefits of village life which the tribe eliminated (Talmon 1980:247–48 n. 17). While the centralization of power in a chief was essential to deliver the tribe from its enemies in the short term, it became devastating to the people in the long term. Theoretically, in the state, all power remained centralized but, in practice, day-to-day affairs were managed by local officials. And theoretically, the authority of the state relied on police power, but soldiers were segregated from civilians, and therefore the state achieved at least a semblance of local autonomy. The book of Judges looks with admiration on the chiefs who fought to keep the people free. But it also admits that to go back to the chaotic days of village society would be suicidal, because "in those days there was no king in Israel; every man did what was right in his own eyes" (Judg 21:25).

Hebrew villages supplemented farming and herding by raiding caravans. Initially, the impact of these raids was negligible, as was the impact of military reprisals taken against the villages. The villagers were not strong or numerous enough to do serious damage to caravan trade, and the standing armies of the day were not equipped to operate in the hills. But, in time, raiders began taking an increasing toll. Following the war between Ramses III (1194–1163 BCE) and the Sea Peoples, the Sea Peoples took over the trade lanes between Egypt and Damascus. The Philistines (Egyptian: perasata; פלשתים, pᵉlištîm; Greek: φυλιστιΐμ and ἀλλόφυλος), as the Bible refers to the Sea Peoples, operated easily in the hills. Their search-and-destroy campaign against the Hebrew villages was relentless. Again and again, they outclassed the warriors mustered by the Hebrews. By the time they massacred Saul and his warriors on Gilboa, victory over the Hebrews was virtually complete.

Faced with annihilation, Israel began the transformation from village to state. The decentralized village way of life gave way to a centralized state. As Israel's first monarch (מֶלֶךְ, *melek*), David raised a standing army to protect its borders. He forged a network of specialized cities and villages which produced and distributed goods year-round. He negotiated covenants for military assistance and trade. He promulgated a code of law administered by full-time judges. And he commissioned teachers and architects to execute the vision of the state in buildings, literature, and other arts.

The key to the successful operation of a state was its bureaucracy, whose makeup and complexity clearly distinguished it from a tribe (Flannery 1972:403; Fried 1967:229; Whybray 1990:133–39; Frick 1985:203). As many as ten different kinds of bureaucracies have been reconstructed by anthropologists (Ahlstrom 1982; Malamat 1965:34–65; Van Selms 1957:118–23; Earle 1989:84–88). The redistribution of power from village to state is apparent in the contrast between the titles of the leaders in the tribe led by Saul (2 Sam 2:8–9; Edelman 1985:88–89) and those in the state of David and Solomon (1 Kgs 4:1–19). The titles of Saul's officials are almost all familial. Jonathan is Saul's son (1 Sam 13:2) and Abner is the son of Saul's uncle (1 Sam 14:50). Few of Solomon's officials carry family titles. Jehoshaphat is recorder and herald. The sons of Seraiah are chief scribes (2 Sam 8:17; 1 Kgs 4:2–6). Adoniram is the director of public labor.

Standing Army

The first sign of the conversion from village to state appeared in the restructuring of the tribe into an army (Talmon 1980:240–44). In Samuel–Kings, David is courageous in battle, cunning in strategy, and loyal to those who fought alongside him. He rises to power as a chief when he answers the call of the warriors who muster to defend their villages from the Philistines. And, as a chief, he is surrounded by brothers, sons, and the sons of uncles (1 Sam 22:1–2; 2 Sam 8:16; 13:32; 17:25; 1 Chron 2:16). But David is also aware of the limitations of the tribe. Without completely abandoning the old ways of defending the people, David begins to centralize the tribe. He alters the way in which plunder is distributed; he hires professional soldiers; and he borrows command patterns from the standing army of Egypt to create a cadre called the "Thirty," which was ready to counter the first Philistine threat. At one point, he distributes command between Joab and Abishai, who are Hebrews, and Ittai of Gath, who is a covenant partner (2 Sam 18:2). At another point, he distributes command between a commander, the three, the commander of the royal bodyguard, and a group of lesser officers (2 Sam 23:8–39; 1 Chron 11:10–47; Na'aman 1988:79; Ahlstrom 1982:27). Again David makes his appointments from both Hebrews and non-Hebrews (Rosenberg 1986:165–68). Benaiah, the commander of the royal bodyguard, is a covenant partner, while Joab is a Hebrew (2 Sam 20:23; Ishida 1982:185; Halpern 1981a:243).

The command structure of the army continues to be refined throughout the reign of David and Solomon (Frick 1985:79). Solomon's elimination of Joab sent a clear signal that he would not be restricted by former loyalties, as does the exile of Abiathar for his association with Solomon's rival Adonijah (Heaton 1974:50–51; Ishida 1982:186). From time to time, the tribes of old still mustered warriors to defend their villages. But once Israel became a state, it was the monarch as commander-in-chief of its standing army who was charged with its defense and expansion.

Production and Distribution

Secondary state formation in Israel was not solely a reaction to the military threat posed by the Philistines, the Ammonites, the Moabites, the Amalekites, and the Midianites. The most important crisis which gave birth to the state was agricultural. The fragile nature of the environment made it impossible for some villages to compete. Consequently, they joined more efficient villages. Burgeoning economic opportunities and the growing market in new horticultural products increased population. More and more land was reclaimed and a smaller and smaller ruling elite wielded all the power (Kipp and Schortman 1989:371; Carneiro 1981:68). By 1000 BCE Hebrew villages in the hills had developed all the land available for farming and herding, but they still needed a more centralized, more efficient, and more aggressive social system to protect their land and feed their children (Halpern 1981b:62–63, 84–85; Frick 1985:99–189).

Villages were made up of households working the same land, exploiting the same natural resources, and facing the same common enemies. There was too much repetition. Every village produced virtually the same products. When the growing or herding season was good for one village it was good for all the villages. But when war, famine, or epidemic destroyed the economy of one village it soon affected the economies of all the rest. States combined villages and cities over a much broader region whose natural resources and external dangers were more diverse (Frick 1985:203). The number of actual square miles in a state was not nearly as important as its number of ecological zones (Hopkins 1983:193–94).

By incorporating more than one ecological zone, a state insured itself against adverse changes in natural resources, weather, and climate. With more than one zone, it expanded crop rotation within a single environment to rotating and mixing from one environment to the other. At its economic peak Israel comprised at least four major ecological zones (Hopkins 1985:53–76). There were plains along the coasts, the hills west of the Jordan River, the valley cut by the Jordan River and the Dead Sea, and the high plains east of the Jordan River. As is clear from Ruth, crop failure in the hills of Judah does not affect the harvest on the plains of Moab to the east, and an epidemic on the plains of Moab does not spread to the villages in the hills of Judah (Ruth 1:1–22).

To take control of production and distribution, states collected taxes from villages and cities in return for improving their infrastructure (Steponaitis: nos. 1, 2, 9, cited in Earle 1989:84–88). The pressure which states brought to bear on agriculture varied as needs varied, and as the power of the state to carry out its land reform varied (Hopkins 1983:194). Not all state policies brought the government into direct control of agriculture (Dybdahl 1981: 39–123). In some cases the state allowed villages to remain in control of production as long as they met their quotas (2 Chron 27:5; Chaney 1981:11–12; Malamat 1979:173–86). The state did not destroy the internal diversity of its villages and cities, but capitalized on the uniqueness of each.

The role of David and Solomon in the specialization of Israel's economy is reflected in the lists of their officials (Heaton 1974:47; Cody 1965:381–93). These officials managed and controlled production and distribution of goods from the land once supervised by the fathers of village households (Zagarell 1986:420). Hushai and Ahithophel are friends of the king or royal advisors (2 Sam 15:12, 32–37). There is also a chief steward, which although well-known in Egypt, was a new office for Israel (Mettinger 1971:63–65). His job was to oversee the palace and state lands, maintaining their productivity and profitability (Heaton 1974:49–50; Mettinger 1971:78–79). The director of public labor was a powerful official who drafted men and women from the villages to perform public works (1 Kgs 5:13–17; Mettinger 1971:9). And there were assistant directors who recruited workers in particular districts. Jeroboam, the son of Nebat, had "charge over all the forced labor of the house of Joseph," and used his power to take over most of the land north of Jerusalem after Solomon's death (1 Kgs 11:26–28; 12:20). His familiarity with state bureaucracy enabled him to make a smooth transition to the new state.

Israel as a state was generally successful. Agricultural yields increased as villages became more efficient in using their land and labor. Its command economy created regional specialization and a consistent surplus (Frick 1985:196–204; Service 1978:31–32). Solomon, for example, divided the state into twelve districts (1 Kgs 4:1–19). The state also introduced technology in the construction of terraced fields, plastered cisterns, and, eventually, in the use of iron (Waldbaum 1978:27). With these resources the state constructed an elaborate infrastructure of roads, fortresses, and public buildings, and initiated joint economic ventures with the Phoenicians (1 Kgs 9:10–21, 26–28).

Soon the state dominated the economy (Kipp and Schortman 1989:373). Some state projects were more successful than others. David's chief steward, for example, was unable to deal with jealousies over the increased influence of the newly annexed areas and the expanded state lands. Furthermore, opposition to taxes and public labor led to the revolts of Amnon, Absalom, and Adonijah against David, and later against Solomon and Rehoboam (1 Kgs 12:4).

Foreign Covenants

The boundaries of villages were ill-defined. States, on the other hand, had clearly defined borders. Ideally, they were marked by clear geographical features such as rivers or ranges of mountains. Samuel–Kings, for example, describes the borders of Israel as Dan in the north, where the Jordan river emerged from a powerful spring at the foot of Mount Hermon, and Beersheba in the south, where the last year-round wells can be found in the Negeb (1 Kgs 4:25; 1 Chron 21:2).

To exercise power beyond state borders, monarchs negotiated covenants. Most were military alliances or trade agreements. The genre of covenant in the Bible parallels the general pattern and technical legal language of the Hittite treaty in many ways. The Treaty of Ramses II and Hattusilis III following the Battle of Kadesh in 1280 BCE is a textbook for treaty style and language. Standard Hittite treaties contain at least six components (McCarthy 1972:12). They open by giving the credentials of the signatories to the treaty and issuing a new and official history of the conflict. Then they lay out the terms. These are followed by a list of witnesses to the treaty, a litany

---

**Treaty of Ramses II and Hattusilis III
(Matthews & Benjamin 1991b:51)**

If a foreign army invades the lands of Ramses, and he sends a message to the Great King of Hatti, . . . the Great King of Hatti shall come and fight against the enemy of Egypt his ally. . . .

Likewise, if Ramses is trying to put down an armed revolt, the Great King of Hatti shall help him until all the rebels have been executed.

When Hattusilis dies, the Son of Hattusilis shall be crowned Great King of Hatti in his father's place. If the officials of Hatti revolt against his son, Ramses shall send infantry and chariots to avenge Hattusilis. Once order has been restored in Hatti, they shall return to Egypt. . . .

The Great King of Hatti shall not grant asylum to any citizen of Egypt who is a fugitive from justice. . . . Likewise, any runaway slave, who escapes to Hatti in search of a new master, shall be extradited to Ramses. . . .

The Pharaoh of Egypt shall not grant asylum to any citizen of Hatti who is a fugitive from justice. The Pharaoh of Egypt shall have the fugitive extradited to the Great King of Hatti. Likewise, any runaway slave who escapes to Egypt in search of a new master shall be extradited to the Great King of Hatti.

of curses for treaty violations and blessings for treaty compliance, and finally, provisions to record and promulgate the treaty.

The history presents the official background to the conflict, which the covenant now settles. Ramses and Hattusilis, for example, declare that Egypt and Hatti are officially at peace with one another and legally identify their states as brothers (אחים, 'ahîm). They promise not to attack or raid one another and to come to each others defense when either faces armed revolt or is attacked by another state (Gen 13:8–18). They also recognize one another's beloved sons and promise to provide military support to insure that these heirs to the throne will be crowned when their patrons died. They also agree to extradite fugitives and runaway slaves (CH articles 15–20). And finally, Ramses and Hattusilis conclude their treaty by blessing compliance with land and population.

The trade agreements which monarchs negotiated with other states provided for the exchange of goods and preferential treatment for each other's caravans. Money did not come into general use in the ancient Near East until the Persians (modern Iran) developed internationally recognized coinage after 537 BCE. When precious metals were used in trade before then, they were not coined, but bullion. The three most common mediums of exchange in the Mediterranean world were grain, wine, and olive oil.

Covenant partners also exchanged wives, troops, and temples. In diplomatic marriages, a woman from the royal household in one state married the monarch of the other. Their relationship was a physical symbol of the unification which the covenant brought about between their two states. These marriages highlighted the role of the covenant in fulfilling the responsibility of the monarch for the children or population of the state. Diplomatic wives exercised significant power in both the state ruled by their parents and in the state of their husband. They were responsible for seeing that the stipulations of the covenant were fulfilled and that all the goods and services promised were, in fact, exchanged. It was also their responsibility to see that the markets in their husbands' states continued to need products from the state of their parents. Because even small states negotiated covenants with many neighboring states, monarchs had many wives (Berlin 1982). Harems in the world of the Bible were not an indication of the sexual appetite of the king but the diplomatic stature of the state. Diplomatic wives competed with one another not just for the sexual attention of the king but for the markets in which to sell the goods and services from the state of their parents.

Soldiers stationed by one state inside the border of its covenant partner ratified the promise of the two states to defend one another. They signified the importance of the covenant in fulfilling the responsibility of the monarch to protect the land. Soldiers also provided intelligence to their home countries on the military strength and tactics of their allies, and served as officers for any additional troops deployed to help their covenant partners in the event of a crisis.

The sanctuaries which covenant partners built in each other's countries were not simply chapels for expatriates. They were symbols of the ability of two people to live as one. A temple was not a building in which a congregation gathered to pray like synagogues, churches, or mosques today. A temple was the residence of a member of the divine assembly; it was the house of a god. Building the house of the divine patron of one state alongside the house of the divine patron of another modeled the goal of the covenant to allow the people of one state to live alongside the people of another. If two members of the divine assembly could peacefully live side by side, hopefully, so could the people whom they had created and protected.

The protocol which monarchs followed in obtaining covenant partners across their borders was carefully designed to allow them to better feed and protect their states. It was refined to produce the best results for both monarchs. Monarchs of Israel and Judah negotiated covenants in a sincere effort to fulfill their commission as the stewards of Yahweh. By distributing the power to negotiate covenants to their monarchs, states could be blessed with a good life if their monarchs were just. But they could just as easily be enslaved by monarchs who were not. Consequently, while Israel and Judah empowered their monarchs to negotiate covenants, they also empowered prophets to monitor the monarchs so that they would use their power to enrich Israel rather than enslave it.

The pioneers of early Israel came from Egypt and its covenant partners in Syria-Palestine. These states were efficient but cruel. When Egypt's empire collapsed, villagers and slaves from the plains along the Mediterranean coast settled the hills west of the Jordan River and north of Jerusalem. Their way of life integrated prohibitions against the social institutions which had caused them so much pain and suffering. Consequently, Israel as villages was a culture without monarchs, without taxes, without soldiers, and without slaves. When Israel became a state with monarchs, taxes, soldiers, and slaves, it commissioned the prophets to safeguard the ideals on which early Israel was incorporated. For the prophets, covenants with other states threatened Israel's commitment to the ideals of its ancestors. While monarchs considered covenants part of their stewardship to feed and protect the people, prophets generally considered them as contrary to the divine covenant with Yahweh. For the prophets, Israel had only one covenant, and that covenant was with Yahweh, who would feed and protect it. Covenants with other states implied that Yahweh either could not or would not take care of Israel. Furthermore, they burdened Israel with the same kind of taxes, soldiers, and slavery from which its ancestors fled, and filled Jerusalem with temples for foreign gods.

Codes of Law

Breakdowns in cooperation between the households of a village were resolved by an assembly of elders. Village assemblies continued to arbitrate the indictments brought by one household against another even after Israel became a state. But they could not resolve all the crises which developed in a state, especially those which arose from a monarch's need to tax the surplus of the villages and cities of the state, and draft its men and women to serve as soldiers and to work on public projects. So, at their coronations, monarchs regularly promulgated a code of law for the state. Codes of law served much the same purpose as the platform of a candidate running for president in the United States today. No code of law was completely new, nor was it the personal invention of a particular monarch. Monarchs promulgated law codes to update traditional patterns of taxation and conscription. They outlined the responsibilities of the villages and cities to the state and the procedures which the state would follow to guarantee their compliance. These procedures were overseen by a state covenant system. But unlike assemblies made up of the fathers of households who temporarily convened to hear complaints, state courts were served by full-time judges appointed by the monarch.

While the ideal of the monarch as a lawgiver remained a cherished ideal, state courts were only modestly successful in keeping the peace. David's state had been held together by his personality and the network of social and economic ties which he constructed before and after becoming king in Jerusalem (1 Sam 25:39–43; 30:26–31; 2 Sam 5:13–16; 8:3–12; Edelman 1988: 254–55; I. Finkelstein 1988b:250–51). Solomon inherited David's state, but he had to deal quickly with the reality that the military threat which had helped David keep the dissident elements in line was no longer present (1 Kgs 5:4). This necessitated an almost frenzied policy of construction projects, new economic ventures, and the extraction of resources which could be redistributed internally and externally. A perception of power was the result, but also a perception of tyranny, which eventually could not be balanced and led to the division of the state (1 Kgs 12:4; Soggin 1982:266–67; Kipp and Schortman 1989:380). Remarkably, revolts against the state did not result in a return to the village society. Even after Jeroboam revolted against Solomon, he used Solomon's state as a model for his own. Both states continued to expand their bureaucracies to control all aspects of production, distribution, worship, and judicial affairs (1 Kgs 12:26–33; 2 Kgs 23:1–20; 2 Chron 19:4–11).

Public Education

Monarchs, like chiefs, used liturgy and storytelling to legalize their centralization of power and solicit both divine and human endorsements (Steponaitis: nos. 7, 8, cited in Earle 1989:84–88). State ideology argued that the divine order of things depended on the monarch. Signs of the status of the ruling elite included their use of exotic items and symbols such as clothing, seals, and court language (Earle 1989:85; Wright 1984:54–55). Annual festivals placed a divine stamp of approval on the monarch and the bureaucracy of the state to guarantee support from the people. Campaigns to unite villages into a state often divided loyalties. Unless monarchs followed their victories in war with victories in public education, their states would collapse.

Following their coronation, monarchs begin the process of consolidation in which literature plays an important role. The educational policies of the monarch, unlike those of the chief, were not limited to storytelling and ritual. Monarchs throughout the ancient Near East made extensive use of architecture to promote the ideology of the state. Public building programs were symbols of power. Monumental architecture like forts, gates, temples, and warehouses graphically represented the ability of the monarch to protect the people and to provide them with a sense of national power and prosperity (Whitelam 1986:169; Dever 1982:290–95).

David set the pattern for the royal ideology followed by later monarchs (Fox 1973:41–42). He turned Jerusalem into a royal city (2 Sam 5:6–12). He prepared to build a state temple for the ark of the covenant (2 Sam 7:1–3), and he commissioned officials to develop a state literature and liturgy (1 Kgs 4:20–21, 34; 5:3–5; 9:20–22; 10:23–29). David's policy of territorial expansion, a developed bureaucracy, and a capital city within an increasingly heterogeneous population identified him as the monarch of a state (I. Finkelstein 1989:48; Flanagan 1981:67). When he first made Jerusalem the capital of Israel, David quickly moved to identify his victory and his right to rule as springing from Yahweh's favor. He did this by bringing the ark of the covenant to that city, joining its power with his claims to legitimacy (2 Sam 6; Whitelam 1989:121). The centerpiece of David's state ideology was the land grant formula which established an everlasting covenant between Yahweh and David. Yahweh adopted David as firstborn with all its attendant privileges (2 Sam 7:8–16; Mendelsohn 1960:38–40; Paul 1979–80:178). The adoption formula was a liturgical endorsement of the eternal right of the household of David to rule Israel (Weinfeld 1970:191).

Solomon further solidified the state. He promoted the worship of Yahweh by constructing the Jerusalem Temple and installing a priesthood, headed by Zadok, who was loyal to his household (1 Kgs 2:35; 6—8). Jerusalem and, by extension, the household of David, became the sacred center of the state (Miller and Hayes 1986:203–4). The centerpiece of Solomon's state ideology describes him using a strategy first employed by Saul, as he draws internal boundaries dividing the state into twelve districts (1 Kgs 4:7–28; 9:15–23; Edelman 1985:85–91). Some boundaries simply redefine old tribal territories, some subdivide tribes like Manasseh and Ephraim, and some incorporate new non-Israelite lands (Heaton 1974:53; Mettinger 1971:112–18; Stager 1985:24). Theoretically, each district had to make provision for one month in the year for state expenses (Mettinger 1971:123–24; Heaton 1974:54). Practically, because of differences in climate and the amount of arable land available in each district, such a program could not work economically. Therefore, the list does not reflect an economic policy but characterizes Solomon as the ideal or wise monarch. The Solomonic ideal also appears in the record of his marriages, massive animal sacrifices, huge stables, and stories like the Parable of the Prostitutes (1 Kgs 3:16–28; 8:63; Miller and Hayes 1986:195).

The Monarch in the Stories of Meriba'al
(2 Sam 9:1–13; 16:1–4; 19:24–30)

The dynamics of state formation in general, and in ancient Israel in particular, are a fascinating study. There is no single story in the Bible which can serve as a case study of state formation in Israel as a whole, but many different stories offer a glimpse into one facet or the other of the process. One of these windows on the monarchy appears in the stories of Meriba'al (2 Sam 9:1–13; 16:1–4; 19:24–30). These stories profile David forging a specialized network of cities and villages to produce and distribute goods year-round (Hopkins 1983:193–97).

In the Bible today, the stories of Meriba'al are part of the argument in Samuel–Kings that the household of Solomon, rather than the household of Absalom, should rule Israel. Meriba'al is the father of the household of Saul to which David once belonged and which supported the household of Absalom against Solomon for control of Israel. The stories of Meriba'al begin when David decides to review its status. David tells Ziba that he wishes to show "kindness" to Saul, using a technical expression for his determination to renegotiate the covenant between their households (Gen 21:22–24; 1 Sam 20:8; 2 Sam 9:1–7; 10:2; 20:14–16; Kenik 1983:58–72).

The struggle between the households of Saul and David for control of Israel was suspended after the battle of Gilboa where the Philistines massacred Saul and Jonathan. Long before his death, Jonathan transferred his status as heir of the household of Saul to David (1 Sam 18:1–5; Ishida, ed. 1982:79). And Saul confirmed the transfer by allowing David to marry his daughter Michal (1 Sam 18:20–29). But at the time of their deaths, David had neither the need, nor the power to take over the household. So, he simply froze its assets. Therefore, Meriba'al is "crippled in his feet" (2 Sam 9:3), "a dead dog" (2 Sam 9:8), and "lame in both his feet" (1 Sam 9:13). Since "feet" in the world of the Bible is a euphemism for male genitals and a phallic symbol of power, the use of these phrases here may indicate that Meriba'al is not simply unable to walk, but the household of Saul no longer works land and gives birth to children in Israel.

David interrogates Meriba'al to determine if he is supporting a contender for the throne. When David calls Meriba'al by name at the beginning of his hearing, he wants to know whether Meriba'al answers to him or to one of his sons. Meriba'al says: "I am your servant," thereby pledging that the household of Saul will support only the heir designated by David.

> ### Stories of Meriba'al
> ### (2 Sam 9:1–13, authors' translation)
>
> . . . David questioned a slave from the household of Saul whose name was Ziba. "Are you Ziba, the slave of Saul?" "I am," he testified.
>
> The king asked: "I wish to renegotiate the covenant between the household of David and the household of Saul. Who is father of the household now?" Ziba testified: "The son of Jonathan, but he is powerless."
>
> The king asked: "Where is he?" "Under the protection of the household of Machir son of Ammiel at Lo-debar," Ziba testified.
>
> So King David ordered the household of Machir to extradite the son of Jonathan from Lo-debar to Jerusalem. The son of Jonathan was brought before David, and he put his face on the ground and David's foot on his neck. "Are you Meriba'al," David asked? "I am," he testified.
>
> So David decreed: "Do not be afraid! For the sake of Jonathan, I will restore the household of Saul to you as long as you eat at my table." Again, Meriba'al put his face on the ground and David's foot on his neck, and accepted the covenant with the words: "This dead dog is not worthy to be your slave."
>
> Then David ordered Ziba to appear before him. "I have restored the household of Saul to your patron's heir. But you shall work the land with your sons and your slaves, and bring the produce to me as along as Meriba'al shall eat at my table." Now Ziba had fifteen sons and twenty slaves. Then Ziba said to the king: "Your word is this slave's command. . . ."

David then recognizes Meriba'al as the heir to the household of Saul. The royal decree not only acknowledges Meriba'al's pledge of allegiance, but also preempts his campaign to increase control of the household by conspiring with one of David's sons. But David does not permit him to exercise his authority immediately. Instead he assigns Meriba'al to "eat at my table" (2 Sam 9:7). David sanctions the title of Meriba'al to the land of his household (Lev 25:8–55; Num 27; Jer 32:6–7; Hos 5:10), while effectively guaranteeing that he cannot use the power against him. It is unlikely David could have done anything else at this point and kept the support of the people (Ben-Barak 1981:83).

Monarchs bring leaders to eat at their tables for two purposes: location and indoctrination (Dan 1:1–10). With Meriba'al at his table, David always knows where he is and has regular opportunity to teach Meriba'al how to support state policy. Patron states today still bring leaders from client states to the mother country for education and military training. As in David's time, the policy facilitates the control which patrons exercise in the states of their clients.

Stories of Daniel
(Dan 1:1–5)

... King Nebuchadnezzar of Babylon ... commanded his palace master Ashpenaz to bring some of the Israelites of the royal family and of the nobility, young men without physical defect and handsome, versed in every branch of wisdom, endowed with knowledge and insight, and competent to serve in the king's palace; they were to be taught the literature and language of the Chaldeans. The king assigned them a daily portion of the royal rations of food and wine. They were to be educated for three years, so that at the end of that time they could be stationed in the king's court.

Finally, until David is satisfied that Meriba'al is loyal enough to exercise the actual authority of father of the household, Ziba will act as his legal guardian to "till the land for him" and "bring in the produce" (2 Sam 9:10). In the villages of Israel, when the father of a household died without an heir, the tribe appointed a legal guardian. By appointing Ziba to administer Saul's property, David uses the tradition of the legal guardian to confiscate the land of Saul. Ziba becomes a state official (1 Chron 6:39–66; 1 Kgs 10:28), and serves David as the "husband's brother" (Deut 25:5–10) for the household. Consequently, Ziba works for David, not Meriba'al. To carry out his responsibility, Ziba negotiates fifteen major labor contracts and twenty minor contracts.

In the reorganization of the household of Saul, David is not a philanthropist granting Meriba'al a benefice whose revenue will pay for his upkeep. David is a monarch renegotiating his covenant with a household to put it back into production by transferring it to the state (Borowski 1979; Hopkins 1983:193–94). But despite his suspicions that Meriba'al is conspiring against him, David himself does not shame Meriba'al, but instead allows him to remain father of the household under the supervision of a legal guardian. Declaring Meriba'al incompetent to feed and protect the household of Saul simply allows David to increase its production and distribution as part of a state network (Sahlins 1968:76; Lenski 1970:263; Chaney 1981:17). He also wants to bring Saul's former supporters to his side (Ben-Barak 1981:77; McCarter 1984:264–65).

In some of the episodes, the name "Meriba'al," which is a label of honor, has been purposefully caricatured to "Mephibosheth," which is a label of shame. At the adoption of Meriba'al as heir to the household of Saul, Jonathan celebrated his son as the "word" (מפי, *mippî*) or "messiah" (מרי, *mᵉrî*) of Yahweh (בעל, *ba'al*). But because it sided with the household of Absalom in its revolt against David, later storytellers labeled Meriba'al as "Mephibosheth," or a "sentence [מפי, *mippî*] of death" (בשת, *bōšet*) for the household of Saul (McCarter 1984:128). The label deprived the household of Saul of all its rights and privileges in Israel.

It was not the first time David appointed a legal guardian for the household of a rival. He had used the same tactic to confiscate the land of Uriah the Hittite (2 Sam 11:1–27). Subsequent monarchs in Israel and Judah follow suit. Ahab and Jezebel use this tradition to confiscate the land of Naboth (1 Kgs 21:1–29). But it is Solomon, who most successfully brings land under state control (1 Kgs 4:7–19; 5:13–18; 9:10–28).

The abuse of power evidenced by this state policy is the target of a verdict against the Monarchs of Israel in Ezekiel (Ezek 34:1–16). The verdict indicts monarchs who foreclose on the property of households in financial difficulty, not to reorganize them, but to seize their lands for the state (Ezek 34:17–18; Allen 1990:163; Brueggemann 1977:71–89).

When David renegotiates his covenant with the household of Saul in the opening episodes of the stories of Meriba'al he carries out only one stage of the protocol used by monarchs in the world of the Bible to centralize production and distribution in the state. As the stories continue, however, they reflect subsequent steps which monarchs take to tighten their control.

Stories of Meriba'al
(2 Sam 16:1–4, authors' translation)

When David had passed a little beyond the summit [of the Mount of Olives as he retreated from Jerusalem], Ziba the slave met him with two donkeys, carrying two hundred loaves of bread, one hundred bunches of raisins, one hundred strings of dried summer fruit, and one skin of wine.

The king asked, "What is all this?" Ziba replied, "The donkeys are for the king to ride, the bread and summer fruit are for his warriors to eat, and the wine is medicine for his casualties who faint in the desert to drink."

Then the king asked, "And where is Meriba'al?" "He stayed in Jerusalem," Ziba replied, "for he said, 'Today Israel will once again belong to the household of Saul.' "

Then the king said to Ziba, "The household of Saul is yours." And Ziba said, "I put my face in the dirt and your foot on my neck. You are my patron and my king. Your wish is my command."

Samuel–Kings recounts three attempts to overthrow David; one by Amnon, one by Absalom, and one by Adonijah. Absalom almost succeeds. When Absalom marches on Jerusalem, David orders a strategic retreat from the city. Since he does not know who in Jerusalem remains loyal to him, he withdraws from the city assuming that only his followers will come with him. Meriba'al is one of those whose loyalties are unmasked (2 Sam 16:1–4). Meriba'al remains in Jerusalem, while Ziba departs. Ziba not only follows David into the field, but he also pays the taxes due to the state from the household of Saul at the precise moment when David and his soldiers need them most.

States tax their cities and villages in order to defend them and to maintain strong markets for their produce (Lenski 1970:268). Tax rates are variable. During wartime, for example, states assess the households on the basis of how many rations (מאכל, ma'ᵃkâl; קמה, qemaḥ) the troops necessary to protect the households require (2 Chron 11:11; 1 Chron 12:41). The register of rations which Ziba delivers to David and his troops is a key to the size of the military contingent protecting Saul's farms and herds. It invoices typical commodities taxed by the state: "loaves of bread, . . . strings of raisins, a hundred summer fruit, and a skin of wine" (2 Sam 16:1–2). Grain, wine, and olive oil are the most common items taxed and traded in the world of the Bible because they can be appraised, stored, transported, and rationed (Hopkins 1983:196; Borowski 1979:171). The same commodities appear elsewhere in the Bible (1 Sam 25:18; 1 Kgs 5:25; Ezek 27:17; 2 Chron 11:11; 1 Chron 12:41).

Donkeys are not typical tax commodities. For farmers, livestock was an asset; for tax collectors, however, it was a liability (Hopkins 1983:197; LaBianca 1979; Antoun 1972; Moore 1972:2–3). Farmers herded livestock to insure their households against crop failure and to supplement available human labor (Hopkins 1985:245–50). However, it was too inconvenient for tax collectors to appraise, store, transport, and ration. Nonetheless, the tax stamp formula "for the king's household" (לבית המלך, lᵉbêt hammelek) identifies the team as a tax payment, not simply transportation for the payment. The tax stamp "for the monarch" appears regularly on storage jars recovered by archaeologists, which contained grain, wine, or olive oil paid by households to the state as taxes (Hopkins 1983:199–200; Borowski 1979:48–49; Lance 1971:315–32; Baly and Tushingham 1971:23–35; Paul and Dever, eds. 1974:186; Diringer 1949:82; Yadin 1961:6–12; Lapp 1960:11–22; Ussishkin 1976:1–13).

David rewards Ziba for his loyalty by removing Meriba'al as father of the household of Saul and designating Ziba to replace him (Mettinger 1971:86). Ziba is no longer simply the legal guardian of the household, he is the father. Although the village assembly follows a lengthy process of discovery and oral testimony in its due process, the court martial of the state does not (Exod 23:1–2; Deut 1:17; 13:14). As a magistrate, David listens to the testimony of Ziba and makes a decision in the case. David's actions have precedents in traditions from states like Alalakh and Ugarit where the lands of traitors were also taken over by the monarch (Ben-Barak 1981:85–86).

In the final episode of the stories of Meriba'al, David makes another attempt to stabilize the relationship between his household and the household of Saul (2 Sam 19:24–30). During his hearing, Meriba'al accuses Ziba of treason, and professes his own loyalty to David. He testifies that he was not in sympathy with Absalom and goes on to argue that he planned to leave Jerusalem and work for David, but that he had been deceived into staying behind by Ziba.

David appears to take the expeditious path, dividing the property between Meriba'al and Ziba in much the same way that Solomon proposes to divide the prostitute's infant (1 Kgs 3:24–25). A fair division of the household of Saul would satisfy that need to heal the nation after Absalom's revolt (Mettinger 1976:119; Ben-Barak 1981:88). But David may not be dividing Saul's property in two, but rather trying to double its yield (Hopkins 1983: 197–202; Boardman 1976:188–89). By adding a second administrator for Saul's property, David could double the harvests from the same amount of land. To offset the risk of such a dramatic increase in production, David appoints Meriba'al to the position. Saul's farmers might work harder for Meriba'al and Ziba together than for Ziba alone. Meriba'al points out that such a reorganization is pointless, since the revolt is over.

Stories of Meriba'al
(2 Sam 19:24–30, authors' translation)

[As David was returning to Jerusalem after putting down the revolt of Absalom . . . ,] Meriba'al came to meet the king. He was dressed as if he had been in mourning since the day David evacuated the city. . . .

The king questioned him: "Why did you not go with me, Meriba'al?" He testified: "Ziba, my slave left without me. Because I am crippled, I ordered him to saddle a donkey for me, so that I might ride out with you, my lord and the king. But the slave tricked me and then lied to you. But you are the Messenger of Yahweh to me. Do what seems good to you. The household of Saul was sentenced to death. But you set your slave among those who eat at your table. What further right have I, then, to appeal to you again for mercy."

So the king decreed: "These charges and counter-charges must stop. You and Ziba will divide the household of Saul." But Meriba'al declined. "As a sign of my gratitude that you have come back to Jerusalem safely, let Ziba keep the household."

Meriba'al's decline is not a simple gesture of piety. Doubling the number of harvests overworks the land and the farmers (Boserup 1965:28–34). In wartime, overplanting farmland is a military necessity; in peacetime, it is economic and political suicide. When farmers plant too many crops in a single year the quantity and quality of each individual harvest drops off; their work doubles, their yield does not. Overworked and underpaid farmers overthrow their governments. Meriba'al refuses to turn Saul's farmland into a dust bowl and to drive his farmers into rebellion. The policy risks destroying David and Meriba'al along with him. Meriba'al, like the prostitute who is willing to give up her child so it may live, shows wisdom and upholds the ideal which promotes life over short-term goals by leaving Ziba in sole control of the land (2 Sam 19:30; 1 Kgs 3:26).

13

The Virgin

The virgin was the most politically significant woman in Israel as a state. In contrast with the way contemporary western cultures use "mother" and "virgin" to describe sexual activity, the Bible focuses on the political connotations of the words. Villages distributed power only to a limited number of households or mothers. States distributed power to a wide variety of cities or virgins. A decentralized village culture, like Israel between 1250 and 1000 BCE, was personified as a mother. A centralized state culture, like Israel between 1000 and 587 BCE, was a personified as virgin. Sexual activity in the world of the Bible was not as much an aspect of personal relationships as an expression of the political power of households.

Protocol for Virgins

In the world of the Bible, "virginity" was not just a woman's physical condition, but her political power. A virgin protected and provided for the household of her father by:

• avoiding promiscuity, which was not simply a lack of sexual indiscretion, but any political maneuver which put the land and children of her household at risk.
• resisting rape, which was not simply an act of sexual violence, but a challenge to the father of her household.
• ratifying a covenant for the household of her father with her marriage.

Virgin as a Married or Marriageable Woman

Only when the word "virgin" is modified by the phrase "who has never known a man" (Gen 24:16; Num 31:18) is the Bible talking primarily about a woman who has never had sexual intercourse (Schmitt 1992:853). Otherwise, "virgin" carries more important connotations. For example, the Teaching on a Breach of Covenant in Deuteronomy (Deut 22:13–21) is not as concerned with the physical integrity of the woman indicted as it is with the status of her household. This teaching directs that if one household falsifies its standing when it negotiates a covenant with another, the woman whose marriage ratified the covenant is to be executed. But if a household brings ungrounded charges of fraud against another, then the husband whose marriage ratifies the covenant is to be flogged. Likewise, when Job testifies:

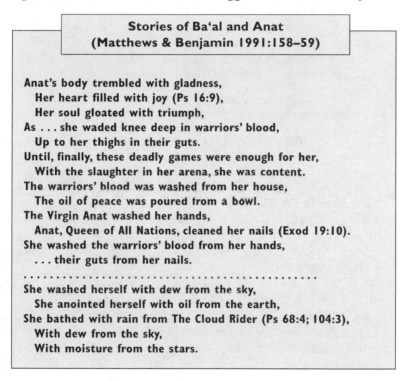

**Stories of Ba'al and Anat
(Matthews & Benjamin 1991:158–59)**

Anat's body trembled with gladness,
  Her heart filled with joy (Ps 16:9),
  Her soul gloated with triumph,
As . . . she waded knee deep in warriors' blood,
  Up to her thighs in their guts.
Until, finally, these deadly games were enough for her,
  With the slaughter in her arena, she was content.
The warriors' blood was washed from her house,
  The oil of peace was poured from a bowl.
The Virgin Anat washed her hands,
  Anat, Queen of All Nations, cleaned her nails (Exod 19:10).
She washed the warriors' blood from her hands,
  . . . their guts from her nails.
. . . .
She washed herself with dew from the sky,
  She anointed herself with oil from the earth,
She bathed with rain from The Cloud Rider (Ps 68:4; 104:3),
  With dew from the sky,
  With moisture from the stars.

"I have made a covenant with my eyes; how then could I look upon a virgin?" (Job 31:1), he is not just referring to lust or voyeurism, but to a desire to worship Anat the Virgin of Ugarit rather than Yahweh the Covenant Partner of Israel (Pope 1965:229).

Sometimes, the word "virgin" in the Bible refers to a woman whose marriage ratifies a significant covenant for her household. For example, the title of a first lady or queen (Isa 7:14) was "Virgin," and her capital city, like Samaria (Jer 31:4, 21; Amos 5:2) or Jerusalem (Jer 18:13), was called the

"Virgin of Israel." Such royal women were important in the distribution of power in the state of Egypt as well as in ancient Israel. For example, an Execration of Traitors indicts queens and princesses along with other defendants for conspiring to overthrow the twelfth dynasty which governed Egypt between 1991 and 1783 BCE (Baines and Malek 1980:36; Pritchard 1969:328–29). Similarly, the Teachings of Amen-em-het (1991–1962 BCE) advise pharaohs against placing too much confidence in royal women who use that misplaced confidence to plot against them (Pritchard 1969:418–19).

Generally, in the world of the Bible, a virgin was a marriageable woman (Schmitt 1992:853). Twelve times in the Bible, "female virgin" or "young woman" (בתולה, beṯûlâh) is parallel with "male virgin" or "young man" (בחור, bāḥûr). The virginity of an unmarried woman was indicative of the political integrity of the household of her father. The village rated a father's fulfillment of his responsibility to feed and protect his household on the basis of how well he cared for and protected its marriageable women. If a father could protect the virgins of his household then he could protect all its members. If he left them in harm's way then he was impeached and someone else took over the land and children of his household.

Virginity as the Honor of a Household

Protecting its virgins was a matter of honor for each household (Baab 1962:788; Tapper 1981:391; Bird 1989:77). The measure of this honor was the evidence of virginity on the part of the bride at the time when the marriage was consummated. Virginity was the legal guarantee of land and children for a household in the world of the Bible (Giovannini 1987). Consequently, households guarded their virgins until they could be married so that their own political status would remain intact (Goody 1976:14). A lack of virginity due to rape or promiscuity threatened a household's social and economic status (Schlegel 1991:724).

Promiscuity in the world of the Bible was not simply a lack of sexual discretion, but a symptom of the risks which a household was taking with its land and children. A Teaching on Breach of Promise in Deuteronomy (Deut 22:23–27) explains the protocol for a virgin when she is threatened with rape (Benjamin 1983:236–42, 301–2). In the city, a virgin must cry out or be considered an accomplice in her assailant's bid to take over the household to which she is promised. In the country she is exonerated from any complicity. "Cry out" is not only a call for help, but also a lawsuit, which begins when the plaintiff stands and cries out for justice at the threshing floor of the village or the gate of the city (2 Sam 15:1–6).

Likewise, rape in the world of the Bible was not simply an act of sexual violence, but a political challenge to the father of a household. People continue to be scandalized by the sex and violence in the Bible. Stories involving rape or adultery, like those of Shechem and Dinah (Gen 34:1–31), David and Bathsheba (2 Sam 11:1—12:25), or Amnon and Tamar (2 Sam

Teachings of Amen-Em-Het
(Pritchard, *ANET*, 1969:418–19)

The Beginning of the instruction which the majesty of the King of Upper and Lower Egypt: Sehetep-ib-Re; the Son of Re: Amen-em-het, the triumphant, made when he spoke in a message of truth to his son, the All-Lord. He said. . . .

Behold, bloodshed occurred while I was without thee, before the courtiers had heard that I was handing over to thee, before I had sat together with thee. Pray let me order thy affairs, inasmuch as I had not prepared for it, I had not (even) thought of it, my heart had not accepted (the idea of) the slackness of servants.

Had women ever marshaled the battle array? Had contentious people been bred within the house? Had the water which cuts the soil (ever) been opened up, so that poor men were frustrated at their work? No mischance had come up behind me since my birth. Never had there been the like of my reputation as a doer of valiant deeds.

13—14:33), seem almost pornographic. But these stories are not novels or soap operas built entirely around romance where a man sees a woman, is infatuated with her, seduces her, and then marriage or revenge follows. Stories involving sex and violence in the world of the Bible were not fundamentally romantic (Patai 1959:47–49). They are not simply describing how men and women feel for each other or explaining why they hurt each other, but are providing an assessment of the political status of the house-

Execrations against Traitors
(Pritchard, *ANET*, 1969:328–29)

All men, all people. all folk, all males, all eunuchs, all women, and all officials, who may rebel, who may plot, who may fight, who may talk of fighting, or who may talk of rebelling, and every rebel who talks of rebelling—in this entire land.

Ameni shall die, the tutor of Sit-Bastet, the chancellor of Sit-Hat-Hor, (daughter of) Nefru.

Sen-Usert the younger, called Ketu, shall die, the tutor of Sit-Ipi, (daughter of) Sit-Hat-Hor, and tutor of Sit-Ipi, (daughter of) Sit-Ameni, the chancellor of Ii-menet, (daughter of) Sit-Hat-Hor. . . .

Ameni, born to Hetep and son of Sen-Usert, shall die.

holds to which these men and women belong. The households of Shechem (Gen 34), Amnon (2 Sam 13:1–22), and Absalom (2 Sam 16:15–22) use sexual violence as a bid to control the households of Jacob, Absalom, and David.

In Israel as a state, political relationships were marked by competition and violence (Schneider 1971:9–11). As households grew in size through birth and marriage friction developed. They used rape to challenge one another and determine who should control land and children in the state (Barth 1961:34, 39). By raping Dinah, the household of Shechem lays claim to her inheritance in the household of Jacob (Schlegel 1991:724). Shechem is not just infatuated with Dinah when he says: "whatever you say of me I will give" (Gen 34:12). The household of Shechem wants control over the animals which the household of Jacob herds (Gen 34:23), and the household of Jacob wants land to settle and graze (Gen 34:10).

Sexual relationships were a measure of the honor and shame of the households to which these men and women belonged (Peristiany 1965:9; Gilmore 1987:3–4). To test the stability or honor of a household, a man from another household attempted to rape one of its women (Giovannini 1987: 69). The challenge itself was an acknowledgment that the household being pressed was honorable, and therefore worthy of the challenge (Abu-Lughod 1986:89). There was a protocol for the challenge (Bourdieu 1979:106; Abu-Lughod 1986:90). Not every wanton act of sexual violence by any man against any woman in ancient Israel qualified as a challenge to the honor of a household (Brandes 1987:126; Zeid 1966:246). When rape met these qualifications it was not only an act of sexual violence but also a hostile takeover bid. The assailant asserted the right of his household to the resources of another. If a household could not protect its women, then it was declared insolvent or shamed and unable to fulfill its responsibilities to the community as a whole (Giovannini 1987:68). Like war, rape was a violent social process for redistributing the limited goods which a society possessed so that it would not be destroyed by the weakness of a single household. The Bible regularly identifies such procedures for social realignment with the formula "so you shall purge the evil from Israel" (Deut 22:22).

Rape as a Political Maneuver

For the challenge protocol to be set in motion the woman in the household targeted for takeover must either be married like Rizpah (2 Sam 3:6–11), Michal (2 Sam 3:12–16), Bathsheba, David's concubines (2 Sam 16:21–22), and Abishag (1 Kgs 2:12–25), or marriageable like Dinah and Tamar. The woman could not, for example, be a widow or a child. Honor and shame were not gender specific, but more than any other members, the women of a household were living symbols of its honor. They were a human portfolio (Schneider 1971:2). Married women or wives were a measure of the fixed assets of a household; marriageable women or virgins measured its potential for growth.

The virginity of a bride was indicative that the household of her father was stable, so that the covenant between her household and the household of her husband would be productive. Her fertility represented the fertility of their covenant. It was a marriage that would produce land and children for both households.

The virginity of a state wife indicated the potential of the stipulations stated in the covenant between her state and the state of her husband to enrich the land and children of both. These women were not things or possessions; they were the incarnation of the status of their households (Zeid 1966:247; Schlegel 1991:727). Consequently, Bathsheba, as a wife, is an official representative of the household of Uriah (2 Sam 11:3); Tamar, as a virgin, is an official representative of the household of Absalom (2 Sam 13:2, 18).

The man needed to be the recognized head or at least a representative of the household. He had to be a son or a prince, a man who would be monarch; the action could not be taken by just any male. To force David to name him heir, Amnon rapes Tamar hoping that his actions will assure him the right of becoming monarch. Similarly, to lay claim to the throne they desire to usurp, Abner asks for Rizpah and Adonijah asks for Abishag. Although neither man consummates his sexual advance, simply asking is equivalent to the act.

The rape must take place in the context of some activity connected with fertility such as harvesting (Gen 34:1–2; Judg 21:17–23), sheep-shearing (2 Sam 13:23–28), eating (2 Sam 13:5–6), or menstruating (2 Sam 11:4). Otherwise, it was treated like any other crime (Deut 22:23–27). The basis for this criterion was the concern over a household's ability to supply food and children to its members. Tying the aggressive act to an event associated with fertility clearly identified the intention of the aggressor.

The household of the assailant became the legal guardian for the shamed household, while negotiations to realign its resources and responsibilities took place (Gen 34:4–24; 2 Sam 11:6–26; 13:15–22). Reigning monarchs played no direct role in the competition between households for political power in the state (Van Seters 1987:122). Their inaction in stories of sexual violence is not simply due to weakness (Ridout 1974:77; Flanagan 1988:261–72). If monarchs expected to retain their position and increase their power as rulers of all Israel, they had to remain neutral in power struggles between its households (Frick 1985:79–80). Removing monarchs from active participation in political challenges also guaranteed that a strong heir would emerge.

The steps which a shamed household followed to reestablish its honor were parallel to the protocol followed to challenge it. A prince or son of the shamed household assassinated a prince or son of the household which had taken over his household. The prince or son had to carry out the assassination while the prince who attacked his household was exercising the power which he had seized (Hoftijzer 1970:58–60). In this way justice and the restoration of honor were matched with attention to place and the symbols of authority.

The Virgin in the Story of Amnon and
Tamar (2 Sam 13:1—14:33)

The story of Amnon and Tamar (2 Sam 13:1—14:33) is an important episode from the stories of David's successor (2 Sam 9—20; 1 Kgs 1—2) in Samuel–Kings. These stories describe the unsuccessful campaigns of Amnon, Absalom, and Adonijah to take over the state. Amnon's strategy against David in the story of Amnon and Tamar is modeled on David's strategy against Uriah in the story of David and Bathsheba (2 Sam 11:2–27). Just as David challenges Uriah's authority as father of a household by sexually abusing Bathsheba, Amnon challenges David by sexually abusing Tamar (Gilmore 1987:3; Gunn 1978:98–100).

Although most translations describe Amnon's ambitions with emotional and romantic language, his actions are political, not simply personal or moral. When he "falls in love" with Tamar, and is so tormented that he "makes himself ill" because of her, Amnon is not just dealing with unrequited love, but political ambition. He is a man who would be king (Pitt-Rivers 1977:78; Davis 1973:160; Gilmore 1987:8).

Amnon is the sole and tragic protagonist. He has no allies and he fails to become king. Every other character in the story, in some way, opposes Amnon. Absalom competes with him to become David's successor. David refuses to designate him heir and allow him to marry Tamar (Gunn 1978: 99). Tamar refuses to support his bid for power. Even Jonadab, whom Amnon considers to be wise and his friend, betrays him. The advice of Jonadab is flawed and his loyalties are divided (Campbell and Flanagan 1990:157; pace McCarter 1984:321; Smith 1990:28). His plan fails, and Jonadab's words to David following Absalom's assassination of Amnon indicate that he supported Absalom all along (2 Sam 13:32–33). But the plot turns on the actions of Amnon and the reactions of Tamar the virgin who defends the household of Absalom with her life.

Amnon launches his campaign for the throne by asking David to assign Tamar to feed him. He is not simply asking for some tender loving care while he is not feeling well. Amnon's request implies that he is fearful of being slowly poisoned and needs Tamar to supervise his kitchen to prevent it from happening again (Ford 1985:381–83; Heaps 1969:17). Tamar belongs to the household of Absalom, Amnon's competitor. Therefore, Amnon's request is not only a risk, it is a challenge. Only the household of Absalom would have made this attempt on his life, so Amnon asks David to make it directly responsible for his safety. Tamar not only serves the probation on which David places the household of Absalom, she is also a hostage on whom Amnon can take revenge if Absalom threatens his life again.

Food plays a literary as well as political role in the story. The story of Amnon begins when he asks for food and ends when he is murdered eating

at the table of Absalom (2 Sam 13:23–29). Storytellers want their audiences
to understand that Amnon, who could neither feed nor protect himself,
should not have become a monarch who must feed and protect the state.

Tamar accepts the task which David the monarch assigns her. The bread
(תלבב, t͏ᵉlabbēḇ; 2 Sam. 13:8) which Tamar prepares says more about the
relationship between the people who eat it together than about its nutri-
tional or medicinal value. The language is both sexual and political (Hackett
1992:93). Tamar and the bread she bakes are samples of the children and
the land which the household of Absalom contribute to the state. By asking
her to prepare this bread for him, Amnon is inviting Tamar to commit
Absalom's resources to his campaign to become monarch in David's place
(Johnson and Earle 1987:208–9).

Having successfully manipulated David to order Tamar to cook for him,
Amnon then orders her directly to have intercourse with him. By eating
and having intercourse together, Amnon and Tamar will ratify an alliance
between their households against David.

Tamar's response to Amnon's ultimatum was quite proper and demonstrates that she is the wise one in this household (Hagan 1979:310): "No,
my brother, do not force me; for such a thing is not done in Israel; do not
do this wanton folly" (2 Sam 13:12). Tamar does not reject their union, only
their union without proper arrangements being made (Pitt-Rivers 1977:165).
Amnon acts contrary to the manners and customs by which his people are
identified (McCarter 1984:322; Gen 20:9; 29:26). Consequently, Tamar accuses him of acting like the fool.

In both the Teachings of Amen-em-ope and Proverbs (Prov 15: 5), for
example, the wise act with deliberation. Fools, on the other hand, are
impulsive. The wise know when to talk and when to listen (Arabic: 'aqal).
Fools are hot-tempered because they let passion run or ruin their lives
(Matthews and Benjamin 1991b:194; Abu-Lughod 1986:90). Tamar assures
Amnon that by following the proper protocol and maintaining social customs, David would arrange the marriage, and thus prevent their being
labeled fools or traitors (2 Sam 13:13).

Tamar's defense also includes a full statement of the legal consequences
of Amnon's suggestion on both of them: "As for me, where could I carry
my shame? And as for you, you would be as one of the wanton fools in
Israel" (2 Sam 13:13; Judg 19:22). If she obeys Amnon, she will shame her

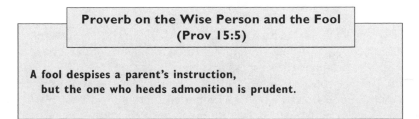

**Proverb on the Wise Person and the Fool
(Prov 15:5)**

A fool despises a parent's instruction,
  but the one who heeds admonition is prudent.

household by depriving it of the opportunity to arrange a marriage for her (Bird 1989:77; Gottlieb 1989:63).

Although Tamar and Amnon address each other as "brother" and "sister," the titles may not indicate that they have two or even one parent in common. Titles which in English are used almost exclusively for people related by blood kinship, in the world of the Bible regularly identify people related by a variety of other relationships. For example, covenant partners in Genesis call each other "father," "son," and "brother." And lovers in the Song of Solomon call each other "brother" and "sister" (Cant 8:18). The characters in the story of Tamar and Amnon are not just solitary figures, they are leading politicians. And their actions do not just reflect personal passion or pain, but distinct strategies in a conscious political campaign.

But even if Tamar and Amnon do have a common parent, the issue in the story is power, not incest (*pace* Smith 1990:24–25, 35). Endogamous marriages between blood relatives were the most common kind of marriage in the biblical world (Murphy and Kasdan 1968:186; Musil 1928:137–40; Cohen 1965:71–75, 121; Daube 1947:77–79; de Vaux 1961:19–20). The marriage of Abraham and Sarah, for example, is endogamous. Like Tamar and Amnon, they are half-brother and sister (Gen 20:12). By contrast, Leviticus and Deuteronomy explicitly forbid endogamous marriages (Lev 18:9, 11; Deut 27:9, 22). It is still not clear when exogamous marriages replaced endogamous marriages in ancient Israel. Therefore, the laws in Leviticus and Deuteronomy may not have been in effect when this telling of the story of Amnon and Tamar became popular (McCarter 1984:323). But even if endogamous marriages were prohibited in general, state marriages were often exempt (Hackett 1992:94).

Amnon ignores Tamar's refusal and rapes her. By raping Tamar, Amnon lays claim to the power, wealth, goods, and service which she represents, and issues a political challenge to David. By forcing her to have sexual relations with him, Amnon breaches a fundamental canon on which ancient Near Eastern society operates (Phillips 1975:241). Honor demands that every member of a household always act with altruism and generosity (Pitt-Rivers 1975:90). Amnon's ultimatum is self-serving. He asks Tamar to violate this fundamental principle to satisfy his sexual desires and to demonstrate his supremacy over the household of Absalom. There is no sense of reciprocity in this suggestion, only personal gratification and political aggrandizement, attainable because of his superior social and physical strength (Frymer-Kensky 1989:98).

Having shamed Tamar, Amnon dismisses her using the legal term for divorce (שלח, *šālaḥ*; McCarter 1984:324; Smith 1990:37). Tamar is sent back to her household in shame to demonstrate that it no longer has status in the state. She becomes the process server.

Again Tamar protests, saying "No, my brother; for this wrong in sending me away is greater than the other which you did to me" (2 Sam 13:16). Once a household is challenged, it is entitled to redeem its honor. In Genesis,

> ### Middle Assyrian Law, article 55
> ### (authors' translation)
>
> If a virgin, who is the daughter of a citizen, who is living in her father's house, who is not engaged to be married, and who is not collateral for any of her father's debts, is kidnapped and raped by another citizen, either in the city, in the country, in the street at night, in a granary or at a city festival, then her father must kidnap and rape the wife of her assailant.
>
> If the assailant has no wife, then the father may give his daughter to her assailant in marriage, and the assailant must pay the bride price and marry her without the opportunity for divorce.
>
> If the father does not wish to marry his daughter to her assailant, then he can keep the bride price and marry his daughter to whomever he wishes.

when the heir of Shechem rapes Dinah, the household of Jacob is allowed to regain its honor by negotiating a covenant with the state (Gen 34:3–4, 8–12; Exod 22:16; MAL 55). Tamar demands the same right for the household of Absalom. Her household has been shamed, but it should not be politically destroyed.

Amnon is unrelenting and refuses to offer either David or Absalom any further opportunity to negotiate with him. Tamar tears her clothes to mourn the honor of Absalom's household (2 Sam 13:19). Tamar, who was the physical symbol of the fertility or honor of the household, now becomes the physical symbol of its infertility or shame (Gen 37:29–35; 39:11–15).

Strangely, David and Absalom further abuse Tamar by refusing to let her cry out. Absalom orders her to be still. He does not answer Amnon's challenge (Hackett 1992:94). The household of Absalom is shamed in Israel. It is powerless. Likewise, David who orders Tamar into harm's way, not only fails to protect her in the household of Amnon, but also does not punish Amnon (Van Seters 1987:53; Trible 1984:422). In fact, David, provisionally confirms or "loves" Amnon as his heir or "firstborn" (2 Sam 13:21). Of all the antagonists who block Amnon's efforts to overthrow David, only Tamar has honor. She serves both David and Amnon obediently. She negotiates unsuccessfully with Amnon both when he threatens her and after he rapes her. She prepares to cry out but is silenced by Absalom. Without witnesses to the assault, and without the opportunity to indict David publicly for failing to protect her, she is a tragic character abused by David, Amnon, and Absalom. Nonetheless, like Uriah she forfeits with honor. Tamar will never regain her status of virgin, nor become the mother of a household. Instead she must spend her days in domestic captivity, a pawn of a much larger political game.

Only after waiting two years does Absalom restore the honor of his household by assassinating Amnon while he is eating at the sheep-shearing (Abu-Lughod 1986:65–66). In addition, by assassinating Amnon, Absalom also makes his own bid to be David's heir and invites the monarch's other sons to endorse him (2 Sam 13:29).

Today sexual behavior is often the only measure of virtue. In the world of the Bible, however, it was social justice which distinguished the saint from the sinner. The Hebrews were no less sensitive to crimes of sexual violence than readers of the Bible today. But the Bible is seldom enthralled with fantasies of sex and violence. In the story of Amnon and Tamar, storytellers do more than voice their outrage against rape. They struggle with questions of justice. They want their audiences to think about how to use power to feed and protect the people.

14

The Priest

In Israel as a state, farmers and herders continued to work the land, but it was the priest (כהן, *kōhēn*) and the Levite (לוי, *lēwî*) who collected the produce from their fields and herds as sacrifices (זבח, *zebaḥ*) or taxes (Wellhausen 1973:121–51; Albright 1968:109, 204–5). The priest was a state official with important economic or financial responsibilities, especially at harvest time. Harvest time was a threshold which marked the end of one growing and herding season and the beginning of another. Priests offered sacrifices marking both the end of the harvest and the beginning of the next planting season. During the first days of a harvest festival, priests determined how much produce could be used by the households which produced it and how much was to be collected by the state. Then they supervised the processing of the sacrifices so that they could be stored in sanctuaries until the beginning of the next agricultural season or until the monarch redistributed them to state workers and soldiers. During the last days of a harvest festival, households borrowed from their sanctuary treasury to pay for animals and seed. Priests set down the conditions for the loans and supervised the transfer of goods from the treasury to the households.

The majority of priests in the state were involved with labeling and collecting sacrifices (1 Chron 23:2–5, 26–32). But there were other distinct categories of priests as well (Levine 1989:xxxiv; Kuhrt 1990:153). There were priests who supervised building funds (2 Chron 24:5–12; 34:9–10; Neh 10:37), and priests who managed estates of land which provided income for the sanctuary (Josh 21:13–19). There were also Levites who served as musicians and singers (1 Chron 15:16–24; 16:4–6) and gatekeepers (1 Chron 9:21–27; 15:23; 16:42). These priests, while not intimately involved in the principal ceremonies of the sanctuary, would have been knowledgeable of them and may well have celebrated rituals and prayers associated with the carrying out of their duties. Priests in the Babylonian sanctuaries performed similar duties (Kuhrt 1990:151). The practical needs of the sanctuary would have been supported by priests who were cooks, janitors, herders, woodcutters, and craftsmen (Cody 1969:78–79).

Priests as State Officials

Today, the separation of church and state in western democracies like the United States and Canada makes it difficult to imagine priests, pastors, or rabbis as state officials. Now they are spiritual leaders, teachers, and counselors. Likewise, to think of tax collectors or bankers as priests seems sacrilegious. But in the world of the Bible there was no separation of church and state. Religion pervaded every activity of daily life, even banking and tax collecting.

The sacredness of banking and tax collecting in the world of the Bible was rooted in an understanding that humans only used or rented land which the divine assembly owned. Even monarchs did not own the land within the borders of their states, they simply managed it. Monarchs were stewards, not landlords. Therefore, no household thought the land belonged to it or that it could do whatever it wanted with the land. Yahweh was the only landlord in Israel; the land of Israel was to be used only as Yahweh prescribed, and only with a commitment to offer Yahweh sacrifices as a commission or tithes for its use (Tylor 1891; Hubert and Mauss 1964). Israel delegated priests to see that the state met these two requirements of correct use and compensation. Consequently, it is priests in the Bible who collect Yahweh's portion at harvest and shearing time, who instruct the people in the correct use of Yahweh's land.

Sacrifices as Taxes and Loans

Today, the rituals described in Leviticus and Numbers are not easy to understand and appreciate. But then it would be difficult to imagine how much an anthropologist, two thousand years from now, could understand about how we redistribute wealth in the United States with only a loan application form or an Internal Revenue Service tax form as evidence. But in the world of the Bible, the rituals in Leviticus and Numbers played a critical role (Anderson 1992:870–86; Anderson 1987). Priests used these rituals to transport goods both from the sanctuary treasury of the divine assembly to the households of Israel and from the households of Israel to the sanctuary treasury. Sacrifice was the central means of revenue collection in the world of the Bible (Anderson 1987:78). The terms employed for sacrifices in the Bible, for example, and those which appear in tax records, are remarkably similar (Levine 1989:xxiii). For instance, the word for a grain sacrifice (מנחה, minḥâh) is the same as the word for a tax collected by a monarch (2 Sam 8:2–6; 1 Kgs 5:1 MT [ET 4:20]; 2 Kgs 8:8–9; 17:3–4). Similarly, the word for the daily sacrifice (תמיד, tāmîd) also means the regular rations or allocations granted by monarchs to their retainers (2 Sam 9:7; 2 Kgs 25:29–30; Jer 52:33).

Protocol for Priests

In the world of the Bible, the priest:

- rules which households in the state have honor or legal standing, and, on the basis of their record of tax payment, which households are shamed or ineligible for benefits;
- assesses the productivity of the fields and herds of the households from the grain and animals they bring to the sanctuary;
- collects sacrifices or taxes;
- offers or processes the sacrifices so that they can be stored;
- deposits sacrifices at the sanctuary treasury until the monarch redistributes them to workers and soldiers at home, or in trade abroad.

The redistribution of goods was not the only function of sacrifice in the world of the Bible. Serious study has been made of the extent to which sacrifice was an antidote for violence. Traditional societies may have prevented the outbreak of mayhem by a collective participation in killing a surrogate or victim (Girard 1977:8, 79–80, 92; Pattison 1991:138). Killing animals may have helped humans refrain from killing one another. Sacrifice channeled violence by reenacting the creation of the world. Many creation stories in the world of the Bible describe the work of creating a world or cosmos as a struggle or battle between the Creator and Chaos. The Creator cuts Chaos into parts and uses them to build a world. By putting these parts in place, the Creator turns Chaos into Cosmos (Matthews and Benjamin 1991b:12–13). Similarly, the priest cut the victim into parts and then distributed them in a carefully prescribed order, thus reaffirming the social order of the state. Sacrifice acknowledged and affirmed the place of each official and household in the state. This, in turn, reduced violence and promoted public generosity, reminding them of the member of the divine assembly and their own ancestors whose blood was shed that they might live.

Sacrifices had to be made carefully, or they would destroy the fertility of Israel's farms and herds rather than enrich them. They were not just offered impulsively and without planning. Consequently, anthropologists have made a sustained effort to reconstruct the protocol (Hubert and Mauss 1964; Evans-Pritchard 1965:70–71).

At harvest and shearing time, each household sent representatives to the sanctuary. Before allowing them to enter, priests purified these representatives by reviewing the status of their household in the state. Priests functioned as diagnosticians. It was their task to determine the ritual purity of households. The state authorized priests to label lepers, eunuchs, women, and resident aliens. Priests also maintained the purity of the sanctuary, purging it through sacrifice when some member of the state, including themselves, contaminated it with some offense (Lev 20:3; Num 19:20; Milgrom 1976:392; 1992).

Some priests used divination to certify the eligibility of a household. When the representatives of the household came before the priest, they asked a question to which the answer "yes" or "no" could be given (Exod 28:30; Num 27:21; 1 Sam 14:41; 28:6; Ezra 2:63). The priest divined the answer by throwing a kind of dice (אורים, 'ûrîm; תֻּמִּים, tummîm). A "yes" indicated the household was in good standing, a "no" that it was not. Other priests interrogated the representatives of the household (תּוֹרה, tôrâh) to certify their eligibility (Ps 15:1–5). If a household was in good standing, its representatives were allowed to enter. If the priests labeled their household with shame, however, they were not. The assets of a household labeled with shame were frozen until it paid its debts to the state with a reparation sacrifice (אשם, 'āšām), and the priest restored its label of honor with a purification sacrifice (חטאת, ḥaṭṭā't).

The sanctuary into which priests admitted the representatives was an architectural compass by which every household in the state could orient itself. A sanctuary marked a geographical point in the state where the sacred space (מקדּשׁ, miqdāš) of the divine plane and the profane space of the human plane intersected (Eliade 1959:20–65). It had specific limits, comprising a series of zones which became increasingly more sacred as one neared the center (Meyers 1992:355–58). Each of these zones was related horizontally to those to its left and right and in front and behind it. They all were also related vertically to the heavens above it and the underworld beneath it as well (Durand 1989:120). Each architectural zone of the sanctuary had corresponding sacrifices which labeled those households eligible to enter and which could be celebrated in each zone's particular realm of sacred

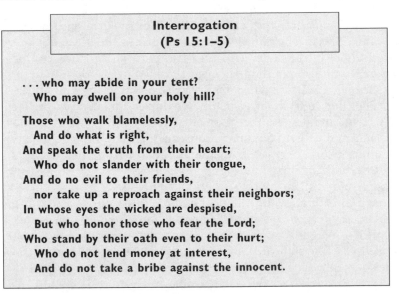

**Interrogation
(Ps 15:1–5)**

. . . who may abide in your tent?
   Who may dwell on your holy hill?

Those who walk blamelessly,
   And do what is right,
And speak the truth from their heart;
   Who do not slander with their tongue,
And do no evil to their friends,
   nor take up a reproach against their neighbors;
In whose eyes the wicked are despised,
   But who honor those who fear the Lord;
Who stand by their oath even to their hurt;
   Who do not lend money at interest,
   And do not take a bribe against the innocent.

space (Detienne 1989:4). Within these set limits, priests orchestrated the performance of all sacrificial rituals for each type of sacrifice—sacrifices of thanksgiving, expiation, or the purgation of ritual impurity.

In the world of the Bible, the temple was not simply the house of God. It was a national treasury and warehouse for goods collected as sacrifices or taxes from the households when they came up to the sanctuary at pilgrimage times. These goods and monies were stored in the temple until they were redistributed (Milgrom 1990:36), generally as rations for state officials and soldiers or in payment for state building projects.

Once the priests had certified the eligibility of the household, they assessed its net worth on the basis of the goods brought by its representatives to the sanctuary. The household was required to send the best samples of its fields and herds. Households could not send crippled or blind animals, nor grain riddled with weevils, nor grapes spotted with blight, in an effort to reduce the value of their appraisal and the amount their produce would be taxed.

Like other specialists, priests reserved certain activities for themselves. This insured their authority as state officials and also provided a legal basis for protecting their portion of the sacrifice and their right to oversee the sacrifice (Lev 17:8–9; Deut 17:12). Leviticus (Lev 17:10–12), for example, prohibits eating meat with blood. The blood must be shed upon the altar. This suggests an expiation of the guilt for taking the life of the animal, sanctioned by Yahweh in Genesis (Gen 9:3), but it also required that the animal be brought to the priests (Pattison 1991:138). A requirement such as this gave the priests an opportunity to examine the animal and to judge its suitability as a sacrifice. It also insured that the household making the sacrifice did not violate the law against eating blood, nor withhold any portion of the animal which would be assigned to Yahweh or the priests. After 700 BCE, all the priests in Judah were stationed at the Temple in Jerusalem, making it difficult for every household in Judah to reach it. Therefore, while still prohibiting the eating of blood, Deuteronomy did allow households simply to drain the blood on the ground like water without priestly supervision (Deut 12:16–24; 15:23; Milgrom 1971:103, n. 32; Levine 1989:116).

The amount which the priest assessed was, by no means, full payment for the blessings of land and children which Yahweh bestowed on the household. Yahweh's blessings were priceless; Israel's sacrifices were merely tokens. The contrast between the blessings of Yahweh and the sacrifices of Israel emphasized the covenant relationship between Yahweh and Israel. Yahweh and the blessings of land and children were great, while Israel and its sacrifices were small (Valeri 1985:66). Yahweh was the father or sovereign covenant partner, Israel the son or vassal partner.

To Sacrifice is to Process, Not to Destroy

When the priests and the household had agreed on what amount of its harvest would be turned over to the state, the priests began the sacrifice.

In harvest rituals the sacrifice was cooked. The stylized actions of the priest during a sacrifice mirrored the actions of the men and women of the household, who slaughtered and roasted animals or parched and seasoned grain. Just as the mother of a household prepared meals for the members of her household, the priest prepared sacrifices for Yahweh.

In the world of the Bible, however, sacrifices were not simply "food for the gods" (Oppenheim 1977:183–98). Not even the tellers of the Gilgamesh story in Mesopotamia thought that the divine assembly would starve to death unless humans fed them (Tigay 1982:224–28, 293–96). Before the bulk of the sacrifices prepared by the priests was placed in storage, they gave the representatives of the household a small portion to eat together at the sanctuary during the days of the festival (1 Sam 1:4–5; McCarter 1980a:52). Some sacrifices had to be eaten on the day of the sacrifice, while others could be extended over at least two days (Lev 7:15–18). The meal was a communion in which Yahweh and the representatives of the household ate together from the fruit of a divine land and the work of human hands (Smith 1889). Without the collaboration represented by the meals which households shared with Yahweh at the sanctuary, the living cosmos would sink back into the lifeless chaos which the opening episode of the stories of Adam and Eve describe. There would be "no plant of the field . . . and no herb . . . for the Lord God had not caused it to rain . . . and there was no one to till the ground" (Gen 2:4–5). If Yahweh did not send the rain, and the men and women of Israel did not work the land, neither would survive.

There is a long-standing tradition of translation and interpretation which considers sacrifice in the world of the Bible as a destruction of farm produce. The "burnt offering" (עלה, 'ōlâh), the "peace offering" (שלמים, šᵉlāmîm), the "grain offering" (מנחה, minḥâh), the "purification offering" (חטאת, ḥaṭṭā'ṯ), and the "reparation offering" (אשם, 'āšām) are consistently described as annihilated. But the wholesale destruction of produce contradicts the strong sense of limited goods that predominated in Mediterranean cultures. For these cultures, natural resources were limited. Once consumed or destroyed they were irreplaceable. And even with their surplus economies it is unlikely that states could afford, much less value, the regular loss of a percentage of their gross national product. Occasionally, laws in Leviticus and Numbers require a holocaust like the cereal sacrifice (Lev 6:23), where total destruction is demanded. But generally, they stipulate that only a portion of a sacrifice be consigned to the flames of the altar (Lev 2:9; 5:13; 7:31–34; Num 5:9–10, 18:25–32; Deut 18:3). In general, it would be better to understand sacrifice in Leviticus and Numbers as processing farm produce to be stored and redistributed rather than destroying it. At sanctuaries throughout Israel, priests slaughtered and butchered livestock, decanted wine and olive oil, and parched grain.

In the closing days of the harvest festival, priests redistributed some of the produce which they had collected in the form of loans. Before they returned to their villages, households needed goods to prepare for the next

---

Story of Gilgamesh
(Matthews & Benjamin 1991b:38)

The ark ran aground on Mount Nisir. It remained grounded for six days and, then, on the seventh day I released a dove. It flew back and forth, but came back without finding a place to rest. Then I released a swallow, but it also returned without finding a place to rest. Finally, I released a raven. Because the flood waters had begun to subside, the raven fed, circled, cawed and flew away. Immediately, I released the rest of the creatures from the ark and they scattered to the four winds.

I prepared a sacrifice,
 I poured a libation on the mountaintop.
I set out my sacred vessels,
 I kindled a sacred fire of reed, cedar and myrtle.
The Gods smelled the aroma,
 They swarmed like flies around the sacrifice.

---

season of herding and planting. The sacrifices which approved the loans and transferred goods from the sanctuary treasury to the household ceremonially exhibited the techniques which farmers and herders were expected to follow in working the land. These sacrifices were exit rituals, commissioning the farmers and herders of Israel to return to their villages and work Yahweh's land (Hubert and Mauss 1964:33–35; de Heusch 1985:5–6).

Besides providing loans to its farmers and herders, the resources of the sanctuary treasury also supported state officials like the priests, who received clothing (Exodus 28), food (Deut 18:1–8), and places to live (Josh 21:1–42). Priests provided an important service to the state, but they could not provide for themselves and still do their primary job. The state paid them for their services from the sanctuary treasury (Milgrom 1970:67, n. 246). In Ugarit, priests, tradespeople, soldiers, and other state officials (Ugaritic: *bnš mlk*) were entitled to a portion of the sacrifice (Anderson 1987:79). In Israel the major portions of the sacrifice, minus the head and fat or a handful of fine flour and oil, were reserved for the use of the priests, their slaves, and Nazirites completing their period of dedication (Lev 2:2–3; 5:12–13; 6:2; 22:11; Num 5:26; 6:19).

In addition to the needs of the priests, other portions of the sacrificial meat and grain would have been processed and redistributed in emergencies in much the same way that Joseph in Genesis (Gen 41:55–57) administered the grain silos of the pharaoh (Anderson 1987:82). This use of the sanctuary as a storehouse of surplus goods and produce is also well-attested in New Kingdom Egypt, serving as a subdepartment of the state, not an independent entity (Janssen 1979).

> ### Stories of Joseph
> ### (Gen 41:46–57)
>
> Joseph was thirty years old when he entered the service of Pharaoh king of Egypt. And Joseph went out from the presence of Pharaoh, and went through all the land of Egypt. During the seven plenteous years the earth produced abundantly. He gathered up all the food of the seven years when there was plenty in the land of Egypt, and stored up food in the cities; he stored up in every city the food from the fields around it. . . .
>
> The seven years of plenty that prevailed in the land of Egypt came to an end; and the seven years of famine began to come. . . . And since the famine had spread over all the land, Joseph opened all the storehouses, and sold to the Egyptians. . . .

Monarchs were interested in the efficient maintenance and operation of sanctuaries because of their function in the state (Kuhrt 1990:154). Sanctuaries were a source of employment and extra income for many. They distributed food and manufactured items from raw materials stored in their treasuries. And finally the daily routine of a sanctuary was a model of the good order which monarchs wished to create in their states. Thus, Jehu solidifies his rule by massacring the worshippers of Ba'al and destroying their sanctuaries (2 Kgs 10:18–28). Similarly, Hezekiah is first credited with cleansing the Temple of foreign influence and foreign gods (2 Kgs 18:3–4). And Josiah in Samuel–Kings begins his public administration by ordering renovation of the Temple in Jerusalem and by appointing various officials to oversee the work (2 Kgs 22:3–7).

There is also some reason for concern by monarchs regarding the potential power and influence exercised by the priests. There were occasions in the ancient Near East when priests contributed to the overthrow of a reigning monarch. For example, the capture of Babylon and its ruler Nabonidus by the Persian forces of Cyrus was aided by the priests of Marduk (Kuhrt 1990:146–50). Similarly, Athaliah's rule of Judah was ended by the actions of Jehoiada the priest, who proclaimed Joash, the seven-year-old son of Joram, as monarch and staged what amounted to a political coup (2 Kgs 11:4–20). In the world of the Bible, improper worship practices were regularly cited as justification for political takeovers, which always needed the cooperation of the priests to succeed (Matthews and Benjamin 1991b:148; 2 Kgs 8:18, 26–27; 9:18).

Temple treasuries, because of their store of food and other necessary items, could also become targets of rapacious officials and kings. For instance, in 169 BCE, Antiochus IV of Syria confiscated the Temple treasury as a fine for Judah's refusal to pay its taxes (1 Macc 1:20–24; Levine

1988:182). He looted 1,800 talents from the temple in Jerusalem and despoiled the sacred vessels and sacrifices within its precincts in order to fund his army and his regime (1 Macc 1:20–24; 2 Macc 5:15–20). Antiochus was not just raiding temples when he stripped the Jerusalem Temple of its wealth, he was robbing banks. Similarly, in earlier periods the Egyptians, Assyrians, and Babylonians looted the Jerusalem Temple of its valuables (1 Kgs 14:25–26; Dan 5:2–4), and when Sennacharib of Assyria laid siege to Jerusalem in 701 BCE, Hezekiah used the Temple treasury to ransom the city (2 Kgs 18:13–16).

The Priest in the Story of Hannah (1 Sam 1:1—2:11)

The story of Hannah in Samuel–Kings (1 Sam 1:1—2:11) shows Eli the priest exercising his responsibility to label those who may and may not enter the sanctuary. Eli and his sons are priests at the sanctuary of Shiloh (Schley 1989:140–42, 152–54; Noth 1963:390; Cohen 1965:66, n. 19; McCarter 1980a:65–66). Both at the beginning of the story of Hannah and at the end of the trial of Eli and his Sons, Eli is sitting at the gate of Shiloh (1 Sam 1:9; 4:18). As the priest of the gate, he sits at its threshold where he can watch the two courtyards between the gate and the Holy of Holies (1 Chron 9:21–27; 15:23; 16:42). During the day, Eli determines who may enter the sanctuary at Shiloh and watches to make sure no inappropriate acts occur there (Durand 1989:120–21; *pace* Cody 1969:69). During the night, he guards it by sleeping nearby (1 Chron 9:26–27). Thus, his person and his office are associated with his responsibility to maintain order within the sanctuary, and his normal place is at the gate. But before the story ends it will be clear that this priest of the gate cannot tell who should enter the sanctuary from those who should not, and is even powerless to stop the inappropriate activities of his own sons within the sanctuary.

In her story, Hannah the wife is the protagonist and Eli the priest is the antagonist. When the story opens, she is infertile. While her household is busy offering sacrifices at Shiloh, Hannah steps quietly into the courtyard reserved for priests. To avoid being detected, she moves her lips as she prays, but does not make a sound with her voice. Eli sees her and mistakenly exercises his authority as priest of the gate by labeling her a drunkard and expelling her (Lev 10:11; Amos 2:8).

Ironically, the prayer which Eli does not hear is for a child who would abstain from wine and beer throughout his life so that he could serve Yahweh worthily in the courtyard where Hannah is praying (1 Sam 1:11; Num 6:3; Judg 13:4). Priests abstained from drinking wine before performing their duties to insure that they could distinguish between the holy and the unholy (Lev 10:9–10; Ezek 44:21–23). Eli is sober, but still so blind that he cannot tell the holy mother-to-be from a common drunk. Eli lacks perception and is always one step behind unfolding events (1 Sam 3:2–9). Consequently, like the sons of Aaron in Leviticus (Lev 10:1–7), Eli and his sons should be expelled from the sanctuary for sacrilege, and the sentence which Eli tries to impose on Hannah and her son should be imposed on him and his sons instead.

Before she leaves the sanctuary Hannah explains her prayer to Eli and asks him to approve the favor she seeks (Ahlstrom 1979:254). Her prayer plays on her name (Brueggemann 1990:36, n. 7). She tells the priest: Yahweh's "favorite" (חנּה, ḥannâh) child needs a "favor" (חן, ḥēn). Eli agrees, endorsing Hannah's prayer and, at the same time, mitigating his own sentence. He labels her in peace or good standing with the sanctuary, which makes her eligible for Yahweh to grant her prayer for a son (Cohen 1965:63, n. 12; Klein 1983:4–5).

When Hannah gives birth to the great man, Hannah names him "Saul" (שאול, šā'ûl) because he was "the answer to a prayer" (שאל, šā'al). Curiously, in the Bible today, Hannah calls him "Samuel," not "Saul." In the world of the Bible, popular leaders were often honored with stories telling of the miraculous events which marked their births. Moses, for example, is a newborn saved from death in the Nile by a daughter of Pharaoh, and Gideon is the only child of a woman who, like Hannah, was infertile. Originally, followers of Saul and Samuel told distinct stories celebrating the birth of each leader in similar ways. But evidently in the protracted struggle between Samuel the prophet and Saul the chief, the supporters of Samuel looted parts of the birth story of Saul to better justify their prophet's claim to the allegiance of Israel. And so now Samuel–Kings explain the name "Samuel" which means "the name of the Lord," as if it were "Saul," which means "the answer to a prayer" (Smith 1929:12–13).

The Priest in the Trial of Eli and his Sons (1 Sam 2:12—4:22)

The trial of Eli and his Sons (1 Sam 2:12—4:22) shows the priest collecting sacrifices. In the trial Yahweh indicts Eli and his sons, Hophni and Phineas, before the divine assembly. Its verdict is subsequently announced at the sanctuary by a prophet. Yahweh accuses the sons of Eli of being fools (בני־בליּעל, bᵉnê bᵉliyyā'al). The same label (בת־בליּעל, baṯ bᵉliyyā'al) which Eli imposed on Hannah is now imposed on him and his sons (1 Sam 1:16).

The sons of Eli are not the only fools in the Bible. The story of the Old Man of Gibeah labels the people who attack his guests as fools (Judg 19:22). The stories of Saul label those who deny his right to be chief as fools (1 Sam

10:27). And the stories of David's rise to power label Nabal a fool for refusing to support David against Saul (1 Sam 25:25).

Hophni and Phineas are fools because they violate their responsibility to collect sacrifices by taking more meat than they are allowed from the pot boiling on the altar (Klein 1983:9; Tsevat 1961:204, n. 78; de Heusch 1985:5). At Shiloh, priests stuck a fork into the pot to draw out their portion "whether it be bad or good" (4QSama; McCarter 1980a:78). By using a fork, the priests at Shiloh did not always receive the prime cuts of meat which were reserved for the priests at other sanctuaries according to stipulations in Leviticus and Deuteronomy (Lev 7:28–36; Deut 18:3; Klein 1983:25; McCarter 1980a:85).

Hophni and Phineas are also fools because they do not wait their turn. Whether the sacrifice was boiled or roasted, priests were required to follow the proper sequence in order for the sacrifice to be effective (Durand 1989: 121). Hophni and Phineas, however, claim their portions before the choice cuts of meat have been removed. Leviticus requires priests to wait until Yahweh's portion of the sacrifice has been set aside (Lev 3:16; 7:23–31; 17:6). Hophni and Phineas take the first part (ראשית, rē'šît) of the sacrifice, which should be reserved for Yahweh (Ezek 20:40; McCarter 1980a:90).

The sacrilege of Hophni and Phineas is compounded by their abuse of power. Instead of allowing each household to present them freely with their portion, they use force to get what they want. They will not compromise, but rather insist on indulging their desires at the expense of Yahweh and the people. Finally, Hophni and Phineas do not just steal meat from the sanctuary treasury occasionally, but every time the households of Israel come to offer sacrifice they abuse their privileges (1 Sam 2:14). They fatten themselves on the choicest parts of every sacrifice (1 Sam 2:29).

Both as the priest of the gate and as the father of the household, Eli places Hophni and Phineas on probation for their repeated extortion of the households of Israel (Matthews and Benjamin 1991b:225). But they ignore him. They do not honor their father or heed his voice (Exod 20:12; Deut 21:18–21). Only when all other legal recourse has been exhausted does Yahweh convene the divine assembly to seek relief from the household of Eli, which neither guards the gate of the sanctuary nor collects and cares for its sacrifice properly.

For its crimes the household of Eli is shamed. Hophni and Phineas are stripped of their position as priests (Jer 33:18; Tsevat 1961:205). Since they despise Yahweh's word they are utterly cut out of the state (Num 15:30–31). For as long as the two men live, the divine assembly forbids them to go up to the altar, to offer incense, and to wear an ephod apron (Klein 1983:26–27). They are no longer entitled to state support, and they are no longer exempt from state labor (Tsevat 1961:193–96; Cohen 1965:90–91; McCarter 1980a:92; Schley 1989:148–51). They lose the privileges which they have abused.

The divine assembly also sentences Eli and his sons to die prematurely (1 Sam 2:27–36; כרת, kārat). They held their own desires above what was due to Yahweh (1 Sam 2:29). This is an intentional offense, one which cannot be atoned (Num 15:22–31). Eli, despite his blindness and other infirmities, is also indicted. He falsely labeled Hannah a fool, and he did not maintain order in the sanctuary of Shiloh (Lev 24:15; Tsevat 1961:203). To die prematurely in the world of the Bible is to die without heirs, and turn your land and children over to legal guardians (Gen 38). The sentence denies Hophni, Phineas, and Eli time to fulfill their role as progenitor and producer and also denies them the chance to reach an age when they will be respected as elders (Tsevat 1961:202). Thus the Sons of Eli not only lose their professional role but also their communal one.

The books of Samuel–Kings use the story of Hannah and the trial of Eli and his Sons to contrast Eli who was a fool with Samuel who was wise (Willis 1971:289–90; Bourke 1954:81–82). Because Samuel was Eli's client, the books of Samuel–Kings want to make it clear that Samuel did not betray his patron. It was the divine assembly which removed Eli and his sons from the office of priest because they did not guard the gate of the sanctuary and collect its sacrifices properly. Samuel took their place in Israel, because he knew how to guard the gate and how to collect sacrifices properly. And as the book of Samuel will go on to tell, it was Samuel who expelled Saul for offering inappropriate sacrifices, and it was Samuel in his role as the gatekeeper who recognized David as the one whom Yahweh anointed to take Saul's place.

15

The Slave

Like the economics of the villages of Israel, the economics of the state of ancient Israel was concerned with land and children. In villages farmers and herders worked the land and midwives delivered the children. But Israel as a state needed more from its land than Hebrew farmers and herders could produce, and more people to work the land than Hebrew midwives could deliver. Therefore, it authorized the priest to manage the land which Hebrew households worked, and to distribute more efficiently the goods which Hebrew households produced. And it used the slave (עֶבֶד, *'ebed*) to work the land which Hebrew farmers and herders could not (Feeley-Harnik 1985:292).

Prisoners of War as Slaves

In the world of the Bible, two continuous sources of slaves were war and debt. States like ancient Israel went to war to conquer land and to take

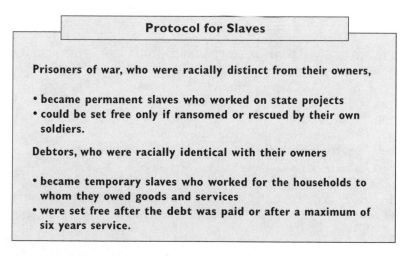

Protocol for Slaves

Prisoners of war, who were racially distinct from their owners,

- became permanent slaves who worked on state projects
- could be set free only if ransomed or rescued by their own soldiers.

Debtors, who were racially identical with their owners

- became temporary slaves who worked for the households to whom they owed goods and services
- were set free after the debt was paid or after a maximum of six years service.

prisoners. War slavery was common throughout the history of Mesopotamia where war between states was frequent. But until 1500 BCE, Egypt relied on its own households to do the bulk of its agricultural and construction work (Gelb 1976:201). Then at the beginning of the New Kingdom, Egypt's armies began to campaign south into Nubia and east into Syria-Palestine bringing home a steady supply of prisoners of war as slaves (Hallo and Simpson 1971:260, 265).

Perpetual slavery was prohibited in the villages of early Israel (Exod 21:2; Deut 15:12; Jer 34:9; Phillips 1984:64, n. 16). The Hebrews were keenly aware of their own heritage. In the world of the Bible, Hebrews (Akkadian: ḫāpiru; עברים, 'ibrîm) were households without land and children who survived as warriors and slaves of the state. The pioneers of early Israel were Hebrews because they had no land and children (Driver 1911:210; Phillips 1984:61; Lemche 1975:138–39; Alt 1966:93–95; Noth 1962:177–80). But then Yahweh blessed them with land and children, and set them free (Akkadian: ḫupšu; hopši).

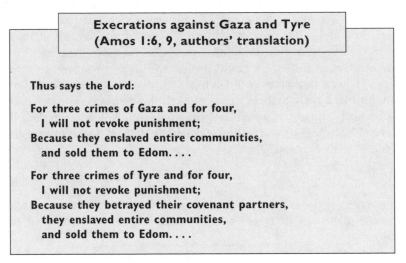

**Execrations against Gaza and Tyre
(Amos 1:6, 9, authors' translation)**

Thus says the Lord:

For three crimes of Gaza and for four,
  I will not revoke punishment;
Because they enslaved entire communities,
  and sold them to Edom. . . .

For three crimes of Tyre and for four,
  I will not revoke punishment;
Because they betrayed their covenant partners,
  they enslaved entire communities,
  and sold them to Edom. . . .

The tribes of early Israel observed their prohibition against slavery by executing most prisoners of war rather than enslaving them. They also destroyed most of the possessions of their captives, and placed their land under interdict. It can certainly be debated whether the violence of killing prisoners of war outright was greater than the violence of enslaving them for life. Nonetheless, the practice did limit the profit motive for war, and so the wars of early Israel were primarily defensive rather than wars of conquest. In Israel as a state, however, slavery became common. Even though slavery in Israel never accounted for the percentage of the labor force that it did in Greece and Rome, the standing army organized by David after 1000 BCE became a source of both land and slaves for the state (van der Ploeg 1972:83; Beavis 1992:38–39).

Most prisoners were racially distinct from their owners, which allowed everyone to easily identify who was a slave and who was free (Lev 25:44–46; Gibson 1990:127–28). The artists who carved records of the pharaohs' victories on Egypt's temple walls carefully portrayed prisoners from each of Egypt's enemies with distinct racial characteristics. Nubian prisoners of war were clearly distinguished, for example, from the Sea Peoples who were prisoners and from the Semitic prisoners of war from Syria-Palestine.

**Teaching on Slaves
(Deut 21:10–14)**

When you go out to war against your enemies, and the Lord your God hands them over to you and you take them captive, suppose you see among the captives a beautiful woman whom you desire and want to marry, and so you bring her home to your house. . . .

[then] . . . she shall shave her head, pare her nails, discard her captive's garb, and shall remain in your house a full month, mourning for her father and mother; after that you may go in to her and be her husband, and she shall be your wife.

But if you are not satisfied with her,

[then] . . . you shall let her go free and not sell her for money. You must not treat her as a slave, since you have dishonored her.

Prisoners of war belonged to the state. Consequently, they became slaves of the state and worked on public projects like palaces, temples, and the farms of the monarch and other officials (Deut 21:10–14; Gelb 1972:83). Prisoners of war provided the state with additional laborers to enhance its infrastructure, expand agricultural production, and compensate for losses due to disease or some other calamity (Ferguson 1990:38, 48, 52).

Few prisoners of war were ransomed or rescued (CH article 32; Matthews 1981b:146–47; Gelb 1973:72–73). Once captured in battle, they became slaves for life. Some slaves, however, earned emancipation because of the services they provided to their owners. A Teaching on Slaves in Deuteronomy (Deut 21:10–14) describes how women taken as prisoners of war can be integrated into the households of Israel, which makes them eligible for marriage. But if they are subsequently divorced, these women cannot be sold as slaves. They must remain free members of society. Similarly, Exodus (Exod 21:7–11) explains that women may be emancipated if their owners fail to treat them with due respect, provide for their needs, or uphold their legal rights. These designated rights include food, clothing, and the sexual rights of the mother of the household. If they are not provided, even when the owner takes another wife, then these women have the right to leave that household free.

Debtors as Slaves

While war was a prolific source of slaves for the state, debt produced slaves for ordinary households as well as for the state. Every household in Israel was entitled to a plot of land (נחלה, *naḥᵃlâh*). This land was the tangible fulfillment of Yahweh's promise: "to you and your descendants I will give this land" (Gen 12:7). Households held title to the land in perpetuity. Legally, land could never be lost or sold. In fact, households easily lost their land and their freedom. Monarchs taxed households into crippling debt. Rich households lent poor households money to pay their taxes, but secured these loans by taking their land and the labor which every member of the household was capable of doing as collateral (Gottwald 1979:769, n. 412; Phillips 1984:55; Levine 1989:179). When households defaulted in repaying their loans, creditors foreclosed on the property and sold the entire household—men, women, and children—as slaves (2 Kgs 4:1; Phillips 1984: 64, n. 16). Legally, creditors were not buying land or selling slaves, just holding the land as collateral and collecting the wages of its owners as interest until the debt was repaid (Lev 25:35–46; 2 Kgs 4:1; Neh 5:1–5).

Debt slaves were racially identical with their owners, but distinguished from them by a label of shame. Because they left their own household to work in the household of their creditors, they were labeled "strangers in the land" (Judg 19:16; Spina 1983:323). Some owners tattooed or pierced the ears of debt slaves in order to make them easily recognizable (Exod 21:6). And some texts describe a distinctive hair style (Akkadian: *abbuttu*) worn by debt slaves which was cut off when they were set free (Harris 1975:333). Nonetheless, Exodus and Deuteronomy reflect an understanding of the reasons for poverty and try to deal with its victims non-violently by protecting the rights of both owners and slaves so that neither would be physically or economically abused (Deut 24:14–15; Fensham 1962:136; Phillips 1984:54). For example, creditors could not charge interest on loans (Exod 22:24 MT [ET v. 25]; Lev 25:35–37; Deut 23:20; Ezek 18:13). They could not accept a millstone as collateral; that would deprive a household of the means of making a living and could subject it to debt slavery (Deut 24:6). And creditors even had to allow their debt slaves to celebrate Israel's festivals with the household they served (Deut 12:18; 16:11–12).

Debt slavery, unlike war slavery, was temporary (Deut 15:12, 17; Phillips 1984:56, 60; Gelb 1972:86). Technically, households in Israel could not borrow more than the members of the household could repay with six years of work, a statute of limitations with the sabbath in mind (Exod 21:2–11; Deut 15:12–18; Phillips 1984:56–58; Lindenberger 1991:482). Households that contracted their members as slaves and clients proved their willingness to

---

Code of Hammurabi, article 117
(Pritchard, *ANET*, 1969:170–71)

If an obligation came due against a seignior and he sold (the services of) his wife, his son, or his daughter, or he has been bound over to service, they shall work (in) the house of their purchaser or obligee for three years, with their freedom reestablished in the fourth year.

---

make good on their debts; they were restored to full political and economic status once the debt was paid (Thompson 1980:610; *pace* Paul 1970:45–46).

Men of a household could be sold as slaves one day at a time to pay a debt. Each day they would take off the clothes or cloak which identified them as free and turn it over to their creditors. Their garments, however threadbare, tied them just as strongly as a sworn contract to the households of their creditors and required them to carry out the agreed upon task. These slaves-for-a-day agreed to become full-fledged slaves if they did not complete the tasks which their creditors set before them. The requirement that the garment be returned during the night as a guard against the evening chill speaks to a society which recognizes those citizens who are on the economic edge (Lev 25:39; van der Ploeg 1972:82). It is also suggestive of a society which is not above violating its own social code and needs to be reminded of its obligations to the community as a whole (Mendelsohn 1949:85 91).

In the trial of Hosiahu from the Yavne-Yam inscription, a slave indicts his creditor for confiscating his cloak for alleged failure to work as con-

---

Trial of Hoshaiahu
(Matthews & Benjamin 1991b:133)

Let my lord the governor pay heed to the words of his servant! Your servant was reaping in Hasar-asam. The work went as usual and your servant completed his reaping and hauling before the others. Despite the fact that your servant had completed his work, Hoshaiahu son of Shobai came and took your servant's garment. All my fellow workers will testify, all those who work in the heat of the day will surely certify that I am not guilty of any breach of contract. Please intercede for me so that my garment will be returned and I will (as always) do my share of the work. The governor should see to it that the garment of your servant is returned and that no revenge be taken against your servant, that he not be fired.

tracted (Matthews and Benjamin 1991b:133). Should it not be returned, he would have no recourse but to sell himself into slavery since the one guard against that status, his garment, had been confiscated (Exod 22:26–27; Deut 24:12–13; Amos 2:8).

Women of a household were sold as slaves more often than men. Mesopotamian sources reveal a large proportion of slaves being female, perhaps reflecting the need for women to perform menial tasks in small households (Harris 1975:333). Women were also sold as wives (Neh 5:5; Turnbaum 1987:545; Phillips 1984:63, n. 15). If the father of a household sold his daughter as a slave the owner could claim her as a wife for himself or his son (Exod 21:7–8; Schwartz 1986:245). If she did not please him she could be redeemed and have her contract voided for a price (Gelb 1972:86; Schwartz 1986:248).

As a condition for a vow or in appreciation for the time a slave had already served, creditors could reduce the actual amount of time due them for a debt. In Jeremiah creditors in Jerusalem freed their slaves as part of a petition to Yahweh to lift the Babylonian siege of the city (Jer 34:8–22). But when, in fact, the siege was lifted they reneged on their oath and placed their debtors back in slavery (Carroll 1986:648–49).

Debt slaves could also voluntarily extend their service. Exodus and Deuteronomy (Exod 21:1–6; Deut 15:12–18) describe the ritual which transformed temporary debt slaves into permanent members of the households which they had served. At the end of the six years of slavery, debt slaves were free to make choices for themselves (Weinfeld 1972:282). Candidates for this change of status set the ritual in motion by making a pledge of allegiance or love for the household of their owners. They renounced their right to go out through the city gate, which meant they could not own land or conduct any other business (CH article 15; Turnbaum 1987:548). The

---

Teaching on Slaves
(Exod 21:1–6)

... When you buy a male Hebrew slave, he shall serve six years, but in the seventh he shall go out a free person without debt. If he comes in single, he shall go out single; if he comes in married, his wife shall go out with him. If his master gives him a wife and she bears him sons or daughters, the wife and her children shall be her master's and he shall go out alone. But if the slave declares, "I love my master, my wife, and my children; I will not go out a free person," then his master shall bring him before God. He shall be brought to the door or the doorpost; and his master shall pierce his ear with an awl; and he shall serve him for life.

significance of the oath of the candidate was similar to that made by Ruth the daughter-in-law in the book of Ruth (Ruth 1:16–17).

In response to candidates' requests, owners brought them to a sanctuary or the doorway to the house so that both the village and the divine assembly could witness the transformation (CH articles 20, 103, 106, 120, 126; Phillips 1984:55–56). Here owners pierced the ears of the candidates with an awl. This final step achieved two aims. It enhanced the significance of the ritual by adding place to action and, like circumcision, it created a distinctive scar (Mendelsohn 1949:49; Matthews 1987:33). A ring or tag of ownership could then be inserted for easy identification of the slave's status (Phillips 1984: 51). Although by this ritual of transformation debt slaves became members of their owner's households, they could still be sold to pay its debts or transferred as part of an inheritance at the death of the owner (CH article 119; Phillips 1984:51; Harris 1975:336).

The Slave in a Story of Abraham and Lot (Gen 13:5—14:24)

The story of Abram and Lot in Genesis (Gen 13:5—14:24) involves both the taking and the freeing of slaves. The state of Sodom defaults on its debts to the state of Elam, which consequently confiscates the land of Sodom and enslaves its people. The household of Lot is taken as prisoners of war to become slaves for Elam, until Abram attacks and delivers them. But in an interesting reversal Abraham, having defeated the armies of Elam, refuses either to enslave the Elamites who are now his prisoners or to take possession of their land.

Abram's riveting Lawrence-of-Arabia character in the story of Abram and Lot is unique among all the other portrayals of him in the Bible. Here, Abram's friends are in danger, so he musters warriors and drives the enemy out of the land. This Abram is powerful, daring, triumphant. In most stories, Abram/Abraham is a gentle herder who cares for his household not with power or wealth but by his wits. The character of Abram is not the only surprise in this story. More than ten percent of all the words here occur rarely or nowhere else in the Bible (Wenham 1987:304). For example, the title "God the Most High" is used only in a few pieces of poetry, and the title "Creator of Heaven and Earth" appears nowhere else (Hamilton 1990:411; Vawter 1986:461–67). Likewise, everywhere else in the Bible the Amorites are Israel's enemies, but here they are Abram's covenant partners. And finally, this story is the only place in the Bible which calls Abram a Hebrew.

If the story of Abram and Lot were the annals of a monarch or a hero story, then the protagonist should be powerful, daring, and triumphant. Great rulers in the ancient Near East developed annals as a public relations tool to celebrate their prowess in war and to remind their people how they protected them from the enemy. The most popular illustrated annals in Egypt, like the Narmer Palette, portrayed pharaohs preparing to crush the heads of their enemies with a war club (Hoffman 1988:42). The same military triumphalism characterizes the annals of the Assyrian emperors from Mesopotamia. Both Tiglath-Pileser III and Sargon II remember their victories with lists of cities conquered, prisoners taken, and plunder seized. If Abram was the ruler of a great state he too may have celebrated his accomplishments in annals like these ancient rulers.

But there are important differences between the story of Abram and Lot and the annals of ancient Near Eastern monarchs. The story does celebrate Abram as a warrior, but as a modest one, and modesty is not characteristic of annals. Technically, Abram does not wage war, he defends Sodom, his covenant partner. And while this story is full of names for verifiable rulers and identifiable geographical locations, there is little of the kind of detail which abounds in the annals of other rulers such as casualty lists and manifests of plunder taken (Sarna 1966:103).

The story of Abram and Lot is an ancestor story which celebrates the household of Abram and Sarai for knowing not only how to make covenants but also how to keep them. It is one of a series reflecting different aspects of the covenant skills of their household. Other stories of Abram and Sarai in Genesis (Gen 11:37—13:4) celebrate Israel's ancestors as negotiators who make covenants with Yahweh their God, Pharaoh their enemy, and with Lot and Melchizedek their friends. This story of Abram and Lot celebrates Abram for fulfilling his covenant with Lot and for making a new covenant with Melchizedek. By placing Abram on the international political stage with the rulers of the most powerful states in Mesopotamia, Syria-Palestine, and Asia Minor (Astour 1966:78), tellers portray him, as storytellers also portray Solomon, as a great ruler (1 Kgs 10:1—11:3). Both Abram and Solomon blessed the states of their time, and these states in turn blessed them (Gen 12:1–3).

Abram and Lot are covenant partners. Lot is not a fool who embarrasses his successful uncle Abram (*pace* Vawter 1977:242; *pace* Coats 1983:142–48). And Lot is not just Abram's foil whose selfishness highlights Abram's generosity when Lot greedily picks the best part of the country, even though his choice turns out to have been disastrous, and his very life depends on the selflessness and loyalty of the uncle he has alienated (*pace* Sarna 1966: 102; *pace* Helyer 1983). Lot's separation from Abram is not the act of a fool who does not realize that only with Abram can he survive. Lot does not separate from Abram, he negotiates a covenant to remain related to Abram. And it is this covenant which allows the household of Lot to survive. Lot is not selfish, he is farsighted.

Although only the history of the conflict, the terms, and the litany are clearly present in the covenant between Abram and Lot (Gen 13:5–18), it still mirrors the characteristic language and content of the genre. The history presents the official background to the conflict, which the covenant now settles. The declaration "No Strife!" announces that Abram and Lot are officially at peace with one another and that they are "kinsmen" (Gen 13:8). Although, the covenant between Abram and Lot no longer preserves the stipulation for a defensive alliance, the story which follows clearly assumes that they establish such an agreement. For example, a foreign army invades Sodom and it sends a message saying: "Come and help me." Abram comes and fights against the enemy of his covenant partner. And finally, once order has been restored, Abram returns to Mamre without staying to exploit the state he delivers. The covenant concludes with blessings, and Abram builds an altar to Yahweh to record and promulgate it.

Consequently, Abram's deliverance of Sodom in chapter 14 may not be as out of place in Genesis as it has often appeared. When Elam's vassals default on their treaty obligations, leading Elam to take reprisals against the Rephaim, Zuzim, Emim, Horites, Amalekites, and Amorites (Gen 14:4–7), Lot is still living at Sodom, and Abram is still at Mamre where preceding stories had left them (Gen 13:12, 18). And unless Abram and Lot make a covenant as they do in chapter 13 (Gen 13:5–18), it would be difficult for storytellers to demonstrate that Abram is an ancestor who keeps his covenants in chapter 14 (Gen 14:1–24).

Some translations give the impression that Elam's covenant partners rebel rather than revolt (מרד, *mārad*). The distinction is important. For example, Americans today refer to the war which began in 1775 as the War of Independence. The British, on the other hand, call it the Rebellion. When a story is told from the perspective of the monarchs it is appropriate to say the slaves rebelled. But the story of Abram and Lot is not told from Elam's perspective. Therefore, Sodom and the household of Lot are fighting for their freedom from slavery to Elam (Hamilton 1990:402). This is Sodom's War of Independence.

Under the terms of its treaty with Elam, Sodom is committed to align itself with Elam's foreign policy and offer logistical and military assistance to Elam's army. The most common declaration of independence in the ancient Near East is defaulting on these obligations to draft soldiers to serve in the sovereign's army and to pay taxes on all crops, herds, raw materials, and manufactured goods. In the ancient Near East every war of independence was a taxpayers' revolt. There was no need to launch a military attack, the first blow was always economic.

In the second episode, Sodom and the other Cities of the Plain prepare to defend themselves against Elam. The armies of Elam rout but do not annihilate Sodom and Gomorrah's army. Their monarchs and some of the soldiers escape (Sarna 1966:108–9). The monarchs of Sodom and Gomorrah do not accidentally fall, nor do they consciously throw themselves into the tar pits to commit suicide (Sarna 1989:10). They crouch down and hide in the tar pits from Elam's soldiers who rush by them in hot pursuit. When Joshua routed the Amorites at Gibeon in Joshua, their monarchs used the same strategy to hide from him in a cave at Makkedah (Josh 10:16). Tellers are wonderfully subtle in their use of language here. They use a word which not only describes the physical position of the monarchs as they crouch down to create a low profile in order to avoid detection by their pursuers, but which also carries the connotation that the monarchs are once again prostrate as vassals before Chedorlaomer, the ruler of Elam (Hamilton 1990:403). Similarly, the armies of Elam do not plunder Sodom wantonly. Destroying Sodom would destroy a rich source of income for Elam. Instead, the armies simply collect their back taxes or exact reparations from Sodom by confiscating the city's grain (אכלם, 'ak^elām) and livestock (רכש, r^ekuš). In addition, Chedorlaomer takes the household of Lot as slaves.

In the climax episode Sodom sends a messenger (פליט, pālîṭ) to Abram. The runner is not simply a survivor of the battle for Sodom, but an official messenger on a diplomatic mission. In the world of the Bible, monarchs carefully maintained corps of messengers to keep them informed of events throughout the state (Meier 1988). Without messengers, monarchs could not make timely decisions and carry out swift responses to a crisis.

Abram responds to the messenger's news by arming the slaves of his household (Wenham 1987:314; Hamilton 1990:406). Abram takes the weapons of his household out of storage, he empties the war chest and draws his own sword (ריק, rîq) to declare war on Elam. The slaves born in his house are the most loyal to Abram since they have not known any other owner (Harris 1975:339).

Abram does not attack Elam at night. He deploys at night and attacks at dawn. Night attacks are possible. Gideon, for example, attacks the Midianites at night (Judg 7:19). However, the story of Gideon in Judges is careful to explain that Gideon's warriors used torches in the darkness. Abram does not. By waiting until nightfall to deploy, Abram prevents the Elamites from knowing an attack is pending and thus from making preparations to defend themselves. This is the same strategy which David used against the Amalekites (1 Sam 30:17; Eph'al 1983:95–96).

After a decisive defeat of Elam, Melchizedek certifies Abram's fulfillment of his covenant with Sodom; and Abram tithes plunder from Elam to the God Most High (עליון, 'elyôn). The appearance of Melchizedek of Salem at the conclusion of the story has often seemed out of place (Schatz 1972:263–89). He has not been mentioned before, and he seems to be from Jerusalem, which is a long way from Sodom. In addition, he seems to interrupt the monarch of Sodom who comes out to greet Abram but does not get a chance to speak. Nonetheless, there are literary connections which weave the Melchizedek episode and the monarch of Sodom episode together. Both the monarch of Sodom and Abram use the same title for God which Melchizedek uses. The God Most High was ruler of the divine assembly. Melchizedek, on behalf of the God Most High, declares Abram eligible for the blessings which the monarch of Sodom attempts to bestow.

The names "Salem" and "Jerusalem" may refer to two different sanctuaries (Ps 76:3). Salem may be a sanctuary for the Cities of the Plain on the east side of the Dead Sea rather than the city of Jerusalem on the west side. But it is the connotations of Salem which are more important here in the story than its geographical location. If Salem is Jerusalem then Jerusalem was the sanctuary where the covenant between Abram and Lot was ratified. Just as David chooses Jerusalem as a neutral city between Israel in the north and Judah in the south, Abram and Lot choose Salem, in contrast to either Moreh or Sodom, to ratify their covenant. It was neutral territory and Melchizedek its priest was recognized by both partners (Smith 1965:141; Hamilton 1990:409–10). Protocol required that Abram return to the same sanctuary where he negotiated the covenant, to verify that he had fulfilled it.

Few war stories in the Bible brag of the military prowess of Israel's warriors. Instead, Israel is only victorious if Yahweh delivers or turns the enemy over to its warriors (נתן, nātan). Melchizedek's blessing carefully reflects this technical language. Melchizedek certifies that Abram has fulfilled his covenant obligations, and therefore is eligible for the blessings which such loyalty deserves.

Literally, the story of Abram and Lot says: "he gave him a tenth of everything" and not "Abram gave Melchizedek a tenth of everything" (Gen 14:20). If Melchizedek and the monarch of Sodom are considered to be two separate rulers of two separate states, Melchizedek and the monarch of Sodom should both be paying Abram for delivering them from Elam, their common enemy. However, there is a tradition of interpretation which regards Abram as the one who pays the tithe, not Melchizedek (Muffs 1982:82–94; Schatz 1972:72). In this interpretation, Melchizedek and the monarch of Sodom are two different officials who are playing separate roles in a single treaty ceremony. Abram gives Melchizedek a tithe on the plunder taken from Chedorlaomer and then returns the balance to Sodom (Fisher 1962:268–69).

The sacrifice which Abram offers fulfills the vow which his household made before going into battle against Elam. His warriors promised, dedicated, banned, or devoted this portion of their plunder to the God Most High in exchange for help in winning the battle. In later tellings, Abram's payment of tithes in this story explained the custom of paying tithes to the priests who served in the Jerusalem Temple (Wenham 1987:317).

When the household of Abram defeats Elam it becomes the legal owner of the household of Lot and all the slaves of Edom. Both Melchizedek and the monarch of Sodom are prepared to recognize that legal right. There is no reason to assume that the intentions of the monarch of Sodom toward Abram are any different than those of Melchizedek. The monarch of Sodom comes out to meet him and Melchizedek brings out bread and wine. These are the ritual foods with which they will break their fast as warriors and officially bring the war to an end. The monarch of Sodom, like the people who greet Saul and David after their victories, is celebrating Abram's victory; he is not about to threaten or attack him. But he does attempt to negotiate: "Give me the persons, but take the goods for yourself" (Gen 14:21). However, Abram declines, having shown his superiority over both Chedorlaomer and his allies and the monarch of Sodom, who had been defeated twice by the Elamites (Wenham 1987:305). He does not wish to be paid for his services in slaves, and therefore he sets all the prisoners of war free. The land and children of Israel are not the spoils of war but Yahweh's gift.

In emancipating the household of Lot and the others, who as foreigners would have become permanent slaves of Elam, Abram reflects Israel's understanding of itself as a people who are slaves set free, and who are themselves emancipators of slaves (Spina 1983:321). Sodom tenders payment of everything but the hostages; however, Abram deducts only his warriors' pay and returns the plunder with the hostages to Sodom. So Abram magnanimously distributes the spoils to Melchizedek, to his soldiers, and to Sodom. He keeps nothing for himself. Abram is a client of the God Most High; to accept goods or land from Sodom would create a conflict of interest and make him a client of Sodom.

Yahweh, the God Most High, alone provides Abram with goods and land. The monarch of Sodom does not bless Abram, only the God Most High blesses him and his household. Abram will not accept a thread or a sandal-thong from the monarch of Sodom as a bounty for recovering Sodom's property. The thread and the sandal-thong do not identify cheap or insignificant property (Speiser 1964:105; Hamilton 1990:413–14). The thread identifies movable and manufactured goods such as cloth. The sandal-thong identifies immovable property such as land walked or surveyed in sandals which then became a title to the land. Abram's choice of words in denouncing the taking of slaves is echoed in Amos which indicts creditors "because they sell . . . the needy for a pair of shoes" (Amos 2:6) and "buy . . . the needy for a pair of sandals" (Amos 8:6). The indictment charges creditors with being ruthless (Giles 1991:14). Instead of extending the borrower's time to pay they foreclose. The creditors auction the land or the sandals, which their debtors have offered as collateral, in order to recover the value of their loan, which is far less than the land itself is worth (Matt 18:21–35). Abram, unlike these ruthless creditors, chooses to show mercy to the weak.

Thus, the story concludes by celebrating not only the faithfulness of Abram to his covenant partners, but also his generosity in victory and his unconditional confidence that the Most High God would feed and protect his household. Each virtue was highly prized in ancient Israel. Each virtue was handed on from generation to generation in stories such as this so that every generation would know that it was not power, nor wealth, but faithfulness, generosity, and confidence in Yahweh which made this people Israel.

16

The Prophet

Villages delegated the host to help them determine which strangers were their friends and which were their enemies. Similarly, states delegated the prophet to help them determine which foreign nations were their friends and which were their enemies. To carry out their responsibilities prophets carefully monitored every covenant a state negotiated and every war it declared. Today the label of "prophet" is given to a psychic who reads the future, an activist whose criticism brings about social change, a poet who warns society of impending doom, a speaker who delivers the Word of the Lord, a precursor who identifies Jesus as the messiah, or a theologian who emphasizes individual responsibility and social morality. In the world of the Bible, however, the prophet (Akkadian: *muḫḫû, nabu*; נביא, *nābî'*; Greek: προφήτης) played a different social and political role (Lang 1983a:60; Lang 1983b:93; Long 1977). The craft of the prophet was learned from a teacher or father in a school or guild (2 Kgs 2:1–18; 4:1–7, 38). The Bible labels a variety of officials as prophets. Origi-

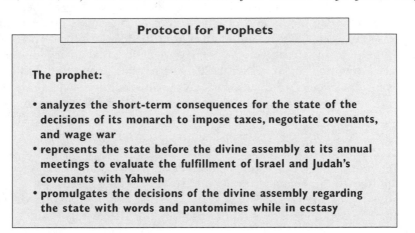

Protocol for Prophets

The prophet:

- analyzes the short-term consequences for the state of the decisions of its monarch to impose taxes, negotiate covenants, and wage war
- represents the state before the divine assembly at its annual meetings to evaluate the fulfillment of Israel and Judah's covenants with Yahweh
- promulgates the decisions of the divine assembly regarding the state with words and pantomimes while in ecstasy

nally, each played a distinct role. Anthropologists continue to chart the relationship between the prophet and a whole field of institutions in Israel and other cultures (Rogerson 1984; Wilson 1980:1–14; McKane 1979; Limburg 1978; Petersen 1987, 1981; Herion 1986; Lang 1985, 1983a; Culley and Overholt 1981).

Classical Prophets

Scholars today refer to prophets whose political and economic positions correspond to those in the books of the Bible where they appear as "classical prophets" (Blenkinsopp 1983:43; Haran 1977). Classical prophets generally opposed the economic and diplomatic policies of monarchs who centralized Israel's economy to produce a surplus, and who negotiated covenants with other states to guarantee military security. Classical prophets considered these military alliances and trade agreements to be direct challenges to Yahweh's power and authority to provide for and to protect the land and its people (Ezek 16:1–63; 23:1–49). Like Israel's legal traditions, the traditions of Israel's classical prophets reserve the power and authority to feed and protect Israel for Yahweh alone. Consequently, for the classical prophets, no social institution, not even the monarchy, was absolute (Greenberg 1990:103–5).

Confrontations between monarchs and prophets in the Bible are not simply personality conflicts or unavoidable political tensions (*pace* Greenberg 1990:110–11). On the contrary, they reflect the exercise of appropriate institutional authority. The confrontation between David the monarch and Gad the prophet, for example, clearly shows the difference between how the prophets understood the authority which the covenant between Yahweh and Israel conferred on the monarch and how the monarchs themselves understood their covenant authority (2 Sam 24:1–25).

Likewise, confrontations between monarchs and prophets do not reflect an understanding in Israel that prophets represent or speak for Yahweh but monarchs do not. The world of the Bible was not divided into sacred and secular realms. Monarchs and prophets were both committed to fulfilling Yahweh's covenant with Israel. They shared the traditions which stressed that ultimately only Yahweh fed and protected Israel. They disagreed, however, on which social system best reflected that conviction. Monarchs argued for the surplus, centralized economic and military system of a state. Prophets, on the other hand, argued for the subsistence, decentralized system attempted by the villages of early Israel (Greenberg 1990:112). Monarchs stressed traditions of stewardship, whereas prophets emphasized the traditions of Israel as a slave-free society (Lang 1983a:77–80). For the prophets, diplomatic policies providing economic security and military preparedness did not lead to peace for Israel and Judah but to disaster.

Prophets thought of themselves as sentries (צפה, *ṣōpeh*), doing for the state as a whole what the lookouts on the walls did for their cities (Ezek 3:17–21;

33:1–9; Lang 1983a:68–69). English uses "watchdog" rather than "watchman" to refer to those who monitor the performance of officials the way the prophets monitored the performance of their monarchs (Hos 11:1; Amos 5:15; cf. 1 Sam 12:14–15; 2 Sam 15:1–33).

In Genesis through Kings, prophecy is a single homogenous movement present from Abraham onward. Consequently, they celebrate Abraham, Moses, Aaron, Miriam, Deborah, and Samuel as prophets (Exod 4:14–16; 7:1–2; 15:20; Deut 18:18; Judg 4:4; Hos 12:13). 1 and 2 Chronicles (1 Chron 25; 2 Chron 12—20), on the other hand, pattern their description of the Levites' liturgical functions in the Jerusalem Temple after 537 BCE on the role of the tribal prophets in the selection of a chief (Rogerson and Davies 1989:281–82). Likewise, the Bible today extends prophecy into the post exilic period after 537 BCE with Haggai, Zechariah, and Malachi. What distinguishes Abraham from Elisha, Miriam from Huldah, Haggai from Hosea, and Zechariah from Ezekiel is that the social world of Elisha, Hosea, Huldah, and Ezekiel is a state, while that of Abraham, Miriam, Haggai, and Zechariah is not. Technically, the differences between the social worlds in which they functioned are too great to identify anthropologically (Rogerson and Davies 1989:274–78). And even though the Bible acknowledges them as honorary prophets, Abraham, Aaron, and Miriam are not as much prophets, as they are ancestors. Likewise, Deborah and Samuel are chiefs, while Haggai, Zechariah, and Malachi are visionaries (חזה, ḥōzeh; ראה, rō'eh) or time travelers (Petersen 1988:37–64; Comaroff 1985; Hanson 1979; Carroll 1973).

Ecstasy

Possession, inspiration, or ecstasy was common to the prophets in the world of the Bible (1 Sam 19:19–24; 1 Kgs 18:1–46). Ecstasy was a trance in which prophets lost control of their emotions and physical movements. This heightened sensitivity appeared in the prophets of Israel, Canaan, and Mari (Malamat 1987:33–52; Lang 1983a:73–74; Ringgren 1982; Ginsberg 1978; Parker 1978; Schmitt 1977; Lewis 1971).

In his memoirs, the Egyptian diplomat Wen-Amon reflects on his encounter with a prophet while traveling in Syria-Palestine between 1100 and 1050 BCE. While in ecstasy the prophet advises the monarch that Wen-Amon is ready to leave the state illegally (pace Lang 1983a:163, n. 132). Even the hieroglyphic letters in the Egyptian word for "prophet" used in Wen-Amon's memoirs show a human figure in violent motion or epileptic convulsion (Pritchard 1969:26, n. 13).

Some prophets induced ecstasy with meditation (1 Kgs 18:41–46). Some fasted until they became ecstatic (1 Kgs 19:1–8). Others produced a trance with music (1 Sam 10:5; 16:14–18; 19:19–24; 2 Kgs 3:15–19). And some prophets danced to stimulate their senses (1 Kgs 18:26–29). In native American cultures prophets induce ecstasy with drugs or lapse into an ecstatic state following a prolonged illness (Overholt 1985, 1986, 1988, 1989).

> ## Memoirs of Wen-Amon
> ## (Matthews & Benjamin 1991b:97)
>
> One day when Prince Tjeker Ba'al was offering sacrifice to his gods, a spirit possessed one of his servants, who became ecstatic. . . . The servant said: "Summon this Egyptian envoy and his statue of Amon, Patron of Travelers, who dispatched him to Syria."
>
> The prophecy occurred on the same night that I had located a freighter headed for Egypt. I had loaded my possessions on board and was only waiting for it to get dark, so that I could smuggle my statue of Amon, Patron of Travelers, on board.

Telling the Future

The impact of the prophets in traditional societies was impressive because of their ability to see the significance of a present crisis for the near future. The prophet did not predict a crisis, but rather responded to it. The kind of crisis which involved the prophet was one which was destroying society's old rules and throwing it into a period without rules (Burridge 1981; 1969: 165–70). The prophet analyzed proposals for social survival, formulating new rules, which were solutions for the short-term. The Iroquois prophet Handsome Lake in 1800, for example, was clearly concerned with short-term, not long-term consequences (Overholt 1985, 1986, 1988, 1989). He did not predict the coming of the Europeans to the Americas, nor even the liquor which they would irresponsibly sell to the Iroquois. Instead he responded to the crisis which the Europeans were creating by prophesying that the Iroquois would survive only by accommodating themselves to the good things which the Europeans brought, such as education and health care, and avoiding the bad things, such as liquor (Wallace 1972).

Prophets and Monarchs

The primary crises to which prophets in Israel responded were the political and economic policies of the monarchs of Israel and Judah between 1000 and 587 BCE (Greenberg 1990:110–13; Hanson 1985; Porter 1982:13–30; Long 1981). Some prophets, like Nathan and Isaiah, were closely aligned with their monarchs. Others, like Elijah and Elisha, were peripheral and were aligned with village households. Nonetheless, all prophets exercised power as the monarchs' loyal opposition, who repeatedly challenged the diplomatic policies of the state (Weinfeld 1986; Crenshaw 1971; Lang 1983a: 63–68; Benjamin 1991:135–44).

After 850 BCE Syria-Palestine fell under Assyria's sphere of influence. Assyrian diplomats, like the Rabshekah in Samuel–Kings, negotiated directly with the soldiers of Judah rather than with Hezekiah their monarch (2 Kgs 18:13–37). About the same time, prophets in Israel and Judah began to employ the same technique by announcing the verdicts of the divine assembly directly to the people, rather than to the monarchs and their courts (Amos 4:4–13).

False Prophets

When Jews living in Alexandria, Egypt translated the Hebrew Bible into Greek sometime after 200 BCE they labeled some of the prophets as "false prophets" (Greek: ψευδοπροφήτης). For example, although the Bible simply refers to Hananiah as a "prophet" (Jer 28:1), the Greek translation or Septuagint introduced him as a "false prophet" (Jer 35:1). False or professional prophets were officials retained as consultants on diplomatic policy by the monarchs of Israel and Judah (Malamat 1989:89–92; Hossfeld and Meyer 1974). They were not necessarily morally degenerate or politically corrupt officials (*pace* Eichrodt [1961]1:332–37). They simply had a different understanding of the obligations which Israel's covenant with Yahweh imposed upon the state and its monarchs than did the books of the Bible in which they appear (Deut 13:1–5; 18:20–22; 1 Kgs 13:11–32; 22:1–28; Jer 14:11–16; 28; Mic 3:5–7; Zeph 3:4; Festinger 1956, 1957; Gross 1979; Hossfeld and Meyer 1973). For example, when Amaziah charges Amos with being a professional prophet paid by the monarch of Judah to destabilize Israel, Amos argues that he makes his living as a herder and farmer, not as a professional prophet (Amos 7:10–17).

Verdicts and Pantomimes

Prophets were masters of both the silent and the sounded arts. They executed not only words, but also symbolic actions (Dick 1984; Lang 1983a: 83–91; Farbridge 1970 [1923]; Lindblom 1973:46, 171–72). Symbolic actions (מופת, *môpēt*) are pantomimes (Bauman 1975). Prophets used three kinds of pantomimes. There were single dramatic gestures, for example, as when Jeremiah buries his clothes in the river bank (Jer 13:1–11; Ezek 4—5); austere practices or asceticism, as when Jeremiah refuses to marry or attend funerals or celebrations (Jer 16:1–13); and the prophet's identification of the silent actions or craft of another, as when Jeremiah, like a docent, draws the attention of his audience to vintners jugging their wine (Jer 13:12–14).

Pantomime is the ancient and universal art of gesture, an expression of social interaction (Broadbent 1964; A. Wilson 1935). Although pantomime first appears in the cave paintings of the stone age and the reliefs of Egypt, Aristotle begins his discussion of pantomime with the Greeks and Romans (Rolfe 1979; Newberry 1893: part ii, plate iv). Anthropologists, sociologists,

Varieties of Prophetic Pantomime		
Prophet-as-Actor	**Prophet-as-Ascetic**	**Prophet-as-Docent**
I Kgs 22:11		
2 Kgs 13:14–19		
Hos 1:1—3:5		
Isa 7:1–9	Isa 20:1–6	Isa 7:10–25
Isa 8:1–4		
Jer 13:1–11	Jer 16:1–4	Jer 13:12–14
Jer 19:1–15	Jer 16:5–7	Jer 18:1–12
Jer 27:1–28:17	Jer 16:8–13	Jer 35:1–19
Jer 32:6–44		
Jer 43:8–13		
Ezek 5:1–5	Ezek 4:1–15	
Ezek 12:1–20	Ezek 24:15–23	
Ezek 21:11–12		
Ezek 21:23–32		
Ezek 24:1–14		
Ezek 37:15–28		
Mic 1:8–16		

and dramatists continue to identify a wide variety of pantomimes in the magic, ritual, and dances of traditional societies (Rolfe 1979). Technically, pantomime is theater without script. Although performers in masks may even use words and music to accompany their gestures (Nobleman 1979:1), mime is primarily a spectacle or "movie," an art whose medium is movement, which appeals to the sense of sight. Pantomime grew from a conviction in traditional cultures that only gestures, acrobatics, and dance can appropriately address human realities whose profundity demands silence (Bourquin 1979:1, 4; Nicoll 1963: 18–19; Hieb 1974; Bellman 1974; Comstock 1974).

Pantomime (אות, 'ôt) for the prophets was not solely representational art describing coming events, but also an act influential in bringing about events (Falk 1960:72–74; Kornfeld 1962:50–57; Ouellette 1967:504–16; Gruber 1977; Gruber 1978:89–97). For them it was a catalyst of social change which highlighted and sometimes ridiculed the faults of the establishment (Bourquin 1979:3; Nobleman 1979; Nicoll 1963:18–19).

Prophetic words borrowed genres from a variety of social institutions (Wolff 1986). The woe or lament portrayed the prophet as a mourner (Ezek 24:9–10; Clifford 1966). The parable and the proverb cast the prophet as a teacher (Isa 5:1–10); the miracle story and the call story as a monarch (2 Kgs 4:1–7; Jer 1:14–19); the covenant lawsuit and the oracle as a member of the divine assembly (1 Kgs 22:10–17; Hos 4:1–4); and oracles against nations as a chief (Jer 48:46).

The miracle stories of Elijah and Elisha were told in villages from which monarchs taxed food and recruited warriors (1 Sam 8:11–17; 1 Kgs 21:1–29). The miracles of these prophets are not so much authorizations of their power as indictments of the monarchs' misuse of power (Overholt 1982; Long 1975). Virtually all the miracles focus on some aspect of feeding and protecting. Miracles demonstrated the effortlessness with which Yahweh could feed and protect the people in contrast to the costly efforts of the monarchs to feed and protect them through covenants with other nations. For example, monarchs took widows' sons for the army, thus putting them to death, whereas Elijah raises the son of the widow of Zarephath to life (1 Kgs 17:17–24). Monarchs taxed widows to death, Elisha gives the widow an endless supply of oil (2 Kgs 4:1–7). And when a borrowed axe necessary to clear the land is lost, Elisha returns it so that the lender would not foreclose on the land in order to pay for the axe (2 Kgs 6:1–7).

The call stories of Isaiah, Jeremiah, and Ezekiel were told by Israelites who had witnessed the coronation of monarchs (Lang 1983a:72–74; Buss 1981; Habel 1965). The literary pattern in these stories includes a divine encounter or lure (Isa 6:1–2), an introductory word or greeting (Isa 6:3–5), an objection or demurrer (Isa 6:4–5), a commission (Isa 6:9–10), and a sign or talisman (Isa 6:11–13). The intention of the stories is to confer authority on the prophet, not to provide an autobiography. Both the coronation of a monarch and the inauguration of a prophet reminded the state that both officials were delegated, not divine. Monarchs were delegated to negotiate covenants, prophets to monitor the state's compliance with its covenants. Because marriages between covenant partners ratified the negotiations for food and arms, "marriage" was a synonym for "covenant" in the world of the Bible. And because classical prophets considered the covenants which the monarchs of Israel and Judah negotiated for food and arms to be violations of Israel's standing covenant or marriage with Yahweh for provisions and protection, they continually indicted these agreements as adultery and prostitution, or covenants without any validity (Hos 1:1—3:5).

Prophets and Elders

There was more than one judicial system in Israel as a state. There was the divine assembly over which Yahweh presided, there were assemblies in the villages and cities over which the elders presided, and there were state courts over which judges appointed by the monarch presided. Although they functioned contemporaneously, one did not review or appeal to the other (*pace* Kohler 1957:139–40). Prophets were associated to some extent with each system but they had a special role in the divine assembly (Isa 1:1–31).

Since village and city assemblies antedated the formation of the state and its courts, they served as rival centers of power. Prophets associated themselves with the city assembly which convened at the gate to emphasize their function in balancing the power of the monarchs. Prophets used the gate court to direct attention to the two standard issues by which the performance of a monarch was evaluated: food and protection (Jer 19:1–13; 20:2). Like any other citizen, prophets stood at the gate to initiate their course of action. But the venue of the trial was regularly transferred to the divine assembly, as it is in Samuel–Kings (1 Kgs 22:1–40), where monarchs and prophets meet on the threshing floor at the city gate to discern whether or not the divine assembly has authorized Israel and Judah to go to war against Aram (Matthews 1987:30–31).

In the world of the Bible, the divine assembly was analogous to the city assembly (Mullen 1980:111–280; Cross 1973:1–76). Both were judicial bodies made up of citizens which met at a threshold to resolve a crisis. Both the city assembly and the divine assembly helped resolve disputes involving land and children. Members of a household appeared before the city assembly; monarchs and prophets stood before the divine assembly. Annually the divine assembly convened at a sanctuary to review the covenants between one state and another. During these festivals, prophets filed a covenant lawsuit (ריב, *rîb*) against any monarch who did not fulfill the covenant obligations of the state to Yahweh (Huffmon 1959; Limburg 1969; Mowinckel 1987). It was the divine assembly which served as the jury before which the prophets indicted the monarchs of Israel and Judah, and it was the decision of the divine assembly which the prophets announced at the end of the trial in their oracles or verdicts (Mic 3).

Prophets and Messengers

The prophet has often been compared to the messenger (מלאך, *mal'āk*) in the world of the Bible (Lang 1983a:70–74; Ross 1962; Westermann 1967). There were similarities between messengers and prophets, but the role of the prophet was more judicial than administrative (Matthews 1991; 1987:26–27; Rogerson and Davies 1989:278). Although Samuel–Kings refer to messengers more than twenty times, only Haggai and Malachi refer to prophets as messengers (1 Sam 23:27; 2 Sam 11:19–24; Hag 1:13; Mal 3:1).

Both messengers and prophets were representatives. But messengers represented monarchs, whereas prophets represented the divine assembly. Both the divine assembly and the monarchs commissioned their representatives with the formula "Go to . . . and say" (Gen 32:3–4; Isa 45:11–13; Jer 2:1–3; Amos 1:3–5). But messengers carried information, whereas prophets delivered a legal verdict. Oracles of judgment are verdicts which impose a sentence; oracles of salvation are verdicts which extend a reprieve or pardon. Both messengers and prophets were treated with the same respect or disdain due those they represented. But messengers played little role in the development of or response to the communications they carried. Prophets, on the other hand, took an active part both in the deliberations of the divine assembly, which led to the verdicts they announced, and in working out Israel's response. In Amos, for example, the prophet mediates several sentence reductions before the divine assembly reaches its final verdict on Israel (Amos 7:1–9).

Prophets and Chiefs

War, too, was an institution which brought monarchs and prophets together over the issue of protecting Israel (Lang 1983a:61–63). In early Israel, war could only be declared by Yahweh, who lifted up a chief to deliver the people from slavery. The state replaced the muster of warriors with a standing professional army, sent into battle as a component of royal strategy and diplomacy. Prophets remained part of the protocol of war used by villages (1 Kgs 22:1–40). Execrations or oracles against foreign nations (Amos 1:3—2:16), the Day-of-Yahweh traditions (Jer 46:10; Amos 5:18), and the enemy-from-the-north motif (Jer 1:15), all played a part in mustering warriors in early Israel (Lang 1983a:76, 78–79).

The Prophet in the Trial of Ahaz
(Isa 7:1–25)

At the trial of Ahaz in Isaiah (Isa 7:1–25), Isaiah uses the children Shear-Jashub and Immanuel in pantomime to indict Ahaz for planning to call on Assyria to help protect Judah against an invasion by Israel and Syria. These pantomimes are poignantly staged in light of the expectation in the world of the Bible that during a military crisis a monarch would offer a human sacrifice (2 Kgs 3:26–27).

Historians call the war which began in 734 BCE the "Syro-Ephraimite War" because Syria and Israel ruled by the household of Ephraim invaded Judah. This military crisis erupted when the foreign policies of Assyria, Syria, Israel, and Judah collided. Assyria wanted to free world trade from raiders and obstructing states. Syria wanted to free Syria-Palestine from Assyria. Israel wanted to free Judah from the isolationist policies of the Davidic monarchy. And Judah wanted to free itself from Israel.

Tiglath-Pileser III (744–727 BCE) formally inaugurated a new age of empires, sometime after 750 BCE, by completely reorganizing Assyria's bureaucracy to gain political and economic control of the trade routes running from the Mediterranean coast inland. Any embargo in these trade lanes cut off Assyria's imports of metals, lumber, and horses, setting off riots among Assyria's citizens (Miller and Hayes 1986:318–19). Under Tiglath-pileser's leadership Assyria ratified three kinds of covenants with foreign states.

Any state willing to align itself with Assyria's foreign policy and offer logistical and military assistance became an Assyrian satellite or ally. These covenant partners retained self-determination in their domestic policies. However, an ally unable to meet its quotas lost its self-determination and became an Assyrian vassal or colony. In a colony, officials retained their titles and offices, but Assyrian personnel reviewed all domestic policies to guarantee that the colony would meet the empire's military and financial budget. These officials functioned much like officials of the International Monetary Fund function in the world today. Their primary responsibility was to design austerity measures for states to implement in order to meet their debt obligations to Assyria. Any reticence or refusal on the part of local officials left the colony subject to outright foreclosure by Assyria. Assyria would deport all state personnel, redistribute its population to developing regions of the empire, and assign the colony an Assyrian military governor, incorporating it completely into the empire as a province.

Assyria preferred to leave states in place rather than to administer countries directly. Local monarchs did a better job of managing commerce than Assyrian officials; local soldiers provoked fewer border incidents with Egypt than Assyrian troops (Miller and Hayes 1986:320–22). However, only states with healthy economies and popular monarchs managed to maintain their self-determination. Assyria's budget requirements increased continually, and few states could meet Assyria's expectations and avoid a taxpayers' revolt. Dethroning and revolution were frequent. For example, Israel went from the status of an Assyrian ally in 738 BCE, to an Assyrian colony in 732 BCE, and finally to an Assyrian province in 721 BCE.

By 742 BCE, Rezin's state of Aram at Damascus in southern Syria was aggressively pursuing an expansionist policy of its own. After Pekah's revolt against the monarch of Israel, Syrian troops occupied Israel's grain producing state of Gilead east of the Jordan River (2 Kgs 15:37; Amos 1:3–5). They also cooperated in the seizure of Judah's Red Sea port at Elat by Edomite troops (2 Kgs 16:6; Tadmor 1962:116–18; Miller and Hayes 1986:323–26). Despite the loss of Gilead and Elat, neither Israel nor Judah were seriously interested in revolting against Assyria.

Without the support of Israel and Judah, Syria had to delay its plans to challenge Assyria and joined Israel and Judah in 738 BCE in paying their assessments to subsidize Tiglath-pileser's war with Urartu in present-day Armenia. During his administration, Tiglath-pileser filed annual reports on the implementation of his foreign policy on the palace walls at Calah-Nimrud (Levine 1972a:19; 1972b:41). He duly reported the financing and supplies which Assyria's covenant partners provided for this campaign (Matthews and Benjamin 1991b:126).

With the help of Syria, Pekah engineered the assassination of Pekahiah in 735 BCE (2 Kgs 15:25). This completed his takeover of Israel and gave Syria a strategic base for invading Judah and forcing Ahaz into an anti-Assyrian coalition. Syria attempted to repeat this strategy of assassination against Ahaz but he escaped (2 Chron 28:7). Consequently, by 734 BCE Syria and Israel were preparing for a full-scale invasion of Judah, strategically targeting the capital city of Jerusalem (2 Kgs 15:29–30, 37; 16:5–9; Isa 7:1—8:8; 2 Chron 28:5–21). Following the military defeat of Judah, Syria and Israel planned to turn Judah over to the household of Tabeel, which had strong ties with Tyre on the Mediterranean coast (Vanel 1974:17–24; Oswalt 1986:193).

Since 885 BCE Judah had been an ally of Israel, and thus was obligated by covenant to follow Israel's foreign policy initiatives. Nonetheless, by putting Judah's military on alert and fulfilling its covenant obligation to Assyria, Ahaz refused to support the anti-Assyrian policies of Pekah and, in effect, abrogated Judah's covenant with Israel (Isa 8:11–15; Miller and Hayes 1986: 329, 344). Some in Judah clearly supported Ahaz' policy of seeking Assyrian aid to gain Judah's independence from Israel; some supported Syria's policy of seeking Israel and Judah's aid to gain independence from Assyria. Isaiah, on the other hand, represented an attempt to keep Judah non-aligned, or at least only minimally compliant with its obligations to Assyria (Dietrich 1976:60–99; Huber 1976:10–34). The interventions which Isaiah makes now appear in Isaiah (Isa 7—8; 9:8–21; 17:1–6; 28:1–4).

The language which Isaiah speaks in the Bible today reflects an education available only to the affluent citizens of Jerusalem (Whedbee 1971:13–22, 149–54). Although it is unlikely that Isaiah was an official serving in the state, he certainly had access to the royal court (Isa 8:2; 22:15 16) and the monarch as well (Isa 7:3; Wilson 1980:271; Fichtner 1949:75–80; Kovacs 1974:171–89). The most powerful intervention which Isaiah makes in support of the coalition's doctrine of non-alignment appears in the trial of Ahaz (Isa 7:1–25).

The crisis which Ahaz and his advisors face is complex. On the one hand, as an Assyrian colony, Judah has a legal responsibility to use military force to put down any rebellion against Assyria. On the other hand, as an ally of Israel, Judah has a legal responsibility to support Israel's struggle for freedom. Regardless of whether Judah decides to support Assyria or Israel it faces dire consequences. If Judah does not join Israel and Syria's struggle against Assyria they will invade. If Judah does join in their struggle Assyria will invade (Vogt 1972:249–55; Cogan 1974:97–103). Ahaz' advisors are unable to reach a decision. The monarch recesses the meeting ostensibly to inspect Jerusalem's defenses and the Kidron Valley reservoirs (Ridderbos 1985:81). Regardless of which decision Judah makes, there will be an invasion and Jerusalem must prepare for siege. But the strategy of a recess is intended primarily to offer the deadlocked participants time to negotiate.

The Gihon spring in the Kidron Valley east of the city is Jerusalem's main water source. Springs were regularly left outside the walls of cities in the ancient Near East to protect them from pollution. Engineers knew that building around or on top of a water source would destroy it. The decision to leave springs outside the walls conserved them during peacetime but exposed them and their cities to destruction during a war. Protecting a city's source of water during a siege was a logistical nightmare. Consequently, Ahaz inspects the Siloam channel with his advisors (Burrows 1958:221–27; Amiran 1975:75–78).

The Siloam channel was an irrigation canal which drew water from the Gihon spring and moved it south along the valley to the upper pool or Siloam reservoir. In the world of the Bible, fullers manufactured cloth from wool. They used large quantities of water to shrink and thicken the cloth, which explains the location of the Fuller's Field adjacent to Jerusalem's major water system. Ahaz' inspection tour takes him outside the city, away from the bulk of his advisors, and gives Isaiah the opportunity to lobby the monarch in virtual privacy. Isaiah proposes that Judah remain non-aligned in this conflict (Gottwald 1985:379; Jensen 1984:93).

A key assumption in Isaiah's argument is the tradition which considers the city of Jerusalem, and Zion, its citadel, impregnable (Clements 1980:72–89; Jensen 1984:93). Yahweh will faithfully (אמת, 'emet) fulfill his commitment to protect Jerusalem from its enemies (Oswalt 1986:201). If Jerusalem is impregnable, then Syria and Israel pose no real threat to Judah (Wilson 1980:272–73). Another important component of Isaiah's argument is the tradition which considers Judah to have only one covenant, its covenant with Yahweh. This covenant with Yahweh recognizes Yahweh alone as monarch of Judah. And as monarch, it is Yahweh's responsibility, not the responsibility of Ahaz, to provide for and to protect the nation (Lust 1971: 464–70). A decision to put Judah's military on alert and endorse its military alliance with Assyria, on the one hand, or a decision for Judah to join the revolt of Syria and Israel, on the other, would both be votes of no-confidence in Yahweh's ability to protect the state. Finally, Isaiah announces the verdict of the divine assembly against Israel and Syria in an effort to convince Ahaz to remain non-aligned. The divine assembly indicts Syria and Israel for attempting to liberate themselves. Yahweh alone is the liberator of the oppressed. Only Yahweh sets slaves free. Assyria is a great state, but certainly no greater than the Egypt from which Yahweh delivered Israel.

Isaiah endorses the words of his proposal with two pantomimes. In one Isaiah is the actor, and in the other he is a docent. Both pantomimes involve children. One focuses on parenting, the other on pregnancy. The non-violent character of these pantomimes contrasts sharply with the sabre-rattling response of Judah's establishment to the threat of invasion (Oswalt 1986: 195). These pantomimes also highlight the short-term consequences of the decision which Ahaz is about to make.

As an actor, Isaiah performs a single dramatic gesture by bringing Shear-jashub along on Ahaz' inspection tour of Jerusalem's water system. Isaiah wants Ahaz to be the leader of the "surviving remnant" (שאר־ישוב, šᵉ'ār-

yāšûḇ). The pantomime is intentionally ambivalent. The good news is that Judah will survive; the bad news is that the damage will be extensive. Judah will survive this crisis but the state will pay a terrible price (Lindblom 1973:424–25; Kaiser 1972:91; Blank 1948:211–15; Hasel 1971:36).

> ### Annals of Ahaz
> ### (2 Kgs 16:1–4)
>
> In the seventeenth year of Pekah son of Remaliah, King Ahaz son of Jotham of Judah began to reign. Ahaz was twenty years old when he began to reign; he reigned sixteen years in Jerusalem. He did not do what was right in the sight of the Lord his God, as his ancestor David had done, but he walked in the way of the kings of Israel. He even made his son pass through fire, according to the abominable practices of the nations whom the Lord drove out before the people of Israel. He sacrificed and made offerings on the high places, on the hills, and under every green tree.

Isaiah's first pantomime is ironic because at the beginning of the crisis Ahaz sacrificed his own son as a gesture of piety to indicate that his fate and the fate of Judah is totally in Yahweh's hands (2 Kgs 16:1–4). Even though the Bible forbids human sacrifice, it admits that it is practiced (Gen 22:1–12; Exod 22:29–30; 34:20; Deut 18:10; Judg 11:30–31, 39; 1 Kgs 16:34; 2 Kgs 16:3; 21:6; Gottwald 1958:36–47). The father of a household who sacrifices his heir forfeits the protection and provision which that child would provide him in his old age. Since it is the heir's responsibility to provide an annuity to the testator, if there is no heir or the heir is irresponsible, the testators die of starvation and neglect (Deut 21:18–21). By sacrificing his son, Ahaz shows that he and Judah are completely dependent upon Yahweh, who alone can deliver them from their enemies.

Child-sacrifice to lift a siege was an orthodox tactic in the world of the Bible (Clemen 1939; Margalit 1986:62–63). A Canaanite creation story, describing El as monarch of a city under siege who sacrifices a child, canonizes the procedure. By 1200 BCE, Ugarit has a prayer to accompany the ritual (Herdner 1978:31–38; Margalit 1981:63–83). In 850 BCE Mesha of Moab, under siege by Israel, sacrifices his son (2 Kgs 3:26–27). In 332 BCE, the monarch of Tyre, under siege by the Macedonians, considers sacrificing a child (Stager and Wolff 1984:30–51). Likewise, in 50 BCE two hundred citizens of Carthage, under siege by Agathocles, sacrifice their children. Leading citizens often join their monarchs in sacrificing their children during a crisis (Spalinger 1978:47–60).

The war memorials of several pharaohs, like the Beit el-Wali relief of Ramses II, portray the citizens of cities under siege sacrificing children. Each relief stages the sacrifice at the peak of an assault (Hoffmeir 1987:60–61). Victims appear in three different postures. Adults dangle a still-living child over the city wall, cut its throat, and then drop its body to the ground. The reliefs clearly demonstrate that child sacrifice symbolizes the complete dependence of the besieged upon their divine patron, not their complete helplessness before their enemy. For example, the Beit el-Wali relief portrays the besieged looking upward toward their divine patron, not down toward their enemy, and includes a prayer addressed to Ba'al, not a plea for mercy addressed to Ramses.

Before his second pantomime Isaiah renews his motion to remain non-aligned, but this time asks Ahaz to choose an appropriate pantomime with which to endorse the proposal. There is a cosmic quality to the sign which Isaiah invites Ahaz to request. Flood rains from above or earthquakes from below are not simply meteorological or seismic confirmation of the Creator's presence in Judah (Kaiser 1972:98). These signs initiate the end-time process by which the existing cosmos is destroyed to prepare for the creation of a new one. The earthquakes and volcanic activity which destroy the world of Lot are "a sign . . . deep as Sheol"; the flood which destroys the world of Noah is "a sign . . . high as heaven" (Job 11:8). Isaiah challenges Ahaz to face the end-time with the confidence of Noah and Lot. Even if war comes, Yahweh will use it to purge the cosmos in preparation for a new creation. Isaiah invites Ahaz to remain calm and exhibit the faith of Noah and Lot, who survive the cataclysm and enter the new world which Yahweh is creating (Ward 1976:329–32).

Requesting a sign can be either an act of piety as it is for Gideon, or an act of presumption as it is for Moses (Exod 17:4; Judg 6:17). Ahaz, however, is neither pious nor hypocritical in refusing to tempt Yahweh. "Tempt" here is a technical term meaning to give a covenant partner legal cause to invoke its sanctions or curses. Yahweh is one of the witnesses to the military alliance between Judah and Assyria. For Judah to violate her covenant with Assyria is to invite or tempt Yahweh to impose the sanctions for violating

---

Trial of Ahaz
(Isa 7:3–4, 14, 16)

Then the Lord said to Isaiah, "Go out to meet Ahaz, you and your son Shear-jashub . . . and say to him, 'Take heed, be quiet, do not fear. . . .' "

[Then Isaiah said] " . . . the Lord himself will give you a sign. Look, the young woman is with child and shall bear a son, and shall name him Immanuel . . . . before the child knows how to refuse the evil and choose the good, the land before whose two kings you are in dread will be deserted."

her covenant with Assyria. But just as Ahaz considers non-alignment presumptuous because it makes Yahweh completely responsible for Judah's defense, Isaiah considers the monarch's decision to fight Israel and Syria presumptuous because it makes the monarch completely responsible for Judah's defense. The majority of Ahaz' advisors want Judah to fulfill its legal obligations to Assyria (Kaiser 1972:97). And eventually, Ahaz will comply with their advice and not the advice of Isaiah (2 Kgs 16:1–20).

Because of his decision to send to Assyria, rather than to Yahweh, for help in repelling the invasion, the divine assembly sentences Ahaz to death. Assyria will invade Judah with plagues of soldiers who are as vicious as killer bees (Deut 1:44). Yahweh will whistle like a beekeeper and they will swarm into the one small hive of Judah, reducing it to the condition of primeval chaos at the dawn of creation (Isa 5:26). Judah's refugees, like the people primeval, will survive on cottage cheese and honey (Isa 7:15, 22). The food of paradise and the food of the poor are identical (Ridderbos 1985:86; Benjamin 1983:39–90, 290–92). But the divine assembly postpones Ahaz' execution until his son is grown. Isaiah marks a woman in the royal family (עלמה, 'almâh; Greek: παρθένος) as a living calendar to count off the days remaining until his execution.

In this second pantomime, Isaiah identifies the silent action of another by drawing attention to the pregnancy of Immanuel's mother and the silent growth of her child as a calendar counting down the time until Ahaz' execution. The actor in the pantomime is not Isaiah but a young woman, who silently goes about her pregnancy (Kaiser 1972:102–3; H. Wolff 1972: 449–56). The pantomime identifies the child and not the manner of the child's birth as significant (Ridderbos 1985:86).

In Christian theology today, the term "virgin birth" refers to the conception of the child Jesus by Mary without sexual intercourse. In comparative religion, the term refers to a child whose mother is human but whose father is divine. In this sense the child is conceived without human sexual intercourse. In the trial of Ahaz, however, the significance of Isaiah's choice of the young woman is not that her child is conceived without sexual intercourse or by intercourse with Yahweh (Willis 1978:1–18). The virgin is a young woman whose marriage ratifies a significant covenant for Judah (Benjamin 1983:300).

What makes this woman significant is that she is close to Ahaz. He will see her every day of her pregnancy and while she is rearing her child. Isaiah converts her pregnancy and delivery from a birthday party to a wake. The book of Hosea uses the same technique when Hosea remembers the birth of his three children, not as days of hope, but as moments of despair (Hos 1:1—3:5). Every time Ahaz looks at this young woman or her son he will see, not the blessing of land and children, but his death sentence. The announcement that this "woman of Judah" is expecting a baby at the same time that the "land of Judah" is expecting an invasion contrasts the prophetic confidence in Yahweh's ability to deliver Judah, infants and all, from

> ## Annals of Ahaz
> ## (2 Kgs 16:7–9)
>
> Ahaz sent messengers to King Tiglath-Pileser of Assyria, saying, "I am your servant and your son. Come up, and rescue me from the hand of the king of Aram and from the hand of the king of Israel, who are attacking me." Ahaz also took the silver and gold found in the house of the Lord and in the treasures of the king's house, and sent a present to the king of Assyria. The king of Assyria listened to him; the king of Assyria marched up against Damascus, and took it, carrying its people captive to Kir; then he killed Rezin.

destruction with Ahaz's confidence only in Judah's own diplomacy and military preparedness (Isa 7:6, 14).

Isaiah announces the verdict of the divine assembly against Pekah and his covenant partners as an attempt to balance the power which Ahaz exercises in Judah. As far as Ahaz and his advisors are concerned, the weak, like the widow, the orphan, and the alien, are the first to suffer and to die during war. Only the strong survive. Consequently, Ahaz decides that not even the strong of Judah will survive an invasion by Israel and Syria without the assistance of Assyria. Isaiah, on the other hand, counters that the invasion and the economic collapse following the war cannot hurt even a child. Yahweh can deliver even a child from the devastating power of monarchs. The war destroys nothing but the armies and supplies which Judah has stockpiled in an effort to protect and feed itself. The child survives because it completely depends upon Yahweh for food and protection; Judah collapses because it does not.

17

The Lawgiver

Lawgivers in western cultures like Greece and Rome began their work by identifying legal principles which people took for granted (Gluckman 1967:354; Llewellyn and Hoebel 1941:29). Then they drafted specific laws to apply these principles to real-life situations (Gluckman 1967:227). But there is still little evidence that the lawgivers in eastern cultures like ancient Israel used a system of general legal principles which they consistently applied to specific situations in the great codes from Exodus, Leviticus, Numbers, and Deuteronomy. Laws in the world of the Bible seldom described typical or average or even ideal behavior in Israel. In fact, average behavior may often have been at variance with these codes (Pospisil 1974:30).

Law and Crisis

In the world of the Bible, the basis of law was not philosophy, but crisis. Lawgivers developed specific laws to deal with households which weakened or threatened the well-being of the state. And households weakened or threatened the well-being of the state when they failed to work their own land, feed their own children, and contribute to the cooperative efforts of the state to collect taxes and raise an army. When Sheba and Jeroboam in Samuel–Kings declare: "We have no portion in David, no share in the son of Jesse! Everyone to your tents, O Israel!" they weaken and threaten the well-being of the state by refusing to pay their taxes (2 Sam 20:1; 1 Kgs 12:16, 32). They forbid the representatives of their households to go up to Jerusalem where the priests determined what portion of the produce from their farms and herds must be turned over to the state for redistribution, and how many members of the household must serve in the army or work on state building projects.

Protocol for Lawgivers

In the world of the Bible, the divine assembly appoints monarchs of states as

- lawgivers with the authority to:
- promulgate a code of law during their coronation
- renew annually the covenant between the divine assembly and the state
- appoint judges to state courts which review complaints from households about their assessments and military service

---

Lawgivers in the Bible do not teach as much about how Israel thought as they do about how Israel as a state worked. For example, laws in the Bible show how Israel reacted to a particular situation or crisis. They also reveal Israel's basic assumptions about human nature, how Israel went about collecting evidence and using it to make legal decisions. And finally, laws outline how Israel as a state distributed power (Rosen 1989:xiv).

Police Power

The anthropology of law in the state differed from the anthropology of law in the villages, even though both functioned alongside one another. The administration of law in the village was decentralized. In villages, the fathers of the households served as its elders or lawgivers (זְקֵנִים, $z^e q\bar{e}n\hat{i}m$; Ruth 4:2; Prov 31:23; Reviv 1989:11). They derived their authority from their own households, and served as an assembly to safeguard the rights of villagers to food and protection (Seeden and Kaddour 1984:502). Assemblies enforced their verdicts through consensus or collective agreement. Cooperation between the households in a village did not result from fear of retribution, but from a shared understanding of what each household needed to do in order for the entire village to survive (pace Malinowski 1959:58–59). A binding consensus was possible only when every household in the village understood who initiated the complaint, what the specific indictment involved, and how the defendant responded (Nader and Metzger 1963:584–92). Consequently, elders talked with plaintiffs and defendants until they all reached an agreement on how the matter should be resolved.

In the state, the administration of law was centralized. The monarch was the lawgiver who appointed judges to hear cases throughout the state. The focus of village law was on the responsibility of the households to feed their members, whereas state law dealt primarily with its responsibility to protect the people. Laws dealing with incest, regulating marriage, and controlling inheritance, for example, developed in villages. Laws dealing with taxes and military or public service, on the other hand, developed in the state (Pospisil

> ## Code of Hammurabi, prologue
> ### (authors' translation)
>
> When . . . Enlil, Lord of the Heavens and the Earth, . . . made
> Marduk the ruler of the Igigi, he created Babylon and made
> Marduk its king. . . . At that time, . . . Enlil named me, Ham-
> murabi, the devout and god-fearing prince, to promote the wel-
> fare of its people, to cause justice to prevail in the land, to
> destroy the wicked and the evil, that the strong might not op-
> press the weak, to rise like the sun over the Mesopotamian
> people with black hair and to light up the land.

1974:xi). In the beginning, state courts only heard complaints from households regarding their assessments, and their obligation to conscript soldiers
for the army (2 Kgs 15:2–4). Gradually, however, they heard cases involving
all areas of public life, including the Gibeonites' call for justice in 2 Sam
21:2–9 and the case of the two prostitutes in 1 Kgs 3:16–28.

State courts used police power, rather than consensus, to guarantee
cooperation. A lawgiver heard the plaintiffs, and then rendered a decision
on the case. Since the decision was based on the judgment of a single
lawgiver there was a greater degree of judicial discretion which was not
necessarily attuned to a broad consensus of opinion within the state as a
whole (Rosen 1989:1–2). While the decision might be based on precedent,
the latitude of interpretation of the precedent was more open to variation.

The centerpiece in the anthropology of state law was its characterization
of the monarch as a lawgiver. Artifacts portraying monarchs as lawgivers
promulgating a code of law during their coronations have been recovered
by archaeologists for more than one ancient Near Eastern culture. Some of
the most exquisite characterizations of both Lipit-Ishtar of Isin and Hammurabi of Babylon, for example, portray them as lawgivers.

Although certainly each new monarch made some changes in state laws,
few monarchs authorized a major restructuring of standing codes of law
(Lemche 1975:138). Monarchs promulgated codes of law to ratify their authority, rather than to inaugurate sweeping judicial reforms. To some
extent the actions of the divine assembly and monarchs during their coronation ceremonies mirrored the actions of the divine assembly and Marduk
in the Enuma Elish story (Matthews and Benjamin 1991a:161). Just as the
divine assembly confirms Marduk as the God Most Honored by announcing
in the story that his word was law and that his command would be obeyed,
the divine assembly confirmed monarchs as lawgivers during their coronation (Enuma iv:1–31). To ratify their appointment as lawgivers, monarchs
then promulgated the code of law by which they promised to maintain order
in the state in order to protect the interests of all the people (Wegner
1992:160).

<table>
<tr><td>

Enuma Elish Story, iv:1–10
(Matthews & Benjamin 1991b:10–11)

You are the God Most Honored . . . ,

Your word shall not be challenged,
   Your word shall speak for all.
Your decree shall not be altered,
   Your word shall build and tear down.
Your word shall be the law,
   Your command shall be obeyed.

</td></tr>
</table>

Monarchs not only promulgated a code of law during their coronations, but also renewed the covenant to which it belonged at least once a year thereafter. In fact, monarchs who did not promulgate a law code at least once a year were subject to rebellion from within or invasion from outside. Without the law the state became lawless. Thus, on the cylinder celebrating his wars in Mesopotamia, Cyrus of Persia claims that his victory over Nabonidus of Babylon was based on Nabonidus' refusal to participate in the annual festival during which the state renewed its loyalty to the divine assembly by once again promulgating its covenant and reaffirming the laws by which the state was to be governed.

The Lawgiver: the Trial of Jehoiakim
(Jer 7:1–15)

In Jeremiah (Jer 7:1–15; 26:1–19), lawgivers play significant roles in both the trial of Jehoiakim the monarch and the trial of Jeremiah the prophet. Jeremiah indicts Jehoiakim and his officials for their failure as lawgivers, who then in turn exercise their authority as lawgivers and indict Jeremiah for lawlessness. Both trials revolve around the question of who is the lawgiver in Judah, and raise questions about jurisdiction, procedure, and sentencing (Pospisil 1974:1). Both trials take place in the Temple of Jerusalem, which is not only the site where the divine assembly convenes but also where the state of Judah tries households charged with treason.

The Bible today recounts only the verdict in the trial of Jehoiakim. The trial itself, which takes place before Yahweh and the divine assembly in the Temple, is assumed but not described. Traditionally, Yahweh and the divine assembly try monarchs who do not fulfill their role as lawgivers by upholding the laws and statutes which made up its covenant with the state.

**Cylinder of Cyrus
(Matthews & Benjamin 1991b:148)**

Marduk, the King of the Gods in Babylon . . . searched through
all the countries for a righteous ruler willing to lead him in the
annual procession. He spoke the name of Cyrus, King of Anshan,
declaring him Ruler of All the World . . . and delivered
Nabonidus, the king who did not worship him, into Cyrus' hands.

The requirements of these rituals were carefully followed at Jehoiakim's
coronation. So, like other monarchs, Jehoiakim would have confirmed his
appointment as a lawgiver in Judah by promulgating the covenant to the
people. This would create the impression that he owed his allegiance to
Yahweh and the divine assembly and to no one else. Practically, however,
Jehoiakim owed his allegiance not to Yahweh but to Pharaoh Necho II
(610–595 BCE).

Necho became pharaoh just as the state of Assyria was being destroyed.
Nabopolassar and the Babylonian army overran Assyria and destroyed
Nineveh in 612 BCE. Before the city fell, Assuruballit and the Assyrian army
moved west to Haran in Syria. Nabopolassar followed. Necho decided to
support Assuruballit in order to create an Assyrian buffer state between
Egypt and Babylon. En route to Haran, Necho marched his soldiers through
Judah along the Coastal Highway and onto the plains of Megiddo where he
was confronted by Josiah and the army of Judah (2 Kgs 23:28–33). Josiah
was not simply defending the territorial integrity of Judah against Egypt but
declaring the state a covenant partner of Babylon. Josiah's decision cost
him his life and Judah its independence. Judah honored Josiah as a hero for
his death on the plains of Megiddo and crowned his heir Jehoahaz as

**Trial of Jehoiakim
(Jer 7:3, 12–15)**

. . . Amend your ways and your doings, and let me dwell with
you in this place. . . . Go now to my place that was in Shiloh
where I made my name dwell at first, and see what I did to it
for the wickedness of my people Israel. And now, because you
have done all these things, says the Lord, and when I spoke to
you persistently, you did not listen, and when I called you, you
did not answer, there I will do to the house that is called by
my name, in which you trust, and to the place that I gave to
you and to your ancestors, just what I did to Shiloh. And I will
cast you out of my sight. . . .

monarch of Judah. The reign of Jehoahaz was brief. Necho returned from Syria, deposed Jehoahaz, and appointed Jehoiakim to govern Judah for Egypt (2 Kgs 24:31–35).

For some in Judah the appointment of Jehoiakim was an expedient compromise, for others it violated Judah's sovereignty. Jehoiakim had no right to function as lawgiver in Judah. He was not a monarch legitimately delegated by the divine assembly but a governor illegitimately appointed by Egypt. Consequently, he was impeached for lawlessness and treason. As an appointee of the pharaoh, Jehoiakim was committed to turn virtually all of Judah's gross national product over to Egypt. Judah became nothing more than a colony whose land and people were exploited by the Egyptians. The system of redistribution established by Yahweh's covenant with Judah became nothing but a device for mining its land and people. Sacrifices ostensibly tendered at the Temple in Jerusalem for the care of the widow, the orphan, and the alien were simply swept away to Egypt. Judah's, households which were ostensibly taxed to protect and provide for the land and its people, were in fact simply having their land and people confiscated. Any father of a household who objected or delayed was summarily executed on some trumped up charge. The members of his household were sold as slaves, and its land confiscated outright by Jehoiakim's government.

While Necho could set the mechanism in motion by which to take control of Judah, ultimately the divine assembly would exercise its right to appoint its own lawgiver, and Yahweh the divine lawgiver would once again be truly represented by a human lawgiver in Jerusalem. When Jeremiah appears, the divine assembly has convened in the Temple and decided to deal with the challenge of Necho by deposing Jehoiakim.

The verdict which Jeremiah announces convicts Jehoiakim of violating the triple mandate: to care for the stranger, the orphan, and the widow; not to shed innocent blood; and not to go after other gods. The verdict frames the oath which Jehoiakim swore at his coronation with the words "amend your ways. . . . then I will dwell with you" (Jer 7:3–7; Ps 72; 132:11–13).

For Jeremiah, this state does not feed and protect the people of Yahweh, but rather teaches them to "steal, murder, commit adultery, swear falsely, make offerings to Ba'al, and go after other gods" (Jer 7:8; Exod 20:3–17). The state is only deluding the people into thinking that it is feeding and protecting them. In reality it is exploiting them. The households of Judah may not see or may not wish to see just how corrupt the state has become, but Yahweh does see that it is no longer fulfilling its covenant obligations. "You may not wish to see what you are really doing, but Yahweh does" (Jer 7:11).

When the trial is over Jeremiah goes to the gate of the Temple to announce the verdict. The site is both strategic and symbolic. He physically stands in the way of those who wish to enter the Temple, creating an obstacle to the fulfillment of their legal obligations to the state. But the gate is also a courthouse where legal proceedings take place. Each connotation weights the verdict which Jeremiah announces with significant implications and evokes a reaction from his audience (Carroll 1986:516).

As the representatives approach the Temple they confess their faith in Yahweh's presence by singing: "This is the Temple of the Lord, the Temple of the Lord, the Temple of the Lord" (Jer 7:4; Ps 122). Jeremiah turns their song of ascent into a taunt by announcing the verdict: "This is . . . a den of thieves" (Jer 7:11). Jeremiah's taunt is brimming with double entendre. On the surface the language of his taunt simply echoes the liturgical language of a psalm being chanted by the representatives of Judah's households coming to the Temple. However, with only subtle changes in spelling, accent, or meaning, Jeremiah's taunt converts a liturgical expression to a vulgar parody.

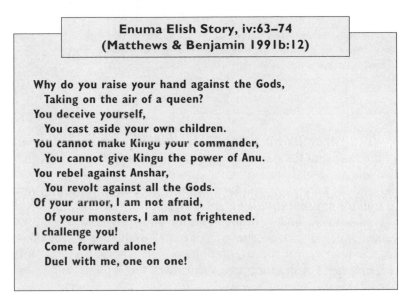

Enuma Elish Story, iv:63–74
(Matthews & Benjamin 1991b:12)

Why do you raise your hand against the Gods,
  Taking on the air of a queen?
You deceive yourself,
  You cast aside your own children.
You cannot make Kingu your commander,
  You cannot give Kingu the power of Anu.
You rebel against Anshar,
  You revolt against all the Gods.
Of your armor, I am not afraid,
  Of your monsters, I am not frightened.
I challenge you!
  Come forward alone!
  Duel with me, one on one!

Taunts are sharply focused insults. In the standard taunt, "who" (מי, *mî*) introduces the first line and "that" (כי, *kî*) introduces the second. For example, "Who is David the son of Jesse, that I should feed his renegades with my wine, my bread, my meat" (1 Sam 25:10) catches the sense, if not the precise grammar, of the genre (Coats 1970:14–26). Taunts are notoriously difficult to translate because of their subtlety. They were a common military strategy in the ancient Near East and ancient Israel. Verbal combat always preceded physical combat. In the Enuma Elish story from Mesopotamia, Tiamat taunts Marduk as he approaches (Enuma 4:63–74). In the story of Gilgamesh, Gilgamesh taunts Ishtar (Gilg 6:31–78). In the story of Aqhat from Ugarit and the story of Ba'al, Aqhat and Anat taunt each other, and Yam or Anat taunt Ba'al repeatedly (AQHT A 6:35–49; Ba'al III.i:20–40).

Although the word "taunt" (שְׁנִינָה, *š^enînâh*) appears only four times, taunting is widely practiced in the Bible (Deut 28:37; 1 Kgs 9:7; 2 Chron 7:20; Jer 24:9). In Genesis, Jacob taunts Laban for falsely accusing him (Gen 31:36–44). In Judges, Gaal taunts Abimelech, his political rival (Judg 9:28–29). And in Samuel–Kings, the Jebusites taunt David and his army at Jerusalem, Ahab taunts the Syrian king Ben-hadad, Jezebel taunts Jehu, and the Rabshakeh taunts Hezekiah (2 Sam 5:6; 1 Kgs 20:11; 2 Kgs 9:31–32; 18:19–37). Elijah is a master of the art. In the trial of Ahab and Jezebel, he taunts Ahab when they first meet, and then Jezebel's prophets of Ba'al (1 Kgs 18:17–18, 27).

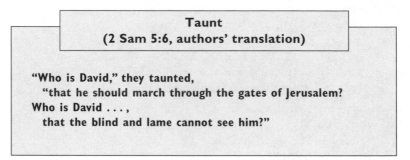

Taunt
(2 Sam 5:6, authors' translation)

"Who is David," they taunted,
  "that he should march through the gates of Jerusalem?
Who is David . . . ,
  that the blind and lame cannot see him?"

The verdict which Jeremiah announces not only questions the religious piety of the state, but the political legitimacy of Jehoiakim to be its monarch. It is not simply a call for religious conversion, but political revolution. Jeremiah indicts Jehoiakim, the king of Judah, for breaching his promise to uphold Judah's covenant with Yahweh (Wegner 1992:176).

Exodus, Leviticus, and Numbers specify a wide range of statutes and ordinances which made up the covenant. Nonetheless, all of these laws could be summarized in the stipulations which Jeremiah cites: "act justly one with another, . . . do not oppress the alien, the orphan, and the widow, . . . [do not] shed innocent blood, . . . do not go after other gods . . ." (Jer 7:5–7). What Jeremiah wants the procession of households entering the sanctuary to do is launch a taxpayers' revolt. Jehoiakim does not deserve the support of the people (Wilcoxen 1977:151).

Jeremiah is not simply an outraged taxpayer, he is an official of the divine assembly. And at the gate, he formally declares the government of Judah illegal, and therefore ineligible for public support. The style in which Jeremiah delivers the verdict is both humorous and shocking. His audience is made up of representatives from the households who have come to pay taxes, priests who are collecting those taxes, and prophets who muster soldiers for the army of Judah. Each group has a vested interest in the state which the Temple represents. Jeremiah does not want the taxpayers to submit the produce of their farms and herds to the priests for assessment, nor to dispatch the men and women of their households to serve in the army or to work on state projects. And he does not want the priests to continue to collect taxes to support the state. To pay and render service to this state, and to work for this state violates every stipulation in the Decalogue. Jehoiakim goes after other gods by serving the divine Necho, who installed him as king of Judah (Wilcoxen 1977:151). Jehoiakim and his priests unjustly collect taxes from the people of Judah and shed innocent blood to confiscate its land. They do not use the taxes they collect to care for the stranger, the orphan, and the widow, but to send to Egypt as tribute. Yahweh led the Hebrews from slavery in Egypt into freedom in the promised land. Jehoiakim is taxing the Hebrews out of their land back into slavery to Egypt. Jehoiakim does not represent Yahweh, and thus does not deserve the support of the people (Jer 26:1). Consequently, Jeremiah stands at the gate to the Temple and announces: "This is not the house of Yahweh, but the treasury of Pharaoh."

Yahweh and the divine assembly are the first to withdraw their support from Judah and the Temple. They leave the Temple of Jerusalem, as Jeremiah encourages the pilgrims to do. If Yahweh no longer dwells in the Temple then the state is no longer authorized to collect taxes and draft soldiers to feed and protect the people. The legal consequences of the verdict can be clearly seen in his call for the soldiers of Judah to surrender and the people of Jerusalem to evacuate the city. Like Shiloh, Jerusalem will be destroyed and the site abandoned, not because its population is weak or its soldiers are cowards, but because Yahweh withdraws his endorsement of Shiloh and Jerusalem (Jer 26:8–9; Ps 78:60). Understandably Jehoiakim and his officials consider the verdict to be treason.

The Lawgiver in the Trial of Jeremiah (Jer 26:1–19)

The trial of Jeremiah takes place in the Temple, where the priests and prophets of the state are the plaintiffs. Priests serve the state by assessing and collecting taxes on the farms and herds of Judah's households. The prophets serve the state by mustering soldiers to fulfill its covenants (Johnson 1962:60–61; Holladay 1989:105). They are paired elsewhere in Jeremiah as his antagonists (Jer 4:9; 5:31; 6:13; 14:18). The princes of Judah in the state court represent Jehoiakim as the lawgiver. They hear the case in the New Gate of the Temple on the charge that Jeremiah has prophesied against the city.

The official and legal character of the trial of Jeremiah is indicated by the use of the phrase "all the people," which does not mean that every last household in the state is present. "All the people" is a technical legal term for a quorum, which means that enough people are present for the trial to be official. Whenever the Bible notes that all the people are present, an action is official, legal, and binding (Gen 19:4). Any other assembly is illegal. Throughout the trial of Jeremiah, it is better to read "all the people" as "officially," rather than as a reference to a group of jurors or spectators (Holladay 1989:105; Thompson 1980:525). Therefore, when "the priests and the prophets and all the people heard Jeremiah speaking these words in the house of the Lord," the priests and the prophets were officially being served with the charges Jeremiah is bringing against them (Jer 26:7). "When Jeremiah had finished speaking all that the Lord had commanded him to speak to all the people," he had officially announced the verdict against the prophets who mustered soldiers and the priests who collected taxes (Jer 26:8). When "all the people gathered around Jeremiah in the house of the Lord," the state court was officially called into session (Jer 26:9).

The priests and prophets ask the state court to label Jeremiah a false prophet, one who does not speak for Yahweh (Holladay 1989:106–7). They charge him with denying the tradition that Jerusalem is to be the sanctuary of Yahweh forever (Ps 132:14). He is therefore subject to a death sentence for speaking against the state and its Temple (Exod 22:27 MT [ET v. 28]; Lev 24:10–16; Deut 18:20). If Yahweh leaves Jerusalem, the state loses the right to collect taxes and to raise an army. The priests and prophets view Jeremiah as a danger to the existence of the state, a man who should be executed for treason.

Jeremiah responds to his indictment by restating "It is the Lord who sent me to prophesy against you" (Jer 26:12). The prophet announces the verdict of the divine assembly. The elders in the trial of Jeremiah not only cite precedents from the trial of Micah of Moresheth, but offer an interpretation of the verdict to assist in the trial of Jeremiah (Mays 1976:37; Holladay 1989:108; Wolff 1981:79–80). Although from a sociological point of view these elders from a village assembly are out of place in a state court, from a literary point of view the book of Jeremiah includes them to emphasize the thoroughness of the trial of Jeremiah. The elders cite the precedent of Micah to remind the court of the harm that will come to the state if innocent blood is shed and a verdict of the divine assembly is ignored (Carroll 1986:518). Consequently, the state court accepts Jeremiah's testimony that he speaks for Yahweh and the divine assembly, and sets aside his death sentence. The lawgivers do not want to shed innocent blood and make the state guilty of murder; thus they unwittingly justify by their own actions the very revolution for which Jeremiah is on trial (Jer 7:9, 24, 28, 30–34).

18

The Storyteller

Ⅰn the world of the Bible, states used an elaborate system of writing and storytelling to preserve and hand on their traditions. The storyteller, the scribe (ספר, sōpēr), and the sage (חכם, ḥākām) performed stories which served two important functions. Storytellers celebrated their monarchs as stewards of the divine assembly, authorized to feed and protect the land and people of the state (Whitelam 1986:166–73; van Leeuwen 1990:297, 301). And storytellers helped monarchs resolve crises which threatened the land and people.

Creation Stories

At coronations and their anniversaries, storytellers performed creation stories describing the birth of the state and the election of its monarch. The Bible does not describe Israel's coronation or covenant renewal ceremony in detail, but it probably contained some of the components found in the inauguration of Moses in Exodus (Exod 19:1—24:18), the covenant between

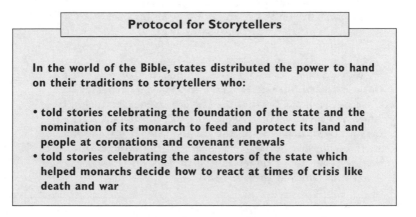

Protocol for Storytellers

In the world of the Bible, states distributed the power to hand on their traditions to storytellers who:

- told stories celebrating the foundation of the state and the nomination of its monarch to feed and protect its land and people at coronations and covenant renewals
- told stories celebrating the ancestors of the state which helped monarchs decide how to react at times of crisis like death and war

Yahweh and Israel in Joshua (Josh 24:1–28), the covenant renewal of Josiah in Samuel–Kings (2 Kgs 23:1–3, 21–23), and the installation of Ezra in Ezra–Nehemiah (Neh 8). On coronation day in Israel the monarch and the people in Jerusalem would have listened to the stories of the deliverance of the Hebrews from slavery like those found today in Exodus. And they would have listened to stories of the settlement of the Hebrew villages in the hills like those found in Joshua and Judges. Storytellers did not simply improvise stories from their own imagination. Every culture in the ancient world shared in a common stock of stories from which they drew and to which they contributed. Ancient Israel was no different. For example, Israel told creation stories like those in Genesis and common to the people of Egypt and Mesopotamia (Gen 1—11). And Israel told its own unique stories of creation like those in Exodus (Exod 5—15). Storytellers in Israel would have performed these stories, just as storytellers in Babylon performed the Enuma Elish story during the Akitu festival.

More than one Mesopotamian text refers to the Akitu festival, which was celebrated at different times and with variations by different cultures. The festival marked the end of the old year and the beginning of a new year (Roaf 1990:201–2; Saggs 1962:365–69; Klein 1992:138–40). In some cultures, the year began when the first crops were sown, in others when the last harvest was collected. Some celebrations lasted for eleven days. Each day was celebrated with rituals which evaluated the performance of monarchs during the year which was ending, before authorizing them to continue to rule for the year which was beginning.

Some three days were dedicated to preparations, prayers, singing, and sacrifices. Special attention was given to the carving of two small wooden statues inlaid with gold and gems, which were used in the dramatization of the Enuma Elish story. One may have represented Tiamat, the antagonist in the story, the other Kingu, Tiamat's helper.

On the fourth day of the festival in Babylon, storytellers began the proclamation of the Enuma Elish story before the statue of Marduk. With the episodes describing the divine assembly recognizing Marduk as the divine

---

Covenant between Yahweh and Joshua (Josh 24:25–27)

So Joshua made a covenant with the people that day, and made statutes and ordinances for them at Shechem. Joshua wrote these words in the book of the law of God; and he took a large stone, and set it up there under the oak in the sanctuary of the Lord. Joshua said to all the people, "See, this stone shall be a witness against us; for it has heard all the words of the Lord that he spoke to us; therefore it shall be a witness against you if you deal falsely with your God."

lawgiver in return for putting down the revolt of Tiamat, storytellers laid down the qualifications for a monarch in the state.

The temple Esagila in the Enuma Elish story is both the center and the model for the new world which Marduk creates, and is the blueprint for state temples throughout Mesopotamia. The condition of the temple at the beginning of each year was a measure of the condition of the state under its monarch. Consequently, on the fifth day of the akitu festival, the temple was thoroughly cleaned. When the statue of Nabu, who ruled the divine assembly in Babylon, arrived from the city of Borsippa, monarchs went into the temple. Then the priests (Akkadian: *urigallu*) stripped them of their royal insignia and tortured them like prisoners of war.

When the priests were satisfied that the monarchs had not betrayed their commission to rule justly, they confirmed the monarch's coronation for another year. On the sixth day of the festival, storytellers carried out the confirmation by telling the conclusion of the Enuma Elish story. Their words were pantomimed by dancers who acted out Marduk's victory over Tiamat and Kingu (Lambert 1968:104–12). Tiamat, who leads the revolt against the divine assembly in the story, is slain by Marduk in combat. Kingu commands the warriors of Tiamat during her revolt. He is executed by Marduk, who uses his blood to thin the clay from which the people primeval are formed. The two small statues prepared during the opening days of the festival were beheaded and burned before a statue of Nabu.

On days seven and eight, representatives from every city in the state arrived with the statues of their divine patrons. Both the human representatives and the statues of the divine patrons which they escorted came to pay their respects to their monarch and to pledge their allegiance for the coming year. Priests audited the records of each delegation's obligations to the state, just as they had audited the record of its monarch. Only delegations in good standing were allowed to renew their membership in the state.

On the ninth day, the monarch engaged in ritual intercourse (Greek: ἱερός γάμος) to celebrate the covenant between the state and its divine patron (Jacobsen 1975:65–77). This sacred marriage between a priest who represented the state and the monarch who represented its divine patron symbolized both the intimacy of the covenant which united the state and its patron and the fertility which resulted from their relationship.

Then on the tenth day, the monarch and the statue of Marduk led the delegations in procession along a sacred highway leading to the Akitu temple on a canal outside of the capital city. Here the first crops would be planted. The participants transported their statues through the fields in wagons and across canals and rivers on barges. It was the climax of the festival. When the entourage arrived at the temple, the monarch showered every city in the state with gifts of gold and silver.

On the eleventh day, the monarch threw a banquet for the representatives from all the cities in the state and their statues. The monarch promulgated the list of officials which would serve the state during the upcoming year.

Every state official was either reappointed or replaced. When the banquet was completed the delegations returned to their own cities. The story of the state had been retold and the new year had begun.

Storytellers, however, were not simply public relations officials for the monarch, trying to give royal decisions their best possible public image. They were responsible for the education or wisdom of the monarch in the ancient Near Eastern skills of government (Gammie and Perdue 1990:x–xi). The book of Proverbs from Israel and the Teachings of Ptah-Hotep from Egypt reflect one kind of syllabus which sages followed with their protégés.

Storytellers were also responsible for educating the people in their responsibilities to the monarch (1 Sam 12). All institutions in the ancient world combined storytelling and ritual. Thus, when the monarch collected taxes, the storytellers explained why the monarch was empowered to collect taxes.

Ancestor Stories

Storytellers in the world of the Bible not only authorized the installation of monarchs at their coronation, they also helped those same monarchs solve problems during the course of their reigns. People in modern western industrial cultures expect future research and future discoveries to solve present problems. People in the world of the Bible looked for solutions to their problems in past experience. Today, a crisis sets research in motion. In the world of the Bible, a crisis set storytelling in motion (Crenshaw 1985:601–15). People today think they live in a world without limits. There are always new worlds and new resources to be discovered. People in the world of the Bible, however, thought they lived in a world of limited goods. Everything had already been discovered. There was nothing left to be explored or uncovered. There was only a forgotten past to be remembered. To prevent a crisis from destroying the state, storytellers searched past traditions for wisdom which had been forgotten or ignored, and retold the stories of the people looking for new directions in past experiences (McCar-

---

**The Tribes of Yahweh
(Gottwald 1979:492)**

Whatever their actual numbers, the Exodus proto-Israelites, who had broken away from the grip of the Egyptian empire and survived a trek through the desert, became a powerful catalyst in energizing and guiding the broad coalition of underclass Canaanites. Their experience became exemplary for all Israel, fundamentally shaping . . . the entire format of the Israelite traditions. Organized as the priestly militarized Levites, spread throughout the tribes, they became intellectual and military-political cadres significantly leavening the whole coalition.

ter 1990:291). No story was repeated word for word. Storytellers always adapted them to the demands of their own day. Storytellers brought insight to a community at an impasse. Their stories showed monarchs a way out. In a seemingly impossible situation, storytellers offered the state words to live by.

In the world of the Bible, death was a time for storytelling. When the Philistines killed Saul and his sons at the battle on Mount Gilboa, the Hebrews were distraught, terrified, uncertain of what was going to happen to them. The death of Saul became the analogy for the death of a much-loved monarch in Israel. Whenever a good monarch died, storytellers sang David's eulogy for Saul in Samuel–Kings (2 Sam 1:17–27). The Song of the

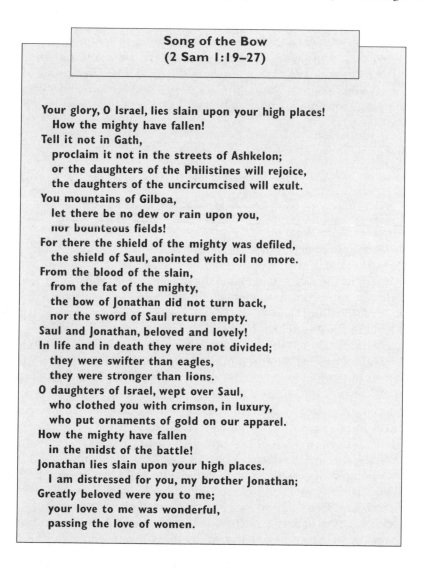

**Song of the Bow
(2 Sam 1:19–27)**

Your glory, O Israel, lies slain upon your high places!
  How the mighty have fallen!
Tell it not in Gath,
    proclaim it not in the streets of Ashkelon;
    or the daughters of the Philistines will rejoice,
    the daughters of the uncircumcised will exult.
You mountains of Gilboa,
    let there be no dew or rain upon you,
    nor bounteous fields!
For there the shield of the mighty was defiled,
    the shield of Saul, anointed with oil no more.
From the blood of the slain,
    from the fat of the mighty,
    the bow of Jonathan did not turn back,
    nor the sword of Saul return empty.
Saul and Jonathan, beloved and lovely!
In life and in death they were not divided;
    they were swifter than eagles,
    they were stronger than lions.
O daughters of Israel, wept over Saul,
    who clothed you with crimson, in luxury,
    who put ornaments of gold on our apparel.
How the mighty have fallen
  in the midst of the battle!
Jonathan lies slain upon your high places.
  I am distressed for you, my brother Jonathan;
Greatly beloved were you to me;
    your love to me was wonderful,
    passing the love of women.

Bow became the standard text which tellers would use to guide the grief of the people.

War was also a time for storytelling. For example, when Joab attacks Abel in Samuel–Kings (2 Sam 20:14–22) a wise woman is able to save her city by telling him a story (McCarter 1990:290). Her story celebrates Abel as a city where justice is dispensed, not where battles are fought. It offers Joab the opportunity to suspend his attack and allow the city assembly to try Sheba for treason. Joab not only enjoys the story, but follows its advice. Sheba is punished and war is avoided.

The role of the storytellers presupposed a thorough education. However, it is not clear that there was at the Israelite court, as in Egypt and Mesopotamia, an institution that can be described as a school for storytellers. There is no direct reference to schools of any kind in the Bible and it may have been left to households, like the House of Shaphan in Jeremiah (Jer 26:24; 29:3), to educate and provide the royal court with a continual supply of storytellers (Whybray 1990:139; Crenshaw 1985:270–81). The annals of both Josiah (640–609 BCE) and Jehoiakim (609–597 BCE) in Samuel–Kings and Jeremiah preserve some memory of how storytellers functioned in a state.

The Storyteller in the Annals of Josiah *(2 Kgs 22:1—23:30)*

At the beginning of Josiah's reign (640–609 BCE), Assyria conquered Syria-Palestine. Judah was first an ally and then a virtual colony of Assyria (Cogan 1974). But in 627 BCE, when Ashurbanipal, the emperor of Assyria, died, civil war broke out as several would-be successors attempted to assume power (Miller and Hayes 1986:382). Judah was at a crossroads. It could remain loyal to the disintegrating Assyrian government or declare its independence. The question in the eighteenth year of King Josiah's was: "Should Judah be faithful or free? Should it fulfill its covenant obligations to Assyria or declare its independence from Assyria?" (2 Kgs 22:3). The annals of Josiah in Samuel–Kings (2 Kgs 22:1—23:30) record the first tentative steps which the monarch takes to test Assyria's actual ability to maintain its control over Judah. Josiah's mentor is the storyteller Shaphan.

Josiah first orders an audit of the Temple treasury to determine just what financial resources are available to him (2 Kgs 22:3–4). Legally, the Temple treasury belonged to Assyria, not to Judah. By ordering an audit, Josiah exceeds his authority as a ruler of an Assyrian colony and acts as if he were the monarch of a free and independent state (Miller and Hayes 1986:397–401). The maneuver is both revolutionary and guarded. If the messengers of the emperor of Assyria question his actions Josiah can describe them simply as those of a good steward who is taking it upon himself to audit his colony's funds.

In many ancient and modern languages the words "count" (ספר, sāpēr) and "recount" (ספר, sōpēr) are closely related. The ability to read and write allowed storytellers to work both as the monarch's book keepers and book readers (2 Kgs 22:3–7; 22:8–10). Storytellers were not only able to count the money in the treasury, but could also recount the stories of Judah. Like the other state officials whom many translations describe as "secretaries" or "scribes," Shaphan serves Josiah as both a storyteller and an accountant (2 Sam 8:17; 20:25; 2 Kgs 12:11 MT [ET v. 10]; 18:18; 25:19; 2 Chron 26:11; Jer 36:20–23; 52:25). Shapan is part of the intellectual community fostered by the royal court and the Temple officials (Whybray 1990:137).

Josiah's second order to repair the Temple is more drastic. The design and decoration of the Temple was a reflection of the policies and covenants of the state. Consequently, after 850 BCE the Temple in Jerusalem reflected Judah's status as a colony of Assyria. The changes in the construction and decoration of the Temple which Josiah orders after 640 BCE are not simply repairs. They reflect fundamental changes in the status of Judah. When Josiah sends Shaphan to contract workers, carpenters, builders, and masons, he is abrogating Judah's treaty with Assyria and declaring Judah an independent state just as Hezekiah had done one hundred years earlier (2 Kgs 18:3–4).

Seemingly, Assyria is unable to challenge Josiah's work on the Temple. Having taken these first steps toward political independence, Josiah renews Judah's covenant with Yahweh. It is the storyteller, Shaphan, who encourages Josiah to take this final step by proclaiming the Torah story given to him by Hilkiah the High Priest. Josiah's reaction to Shaphan's proclamation is to tear his clothes. This sign of mourning and shame is Josiah's admission of guilt for having enslaved Judah to Assyria. Josiah is a monarch who has been called to justice (Matthews 1988b, 1991). Once Shaphan's story makes him aware of his failure to fulfill Judah's commitment to Yahweh, Josiah repents (2 Kgs 22:11–13; cf. 1 Kgs 21:27–29). By destroying the royal garments which identify him as the ruler of a colony for Assyria he declares Judah independent.

The prophet Huldah ratifies Judah's declaration of independence and assures Josiah of success in his attempt to reunite the colonies into which Assyria divided Israel and Judah (2 Kgs 22:13). Huldah certifies that Shaphan's story is authentic, and carries out the role of the prophet who confirms the election of a chief to deliver the people from slavery (Priest 1980:367). Josiah follows this ancient protocol for the selection of a chief to demonstrate that, unlike Jeroboam and Manasseh, who were lifted up by the emperors of Assyria to enslave the Hebrews, he is like the chiefs of Israel's early days who were lifted up by Yahweh to set the people free (Christensen 1984:402).

The Storyteller in the Annals of Jehoiakim (Jer 36:1–32)

International power had been redistributed to new states by the time of Josiah's death in 609 BCE. Assyria was now off the world stage and had been replaced by Egypt and Babylon. During Jehoiakim's brief reign (609–599 BCE), Judah was a colony first of Egypt and then of Babylon. Nonetheless, the question which faced Jehoiakim was the same as the question which faced Josiah: Should Judah be faithful or free; should Judah fulfill its covenant obligations to Babylon and Egypt or declare its independence from both? And the mentor who guides the monarch is the storyteller Baruch.

In the Bible today, the relationship between Jehoiakim and Baruch is subordinated to the relationship between Jehoiakim and Jeremiah. The book of Jeremiah portrays Baruch more as a secretary to Jeremiah than as a storyteller for Jehoiakim. He records the words of the prophet and officially promulgates them to Jehoiakim (Jer 36:4–8). And he executes the title by which Jeremiah takes over control of the ancestral land of his household (Jer 32:11–14). The book of Jeremiah portrays Jehoiakim's decisions to declare Judah's independence from Babylon and to take back control of its own land more as the result of the words and deeds of Jeremiah the prophet than as the result of the advice of Baruch the storyteller.

Nonetheless, the distinct role of the storyteller is not completely absorbed by the role of the prophet here. For example, the prophet indicts Jehoiakim for choosing to be faithful to one foreign monarch after the other, but it is Baruch the storyteller who, in 605 BCE, actually records the words of the prophet and promulgates the indictment of Jehoiakim to a crowd at the Temple on a day of mourning. It would be more consistent with the protocol for the prophet if Jeremiah himself promulgated his own indictment. And it would also be more consistent with the protocol for the storyteller if Baruch, like Shaphan, proclaimed the words of the Torah story instead of the words of Jeremiah. In order to decide how to respond to Jeremiah's indictment, Jehoiakim listens to Baruch retell the story of Yahweh's covenant with Judah. Both events center on the written word of Yahweh and involve reading from a holy book (Kessler 1969:381; Isbell 1978).

Micaiah is the first royal official to hear Baruch's performance of Judah's story in the chamber of Gemariah, a place open only to officials like Baruch (Jer 36:11; Muilenberg 1970:227–28). He discusses it with other royal officials who become alarmed (Jer 36:16). They order Baruch to retell parts of the story for them before deciding to report all these words to the monarch (Jer 36:12–18). They also quite apprehensively ask him to certify that his story is authentic (Jer 36:17). They want to be sure that both the scroll and Jeremiah the prophet are authentic (Muilenberg 1970:225; Isbell 1978:34).

After due deliberation, they report the substance of his story to the monarch (Jer 36:20). Jehoiakim decides to get a second storyteller, Jehudi, to retell the story for him (Jer 36:21).

Publicly, in the presence of the Babylonian messengers, Jehoiakim haughtily denies Jeremiah's indictment. Using a nearby charcoal heater, Jehoiakim burns the scroll piece by piece as it is read, thereby disputing its contents as being the word of Yahweh (Jer 36:22–23). For a monarch of Judah to burn the words of the prophet does not nearly constitute the sacrilege it does for him to burn a Torah scroll. Jehoiakim's pantomime is as convincing to the messengers from Babylon as it is scandalous to the people of Judah who are loyal to their covenant with Yahweh. He does not want to provide the Babylonian messengers with any evidence of his disloyalty to Nebuchadnezzar.

There is a long-standing tradition in the ancient Near East that emperors are suspicious of their colonies and that vassal rulers are always protesting their innocence. The El Amarna Letters, dictated by officials of the pharaohs Amenophis III and Akhenaten after 1400 BCE, are filled with protests of innocence as well as hints that the rulers will take advantage of every perceived weakness in their pharaohs.

No one in the court of Jehoiakim tears off the uniforms which identify them as officials appointed by Nebuchadnezzar. They are not alarmed, nor do they tear their garments (Jer 36:24; Carroll 1986:660). Publicly Judah remains faithful to its covenant with Nebuchadnezzar and abrogates its treaty with Yahweh. For his crime, Jeremiah sentences Jehoiakim to a shameful death (Jer 36:32; Carroll 1986:663).

Privately, however, the political overtures of Egypt, Jeremiah's indictment, and the stories of Baruch and Jehudi move Jehoiakim to declare Judah's independence from Babylon (Miller and Hayes 1986:407–8). By 600 BCE Judah is free. Soon, however, the Babylonians lay siege to Jerusalem and Jehoiakim dies the monarch of an independent but embattled state.

El Amarna Letter no. 254
(Matthews & Benjamin 1991b:78–79)

Your servant, who is less than the dust under your feet, renews his oath of loyalty to Pharaoh by bowing seven times seven times. I have received Pharaoh's letter. Your fears are unfounded. I am far too insignificant to be a threat to my Pharaoh's lands. . . . The proof that I am neither a criminal nor a rebel can be seen in my regular payment of tribute and my willingness to obey all of the commands of your provincial governor.

The Storyteller in the Bible Today

Although monarchs virtually disappeared from Israel and Judah after the Babylonians destroyed Jerusalem in 587 BCE, storytellers survived. The monarchs to whom they had spoken in the past were gone but the people themselves remained. The Bible today is basically the work of storytellers whose patient performance of their task has served generation after generation in their struggle to understand what to believe and how to live. Judaism, Christianity, and Islam today all preserve different performances which storytellers from the world of the Bible developed. Some of these stories were first told as long ago as the Bronze Age (3000–1250 BCE). During the formative periods of Judaism, Christianity, and Islam, certain stories became normative for expressing the beliefs of each religious movement and evaluating the behavior of their believers. Today these religions preserve their normative stories in writing and identify them as the word of God, the Bible, or Scripture.

The "Tanak," as Jews today often refer to the Bible, or "Old Testament," as Christians prefer to call it, was already taking shape between 700 and 600 BCE when Josiah listened to the scroll proclaimed for him by Shaphan. By 100 CE, when their positions during the war between Judah and Rome had alienated Jews from Christians, the Bible was in virtually the same form in which it is proclaimed and preached in temples and churches today. Jews generally refer to the sections of the Bible as "scrolls." Christians refer to them as books. Neither the word "scroll" nor the word "book" (Latin: *codex*) identifies a literary genre, but rather the most familiar physical format in which particular stories were preserved and handed on from one generation to the next. Scrolls and books were manufactured either from plants or animals. Vellum or parchment was a specially tanned leather; papyrus was woven from a reed plant.

The most common genres in the Bible today are law and story. Storytellers did not compose the Bible like modern authors write books. Originally, they developed stories orally. Storytellers were careful observers of Israel's common experience. Their memories and reflections slowly formed a rich archive (*midrash*) of quite simple laws (*halakah*) and stories (*haggadah*). Their archive continued to grow and develop from repeated performances at the annual harvest festivals where taxes were collected, and in times of crisis when decisions needed to be made. Simple laws and stories were soon woven together into more complex cycles of stories and codes of law. It was from this archive that tellers drew the first stories like the Song of Miriam at the Red Sea (Exod 15:20–21), and laws like the decree of David: "the share of the one who goes down into the battle shall be the same as the share of the one who stays by the baggage," from which the Bible today would develop (1 Sam 30:24).

Hymn to Yahweh as a Chief
(Exod 15:20–21)

Then the prophet Miriam, Aaron's sister, took a tambourine in her hand; and all the women went out after her with tambourines and with dancing. And Miriam sang to them:

"Sing to the Lord, for he has triumphed gloriously;
  horse and rider he has thrown into the sea."

Not all Hebrews in ancient Israel understood their responsibility to Yahweh in the same way. Some Hebrews were committed to forming a decentralized village culture without a monarch, without an army, without taxes, and without slaves, whereas other Hebrews formed a centralized state with a monarch, an army, taxes, and slaves. Although the Hebrews who lived in states certainly considered themselves followers of Yahweh, their world view was much different from the Hebrews who pioneered the villages of early Israel before them. Therefore, the stories told in Hebrew villages were different from those told by the monarchs of Hebrew states. And more than one kind of story was told in Israel as a state. Scholars have studied four of these royal stories from the Bible today in some detail (Noth 1972:261–76).

Between 1250 and 1000 BCE, Hebrews in the area of Samaria told a story intended to help build the Hebrew villages in their region into a state. Because it describes the God of ancient Israel as Elohim, the powerful and triumphant creator of the cosmos, scholars labeled it the "Elohists' story" which is abbreviated "E."

Hebrews living around Jerusalem between 1000 and 900 BCE were telling a somewhat different story from their neighbors to the north. Its storytellers wanted to build the state of Israel into a empire. Consequently, their story provides an unconditional endorsement for the state founded by David and Solomon, which created a state with the Hebrew villages north of Jerusalem and the non-Hebrew states of Moab, Ammon, Edom, and Syria before forging covenants with major powers like Egypt. Because the God of ancient Israel reveals the name "Yahweh" to the man and the woman in the stories of Adam and Eve (Gen 4:26), scholars identify it as the "Yahwists' story." The Yahwists' story is abbreviated "J" from the German spelling of Yahweh as "Jahve." Unlike the courtly descriptions of the God of ancient Israel in the Elohists' story, the descriptions of the God of ancient Israel in the Yahwists' story are very down-to-earth. For example, in the Elohists' story, the God of ancient Israel creates by decree and promulgates these decrees through angels and dreams. In the Yahwists' story, on the other hand, the God of ancient Israel creates like a potter working the clay by hand, and visits the Hebrews in person.

Beatitudes for Storytellers
(Sir 39:1–11)

... the one who devotes himself
  to the study of the law of the Most High. ...
... seeks out the wisdom of all the ancients,
  and is concerned with prophecies;
he preserves the sayings of the famous
  and penetrates the subtleties of parables;
he seeks out the hidden meanings of proverbs
  and is at home with the obscurities of parables.
He serves among the great
  and appears before rulers;
he travels in foreign lands
  and learns what is good and evil in the human lot.
He sets his heart to rise early
  to seek the Lord who made him,
and to petition the Most High;
  he opens his mouth in prayer
and asks pardon for his sins.

If the great Lord is willing,
  he will be filled with the spirit of understanding;
he will pour forth words of wisdom of his own
  and give thanks to the Lord in prayer.
The Lord will direct his counsel and knowledge,
  as he meditates on his mysteries.
He will show the wisdom of what he has learned.
  and will glory in the law of the Lord's covenant.
Many will praise his understanding;
  it will never be blotted out.
His memory will not disappear,
  and his name will live through all generations.
Nations will speak of his wisdom,
  and the congregation will proclaim his praise.
If he lives long, he will leave a name ... ,
  and if he goes to rest, it is enough for him.

The Yahwists' story appears when the cities and states which made up the state of Israel under David and Solomon began to declare their independence (Hayes and Miller 1977:375–76). For example, sometime before 900 BCE the region of Cabul north of the Carmel mountains moved from Israel's sphere of influence to that of Tyre (1 Kgs 9:10–14) and Syria won its independence (1 Kgs 11:23–25). Edom followed (1 Kgs 11:14–22), and then even the Hebrews in the northern part of the country declared their independence from Jerusalem (1 Kgs 12). During his reign, Solomon added only

Gezer to Israel (1 Kgs 9:16). In this climate of emerging nationalism, story-tellers proclaimed the Yahwists' story to shore up Israel as a state. It promises military security and economic aid to those who remain loyal. In the story, Yahweh commands Abraham, David's ancestor, to live as a guest among many different peoples in order to bless them and to make their life flourish. To have Abraham as a guest is tantamount to belonging to Israel. Abraham cares for the resources of the people who are his hosts just as the state cares for those who belong to it. Israel, like Abraham, serves as their legal guardian (Gen 18:16–33), the father of their household (Gen 13:1–18), and their chief (Gen 14:1–24).

The "Deuteronomists' story," abbreviated "D," was named for its master-piece: Deuteronomy. The Deuteronomists' story downsizes the empire of David and Solomon into the state of Judah. It developed in Judah between 700 and 600 BCE. The Deuteronomists' story helps Judah avoid the complete destruction of its social institutions by the Babylonians. Israel's foreign entanglements became a liability. In the Deuteronomists' story, the statutes and ordinances of Yahweh call Israel to a cloistered and isolated life, apart from the other nations. Israel is to be totally self-contained. Isolationism replaces colonialism (McCarter 1990:292).

Finally, the "Priests' story" or "P" developed in Babylon between 600 and 400 BCE. The Priests' story converts the state of Judah into the religion of Judaism. Because this story has a special concern for laws and calendars dealing with worship it was named for the priests who were responsible for the liturgy of ancient Israel.

The great stories of ancient Israel are now artfully combined in Genesis, Exodus, Leviticus, Numbers, and Deuteronomy into a genre which Jews today call "Torah" and Christians generally refer to as the Pentateuch. "Pentateuch" is a Greek word meaning the "five books." "Torah" is a Hebrew word which is often translated "law," but "teaching" carries more accurate connotations in English. The Torah story is the core of the Bible. It contains the basic law codes and cycles of stories by which the identity

of ancient Israel and by which subsequent biblical communities gauge their
authenticity. If it is not Torah, it is not biblical.

Today, creeds and other theological writings are rigorously logical. Churches
and theologians attempt to eliminate any possible contradictions in the way
they express their faith in God and the outlook on daily life which it informs.
Torah, on the other hand, is much more tolerant of diversity. As Torah took
shape in ancient Israel, stories with very different ways of understanding
the God of ancient Israel and looking at life were included. Torah valued
the richness of its various traditions over uniformity. The Bible today is by
no means a textbook. It is a testimony to the continuing struggle of diverse
communities in ancient Israel and early Christianity who responded to the
challenges of their day in different ways.

Torah developed from cycles of stories and codes of laws with common
motifs. These laws and stories almost all dealt with the promise of land
and children, the exodus from slavery, the covenant between Yahweh
and Israel, wandering in the desert, and the settlement of the villages in
the hill country. The sequence of these laws and stories in Torah is
neither historical nor chronological. But the sequence is also not hap-
hazard like a scrapbook or collage. It artistically displays the experience
of the Hebrews and emphasizes their particular characteristics as a chosen
people at different times and in different places in the promised land and
outside it.

The pattern which first appeared in the Deuteronomists' story after 700
BCE became standard for the structure of the Bible today. The Deuteronomists' story used Deuteronomy as a command against which it measures Israel's compliance in Joshua, Judges, and Samuel–Kings. Likewise,
the Bible uses the Torah story in Genesis, Exodus, Leviticus, Numbers, and
Deuteronomy as a command against which it evaluates Israel's compliance.
The Torah or Pentateuch became a constitution or point of reference for
storytellers in Israel and the standard against which all subsequent stories
were measured and on which all subsequent stories commented.

Virtually every other tradition in the Bible today in some way evaluates
Israel's performance in light of the Torah story. It remained constant in
Israel while traditions commenting on it continued to change. Today the
Bible reflects the ongoing process which Israel used to update and revise
the way it understood itself and its relationship to the God of Israel. The
prophetic books, the writings or wisdom literature, and even the New
Testament all update and revise the Torah story for their own time and their
own communities, and, to some degree, tellers in each tradition altered the
understanding which previous stories had proposed.

The prophets, for example, understand the Torah story in a different way
than the Yahwists' story. The monarchs of Israel and Judah continued to
increase taxes forcing more and more of their people to sell themselves into
slavery to pay their taxes. With the Torah story as their benchmark, the
prophets issue indictment after indictment against the monarchs of Israel

and Judah for their foreign alliances and policies of domestic exploitation. In the prophets' reading of the Torah story, Israel is called not to be the provider and protector of the family of nations, but rather to be provided for and protected by Yahweh. The taxes which the monarchs use to warehouse supplies and build armies are sacrilegious to the prophets, who stress the gratuitous generosity of Yahweh in providing for and protecting Israel.

Even among the Jews who migrated or were deported from Syria-Palestine into the Greek speaking world of Egypt, the process of problem-solving the in present by rereading the past continued. Faced with a new language and a new culture, these Jews read the Torah story in a new way. They not only translated their Bible from Hebrew into Greek, but included new works like the Wisdom of Solomon, the Wisdom of Sirach, Tobit, and Judith. These works, today called the "apocrypha" or the "pseudepigrapha," reflect the way in which these Jews adapted their eastern Mediterranean heritage, culture, and faith to the western Mediterranean way of life. Today this Greek language version of the Bible is called the "Septuagint" because of an early tradition which attributed the translation to a group of seventy (Latin: *septuaginta*) scholars (Sundberg 1964). It was the Septuagint story which became the Christian Old Testament (Hayes 1979:43).

And finally Christians understood the Torah story in a different way than their predecessors. Christians began to tell their story in the New Testament between 50 and 100 CE. Not long after, both Jews and Christians closed their canons. From 100 CE onward, no writings were considered normative, inspired, or canonical.

A certain amount of tolerance is always necessary to adapt stories to specific cases. However, when the variance in application becomes too wide, a series of quality controls is established in order to limit the number of applications which can be made and thus reduce the variation between one story and the other. Canon is a control on storytelling. "Canon" comes from a Hebrew word meaning a "cane" (קָנֶה, *qāneh*) or a "reed" (Latin: *rundo donax*; 1 Kgs 14:15; Holladay 1971: s.v. "קָנֶה"; Abbott-Smith 1937: s.v. "κανών"). For Egyptians, the canon was a common measurement like a meter or a yardstick. In Ezekiel, however, the canon measures three-meters or 10 ft. 4 in. (Ezek 40:5; 42:16). When used in reference to the Bible, canon identifies stories which are normative for teaching and morality in the community of faith.

However, even with a canon, storytelling is still used today to initiate new members into the community and to teach and preach to them during worship. The ability to tell the story remains a requirement for membership. In the ceremonies of bar mitzvah, as well as baptism, candidates retell the official stories of their religious communities by telling their own stories in order to demonstrate a familiarity with the past and an ability to live in the present (Chicago Studies 1982:1–101). Preachers and teachers are now the storytellers in Judaism, Christianity, and Islam. Some preaching and teaching traditions like the Mishnah (200 CE) and the Talmud (400 CE) for Judaism and the work of the church fathers (100–800 CE) for Christianity were written down. But it is the weekly preaching and teaching carried on in temples, churches, and mosques which has the strongest impact on the way believers understand their faith and tell their stories. Thus, each generation of believers must learn the ancient craft of the storyteller in order to face the new challenges and the unique crises of their own day.

Abbreviations

AA	*American Anthropologist*
ABD	Anchor Bible Dictionary
AJS	*American Journal of Sociology*
AmEth	*American Ethnologist*
ANET	J. Pritchard, *Ancient Near Eastern Texts*
AOAT	Alter Orient und Altes Testament
AQ	*Anthropological Quarterly*
ARA	*Annual Review of Anthropology*
Arch	*Archaeology*
AS	*Assyriological Studies*
ASR	*American Sociological Review*
AUSS	*Andrews University Seminary Studies*
BA	*Biblical Archaeologist*
BAR	*Biblical Archaeology Review*
BASOR	*Bulletin of the American Schools of Oriental Research*
Bib	*Biblica*
BN	*Biblische Notizen*
BRev	*Bible Review*
BRT	*Baptist Review of Theology*
BTB	*Biblical Theology Bulletin*
BZ	*Biblische Zeitschrift*
BZAW	Beihefte zur ZAW
CA	*Current Anthropology*
CBQ	*Catholic Biblical Quarterly*
ETL	*Ephemerides theologicae lovanienses*
ExT	*Expository Times*
FB	Forschung zur Bibel
FEH	*Fides et Historia*
HBD	*Harper's Bible Dictionary*

HTR	*Harvard Theological Review*
HUCA	*Hebrew Union College Annual*
IDB	*Interpreters Dictionary of the Bible*
IEJ	*Israel Exploration Journal*
Int	*Interpretation*
IOS	*Israel Oriental Society*
ISSB	*International Social Science Bulletin*
JAAR	*Journal of the American Academy of Religion*
JANES	*Journal of the Ancient Near Eastern Society*
JAOS	*Journal of the American Oriental Society*
JBL	*Journal of Biblical Literature*
JCS	*Journal of Cuneiform Studies*
JESHO	*Journal of the Economic and Social History of the Orient*
JJS	*Journal of Jewish Studies*
JNES	*Journal of Near Eastern Studies*
JNSL	*Journal of Northwest Semitic Languages*
JPOS	*Journal of the Palestine Oriental Society*
JQR	*Jewish Quarterly Review*
JRAI	*Journal of the Royal Academy of Ireland*
JSOT	*Journal for the Study of the Old Testament*
JSS	*Journal of Semitic Studies*
JTS	*Journal of Theological Studies*
OTS	*Oudtestamentische Studiën*
PEQ	*Palestine Exploration Quarterly*
PRS	*Perspectives in Religious Studies*
RA	*Revue d'assyriologie et d'archéologie orientale*
RAI	*Rencontre d'Assyriologique*
RB	*Revue Biblique*
RES	*Répertoire d'épigraphie sémitique*
RHA	*Revue hittite et asianique*
RQ	*Römische Quartalschrift für christliche Altertumskunde und Kirchengeschichte*
SH	*Scripta Hierosolymitana*
SJOT	*Scandinavian Journal of Old Testament*
SJT	*Scottish Journal of Theology*
TBT	*The Bible Today*
TDOT	*Theological Dictionary of the Old Testament*
TLZ	*Theologische Literaturzeitung*
UF	*Ugarit Forschungen*
USQR	*Union Seminary Quarterly Review*
VT	*Vetus Testamentum*
WA	*World Archaeology*
ZAW	*Zeitschrift für die alttestamentliche Wissenschaft*
ZTK	*Zeitschrift für Theologie und Kirche*

Bibliography

Abbott-Smith, G.
  1937   *A Manual Greek Lexicon of the New Testament.* Edinburgh: T & T
                Clark.
Abrahams, R. G.
  1973   "Some Aspects of Levirate." In *The Character of Kinship.* Edited
                by J. Goody. Cambridge: Cambridge University Press. Pages
                163–74.
Abu-Lughod, L.
  1986   *Veiled Sentiments: Honor and Poetry in a Bedouin Society.*
                Berkeley: University of California Press.
Achtemeier, P. J., ed.
  1985   *The Harper's Bible Dictionary.* San Francisco: Harper & Row.
Ackerman, S.
  1992   "Isaiah." In *The Women's Bible Commentary.* Edited by C. A.
                Newsom and S. H. Ringe. Louisville: Westminster/ John Knox.
                Pages 161–68.
Adams, R. McC.
  1972   "The Mesopotamian Social Landscapes: A View from the
                Frontier." In *Reconstructing Complex Societies.* Edited by C. B.
                Moore. Cambridge: Cambridge Archaeology Seminar. Pages
                1–20.
  1981   *Heartland of Cities.* Chicago: University of Chicago Press.
  1984   "Mesopotamian Social Evolution: Old Outlooks, New Goals." In
                *On the Evolution of Complex Societies, Essays in Honor of Harry
                Hoijer.* Edited by T. Earle. Malibu, Calif.: Undena. Pages 79–129.
Adams, R. N.,
  1977   "Power in Human Societies: A Synthesis." In *The Anthropology
                of Power.* Edited by R. D. Fogelson and R. N. Adams. New York:
                Academic Press. Pages 387–410.
Aharoni, Y.
  1967   *The Land of the Bible: A Historical Geography.* Philadelphia:
                Westminster.
Ahlstrom, G. W.
  1977   "King Jehu—a Prophet's Mistake." In *Scriptures in History and
                Theology: Essays in Honor of J. Coert Rylaarsdam.* Edited by A. L.
                Merrill and T. W. Overholt. Pittsburgh: Pickwick Press. Pages
                47–69.

1979   "1 Samuel 1:15." *Bib* 60:254.
1982   *Royal Adminstration and National Religion in Ancient Palestine.*
                Leiden: E. J. Brill.
1984   "Giloh: A Judahite or Canaanite Settlement." *IEJ* 34: 170–72.

Ahmed, A. M. A.
1973   "Tribal and Sedentary Elites: A Bridge Between Two
                Communities." In *The Desert and the Sown: Nomads in a Wider
                Society.* Edited by C. Nelson. Berkeley: University of California
                Press. Pages 75–96.

Ahroni, R.
1984   "The Levirate and Human Rights." In *Jewish Law and Current
                Legal Problems.* Edited by N. Rakover. Jerusalem: Library of
                Jewish Law. Pages 67–76.

Albright, W. F.
1966   *Archaeology, Historical Analogy and Early Biblical Tradition.* Baton
                Rouge: Louisiana University Press.
1968   *Archaeology and the Religion of Israel.* 5th ed. Baltimore, Md.:
                Johns Hopkins University Press.

Alexander, T. D.
1985   "Lot's Hospitality." *JBL* 104:289–91.
Allen, L. C.
1990   *Ezekiel 20–48.* Dallas: Word Books.
Alon, D. and T. E. Levy.
1983   "Chalcolithic Settlement Patterns in the Northern Negev
                Desert." *Current Anthropology* 24:105–7.

Alt, A.
1968   "Die Landnahme der Israeliten in Palastina."
                Reformationsprogramm der Universitat. Leipzig, 1925; Translated
                by R. A. Wilson in *Essays on Old Testament History and Religion.*
                Garden City, N.Y: Doubleday. Pages 173–221.
1929   "Der Gott der Vater." *Beitrage zur Wissenschaft vom Alten und
                Neuen Testament.* Stuttgart. In *Essays on Old Testament History
                and Religion.* Oxford: Oxford University Press. Pages 1–86.
1930   "The Origins of Israelite Law." In *Essays on Old Testament
                History and Religion.* Oxford: Oxford University Press. Pages
                101–71.
1966   "Die Staatenbilding der Israeliten in Palästina."
                Reformationsprogramm der Universität. Leipzig. In *Essays on Old
                Testament History and Religion.* Oxford: Oxford University Press.
                Pages 223–309.

Alter, R.
1978   "Character in the Bible." *Commentary* 66, 4:58–65.
Amiran, D. H. K. and Y. Ben-Arieh.
1963   "Sedentarization of Beduin in Israel." *IEJ* 13:161–81.
Amiran, R.
1975   "Water Supply at Ancient Jerusalem." In *Jerusalem Revealed.*
                Edited by Y. Yadin. Jerusalem: Israel Exploration Society. Pages
                75–78.

Amit, Y.
1987   "Judges 4: Its Contents and Form." *JSOT* 39:89–111.
Amsler, S.
1979   "La sagesse de la femme." In *La sagesse de l'ancien testament.*
                Edited by M. Gilbert. Bibliotheca Ephermeridum Theologicarum

Lovaniensium. Vol. 51. Leuven: Leuven University Press. Pages 112–16.

1980   "Le prophetes et la communication par les actes." In *Werden und Wirken des Alten Testaments. Festschrift für Claus Westermann zum 70. Geburtstag.* Göttingen: Vandenhoeck and Ruprecht. Pages 194–201.

Anati, E.
1987   *I Siti A Plaza Di Har Karkom.* Brescia: Centro Camuno Di Studi Preistorici.

Andersen, F. I.
1966   "The Socio-Juridical Background of the Naboth-Incident." *JBL* 85:46–57.

Andersen, J.
1969   "Studies in the Medieval Diagnosis of Leprosy in Denmark: An Archaeological, Historical and Clinical Study." *Danish Medical Bulletin* 12. Suppl. 9.

Anderson, A. A.
1989   *2 Samuel.* Dallas: Word Books.

Anderson, G. A.
1987   *Sacrifices and Offerings in Ancient Israel.* Atlanta: Scholars Press.
1992   "Sacrifice and Sacrifical Offerings: Old Testament." *ABD* 5:870–86.

Andrae, T.
1926   *Mystikens Psykologi.* Stockholm.

Andreasen, N. E. A.
1983   "The Role of the Queen Mother in Israelite Society." *CBQ* 45:179–94.

Angel, J. L.
1972   "Ecology and Population in the Eastern Mediterranean." *WA* 4:88–105.

Antoun, R. T.
1972   *Arab Village: A Social Structural Study of a Trans-Jordanian Peasant Community.* Bloomington: University of Illinois Press.

Ardener, E.
1975   "The 'Problem' Revisited." In *Perceiving Females.* Edited by S. Ardener. London: Malaby Press. Pages 19–27.

Ashby, G.
1988   *Sacrifice: Its Nature and Purpose.* London: SCM.

Ashley, D. and D. M. Orenstein.
1985   *Sociological Theory: Classical Statements.* Boston: Allyn and Bacon.

Astour, M. C.
1966   "Political and Cosmic Symbolism in Genesis 14 and Its Babylonian Sources." In *Biblical Motifs: Origins and Transformations.* Edited by A. Altmann. Cambridge, Mass.: Harvard University Press. Pages 65–112.

Awad, M.
1959   "Settlement of Nomadic and Semi-Nomadic Tribal Groups in the Middle East." *International Labor Review* 79:25–56.

Baab, O. J.
1962a   "Birth." *IDB.* 1:440.
1962b   "Virgin." *IDB.* 4:787–88.
1962c   "Widow." *IDB.* 4:842–43.

Bailey, C.
1984   "Bedouin Place-Names in Sinai: Towards Understanding a
                   Desert Map." *PEQ* 116:42–57.
Bailey, F. G.
1969   *Stratagems and Spoils. A Social Anthropology of Politics.* Oxford:
                   Blackwell.
Baines, J. and J. Malek.
1980   *Atlas of Ancient Egypt.* New York: Facts on File.
Bal, M.
1988   *Murder and Difference: Gender, Genre, and Scholarship On Sisera's
                   Death.* Bloomington: Indiana University Press.
Balch, D. L.
1981   "Let Wives be Submissive: The Domestic Code in 1 Peter." *SBL
                   Monograph Series* 26. Chico, Calif.: Scholars Press. Pages 1-20,
                   81–116.
1988   "Household Codes." In *Greco-Roman Literature and the New
                   Testament: Selected Forms and Genres.* Edited by D. E. Aune.
                   Atlanta: Scholars Press.
Baldwin, J.
1988   *1 and 2 Samuel: An Introduction and Commentary.* Leicester:
                   InterVarsity.
Balikci, A.
1990   "Tenure and Transhumance: Stratification and Pastoralism
                   among the Lankenkhel." In *The World of Pastoralism: Herding
                   Systems in Comparative Perspective.* Edited by J. G. Galaty and D.
                   L. Johnson. London: Guilford Press. Pages 301–22.
Baltzer, K.
1968   "Considerations Regarding the Office and Calling of the
                   Prophet." *HTR* 61:567–81.
Baly, D.
1965   *Geographical Companion to the Bible.* London: Butterworth.
Baly, D. and A. D. Tushingham.
1971   *Atlas of the Biblical World.* New York: World Publishing.
Barstad, H. M.
1984   *The Religious Polemics of Amos.* VTSupp 34; Leiden: E. J. Brill.
Barth, F.
1954   "Father's Brother's Daughter Marriage in Kurdistan."
                   Southwestern Journal of Anthropology 10:164–71.
1961   *Nomads of South Persia. The Basseri Tribe of the Khamseh
                   Confederacy.* Oslo, Boston: Little, Brown and Company.
1962   "Nomadism in the Mountain and Plateau Areas of South West
                   Asia." In *The Problems of the Arid Zone.* UNESCO: Arid Zone
                   Research, XVIII. Pages 341–55.
1973a   "A General Perspective on Nomad-Sedentary Relations in the
                   Middle East." In *The Desert and the Sown.* Edited by C. Nelson.
                   Berkeley: University of California Press. Pages 11–21.
1973b   "Descent and Marriage Reconsidered." In *The Character of
                   Kinship.* Edited by J. Goody. Cambridge University Press. Pages
                   3–19.
1981   *Process and Form in Social Life.* London: Routledge & Kegan Paul.
Bar-Yosef, O. and A. Khazanov, eds.
1992   "Introduction." In *Pastoralism in the Levant, Archaeological
                   Materials in Anthropological Perspective.* Madison, Wis.:
                   Prehistory Press. Pages 1–10.

Batchelor, J.
1892   *The Ainu of Japan: The religion, superstitions, and general history of the hairy aborigines of Japan.* London: Religious Tract Society.

Bates, D. G.
1971   "The Role of the State in Peasant-Nomad Mutualism." *Anthropological Quarterly* 44:109–31.
1972   "Differential Access to Pasture in a Nomadic Society: The Yoruk of Southeastern Turkey." In *Perspectives on Nomadism.* Edited by W. G. Irons and N. Dyson-Hudson. Leiden: E. J. Brill. Pages 48–59.
1974   "Shepherd Becomes Farmer, A Study of Sedentarization and Social Change in Southeastern Turkey." In *Turkey, Geographic and Social Perspective.* Edited by P. Benedict et al. Leiden: E. J. Brill. Pages 92–133.

Bates, D. G. and A. Rassam.
1983   *Peoples and Cultures of the Middle East.* Englewood Cliffs, N.J.: Prentice-Hall.

Batto, B. F.
1974   *Studies on Women at Mari.* Baltimore, Md.: Johns Hopkins University Press.

Bauman, R.
1975   "Verbal Art as Performance." *AA* 77:290–311.

Beals, R. L. and H. Hoijer.
1971   *An Introduction to Anthropology.* 4th ed. New York: Macmillan.

Beattie, D. R. G.
1974   "The Book of Ruth as Evidence for Israelite Legal Practice." *VT* 24:251–67.

Beaumont, P., G. H. Blake, and J. M. Wagstaff.
1976   *The Middle East: A Geographical Study.* New York: John Wiley & Sons.

Beavis, M. A.
1992   "Ancient Slavery as an Interpretive Context for the New Testament Servant Parables with Special Reference to the Unjust Steward (Luke 16:1-8)." *JBL* 111:37–54.

Becker, H. S.
1973   *Outsiders: Studies in the Sociology of Deviance.* New York: The Free Press.

Beckling, B. E. J. H.
1989   "I Will Break His Yoke From Off Your Neck: Remarks on Jeremiah 30:4–11." *OTS* 25:63–76.

Bellefontaine, E.
1979   "Deuteronomy 21:18–21: Reviewing the Case of the Rebellious Son." *JSOT* 13:13–31.
1987   "Customary Law and Chieftainship: Judicial Aspects of 2 Samuel 14.4–21." *JSOT* 38:47–72.

Bellman, B.
1974   "The Socio-Linguistics of Ritual Performance." In *New Dimensions in Dance Research—anthropology & dance: The American Indian.* CORD Research Annual 6:131–46.

Ben-Barak, Z.
1979   "The Legal Background to the Restoration of Michal to David." *SVT* 30:15–29.
1981   "Meribaal and the System of Land Grants in Ancient Israel." *Biblica* 62:73–91.

Benedict, R.
  1934   *Patterns of Culture.* Boston: Houghton Mifflin.
Benjamin, D. C.
  1983   *Deuteronomy and City Life.* Lanham, Md.: University Press of
                        America.
  1989   "Israel's God: Mother and Midwife." *BTB* 19:115–20.
  1990   "The Persistant Widow—Parables in Ruth and Luke." *TBT*
                        28:213–19.
  1991   "An Anthropology of Prophecy." *BTB* 21:135–44.
  1992   "Stories of Elijah." In *The Land of Carmel: A Festschrift for
                        Joachim Smet on his 75th birthday.* Rome: Institutum
                        Carmelitanum. Pages 19–28.
  1993   "Stories of Adam and Eve." In *Problems of Old Testament
  (forthcoming)   Theology: A Festschrift for Rolf P. Knierim on his 65th Birthday.*
                        Leiden: E. J. Brill.
Bergman, J., H. Ringgren, and M. Tsevat.
  1975   "*Betulim.*" *TDOT.* Grand Rapids: Eerdmans. 2.338–43.
Berlin, A.
  1982   "Characterization in Biblical Narrative: David's Wives." *JSOT*
                        23:69–85.
Berreman, G.
  1971   *Anthropology Today.* Del Mar, Calif.: Communications Research
                        Machines, Inc.
Bertholet, A.
  1919   *Kulturgeschichte Israels.* Göttingen: Vandenhoeck & Ruprecht.
Bertramus, C.
  1574   *De politica Judaica tam civili quam ecclesiastica.*
Bird, P.
  1974   "Images of Women in the Old Testament." In *Religion and
                        Sexism.* Edited by R. R. Ruether. New York: Simon and
                        Schuster. Pages 41–88.
  1989   " 'To Play the Harlot': An Inquiry into an Old Testament
                        Metaphor." In *Gender and Difference in Ancient Israel.* Edited by
                        P. Day. Philadelphia: Fortress Press. Pages 75–94.
Black-Michaud, J.
  1975   *Cohesive Force: Feud in the Mediterranean and the Middle East.*
                        New York: St. Martin's Press.
Blank, S.
  1948   "The Current Misinterpretation of Isaiah's šeʾār yāšûb." *JBL*
                        67:211–15.
  1962   "Youth." *IDB.* 4:925.
Blenkinsopp, J.
  1972   *Gibeon and Israel: The Role of Gibeon and the Gibeonites in the
                        Political and Religious History of Early Israel.* Cambridge:
                        Cambridge University Press.
  1974   "Did Saul Make Gibeon His Capital?" *VT* 24:1–7.
  1983   *A History of Prophecy in Israel.* Philadelphia: Westminster.
Bloch, M.
  1973   "The Long Term and the Short Term: The Economic and
                        Political Significance of the Morality of Kinship." In *The
                        Character of Kinship.* Edited by J. Goody. Cambridge: Cambridge
                        University Press. Pages 75–87.

Blok, A.
1981   "Rams and Billy-Goats: A Key to the Mediterranean Code of
                    Honour." *Man* 16:427–40.
Blumer, H.
1969   *Symbolic Interactionism: Perspective and Method.* Englewood Cliffs,
                    N.J.: Prentice-Hall.
Boardman, J.
1976   "The Olive in the Mediterranean: Its Culture and Use."
                    Philosophical Transactions of the Royal Society of London, series B,
                    275:187–96.
Bohannan, P. and L. Bohannan.
1968   *Tiv Economy.* Evanston, Ill.: Northwestern University Press.
Boling, R. G.
1975   *Judges.* Garden City, N.Y.: Doubleday.
Bonte, P.
1977   "Non-Stratified Social Formations Among Pastoral Nomads." In
                    The Evolution of Social Systems. Edited by J. Friedman and M. J.
                    Rowlands. London: Duckworth. Pages 173–200.
Borowski, O.
1979   *Agriculture in Iron Age Israel.* Ph.D. dissertation, University of
                    Michigan.
1987   *Agriculture in Iron Age Israel.* Winona Lake, Ind.: Eisenbrauns.
Bos, J. W. H.
1988   "Out of the Shadows: Genesis 38; Judges 4:17–22; Ruth 3."
                    Semeia 42:37–67.
Boserup, E.
1965   *The Conditions of Agricultural Growth: The Economics of Agrarian
                    Change under Population Pressure.* Chicago: Aldine.
Bott, E.
1971   *Family and Social Network: Roles, Norms, and External
                    Relationships in Ordinary Urban Families.* 2d ed. New York: Free
                    Press.
Botterweck, G. J. and H. Ringgren, eds.
1974–90   *Theological Dictionary of the Old Testament.* 6 vols. Grand Rapids,
                    Mich.: Eerdmans.
Bourdieu, P.
1979   "The Sense of Honour." In *Algeria 1960.* Cambridge: Cambridge
                    University Press. Pages 95–132.
Bourke, J.
1954   "Samuel and the Ark: A Study in Contrasts." *Dominican Studies*
                    7:81–82.
Bourquin, D.
1979   "To Talk of Mime." In *Mimes on Miming.* Edited by B. Rolfe. Los
                    Angeles: Panjandrum. Pages 3–5.
Bowman, R. G.
1991   "The Fortune of King David/The Fate of Queen Michal: A
                    Literary Critical Analysis of 2 Samuel 1–8." In *Telling Queen
                    Michal's Story: An Experiment in Comparative In- terpretation.*
                    Edited by D. J. A. Clines and T. C. Eskenazi.
1991   Sheffield: JSOT Press. Pages 97–120.
Braithwaite, J.
1991   "Forward." In *Emotions and Violence: Shame and Rage in
                    Destructive Conflicts.* Edited by T. J. Scheff and S. M. Retzinger.
                    Lexington, Mass.: D. C. Heath. Pages ix–xv.

Brandes, S.
    1987   "Reflections on Honor and Shame in the Mediterranean." In
                    Honor and Shame and the Unity of the Mediterranean. Edited by D.
                    D. Gilmore. Washington, D.C.: American Anthropological
                    Association. Pages 121–34.
Brandfon, F. R.
    1987   "The Limits of Evidence: Archaeology and Objectivity."
                    MAARAV 4:5–43.
Braudel, F.
    1972   *The Mediterranean and the Mediterranean World in the Age of
                    Philip II, Vols. I–II.* London: Collins.
Breasted, J. H.
    1986 [1912]   *Development of Religion and Thought in Ancient Egypt.* Reprint.
                    Philadelphia: University of Pennsylvania Press.
Brenner, A.
    1985   *The Israelite Woman.* Sheffield: JSOT Press.
Brew, J. O.
    1956   "The Metal Ages: Copper, Bronze, and Iron." In *Man, Culture,
                    and Society.* Edited by H. L. Shapiro. New York: Oxford
                    University Press. Pages 111–38.
Brichto, H. C.
    1973   "Kin, Cult, Land and Afterlife–A Biblical Complex." *HUCA*
                    44:1–54.
Bright, J.
    1981   *A History of Israel.* 3d ed. London: SCM.
Broadbent, R. J.
    1964   *History of Pantomime.* New York: B. Blom.
Brody, S. N.
    1974   *The Disease of the Soul.* Ithaca: Cornell University Press.
Broshi, M.
    1984   "Legal Document from Babatha's Archives." In *Highlights of
                    Archaeology: The Israel Museum Jerusalem.* Jerusalem: The Israel
                    Museum. Pages 158–59.
Brown, J.
    1970   "A Note on the Division of Labor." *American Anthropologist*
                    72:1073–78.
Brueggemann, W.
    1977   *The Land.* Philadelphia: Fortress Press.
    1990   "I Samuel 1: A Sense of a Beginning." *ZAW* 102:33–48.
Buckley, T.
    1988   "Menstruation and the Power of Yurok Women." In *Blood
                    Magic: The Anthropology of Menstruation.* Edited by T. Buckley
                    and A. Gottlieb. Berkeley: University of California Press. Pages
                    187–209.
Buckley, T. and A. Gottlieb.
    1988   "A Critical Appraisal of Theories of Menstrual Symbolism." In
                    Blood Magic: The Anthropology of Menstruation. Edited by T.
                    Buckley and A. Gottlieb. Berkeley: University of California Press.
                    Pages 3–50.
Burridge, K. O. L.
    1969   *New Heaven, New Earth: A study of millenarian activities.* New
                    York: Schocken.
    1981   "Reflections on Prophecy and Prophetic Groups." *Semeia*
                    21:99–102.

Burrows, M.
1940   "The Ancient Oriental Background of Hebrew Levirate
                Marriage." *BASOR* 77:2–15.
1940   "The Marriage of Boaz and Ruth." *JBL* 69:445–54.
1958   "The Conduit of the Upper Pool." *ZAW* 70:221–27.
Burton, R. F.
1961   *The Lake Regions of Central Africa, a Picture of Exploration.* 2 vols.
                New York: Horizon.
Buss, M.
1981   "An Anthropological Perspective on Prophetic Call Narratives."
                Semeia 21:9–30.
Buttrick, G. A., ed.
1962–76   *The Interpreter's Dictionary of the Bible.* 4 vols. and suppl.
                Nashville: Abingdon Press.
Butzer, K.
1982   *Archaeology as Human Ecology: Method and Theory for a
                Contextual Approach.* Cambridge: Cambridge University Press.
Callaway, J. A.
1974   "Khirbet Raddana." *RB* 81:91–94.
1983   "A Visit with Ahilud: A Revealing Look at Village Life When
                Israel First Settled the Promised Land." *BAR* 9,5. Pages 42–53.
1984   "Village Subsistence at Ai and Raddana in Iron Age I." In *The
                Answers Lie Below, Essays in Honor of L. E. Toombs.* Edited by H.
                O. Thompson. Lanham, Md.: University Press of America. Pages
                51–66.
Camp, C. V.
1981   "The Wise Women of 2 Samuel: A Role Model for Women in
                Early Israel?" *CBQ* 43:14–29.
1985   *Wisdom and the Feminine in the Book of Proverbs.* Decatur, Ga.:
                Almond Press.
Campbell, A. F. and J. W. Flanagan.
1990   "1–2 Samuel." *The New Jerome Biblical Commentary.* Englewood
                Cliffs, N.J.: Prentice-Hall. Pages 145–59.
Campbell, E. F., Jr.
1975   *Ruth.* Garden City: Doubleday.
Campbell, J.
1972 [1949]   *The Hero with a Thousand Faces.* Reprint. Princeton, N.J.:
                Princeton University Press.
Carmichael, C. M.
1974   *The Laws of Deuteronomy.* Ithaca, N.Y.: Cornell University Press.
1977   "A Ceremonial Crux: Removing a Man's Sandal as a Female
                Gesture of Contempt." *JBL* 96:321–26.
Carneiro, R.
1970   "A Theory of the Origin of the State." *Science* 169:733–38.
1978   "Political Expansion as an Expression of the Principle of
                Competitive Exclusion." In *Origins of the State: The Anthropology
                of Political Evolution.* Edited by R. Cohen and E. R. Service.
                Philadelphia: Institute for the Study of Human Issues, Inc.
                Pages 205–23.
1981   "The Chiefdom as Precursor of the State." In *The Transition to
                Statehood in the New World.* Edited by G. Jones and R. Krautz.
                Cambridge: Cambridge University Press. Pages 37–79.

Carroll, B. A., ed.
1976   *Liberating Women's History: Theoretical and critical essays.*
                Urbana: University of Illinois Press.
Carroll, R. P.
1973   *When Prophecy Failed: Cognitive dissonance in the pro- phetic
                traditions of the Old Testament.* New York: Seabury.
1986   *Jeremiah.* Philadelphia: Westminster.
Chaney, M. L.
1981   "Systematic Study of the Sociology of the Israelite Monarchy."
                Paper presented at the SBL Annual Meeting, San Francisco,
                Calif.
1983   "Ancient Palestinian Peasant Movements and the Formation of
                Premonarchic Israel." In *Palestine in Transition: The Emergence of
                Ancient Israel.* Edited by D. N. Freedman and D. F. Graf.
                Sheffield: Almond Press. Pages 39–90.
Chang, C. and H. A. Koster.
1986   "Beyond Bones: Toward an Archaeology of Pastoralism." In
                Advances in Archaeological Method and Theory 9. Edited by M. B.
                Schiffer. Orlando, Fla.: Academic Press. Pages 97–147.
Childs, B. S.
1974   *Exodus.* London: SCM.
Christensen, D. L.
1984   "Huldah and the Men of Anathoth: Women in Leadership in the
                Deuteronomic History." *SBL Seminar Papers* 23:399–404.
Claessen, H. J. M. and P. Skalnik, eds.
1978   "The Early State: Theories and Hypotheses." In *The Early State.*
                The Hague: Mouton. Pages 3–29.
Clark, E. and H. Richardson, eds.
1977   *Women and Religion: Readings in the Western Tradition from
                Aeschylus to Mary Daly.* San Francisco: Harper & Row.
Clemen, C.
1939   *Die Phonikische Religion.* Leipzig: J. C. Hinrichs.
Clements, R. E.
1980   *Isaiah and the Deliverance of Jerusalem: A Study of the
                Interpretation of Prophecy in the Old Testament.* Sheffield: JSOT
                Press.
Clifford, R. J.
1966   "The use of *hôy* in the Prophets." *CBQ* 28:458–64.
Coats, G. W.
1970   "Self-Abasement and Insult Formulas." *JBL* 89:14–26.
1972   "Widow's Rights: A Crux in the Structure of Genesis 38." *CBQ*
                34:461–66.
1973   "Abraham's Sacrifice of Faith: A Form-Critical Study of Genesis
                22." *Int* 27:389–400.
1983   *Genesis, with an Introduction to Narrative Literature.* Grand
                Rapids, Mich.: Eerdmans.
Cockerham, W.
1981   *Sociology of Mental Disorder.* Englewood Cliffs, N.J.: Prentice-Hall.
Cody, A.
1965   "Le titre Egyptien et le nom propre du scribe de David." *RB*
                72:381–93.
1969   *A History of Old Testament Priesthood.* Rome: PBI.

Cogan, M.
1974   *Imperialism and Religion: Assyria, Judah and Israel in the Eighth and Seventh Centuries B.C.E.* Missoula, Mont.: Scholars Press.
Cohen, A.
1965   *Arab Border-Villages in Israel: A Study of Continuity and Change in Social Organization.* Manchester: Manchester University Press.
Cohen, C.
1973   "The Widowed City." *JANES* 5:75–81.
Cohen, M. A.
1965   "The Role of the Shilonite Priesthood in the United Monarchy of Ancient Israel." *HUCA* 36:59–98.
Cohen, N. G.
1992   Personal Communication, June 25.
Cohen, R.
1979   "The Iron Age Fortresses in the Central Negev." *BASOR* 236:61–79.
Cohen, R. and W. G. Dever.
1978   "Preliminary Report of the Pilot Season of the 'Central Negev Highlands Project.'" *BASOR* 232:29–45.
Cohn, R. L.
1983   "Form and Perspective in 2 Kings V." *VT* 33:171–84.
Cole, D. P.
1975   *Nomads of the Nomads. The Al Murah Bedouin of the Empty Quarter.* Chicago: Aldine.
Comaroff, J.
1985   *Body of Power, Spirit of Resistance: The culture and history of a South African people.* Chicago: University of Chicago Press.
Combs-Schilling, M. E.
1989   *Sacred Performance: Islam, Sexuality and Sacrifice.* New York: Columbia University Press.
Comstock, T. ed.
1974   *New Dimensions in Dance Research—anthropology & dance: The American Indian.* CORD Research Annual 6.
Coote, R. B.
1981   *Amos Among the Prophets.* Philadelphia: Fortress Press.
Coote, R. B. and K. W. Whitelam.
1986   "The Emergence of Israel: Social Transformation and State Formation Following the Decline in Late Bronze Age Trade." *Semeia* 37:107–47.
1987   *The Emergence of Early Israel in Historical Perspective.* Sheffield: Almond Press.
Cornelius, I.
1984   "Genesis XXVI and Mari: The Dispute Over Water and the Socio-Economic Way of Life of the Patriarchs." *JNSL* 12:53–61.
Cowling, G.
1988   "The Biblical Household." In *Wuenschet Jerusalem Frieden: Collected Communications to XIIth Congress of International Organization for Study of the Old Testament, Jerusalem, 1986.* Edited by M. Augustin and K. Schnunck. New York: Peter Lang. Pages 179–92.
Crenshaw, J. L.
1971   *Prophetic Conflict: Its effects upon Israelite religion.* BZAW 124. Berlin: Walter de Gruyter.
1985   "Education in Ancient Israel." *JBL* 104:601–15.

1990   "The Sage in Proverbs." In *The Sage in Israel and the Ancient Near East*. Edited by J. G. Gammie and L. G. Perdue. Winona Lake, Ind.: Eisenbrauns. Pages 205–16.

Cresswell, R.
1976   "Lineage Endogamy Among Maronite Mountaineers." In *Mediterranean Family Structures*. Edited by J. G. Peristiany. Cambridge: Cambridge University Press. Pages 101–14.

Cronk, L.
1989   "Strings Attached." *The Sciences* 5/6:2–4.
1990   Personal Communication, May 10.

Cross, F. M.
1973   *Canaanite Myth and Hebrew Epic: Essays in the History of the Religion of Israel*. Cambridge, Mass.: Harvard University Press.
1985   "New Directions in Dead Sea Scroll Research: II, Original Biblical Text Reconstructed from Newly Found Fragments." *BRev* 1,3:16–35.

Crusemann, F.
1980   "Zwei altestamentliche Witze: I Sam 21:11–15 und II Sam 6:16, 20–23." *ZAW* 92:215–27.

Culley, R. C.
1981   "Anthropology and Old Testament: An introductory comment." *Semeia* 21:1–5.

Culley, R. C. and T. W. Overholt, eds.
1981   *Anthropological perspectives on Old Testament Prophecy. Semeia* 21.

Cundall, A. E.
1968   *Judges, An Introduction and Commentary*. Leicester: InterVarsity.

Dalley, S.
1984   *Mari and Karana: Two Old Babylonian Cities*. New York: Longman.

Dalman, G.
1928–39   *Arbeit und Sitte in Palastina*. Gütersloh: C. Bertelsmann.

Dar, S.
1986   *Landscape and Pattern: An Archaeological Survey of Samaria 800 B.C.E.–636 C.E.* BAR International Series 308[i]. Oxford: British Archaeological Reports.

Daube, D.
1947   *Studies in Biblical Law*. Cambridge: Cambridge University Press.
1969   "The Culture of Deuteronomy." *Orita* 3:27–53.

Davies, D.
1977   "An Interpretation of Sacrifice in Leviticus." *ZAW* 89:387–98.

Davies, E. W.
1981a   "Inheritance Rights and the Hebrew Levirate Marriage, part 2." *VT* 31 3. Pages 257–68.
1981b   *Prophecy and Ethics: Isaiah and the Ethical Traditions of Israel*. Sheffield: JSOT Press.
1983   "Ruth IV 5 and the Duties of the *gō'ēl*." *VT* 33:231–34.

Davies, M. L.
1988   "Levitical Leprosy: Uncleanness and the Psyche." *ExpT* 99:136–39.

Davis, J.
1973   *Land and Family in Pisticci*. London: Athlone Press.

Day, J.
1989   *Molech: A God of Human Sacrifice in the Old Testament*. Cambridge: Cambridge University Press.

Deatrick, E. P.
1962   "Salt, Soil, Savior." *BA* 25,2:41–48.
de Geus, C. H. J.
1976   *The Tribes of Israel. An Investigation into some of the Presuppositions of Martin Noth's Amphictyonic Hypothesis.* Assen: Van Gorcum.
de Heusch, L.
1985   *Sacrifice in Africa: A Structuralist Approach.* Bloomington: Indiana University Press.
Delaney, C.
1988   "Mortal Flow: Menstruation in Turkish Village Society." In *Blood Magic, The Anthropology of Menstruation.* Edited by T. Buckley and A. Gottlieb. Berkeley: University of California Press. Pages 75–93.
Dentler, R. A. and K. T. Erikson.
1984   "The Functions of Deviance in Groups." In *Deviant Behavior.* 2d ed. Edited by D. H. Kelly. New York: St. Martin's Press. Pages 90–103.
Destro, A.
1989   *The Law of Jealousy: Anthropology of Sotah.* Atlanta: Scholars Press.
Detienne, M.
1989   "Culinary Practices and the Spirit of Sacrifice." In *The Cuisine of Sacrifice among the Greeks.* Edited by M. Detienne and J.-P. Vernant. Chicago: University of Chicago Press. Pages 1–20.
de Vaux, R.
1961   *Ancient Israel.* New York: McGraw-Hill.
Dever, W. G.
1982   "Monumental Architecture in Ancient Israel in the Period of the United Monarchy." In *Studies in the Period of David and Solomon and other Essays.* Edited by T. Ishida. Winona Lake, Ind.: Eisenbrauns. Pages 269–306.
de Vries, S.
1978   *Prophet against Prophet.* Grand Rapids, Mich.: Eerdmans.
De Waard, J.
1989   "Jotham's Fable: An Exercise in Clearing Away the Unclear." In *Wissenschaft und Kirche: Festschrift fur Eduard Lohse.* Edited by K. Aland and S. Meurcr. Bielefeld: Luther Verlag. Pages 362–70.
de Ward, E. F.
1977   "Superstitution and Judgment: Archaic Methods of Finding a Verdict." *ZAW* 89:1–19.
Dick, M. B.
1984   "Prophetic Poetics and the Verbal Icon." *CBQ* 46:226–46.
Dieterich, A.
1905   *Mutter Erde.* Leipzig: Teubner.
Dietrich, W.
1976   *Jesaja und die Politik.* Beiträge zur evangelischen Theologie, 74. Munich: Chr. Kaiser Verlag.
Diringer, D.
1949   "The Royal Jar Handle Stamps." *BA* 12:73–86.
Donaldson, M.
1981   "Kinship Theory in the Patriarchal Narratives: The Case of the Barren Wife." *JAAR* 49:77–87.

Donegan, J. B.
  1978   *Women and Men Midwives: Medicine, Morality and Misogyny in
                  Early America*. Westport, Conn.: Greenwood Press.
Douglas, M.
  1966   *Purity and Danger*. New York: Praeger.
  1973   *Natural Symbols*. New York: Pantheon.
  1960   *Implicit Meanings: Essays in Anthropology*. London: Routledge &
                  Paul.
Driver, G. R. and J. C. Miles
  1952–55   *The Babylonian Laws*. Oxford: Clarendon Press.
Driver, S. R.
  1895   *Deuteronomy*. 3d ed. Edinburgh: T & T Clark.
  1911   *The Book of Exodus*. Cambridge: Cambridge University Press.
Durand, J.-L.
  1989   "Ritual as Instrumentality." In *The Cuisine of Sacrifice among the
                  Greeks*. Edited by M. Detienne and J.-P. Vernant. Chicago:
                  University of Chicago Press. Pages 119–28.
Dybdahl, J. L.
  1981   *Israelite Village Land Tenure: Settlement to Exile*. Ph.D.
                  dissertation, Fuller Theological Seminary.
Dyson-Hudson, N.
  1971   "The Study of Nomads." In *Perspectives on Nomadism*. Edited by
                  W. G. Irons and N. Dyson-Hudson. Leiden: E. J. Brill. Pages 2–27.
Earle, T.
  1977   "A Reappraisal of Redistribution: Complex Hawaiian
                  Chiefdoms." In *Exchange Systems in Prehistory*. Edited by T.
                  Earle and J. Ericson. New York: Academic Press. Pages 213–29.
  1987   "Chiefdoms in Archaeological and Ethnohistorical Perspective."
                  ARA 16:279–308.
  1989   "The Evolution of Chiefdoms." *CA* 30:84–88.
Earle, T., ed.
  1991   "The Evolution of Chiefdoms." In *Chiefdoms: Power, Economy,
                  and Ideology*. Cambridge: Cambridge University Press. Pages 1–15.
Edelman, D.
  1984   "Saul's Rescue of Jabesh-Gilead (1 Sam. 11.1–11: Sorting Story
                  from History." *ZAW* 96:195–209.
  1985   "The 'Ashurites' of Eshbaal's State." *PEQ* 117:85–91.
  1988   "Tel Masos, Geshur, and David." *JNES* 47:253–58.
  1991   "The Manassite Genealogy in 1 Chronicles 7:14–19: Form and
                  Source." *CBQ* 53:179–201.
Edelstein, G. and Gibson, S.
  1982   "Ancient Jerusalem's Rural Food Basket." *BAR* 8,4:46–54.
Edwards, D. R.
  1985   "Heart." *HBD*, 377.
Edwards, I. E. S.
  1961   *The Pyramids of Egypt*. New York: Penguin Books.
Eichrodt, W.
  1961   *Theology of the Old Testament*. 2 vols. Philadelphia: Westminster.
Eilberg-Schwartz, H.
  1990   *The Savage in Judaism: An Anthropology of Israelite Religion and
                  Ancient Judaism*. Bloomington: Indiana University Press.
  1990   "Israel in the Mirror of Nature: Animal metaphors in the rituals
                  and narratives of Israelite religion." In *The Savage in Judaism: An*

Anthropology of Israelite Religion and Ancient Judaism.
Bloomington: Indiana University Press. Pages 115–40.
El-Barghuthi, O. S.
1924   "Rules of Hospitality (QANUN YD-DIYAFEH)." *JPOS* 4:175–203.
Eliade, M.
1959   *The Sacred and the Profane: The Nature of Religion.* New York:
             Harcourt, Brace & World, Inc.
1964   *Shamanism: Archaic Techniques of Ecstasy.* New York: Pantheon.
1969   *Images and Symbols: Studies in Religious Symbolism.* New York:
             Sheed & Ward.
1972   *The Forge and the Crucible.* Chicago: University of Chicago Press.
Elliger, K.
1955   "Das Gesetz Leviticus 18." *ZAW* 67:1–25.
1966   *Leviticus.* Tübingen: J. C. B. Mohr.
Elliott, J. H.
1981   *A Home for the Homeless: A Sociological Exegesis of 1 Peter, its
             Situation and Strategy.* Philadelphia: Fortress. Pages 207–37.
1986   "1 Peter, Its Situation and Strategy: A Discussion with David
             Balch." In *Perspectives in First Peter.* Edited by C. Talbert.
             Macon, Ga.: Mercer University Press. Pages 61–78.
Emmerson, G. I.
1989   "Women in Ancient Israel." In *The World of Ancient Israel:
             Sociological, Anthropological, and Political Perspectives.* Edited by
             R. E. Clements. Cambridge: Cambridge University Press. Pages
             371–94.
Eph'al, I.
1983   "On Warfare and Military Control in the Ancient Near Eastern
             Empires: A Research Outline." In *History, Historiography and
             Interpretation: Studies in Biblical and Cuneiform Literatures.* Edited
             by H. Tadmor and M. Weinfeld. Jerusalem: Magnes Press. Pages
             88–106.
Erikson, K. T.
1962   "Notes on the Sociology of Deviance." *Social Problems* 9:307–14.
Eslinger, L.
1985   *Kingship of God in Crisis: A Close Reading of 1 Samuel 1–12.*
             Decatur, Ga.: Almond Press.
Evans, G.
1963   "The Incidence of Labour-Service at Mari." *RA* 57:65–78.
1966   "Rehoboam's Advisers at Shechem, and Political Institutions in
             Israel and Sumer." *JNES* 25:273–79.
Evans-Pritchard, E. E.
1964   *Social Anthropology and Other Essays.* New York: Free Press.
1965   *Theories of Primitive Religion.* Oxford: Oxford University Press.
Exum, J. C.
1989   "Murder They Wrote: Ideology and the Manipulation of Female
             Presence in Biblical Narrative." *USQR* 43,1–4:19–39.
Falk, Z. W.
1960   "Two Symbols of Justice." *VT* 10:72–74.
Farbridge, M. H.
1970 [1923]   *Studies in Biblical and Semitic Symbolism.* New York: KTAV.
Fares, B.
1932   *L'honneur chez les Arabes avant l'Islam.* Paris.
Feeley-Harnik, G.
1985   "Issues In Divine Kingship." *ARA* 14:273–313.

Feil, D. K.
  1988   "The Morality of Exchange." In *Choice and Morality in
                    Anthropological Perspective*. Edited by G. N. Appell and T. N.
                    Madan. Albany: State University of New York Press. Pages
                    99–109.
Feldman, Y.
  1966   "Dermatology in the Hebrew Bible." *Cutis* 2:984–88.
Fensham, F. C.
  1962   "Salt as Curse in the Old Testament and the Ancient Near East."
                    BA 25 2. Pages 48–50.
  1964   "Did a Treaty Between the Israelites and the Kenites Exist?"
                    BASOR 175:51–54.
Ferguson, R. B.
  1990   "Explaining War." In *The Anthropology of War*. Edited by J.
                    Haas. Cambridge: Cambridge University Press. Pages 26–55.
Festinger, L.
  1957   *A Theory of Cognitive Dissonance*. Evanston, Ill.: Row, Peterson.
Festinger, L., et al.
  1956   *When Prophecy Fails: A Social and Psychological Study of a
                    Modern Group that Predicted the Destruction of the World*.
                    Minneapolis: University of Minnesota Press.
Fichtner, J.
  1949   "Jesaja unter den Weisen." *TLZ* 74:75–80.
Finkelstein, I.
  1984   "The Iron Age 'Fortresses' of the Negev Highlands:
                    Sedentarization of the Nomads." *Tel Aviv* 11:189–209.
  1985   "Summary and Conclusions: History of Shiloh from Middle
                    Bronze Age II to Iron Age II." *Tel Aviv* 2:159–77.
  1988a   *The Archaeology of the Settlement of Israel*. Jerusalem: Israel
                    Exploration Society.
  1988b   "Arabian Trade and Socio-Political Conditions in the Negev in
                    the Twelfth-Eleventh Centuries B.C.E." *JNES* 47:241–52.
  1989   "The Emergence of the Monarchy in Israel: The Environmental
                    and Socio-Economic Aspects." *JSOT* 44:43–74.
Finkelstein, J. J.
  1966   "The Genealogy of the Hammurapi Dynasty." *JCS* 20:95–118.
  1968   "An Old Babylonian Herding Contract and Genesis 31:38ff."
                    JAOS 88:30–36.
Fishbane, M.
  1986   "Biblical Prophecy as a Religious Phenomenon." In *Jewish
                    Spirituality*. Edited by A. Green. Vol. 1. New York: Crossroad.
                    Pages 62–81.
Fisher, L. R.
  1962   "Abraham and His Priest-King." *JBL* 81:264–70.
Flanagan, J. W.
  1981   "Chiefs in Israel." *JSOT* 20:47–73.
  1988   *David's Social Drama: A Hologram of Israel's Early Iron Age*.
                    Sheffield: Almond Press.
Flandrin, J. L.
  1979   *Families in Former Times: Kinship, Household, and Sexuality*.
                    Translated by R. Southern. Cambridge: Cambridge University
                    Press.

Flannery, K. V.
1972   "The Cultural Evolution of Civilizations." *Annual Review of Ecology and Systematics* 3:399–426.

Fleming, S.
1988   "Musings on Midwifery." *Arch* 41:68–69, 86.

Flesher, P. V. McC.
1988   *Oxen, Women, or Citizens? Slaves in the System of the Mishnah.* Brown Judaic Studies 143. Atlanta: Scholars Press.

Fohrer, G.
1952   "Die Gattung der Berichte über symbolische Handlungen der Propheten." *ZAW* 64:101–20.

Fontaine, C. R.
1982   *Traditional Sayings in the Old Testament.* Sheffield: Almond Press.
1990   "The Sage in Family and Tribe." In *The Sage in Israel and the Ancient Near East.* Edited by J. Gammie and L. Perdue. Winona Lake, Ind.: Eisenbrauns. Pages 155–64.

Ford, F. L.
1985   *Political Murder: From Tyrannicide to Terrorism.* Cambridge, Mass.: Harvard University Press.

Fortes, M.
1967   "Of Installation Ceremonies." *PRAI:*5–20.
1969   *Kinship and the Social Order.* London: Routledge & Kegan Paul.

Fox, M.
1973   "*Tob* as Covenant Terminology." *BASOR* 209:41–42.

Fox, R.
1967   *Kinship and Marriage: An Anthropological Perspective.* Harmondsworth, England: Penguin Books.

Frazer, J. G.
1910 [1974]   *Darwin and Modern Science.* Edited by A. C. Seward. Cambridge: Cambridge University Press. Pages 152–70. Reprinted as "Some Primitive Theories of The Origin of Man." In *Frontiers of Anthropology.* Edited by Ashley Montagu. New York: G. P. Putnam's Sons. Pages 297–314.
1935 [1974]   *The Golden Bough: The magic art.* Vol. 1. New York: Macmillan. Pages 1–23. Reprinted as "Anthropology into Literature." In *Frontiers of Anthropology.* Edited by Ashley Montagu. New York: G. P. Putnam's Sons. Pages 278–96.

Freedman, D. N., ed.
1992   *The Anchor Bible Dictionary.* 6 vols. New York: Doubleday.

Freeman, S. T.
1970   *Neighbors: Social Contract in a Castilian Hamlet.* Chicago: University of Chicago Press.

Frick, F. S.
1971   "The Rechabites Reconsidered." *JBL* 90:379–87.
1972   "Rechabites." *IDB.* 4.726–28.
1985   *The Formation of the State in Ancient Israel.* Sheffield: JSOT Press.
1986   "Social Science Methods and Theories of Significance for the Study of the Israelite Monarchy: A Critical Review Essay." *Semeia* 37:9–52.
1989   "Ecology, Agriculture and Patterns of Settlement." In *The World of Ancient Israel.* Edited by R. E. Clements. Cambridge: Cambridge University Press. Pages 67–93.

Fried, M. H.
1967   "On the Concepts of 'Tribe' and 'Tribal Society.' " In *Essays on
                the Problem of Tribe*. Edited by J. Helm. Seattle: University of
                Washington Press. Pages 3–20.
1978   "The State, the Chicken, and the Egg; or, What Came First?" In
                Origins of the State: The Anthropology of Political Evolution. Edited
                by R. Cohen and E. R. Service. Philadelphia: Institute for the
                Study of Human Issues, Inc. Pages 35–47.
Friedl, E.
1975   *Women and Men: An anthropologist's view*. New York: Rinehart
                and Winston.
Friedman, J. and M. J. Rowlands, eds.
1977   "Notes towards an Epigenetic Model of 'Civilization.' " In *The
                Evolution of Social Systems*. London: Duckworth. Pages 201–76.
Fries, N. K.
1904   *Das philosophische Gesprach von Hiob bis Platon*. Tübingen.
Frymer, T. S.
1962   "Ordeal, Judicial." *IDB*. 3:638–40.
Frymer-Kensky, T.
1985   "Review: *Texts of Terror: Literary feminist readings of Biblical
                narrativies*." *BRev* 1:6–7.
1989   "Law and Philosophy: The Case of Sex in the Bible." *Semeia*
                45:89–102.
Galaty, J. G. and D. L. Johnson.
1990   "Introduction: Pastoral Systems in Global Perspective." In *The
                World of Pastoralism: Herding systems in comparative perspective*.
                Edited by J. G. Galaty and D. L. Johnson. New York: Guilford
                Press/London: Belhaven Press. Pages 1–31.
Gammie, J. G. and L. G. Perdue.
1990   "Preface." In *The Sage in Israel and the Ancient Near East*.
                Winona Lake, Ind.: Eisenbrauns. Pages ix–xii.
Garfinkel, H.
1950   "Conditions of Successful Degradation Ceremonies." *American
                Journal of Sociology* 61:420–24.
Gaster, T. H.
1956   *Thespis: Ritual, Myth and Drama in the Ancient Near East*. New
                York: Schuman.
1975 [1969]   *Myth, Legend and Custom in the Old Testament*. New York: Harper
                & Row.
Geertz, C.
1973   *The Interpretation of Cultures: Selected essays*. New York: Basic
                Books.
1980   *Negara: The theatre state in nineteenth-century Bali*. Princeton:
                Princeton University Press.
1983   *Local Knowledge: Further essays in interpretative anthropology*.
                New York: Basic Books.
Geier, M.
1656   *De Ebraeorum luctu lugentiumque ritibus*.
Gelb, I. J.
1972   "From Freedom to Slavery." *RAI* 18:81–92.
1973   "Prisoners of War in Early Mesopotamia." *JNES* 32:72–73.
1976   "Quantitative Evaluation of Slavery and Serfdom." *AOAT*
                25:195–207.

Gellner, E.
1977   "Patrons and Clients." In *Patrons and Clients in Mediterranean Societies.* Edited by E. Gellner and J. Waterbury. London: Duckworth. Pages 1–51.

Gerstenberger, E. S.
1988   "Introduction to Cultic Poetry." In *Psalms, part I: With an Introduction to Cultic Poetry.* Grand Rapids, Mich.: Eerdmans. Pages 1–22, 30–34.

Gibson, T.
1990   "Raiding, Trading, and Tribal Autonomy in Insular Southeast Asia." In *The Anthropology of War.* Edited by J. Haas. Cambridge: Cambridge University Press. Pages 125–45.

Gilbert, A. S.
1975   "Modern Nomads and Prehistoric Pastoralists: The Limits of Analogy." *JANES* 7:53–71.

Giles, T.
1991   "*dāl* and *'ebyôn*: The Poor and the Needy in the Book of Amos." *BRT* 1:12–20.

Gilmore, D. D.
1987   "Introduction: The Shame of Dishonor." *In Honor and Shame and the Unity of the Mediterranean.* Edited by D. D. Gilmore. Washington, D.C.: American Anthropological Association. Pages 2–21.

Gilula, M.
1967   "An Egyptian Parallel to Jeremia I 4-5." *VT* 17:114.

Ginsberg, H. L.
1978   "The Oldest Record of Hysteria with Physical Stigmata, Zech 13:2–6." In *Studies in the Bible and the Ancient Near East: Presented to S. E. Lowenstamm.* Jerusalem: Magnes Press. Pages 23–27.

Giovannini, M. J.
1987   "Female Chastity Codes in the Circum-Mediterranean: Comparative Perspectives." In *Honor and Shame and the Unity of the Mediterranean.* Edited by D. D. Gilmore. Pages 61–74.

Girard, R.
1977   *Violence and the Sacred.* Baltimore, Md.: Johns Hopkins University Press.

Gluckman, M.
1967   *The Judicial Process among the Barotse of Northern Rhodesia.* Manchester: Manchester University Press.

Gnuse, R.
1991   "Israelite Settlement of Canaan: A Peaceful Internal Process." *BTB* 21:56–66 and 109–17.

Goode, E.
1975   "On Behalf of Labeling Theory." *Social Problems* 22:570–83.
1990   *Deviant Behavior.* 3d ed. Englewood Cliffs, N.J.: Prentice-Hall.

Goody, J.
1972   "The Evolution of the Family." In *Household and Family in Past Time.* Edited by P. Laslett and R. Wall. Cambridge: Cambridge University Press. Pages 103–24.
1973a   "Bridewealth and Dowry in Africa and Eurasia." In *Bridewealth and Dowry.* Edited by J. Goody and S. Tambiah. Cambridge: Cambridge University Press. Pages 1–58.

1976   *Production and Reproduction.* Cambridge: Cambridge University Press.

1982   *Cooking, Cuisine, and Class.* Cambridge: Cambridge University Press.

Goody, J. and S. Tambiah, eds.
1973b   *Bridewealth and Dowry.* Cambridge: Cambridge University Press.

Gordis, R.
1974   "Love, Marriage, and Business in the Book of Ruth: A Chapter in Hebrew Customary Law." In *A Light unto My Path: Old Testament Studies in Honor of Jacob M. Myers.* Edited by H. N. Bream, R. D. Heim and C. A. Moore. Gettysburg Theological Studies, 4. Philadelphia: Temple University Press. Pages 241–64.

Gordon, M. M.
1964   *Assimilation in American Life: The Role of Race, Religion, and National Origins.* New York: Oxford University Press.

Gottlieb, C.
1989   *Varieties of Marriage in the Bible and Their Analogues in the Ancient World.* Ph.D. dissertation, New York University.

Gottwald, N. K.
1958   "Immanuel as the Prophet's Son." *VT* 8:36–47.
1976   "War, Holy." *IDB.* 4:942–44.
1979   *The Tribes of Yahweh. A Sociology of the Religion of Liberated Israel 1250-1050 B.C.E.* New York: Orbis Books.
1983   "Early Israel and the Canaanite Socio-Economic System." In *Palestine in Transition: The Emergence of Ancient Israel.* Edited by D. N. Freedman and D. F. Graf. Sheffield: Almond Press. Pages 25–37.
1985   *The Hebrew Bible: A Socio-Literary Introduction.* Philadelphia: Fortress Press.

Gove, W. R.
1975   "The Labelling Theory of Mental Illness: A Reply to Scheff." *American Sociological Review* 40:242–48.
1980   *Labeling of Deviance: Evaluating a Perspective.* 2d ed. Beverly Hills: Sage Publications.

Granqvist, H.
1947   *Birth and Childhood Among the Arabs.* Helsinki: Soderstrom & Co.

Gray, G. B.
1971 [1925]   *Sacrifice in the Old Testament.* Reprint. New York: KTAV.

Gray, J.
1975   *I and II Kings.* 2d ed. Philadelphia: Westminster.
1982 [1969]   *Near Eastern Mythology.* New revised ed. New York: Peter Bedrick.

Grayson, A. K.
1972–76   *Assyrian Royal Inscriptions.* Wiesbaden: Harrassowitz.

Greenberg, M.
1990   "Biblical Attitudes Toward Power: Ideal and Reality in Law and Prophets." In *Religion and Law: Biblical-Judaic and Islamic Perspectives.* Edited by E. B. Firmage et al. Winona Lake, Ind.: Eisenbrauns. Pages 101–12.

Gross, W.
1979   "Lying Prophet and Disobedient Man of God in 1 Kings 13: Role Analysis." *Semeia* 15:97–135.

Grosz, K.
 1983   "Bridewealth and Dowry in Nuzi." In *Images of Women in
             Antiquity*. Edited by A. Cameron and A. Kuhrt. Detroit: Wayne
             State University Press. Pages 193–206.
Gruber, M. I.
 1989   "Breast-Feeding Practices in Biblical Israel and in Old
             Babylonian Mesopotamia." *JANES* 19:61–83.
 1977   "Aspects of Non-Verbal Communication in the Ancient Near
             East." Ph.D. diss. Columbia University.
 1978   "Tragedy of Cain and Abel." *JQR* 69:89–97.
Gunkel, H.
 1917   *Das Marchen im Alten Testament*. Tübingen: Mohr.
 1987   *The Folktale in the Old Testament*. Translated by M. D. Rutter.
             Sheffield: Almond Press.
Gunn, D. M.
 1978   *The Story of King David: Genre and interpretation*. JSOT suppl. 6.
             Sheffield: JSOT Press.
 1980   *The Fate of King Saul*. Sheffield: Sheffield University Press.
Haas, J.
 1982   *The Evolution of the Prehistoric State*. New York: Columbia
             University Press.
Habel, N. C.
 1965   "The Form and Significance of the Call Narratives." *ZAW*
             77:297–323.
Habicht, J. P., J. Davanzo, W. P. Butz, and L. Meyers.
 1985   "The Contraceptive Role of Breast Feeding." *Population Studies*
             39:213–32.
Hackett, J. A.
 1992   "1 and 2 Samuel." In *The Women's Bible Commentary*. Edited by
             C. A. Newsom and S. H. Ringe. Louisville, Ky.:
             Westminster/John Knox. Pages 85–95.
Hagan, H.
 1979   "Deception as Motif and Theme in 2 Sm 9–20; 1 Kgs 12." *Bib*
             60:301–26.
Hallo, W. W. and W. K. Simpson.
 1971   *The Ancient Near East: A History*. New York: Harcourt Brace
             Jovanovich.
Halpern, B.
 1981a   *The Constitution of the Monarchy in Israel*. Chico, Calif.: Scholars
             Press.
 1981b   "The Uneasy Compromise: Israel Between League and
             Monarchy." In *Traditions in Transformation, Turning Points in
             Biblical Faith*. Edited by B. Halpern and J. D. Levenson. Winona
             Lake, Ind.: Eisenbrauns. Pages 59–96.
 1988   *The First Historians: The Hebrew Bible and History*. San
             Francisco: Harper & Row.
Hals, R. M.
 1969   *The Theology of the Book of Ruth*. Philadelphia: Fortress Press.
 1985   "Legend." In *Saga, Legend, Tale, Novella, Fable*. Edited by G.
             Coats. Sheffield: JSOT Press. Pages 45–55.
Hamerton-Kelly, R. C.
 1987   *Violent Origins*. Stanford, Calif.: Stanford University Press.

Hamilton, V. P.
  1990   *The Book of Genesis Chapters 1–17*. Grand Rapids, Mich.:
                 Eerdmans.
Hanson, K. C.
  1989   "The Herodians and Mediterranean Kinship." *BTB* 19:75–84.
Hanson, P. D.
  1979   *The Dawn of Apocalyptic*. Philadelphia: Fortress Press.
  1985   "Conflict in Ancient Israel and Its Resolution." In *Understanding
                 the Word*. Edited by J. Butler, E. Conrad, and B. Ollenburger.
                 Pages 185–205.
  1987   "The Prophets as Writers and Poets." In *Prophecy in Israel:
                 Search for an identity*. Edited by D. Petersen. Philadelphia:
                 Fortress Press. Pages 22–73.
Haran, M.
  1977   "From Early to Classical Prophecy: Continuity and change." *VT*
                 27:385–97.
  1978   *Temples and Temple Service in Ancient Israel*. Oxford: Oxford
                 University Press.
  1979   "Seething a Kid in its Mother's Milk." *JSS* 30:23–35.
Harper, R. F.
  1892–1914   *Assyrian and Babylonian Letters*. Chicago: University of Chicago
                 Press.
Harris, M.
  1979   *Cultural Materialism: The Struggle for a Science of Culture*. New
                 York: Random House.
  1980   *Cultural Materialism*. New York: Vintage Books.
Harris, R.
  1964   "The *Naditu* Woman." In *Studies Presented to A. Leo Oppenheim*.
                 Chicago: University of Chicago Press. Pages 107–35.
  1975   *Ancient Sippar: A Demographic Study of an Old Babylonian City
                 (1894-1595 B.C.)*. Istanbul: Nederlands
                 Historisch-Archaeologisch Instituut.
Harrison, R. K.
  1962   "Madness." *IDB*. 3:220–21.
Hartman, C. G.
  1974   "The Solution of the Problem of the Infertility of the Unmarried
                 in Nonliterate Societies." In *Frontiers of Anthropology*. Edited by
                 Ashley Montagu. New York: G. P. Putnam's Sons. Pages 463–67.
Hasel, G.
  1971   "Linguistic Considerations Regarding the Translation of Isaiah's
                 Shear-Jashub. A Reassessment." *AUSS* 9:36–46.
Hauer, C., Jr.
  1986   "From Alt to Anthropology: The Rise of the Israelite State."
                 JSOT 36:3–15.
Hauser, A. J.
  1978   "Israel's Conquest of Palestine: A Peasant's Rebellion?" *JSOT*
                 7:2–19.
Hayes, J. H.
  1979   *An Introduction to Old Testament Study*. Nashville: Abingdon
                 Press.
Hayes, J. H. and J. M. Miller, eds.
  1977   *Israelite and Judean History*. Philadelphia: Westminster.
Hayter, M.
  1987   *The New Eve in Christ*. London: SPCK.

Heaps, W. A.
1969   *Assassination: A Special Kind of Murder.* New York: Meredith
            Press.
Heaton, E. W.
1974   *Solomon's New Men: The Emergence of Ancient Israel as a National
            State.* New York: Pica Press.
Heilbroner, R.
1962   *The Making of Economic Society.* Englewood Cliffs, N.J.:
            Prentice-Hall.
Helyer, L. R.
1983   "The Separation of Abram and Lot: Its Significance in the
            Patriarchal Narratives." *JSOT* 26:77–88.
Hendel, R. S.
1987   *The Epic of the Patriarch: The Jacob Cycle and the Narrative
            Traditions of Canaan and Israel.* Atlanta: Scholars Press.
Herdner, A.
1978   "Nouveaux Textes Alphabétiques de Ras Shamra." *Ugaritica*
            7:31–38.
Herion, G. A.
1986   "The Impact of Modern and Social Science Assumptions on The
            Reconstruction of Israelite History." *JSOT* 34:3–33.
Herskovits, M. J.
1940   *The Economic Life of Primitive Peoples.* New York: Knopf.
Hertzberg, H. W.
1964   *I and II Samuel. A Commentary.* Tr. J. S. Bowden. Philadelphia:
            Westminster.
Herzfeld, M.
1987   " 'As in your own house': Hospitality, Ethnography, and the
            Stereotype of Mediterranean Society." In *Honor and Shame and
            the Unity of the Mediterranean.* Edited by D. D. Gilmore.
            Washington, D.C.: American Anthropological Association.
            Pages 75–89.
Hieb, L.
1974   "Rhythms of Significance: Toward a symbolic analysis of dance
            in ritual." In *New Dimensions in Dance Research—Anthropology &
            dance: The American Indian.* CORD Research Annual 6:225–32.
Hiebert, P. S.
1989   " 'Whence Shall Help Come to Me?' " In *Gender and Difference.*
            Edited by Peggy L. Day. Minneapolis: Fortress Press. Pages
            125–41.
Hobbs, T. R.
1985   *2 Kings.* Waco, Tex.: Word Books.
Hoebel, E. A.
1972   *Anthropology: The Study of Man.* 4th ed. New York: McGraw-Hill.
Hoens, D.
1975   "Rites of Initiation: A contribution to the methodology of
            comparative religion." In *Explorations in the Anthropology of
            Religion: Essays in honour of Jan van Baal.* Edited by W. E. A. van
            Beek and J. H. Scherer. The Hague: Nijhoff. Pages 29–45.
Hoffman, M. A.
1988   "Prelude to Civilization: The Predynastic Period in Egypt." In
            The First Egyptians. Columbia, S.C.: University of South Carolina
            Press. Page 42.

Hoffmeir, J. K.
  1987   "Queries and Comments." *BAR* 13,2:60–61.
Hoffner, H. A.
  1975   "Propaganda and Political Justification in Hittite
                  Historiography." In *Unity and Diversity: Essays in the History,
                  Literature, and Religion of the Ancient Near East*. Edited by H.
                  Goedicke and J. J. M. Roberts. Baltimore, Md.: Johns Hopkins
                  University Press. Pages 49–62.

Hoftijzer, J.
  1970   "Absalom and Tamar: A Case of Fratriarchy?" In *Schrift en
                  Uitleg*. Kampen: J. H. Kok. Pages 54–61.

Hoijer, H.
  1956   "Language and Writing." In *Man, Culture, and Society*. Edited by
                  H. L. Shapiro. New York: Oxford University Press. Pages
                  198–223.

Hole, F.
  1979   "Rediscovering the Past in the Present: Ethnoarchaeology in
                  Luristan, Iran." In *Ethnoarchaeology: Implications of Ethnography
                  for Archaeology*. Edited by C. Kramer. New York: Columbia
                  University Press. Pages 192–218.

Holladay, W. L.
  1971   *A Concise Hebrew and Aramaic Lexicon of the Old Testament*.
                  Grand Rapids, Mich.: Eerdmans.
  1986   *Jeremiah 1: A Commentary on the Book of the Prophet Jeremiah
                  Chapters 1–25*. Philadelphia: Fortress Press.
  1989   *Jeremiah 2: A Commentary on the Book of Jeremiah Chapters
                  26–52*. Minneapolis: Fortress Press.

Holy, L.
  1989   *Kinship, Honour and Solidarity: Cousin Marriage in the Middle
                  East*. Manchester: Manchester University Press.

Hooks, M.
  1985   *Sacred Prostitution in Israel and the Ancient Near East*. Ph.D.
                  dissertation, Hebrew Union College.

Hopkins, D. C.
  1983   "The Dynamics of Agriculture in Monarchical Israel." *SBL
                  Seminar Papers* 17:177–202.
  1985   *The Highlands of Canaan*. Sheffield: Almond Press.
  1987   "Life on the Land: The Subsistence Struggles of Early Israel." *BA*
                  50:178–91.

Hossfeld, F. L. and I. L. Meyer.
  1973   *Prophet gegen Prophet*. Göttingen: Verlag Schweizerisches
                  Katholisches Bibelwerk.
  1974   "Der Prophet vor dem Tribunal, Neuer Auslegungsversuch von
                  Jer 26." *ZAW* 86:30–50.

Houtman, C.
  1977   "Zu 1 Samuel 2:25." *ZAW* 89:412–17.
Huber, F.
  1976   *Jahwe, Juda und die anderen Volker beim Propheten Jesaja*. Berlin:
                  Walter de Gruyter.

Hubert, H. and M. Mauss.
  [1899] 1964   *Sacrifice: Its Nature and Function*. Chicago: University of Chicago
                  Press.
  1902/03   "Théorie générale de la magie." *Année Sociologique* 7:1–146.

Huffmon, H.
1959   "The Covenant Lawsuit in the Prophets." *JBL* 78:285–95.
Hulse, E. V.
1975   "The Nature of Biblical 'Leprosy' and the Use of Alternative
            Medical Terms in Modern Translations of the Bible." *PEQ*
            107:87–105.
Ibrahim, M. M.
1978   "The Collared-Rim Jar of the Early Iron Age." In *Archaeology in
            the Levant: Essays for Kathleen Kenyon.* Edited by R. Moorey and
            P. Parr. Warminster: Aris & Phillips. Pages 116–26.
Irons, W. G.
1971   "Variation in Political Stratification among the Yomut
            Turkmen." *AQ* 44:143–56.
1974   "Nomadism as a Political Adaptation: The Case of the Yomut
            Turkmen." *American Ethnologist* 1:635–58.
Isbell, C. D.
1978   "2 Kings 22:3–23:24 and Jeremiah 36: A Stylistic Comparison."
            JSOT 8:33–45.
Ishida, T.
1977   *Royal Dynasties in Ancient Israel.* Berlin: Walter de Gruyter.
1982   "Solomon's Succession to the Throne of David—A Political
            Analysis." In *Studies in the Period of David and Solomon and other
            Essays.* Edited by T. Ishida. Winona Lake, Ind.: Eisenbrauns.
            Pages 175–87.
Isserlin, B. S. J.
1983   "The Israelite Conquest of Canaan: A Comparative Review of
            the Arguments Applicable." *PEQ* 115:85–94.
Jackson, B. S.
1984   "The Ceremonial and the Judicial: Biblical Law as Sign and
            Symbol." *JSOT* 30:25–50.
Jacobsen, T.
1949   "Mesopotamia: The Cosmos as a State." In *Before Philosophy:
            The Intellectual Adventure of Ancient Man.* Baltimore, Md.:
            Penguin Books. Pages 137–99.
1975   "Religious Drama in Ancient Mesopotamia." In *Unity and
            Diversity; Essays in History, Literature, and Religion of the Ancient
            Near East.* Edited by H. Goedicke and J. J. M. Roberts. Baltimore,
            Md.: Johns Hopkins University Press. Pages 65–77.
Jakobson, R. D.
1950   "Umbilical Cord." In *Funk and Wagnalls Standard Dictionary of
            Folklore, Mythology, and Legend.* Edited by M. Leach. New York:
            Funk & Wagnalls. Pages 1149.
James, E. O.
1962   *Sacrifice and Sacrament.* New York: Barnes & Noble.
Jameson, R. D.
1989   "Shoes." *Standard Dictionary of Folklore, Mythology and Legend.*
            Edited by M. Leach. San Francisco: Harper & Row. Pages 1008–9.
Janeway, E.
1980   "Who is Sylbia? On the Loss of Sexual Paradigms." In *Women:
            Sex and Sexuality.* Edited by C. R. Stimpson and E. W. Person.
            Chicago: University of Chicago Press. Pages 4–20.
Janssen, J. J.
1979   "The Role of the Temple in the Egyptian Economy During the
            New Kingdom." In *State and Temple Economy in the Ancient Near*

East. Edited by E. Lipinski. Leuven: Departement Orientalistiek. Pages 505–15.

Jensen, J.
1984   *Isaiah, 1–39.* Wilmington, Del.: Michael Glazier.
1990   "Isaiah 1–39." In *The New Jerome Biblical Commentary.* Edited by R. E. Brown, J. A. Fitzmyer, R. E. Murphy. Englewood Cliffs, N.J.: Prentice-Hall. Pages 229–48.

Jensen, M. D., R. C. Benson, and I. M. Bobak.
1977   *Maternity Care, the Nurse and the Family.* St. Louis, Mo.: C. V. Mosby.

Johnson, A. and T. Earle.
1987   *The Evolution of Human Society: From Forager Group to Agrarian State.* Stanford: Stanford University Press.

Johnson, A. R.
1962   *The Cultic Prophet in Ancient Israel.* Cardiff: University of Wales Press.
1964   *The Vitality of the Individual in the Thought of Ancient Israel.* 2d ed. Cardiff: University of Wales Press.
1983 [1970]   "Psalm 23 and the Household of Faith," In *Proclamation and Presence: Old Testament Essays in Honour of Gwynne Henton Davies.* Edited by J. I. Durham and J. R. Porter. Macon, Ga.: Mercer University Press. Pages 255–71.

Johnson, M. D.
1969   *The Purpose of Biblical Genealogies.* SNTSMS 8; Cambridge: Cambridge University Press.

Jordan, B.
1983   *Birth in Four Cultures.* Montreal: Eden.

Junker, H.
1959   "Die literarische Art von Is 5.107." *Biblica* 40: 259–66.

Kaiser, O.
1972   *Isaiah 1–12: A Commentary.* Philadelphia: Westminster.
1974   *Isaiah 13–39: A Commentary.* Philadelphia: Westminster.

Kalmin, R.
1992   "Levirate Law." *ABD* 4:296–97.

Kapelrud, A. S.
1967   "Shamanistic Features in the Old Testament." In *Studies in Shamanism.* Edited by Carl-Martin Edsman. Stockholm: Almqvist and Wiksell. Pages 90–96.

Kay, M. A.
1982   *Anthropology of Human Birth.* Philadelphia: F. A. Davis.

Keel, O.
1985   *The Symbolism of the Biblical World: Ancient Near Eastern Iconography and The Book of Psalms.* Translated by T. J. Hallett; New York: Crossroad.

Keesing, R. M.
1971   *New Perspectives in Cultural Anthropology.* New York: Holt, Rinehart and Winston.

Kelly, J.
1984   *Women, History and Theory.* Chicago: University of Chicago Press.

Kenik, H. A.
1983   *Design for Kingship: The Deuteronomistic Narrative Technique in 1 Kings 3:4–15.* Chico, Calif.: Scholars Press.

Kessler, M.
1969   "The Significance of Jer 36." *ZAW* 81:381–83.

Khazanov, A. M.
1984   *Nomads and the Outside World.* Cambridge: Cambridge University
               Press.
Kipp, R. S. and E. M. Schortman.
1989   "The Political Impact of Trade in Chiefdoms." *AA* 91:370–85.
Kitsuse, J.
1962   "Societal Reactions to Deviant Behavior: Problems of Theory
               and Method." *Social Problems* 9:247–56.
Klein, I.
1979   *A Guide to Jewish Religious Practice.* New York: Jewish
               Theological Seminary of America.
Klein, J.
1992   "Akitu." *ABD* 1:138–40.
Klein, R. W.
1983   *1 Samuel.* Waco, Tex.: Word Books.
Knierim, R. P.
1981   "Cosmos and History in Israel's Theology." *Horizons in Biblical
               Theology* 3:59–123
Koch, K.
1983   *The Prophets: The Assyrian Period.* Philadelphia: Fortress Press.
1984   *The Prophets: The Babylonian and Persian Periods.* Philadelphia:
               Fortress Press.
Kochavi, M., ed.
1972   *Judea, Samaria and the Golan: Archaeological Survey 1967–1968.*
               Jerusalem: Carta (Hebrew).
Kohler, L. H.
1957   *Hebrew Man.* Nashville: Abingdon Press.
Kornfeld, W.
1962   "Der Symbolismus der Tempelsaulen." *ZAW*:52–57.
Koster H. A. and J. B. Koster.
1976   "Competition or Symbiosis?: Pastoral Adaptive Strategies in the
               Southern Argolid, Greece." In *Regional Variation in Modern
               Greece and Cyprus.* Edited by M. Dimen and E. Friedl. New York:
               N.Y. Academy of Sciences. Pages 275–85.
Kovacs, B. W.
1974   "Is There a Class-Ethic in Proverbs?" In *Essays in Old Testament
               Ethics,* Edited by J. L. Crenshaw and J. T. Willis. New York:
               KTAV. Pages 171–89.
Kraeling, C. H. and R. M. Adams, eds.
1960   *City Invincible.* Chicago: University of Chicago Press.
Kramer, S. N.
1942   "The Oldest Literary Catalogue." *BASOR* 88:10–19.
1956   "Man's First Cosmogony and Cosmology." In *From the Tablets of
               Sumer.* Indian Hills, Colorado: Falcon's Wing Press. Pages 71–96.
Kraus, H.-J.
1988   *Psalms 1–59.* Minneapolis, Minn.: Augsburg.
Kristiansen, K.
1982   "The Formation of Tribal Systems in Later European Prehistory:
               Northern Europe, 4000–500 B.C." In *Theory and Explanation in
               Archaeology, The Southhampton Conference.* Edited by C. Renfrew
               et al. New York: Academic Press. Pages 241–80.
Kroeber, A. L.
1948   *Anthropology.* New York: Harcourt Brace Jovanovich.

Kruger, P. A.
   1988   "The Symbolic Significance of the Hem (KANAF) in 1 Samuel
                     15.27." In *Text and Context: Old Testament and Semitic Studies for
                     F. C. Fensham*. Edited by W. Claassen. Sheffield: JSOT Press.
                     Pages 105–16.
Kurht, A.
   1990   "Nabonidus and the Babylonian Priesthood." In *Pagan Priests:
                     Religion and Power in the Ancient World*. Edited by M. Beard and J.
                     North. London: Duckworth. Pages 117–55.
LaBianca, O. S.
   1979   "Agricultural Production on Hesban's Hinterland in the Iron
                     Age." Paper presented to the annual meeting of the ASOR
                     (November 15, 1979).
   1990   *Sedentarization and Nomadization: Food System Cycles at Hesban
                     and Vicinity in Transjordan*. Berrien Springs, Mich.: Andrews
                     University Press.
Lakoff, G. and M. Johnson
   1980   *Metaphors We Live By*. Chicago: University of Chicago Press.
   1987   *Women, Fire, and Dangerous Things: What Categories Reveal About
                     the Mind*. Chicago: University of Chicago Press.
Lambert, W. G.
   1968   "Myth and Ritual as Conceived by the Babylonians." *JSS*
                     13:104–12.
Lance, H. D.
   1971   "Royal Stamps and the Kingdom of Josiah." *HTR* 64:315–32.
Landsberger, H. A.
   1973   "Peasant Unrest: Themes and Variations." In *Rural Protest:
                     Peasant Movements and Social Change*. Edited by H. A.
                     Landsberger. New York: Barnes & Noble. Pages 1–64.
Lane, E. W.
   1878   *An Account of the Manners and Customs of the Modern Egyptians*.
                     2 vols. London.
Lang, B.
   1981   *Kein Aufstand in Jerusalem: die Politik des Propheten Ezechiel*.
                     Stuttgart: Katholisches Bibelwerk.
   1983a   "What is a Prophet?" In *Monotheism and the Prophetic Minority*.
                     Sheffield: Almond Press. Pages 60–91.
   1983b   "The Making of Prophets in Israel." In *Monotheism and the
                     Prophetic Minority*. Sheffield: Almond Press. Pages 92–113.
   1983c   "Old Testament and Anthropology: A preliminary bibliography."
                     Biblische Notizen: Beitraege zur exegetischen diskussion 20:37–46.
   1985   "Introduction: Anthropology as a new model for biblical
                     studies." In *Anthropological Approaches to the Old Testament*.
                     Edited by B. Lang. *Issues in Religion and Theology* 8:1–20.
   1986   "Street Theater, Raising the Dead, and the Zoroastrian
                     Connection in Ezekiel's Prophecy." In *Ezekiel and His Book.
                     Textual and Literary Criticism and Their Interrelation*. Edited by J.
                     Lust. *BETL* 74; Leuven: Leuven University Press. Pages 297–316.
   1988   "Afterlife: Ancient Israel's Changing Vision of the World
                     Beyond." *BRev* 4, 1:12–23.
Lapp, P. W.
   1960   "Late Royal Seals from Judah." *BASOR* 158:11–22.

Lasine, S.
1984   "Guest and Host in Judges 19: Lot's Hospitality in an Inverted
               World." *JSOT* 29:37–59.
Laughlin, J. C. H.
1976   "The 'Strange Fire' of Nadab and Abihu." *JBL* 95:559–65.
Leach, E. R.
1951   "The Structural Implications of Matrilateral Cross-Cousin
               Marriage." *JRAI* 81:23–55.
1958   "Magical Hair." *JRAI* 88:147–64.
1976   *Culture and Communication.* Cambridge: Cambridge University
               Press.
Leavitt, J. W.
1986   *Brought to Bed: Child-Bearing in America, 1750-1950.* New York:
               Oxford University Press.
Lees, S. H.
1979   "Ethnoarchaeology and the Interpretation of Community
               Organization." In *Ethnoarchaeology: Implications of Ethnography
               for Archaeology.* Edited by C. Kramer. New York: Columbia
               University Press. Pages 265–76.
Lemche, N. P.
1975   "The 'Hebrew Slave': Comments on the Slave Law, Exodus
               21:2–11." *VT* 25:129–44.
1983   "On Sociology and the History of Israel." *BN* 21:48–58.
1985   *Early Israel: Anthropological and Historical Studies on the Israelite
               Society Before the Monarchy.* SVT 37; Leiden: E. J. Brill.
1988   *Ancient Israel: A New History of Israelite Society.* Sheffield: JSOT
               Press.
Lemert, E. M.
1972 [1967]   *Human Deviance, Social Problems, and Social Control.* 2d ed.
               Englewood Cliffs, N.J.: Prentice-Hall.
Lenski, G.
1970   *Human Societies: A Macrolevel Introduction to Sociology.* New
               York: McGraw-Hill Book Co.
Lenski, G. and J. Lenski.
1978   *Human Societies: An Introduction to Macrosociology.* 3d ed. New
               York: McGraw-Hill.
Lerner, G.
1986   *The Creation of Patriarchy.* New York: Oxford University Press.
Levine, A.-J.
1992   "Ruth." In *The Women's Bible Commentary.* Edited by C. A.
               Newsom and S. H. Ringe. Louisville: Westminster/John Knox.
               Pages 78–84.
Levine, B. A.
1983   "In Praise of the Israelite *Mispaha*: Legal Themes in the Book of
               Ruth." In *The Quest for the Kingdom of God: Studies in Honor of
               George E. Mendenhall.* Edited by H. B. Huffmon et al. Winona
               Lake, Ind.: Eisenbrauns. Pages 95–106.
1989   *Leviticus.* Philadelphia: The Jewish Publication Society.
Levine, L. B.
1972a   *Two Neo-Assyrian Stelae from Iran.* Toronto: Royal Ontario
               Museum.
1972b   "Menahem and Tiglath-Pileser: A New Symchronism." *BASOR*
               206:40–42.

Levine, L. I. A.
  1988   "The Age of Hellenism." In *Ancient Israel: A short history from
                    Abraham to the Roman destruction of the Temple*. Edited by H.
                    Shanks. Englewood Cliffs, N.J.: Prentice-Hall. Pages 177–204.
Levinson, J. and B. Halpern.
  1980   "The Political Import of David's Marriages." *JBL* 99:507–18.
Levi-Strauss, C.
  1963   *Structural Anthropology*. New York: Basic Books.
  1966   *The Savage Mind*. Chicago: University of Chicago Press.
  1967   *The Scope of Anthropology*. Translated by S. O. Paul and R. A.
                    Paul. London: Cape.
  1969   *The Elementary Structures of Kinship*. Boston: Beacon Press.
  1979   *Myth and Meaning*. New York: Schocken Books.
Lewis, G.
  1987   "A Lesson From Leviticus: Leprosy" *Man* 22:593–612.
Lewis, I. M.
  1971   *Ecstatic Religion: An anthropological study of spirit possession and
                    shamanism*. Baltimore, Md.: Penguin Books.
  1980   "What is a Shaman." *Folk* 23:25–35.
Lillie, W.
  1975   "Pauline House-Tables." *ExpT* 86:179–83.
Limburg, J.
  1969   "The Root *ryb* and the Prophetic Lawsuit Speeches," *JBL*
                    88:291–304.
  1978   "The Prophets in Recent Study." *Interpretation* 32:56–68.
Lindars, B.
  1965   "Elijah, Elisha and the Gospel Miracles." In *Miracles*. Edited by
                    C. F. D. Moule. London: A. R. Mowbray & Co. Pages 61–79.
Lindblom, J.
  1973   *Prophecy in Ancient Israel*. Philadelphia: Fortress Press.
Lindenberger, J. M.
  1991   "How Much for a Hebrew Slave? The Meaning of *MINEH* in
                    Deut 15:18." *JBL* 110:479–82.
Link, B. G. et al.
  1987   "The Social Rejection of Former Mental Patients: Understanding
                    Why Labels Matter." *AJS* 92,6:1461–500.
Linsky, A.
  1975   "An Inventory of Propositions from the Societal Reaction
                    Perspective." Unpublished paper. Annual meeting of the Society
                    for the Study of Social Problems. San Francisco, August.
Liverani, M.
  1992   "Nationality and Political Identity." *ABD* 4.1031–37.
Llewellyn, K. N. and E. A. Hoebel.
  1941   *The Cheyenne Way*. Norman: University of Oklahoma Press.
Lofland, J.
  1969   *Deviance and Identity*. Englewood Cliffs, N.J.: Prentice-Hall.
Long, B. O.
  1975   "Social Setting for Prophetic Miracle Stories." *Semeia* 3:46–63.
  1977   "Prophetic Authority as Social Reality." In *Canon and Authority*.
                    Edited by G. W. Coats et al. Philadelphia: Fortress Press. Pages
                    3–20.
  1981   "Social Dimensions of Prophetic Conflict." *Semeia* 21:31–53.

Long, V. P.
    1989   *The Reign and Rejection of King Saul: A Case for Literary and
                Theological Coherence.* Atlanta: Scholars Press.
Luria, B. Z.
    1969–70   *Saul and Benjamin: Studies in the History of the Tribe of Benjamin.*
                Jerusalem: Magnes Press.
    1985-86   "What is the Vineyard in Isaiah's Parable?" *Beth Mikra*
                31:289–92 (Hebrew).
Lust, J.
    1971   "The Immanuel Figure: A Charismatic Judge-Leader." *ETL*
                42:464–70.
McCarter, P. K.
    1973   "The River Ordeal in Israelite Literature." *HTR* 66:403–12.
    1980a   *I Samuel.* New York: Doubleday.
    1980b   "The Apology of David." *JBL* 99:489–504.
    1984   *II Samuel.* New York: Doubleday.
    1986   "A Major New Introduction to the Bible." *BRev* 2,2:42–50.
    1988   "The Patriarchal Age." In *Ancient Israel: A Short History from
                Abraham to the Roman Destruction of the Temple.* Edited by H.
                Shanks. Englewood Cliffs, N.J.: Prentice-Hall. Pages 1–29.
    1990   "The Sage in the Deuteronomistic History." In *The Sage in Israel
                and the Ancient Near East.* Edited by J. G. Gammie and L. G.
                Perdue. Winona Lake, Ind.: Eisenbrauns. Pages 289–93.
McCarthy, D. J.
    [1972] 1978 *Old Testament Covenant: A Survey of Current Opinions.* Atlanta:
                John Knox.
McEvenue, S. E.
    1975   "A Comparison of Narrative Styles in the Hagar Stories." In
                Classical Hebrew Narrative. Edited by R. C. Culley. *Semeia*
                3:64–80.
McKane, W.
    1979   "Prophecy and the Prophetic Literature." In *Traditions and
                Interpretation.* Edited by G. W. Anderson. Oxford: Oxford
                University Press. Pages 163–88.
    1982   "Prophet and Institution." *ZAW* 94:251–66.
McKenzie, D.
    1907   "Children and Wells." *Folklore* 18:253–82.
McKenzie, J. L.
    1959   "The Elders in the Old Testament." *Biblica* 40:523–27.
    1965   "Sandals." *Dictionary of the Bible.* Milwaukee: Bruce. Pages
                772–73.
McNutt, P. M.
    1990   *The Forging of Israel: Iron Technology, Symbolism, and Tradition in
                Ancient Society.* Sheffield: Almond Press.
Malamat, A.
    1965   "Organs of Statecraft in the Israelite Monarchy." *BA* 28:34–65.
    1968   "King Lists of the Old Babylonian Period and Biblical
                Genealogies." *JAOS* 88:163–73.
    1973   "Tribal Societies: Biblical Genealogies and African Lineage
                Systems." In *Archives européennes de sociologie* 14:126–36.
    1979   "*UMMATUM* in Old Babylonian Texts and its Ugaritic and
                Biblical Counterparts." *UF* 11:527–36.

| 1987 | "A Forerunner of Biblical Prophecy: The Mari documents." In *Ancient Israelite Religion*. Edited by P. Miller, Jr, P. Hanson et al. Philadelphia: Fortress Press. Pages 33–52. |
| 1989 | *Mari and the Early Israelite Experience*. Oxford: Oxford University Press. |

Malina, B. J.
1981	*The New Testament World: Insights from Cultural Anthropology*. Atlanta: John Knox.
1981	"Clean and Unclean: Understanding Rules of Purity." In *The New Testament World: Insights from Cultural Anthropology*. Atlanta: John Knox. Pages 122–52.
1986	*Christian Origins and Cultural Anthropology*. Atlanta: John Knox.

Malina, B. J. and J. H. Neyrey.
| 1988 | *Calling Jesus Names: The Social Value of Labels in Matthew*. Sonoma, Calif.: Polebridge Press. |

Malinowski, B.
| 1959 | *Crime and Custom in Savage Society*. Paterson, N.J.: Littlefield, Adams and Company. |

March, E.
| 1974 | "Prophecy." In *Old Testament Form Criticism*. Edited by J. H. Hayes. San Antonio: Trinity University Press. |

Marcus, D.
| 1989 | "The Bargaining between Jephthah and the Elders (Judges 11:4–11)." *JANES* 19:95–100. |

Marcus, G. E. and M. M. J. Fischer.
| 1986 | *Anthropology as Cultural Critique: An experimental moment in the human sciences*. Chicago: University of Chicago Press. |

Marcus, G. E. and J. Clifford, eds.
| 1986 | *Writing Culture: The poetics and politics of ethnography: A School of American Research Advanced Seminar*. Berkeley: University of California Press. |

Marfoe, L.
| 1979 | "The Integrative Transformation: Patterns of Socio-political Organization in Southern Syria." *BASOR* 234:1–42. |

Margalit, B.
| 1981 | "A Ugaritic Prayer for a City Under Siege." *Proceedings of the Seventh World Congress of Jewish Studies: Studies in the Bible and the Ancient Near East* 177:63–83 (Hebrew). |
| 1986 | "Why King Mesha of Moab Sacrificed his Oldest Son." *BAR* 12,6:62–63, 76. |

Martin, J. D.
| 1989 | "Israel as a Tribal Society." In *The World of Ancient Israel: Sociological, Anthropological and Political Perspectives: Essays by Members of the Society for Old Testament Study*. Edited by R. E. Clements. Cambridge [England]/New York: Cambridge University Press. Pages 95–118. |

Matheney, M. P.
| 1986 | "Current Status of Old Testament Studies." *American Library Association: Proceedings* 40. Pages 119–33. |

Matthews, V. H.
1981a	"Pastoralists and Patriarchs." *BA* 44:215–18.
1981b	"Legal Aspects of Military Service in Ancient Mesopotamia." *Military Law Review* 94:135–51.
1986	"The Wells of Gerar." *BA* 49:118–26.

1987	"Entrance Ways and Threshing Floors: Legally Significant Sites in the Ancient Near East." *FEH* 19:25–40.
1988a	*Manners and Customs in the Bible.* Peabody, Mass.: Hendrickson Publishers.
1988b	"Kings of Israel: A Question of Crime and Punishment." *SBL Seminar Papers.* Atlanta: Scholars Press. Pages 517–26.
1991	"The King's Call to Justice," *BZ* 35:204–16.

Matthews, V. H. and D. C. Benjamin.

1991a	"The Divine Assembly: Ancient Israel's Understanding of God." *TBT* 29,3:157–62.
1991b	*Old Testament Parallels: Laws and Stories from the Ancient Near East.* Mahwah, N.J.: Paulist Press.

Matthews, V. H. and F. Mims.

1985	"Jacob the Trickster and Heir of the Covenant: A Literary Interpretation." *PRS* 12:185–95.

Mattingly, G. L.

1985	"Farming." *Harper's Bible Dictionary.* Edited by P. J. Achtemeier. San Francisco: Harper & Row. Pages 303–4.

Mauss, M.

1967	*The Gift: Forms and Functions of Exchange in Archaic Societies.* New York: Norton & Company.
1968	*Les fonctions sociale du sacre.* Vol. 1. Edited by V. Karady. Paris.

Mayes, A. D. H.

1969	"The Historical Context of the Battle Against Sisera." *VT* 19:353–60.

Mays J. L.

1976	*Micah.* Philadelphia: Westminster.

Mazar, A.

1990	*Archaeology of the Land of the Bible 10,000–586 B.C.E.* New York: Doubleday.

Mazar, B.

1965	"The Sanctuary of Arad and the Family of Hobab the Kenite." *JNES* 24:297–303.

Meier, S. A.

1988	*The Messenger in the Ancient Semitic World.* Atlanta: Scholars Press.

Mendelsohn, I.

1949	*Slavery in the Ancient Near East.* New York: Oxford University Press.
1960	"On the Preferential Status of the Eldest Son." *BASOR* 156:38–40.
1970	"Slavery in the Ancient Near East." In *The Biblical Archaeologist Reader 3.* Edited by E. F. Campbell and D. N. Freedman. Garden City, N.Y.: Doubleday. Pages 127–43.

Mendenhall, G. E.

1973	*The Tenth Generation. The Origins of the Biblical Tradition.* Baltimore, Md.: Johns Hopkins University Press.
1975	"The Monarchy." *Int* 29:155–70.
1976a	" 'Change and Decay All Around I See': Conquest, Covenant, and *The Tenth Generation.*" *BA* 39:152–57.
1976b	"Social Organization in Early Israel." In *Magnalia Dei: The Mighty Acts of God.* Edited by F. M. Cross et al. Garden City, N.Y.: Doubleday. Pages 132–51.

Mernissi, F.
1975   *Beyond the Veil: Male-Female Dynamics in a Modern Muslim
               Society*. Cambridge, Mass.: Schenkman.
Mettinger, T. N. D.
1971   *Solomonic State Officials, A Study of the Civil Government Officials
               of the Israelite Monarchy*. Lund: CWK Gleerups Forlag.
1976   *King and Messiah, The Civil and Sacral Legitimation of the Israelite
               Kings*. Lund: CWL Gleerups Forlag.
Meyers, C. L.
1978   "The Roots of Restriction: Women in Early Israel."*BA* 41:91–103.
1983   "Procreation, Production, and Protection: Male-Female Balance
               in Early Israel." *JAAR* 51:568–93.
1988   *Discovering Eve: Ancient Israelite Women in Context*. New York:
               Oxford University Press.
1989   "Women and the Domestic Economy of Early Israel." In
               Women's Earliest Records From Ancient Egypt. Atlanta: Scholars
               Press. Pages 265–78.
1991   "Of Drums and Damsels: Women's Performance in Ancient
               Israel." *BA* 54:16–27.
1992   "Temple, Jerusalem." *ABD* 6:350–69.
Milgrom, J.
1970   "The Term '*Aboda*.' " In *Studies in Levitical Terminology*.
               Berkeley: University of California Press. Pages 60–87.
1971   "A Prolegomenon to Leviticus 17:11." *JBL* 90:149–56.
1976a   *Cult and Conscience: The Asham and the Priestly Doctrine of
               Repentence*. Leiden: E. J. Brill.
1976b   "Israel's Sanctuary: The Priestly 'Picture of Dorian Gray.' "*RB*
               83:390–99.
1983   "Of Hems and Tassels." *BAR* 9,3:61–65.
1990   *The JPS Torah Commentary: Numbers*. Philadelphia: Jewish
               Publication Society.
1991   *Leviticus 1–16*. New York: Doubleday.
1992   "The Priestly Laws of Sancta Contamination." In *"Sha'arei
               Talmon": Studies in the Bible, Qumran, and the Ancient Near East
               Presented to Shemaryahu Talmon*. Edited by M. Fishbane and E.
               Tov. Winona Lake, Ind.: Eisenbrauns. Pages 137–46.
Miller, J. M.
1974   "Saul's Rise to Power: Some Observations Concerning 1 Sam.
               9:1–10:16; 10:26–11:15; 13:2–14:16." *CBQ* 36:157–74.
1977   "The Israelite Occupation of Canaan." In *Israelite and Judean
               History*. Edited by J. H. Hayes and J. M. Miller. Philadelphia:
               Westminster. Pages 213–84.
Miller, J. M. and J. H. Hayes.
1986   *A History of Ancient Israel and Judah*. Philadelphia: Westminster.
Miller, P. D. and J. J. M. Roberts.
1977   *The Hand of the Lord*. Baltimore, Md.: Johns Hopkins University
               Press.
Miscall, P. D.
1989   "Elijah, Ahab and Jehu: A Prophecy Fulfilled." *Prooftexts*
               9:73–83.
Misgeld, D.
1976   "Critical Theory and Hermeneutics: The Debate between
               Habermas and Gadamer." In *On Critical Theory*. Edited by J.
               O'Neill. New York: Seabury Press. Pages 164–83.

Mitchell, W. A.
  1971   "Movement and Pastoral Nomadism: A Tentative Model." *Rocky Mountain Social Science Journal* 8:63–72.

Mohammed, A.
  1973   "The Nomadic and the Sedentary: Polar Complimentaries—Not Polar Opposites." In *The Desert and the Sown: Nomads in a Wider Society*. Edited by C. Nelson. Berkeley: University of California Press. Pages 97–112.

Mohlenbrink, K.
  1940–41   "Sauls Ammoniterfeldzug und Samuels Beitrag zum Konigtum des Saul." *ZAW* 58:57–70.

Mollenkott, V. R.
  1983   *Divine Feminine: Biblical Imagery of God as Female*. New York: Crossroad.

Moller-Christensen, V.
  1967   "Evidence of Leprosy in Earlier People." In *Diseases in Antiquity*. Edited by D. Brothwell and A. T. Sandison. Springfield, Ill.: C. C. Thomas. Pages 295–306.

Moore, C. B., ed.
  1972   *Reconstructing Complex Societies*. Cambridge, Mass.: Cambridge Archaeology Seminar.

Montagu, A., ed.
  1974   *Frontiers of Anthropology*. New York: G. P. Putnam's Sons.

Morrison, M. A.
  1981   "Evidence for Herdsmen and Animal Husbandry in the Nuzi Documents." In *Studies on the Civilization and Culture of Nuzi and the Hurrians: In Honor of Ernest R. Lacheman*. Edited by M. A. Morrison and D. I. Owen. Winona Lake, Ind.: Eisenbrauns. Pages 257–96.
  1983   "The Jacob and Laban Narrative in Light of Near Eastern Sources." *BA* 46:155–64.

Mowinckel, S.
  1987   "Cult and Prophecy." In *Prophecy in Israel: Search For an Identity*. Edited by D. Petersen. Philadelphia: Fortress Press. Pages 74–98.

Muffs, Y.
  1982   "Abraham the Noble Warrior: Patriarchal Politics and Laws of War in Ancient Israel." *JJS* 33:81–107.

Muilenberg, J.
  1970   "Baruch the Scribe." In *Proclamation and Presence: Old Testament Essays in Honour of Gwynne Henton Davies*. Edited by J. I. Durham and J. R. Porter. Macon, Ga.: Mercer University Press. Pages 215–38.

Mullen, E. T., Jr.
  1980   *The Divine Council in Canaanite and Early Hebrew Literature*. Chico, Calif.: Scholars Press.

Murdock, G. P.
  1965   *Social Structure*. New York: Free Press.
  1981   *Atlas of World Cultures*. Pittsburgh: University of Pittsburgh Press.

Murphy, R. F. and L. Kasdan.
  1968   "The Structure of Parallel Cousin Marriage." In *Marriage, Family and Residence*. Edited by P. Bohanan and J. Middleton. Garden City, N.Y.: Natural History Press. Pages 185–201.

Murray, D. F.
1979   "Narrative Structure and Technique in the Deborah- Barak
            Story, Judges iv 4-22." In *Studies in the Historical Books of the
            Old Testament*. Edited by J. A. Emerton. Leiden: E. J. Brill. Pages
            155–89.
Musil, A.
1928   *Manners and Customs of the Rwala Bedouins*. New York: AMS
            Press.
Myres, J. L.
1974   *Anthropology and The Classics*. Edited by R. R. Marett. Oxford:
            Clarendon, 1908. Reprinted as "Herodotus [484–425 BC]: The
            'Father' of Anthropology." In *Frontiers of Anthropology*. Edited
            by Ashley Montagu. New York: G. P. Putnam's Sons. Pages
            19–45.
Na'aman, N.
1988   "The List of David's Officers šālîšîm." *VT* 38:71–79.
Nadel, S. F.
1956   "The Concept of Social Elites." *ISSB* 8,3:413–24.
Nader, L. and D. Metzger.
1963   "Conflict Resolution in Two Mexican Communities." *AA*
            65,3.584–92.
Nagi, S. Z.
1969   *Disability and Rehabilitation*. Columbus: Ohio State University
            Press.
Nelson, R.
1987   *First and Second Kings*. Atlanta: John Knox.
Netting, R. McC., R. R. Wilk, and E. J. Arnould, eds.
1984   *Household: Comparative and Historical Studies of the Domestic
            Group*. Berkeley: University of California Press.
Neufeld, E.
1944   *Ancient Hebrew Marriage Laws*. London: Longmans, Green & Co.
1960   "The Emergence of a Royal-Urban Society in Ancient Israel."
            HUCA 31:31–53.
Newberry, P. E.
1893   *Beni Hassan*. London: Egypt Exploration Society.
Nicoll, A.
1963   *Masks, Mimes and Miracles: Studies in popular theatre*. New York:
            Cooper Square.
Niditch, S.
1979   "The Wronged Woman Righted: An Analysis of Genesis 38."
            HTR 72:143–49.
1985   "Legends of Wise Heroes and Heroines." In *The Hebrew Bible and
            Its Modern Interpreters*. Edited by D. A. Knight and G. M.
            Tucker. Philadelphia: Fortress Press. Pages 445–64.
Niehr, H.
1986   "Zur Gattung von Jes 5, 1–7." *BZ* 30:99–104.
Nobleman, R.
1979   *Mime and Masks*. Rowayton, Conn.: New Plays.
Noth, M.
1957   *Überlieferungsgeschichtliche Studien: Die sammelnden und
            bearbeitenden Geschichtswerke im Alten Testament*. 2d unchanged
            edition; Tübingen: Max Niemeyer Verlag.
1960   *The History of Israel*. Translated by P. R. Ackroyd. 2d edition.
            New York: Harper & Row.

1962   *Exodus*. Philadelphia: Westminster.
1963   "Samuel und Silo." *VT* 13:390–400.
1968   *Das vierte Buch Mose*. Göttingen, 1966. English edition translated
                by J. D. Martin. London: SCM.
1972   *A History of Pentateuchal Traditions*. Translated by B. W.
                Anderson. Englewood Cliffs, N.J.: Prentice-Hall.
Oakman, D. E.
1986   *Jesus and the Economic Questions of His Day*. Lewiston, N.Y.:
                Edwin Mellen Press.
1991   "The Ancient Economy in the Bible." *BTB* 21:34–39.
Oden, R. A.
1983   "Jacob as Father, Husband, and Nephew: Kinship Studies and
                the Patriarchal Narratives." *JBL* 102:189–205.
Olrik, A.
1965   "Epic Laws of Folk Narrative." In *The Study of Folklore*. Edited by
                A. Dundes. Englewood Cliffs, N.J.: Prentice-Hall. Pages 129–41.
Oppenheim, A. L.
1939   "Métiers et Professions à Nuzi." *RES*: 49–61.
1977   *Ancient Mesopotamia: Portrait of a dead civilization*. Edited by E.
                Reiner. Chicago: University of Chicago Press.
Ortner, S. B.
1974   "Is Male to Female as Nature is to Culture?" In *Women, Culture,
                and Society*. Edited by M. Z. Rosaldo and L. Lamphere. Stanford:
                Stanford University Press. Pages 67–80.
Oswalt, J. N.
1986   *The Book of Isaiah, Chapters 1–39*. Grand Rapids, Mich.:
                Eerdmans.
Otwell, J. H.
1977   *And Sarah Laughed: The Status of Women in the Old Testament*.
                Philadelphia: Westminster Press.
Ouellette, J.
1967   "La deuxieme commandement et le rôle de l'image dans la
                symbolique religieuse de l'Ancien Testament; essai
                d'interprétation." *RB* 74:504–16.
Overholt, T. W.
1981   "Prophecy: The Problem of Cross-Cultural Comparison." *Semeia*
                21:55–78.
1982   "Seeing is Believing: The social setting of prophetic acts of
                power." *JSOT* 23:3–31.
1985   "Prophecy, the problem of cross-cultural comparison." In
                Anthropological Approaches to the Old Testament. Edited by B.
                Lang. Philadelphia: Fortress Press. Pages 60–82.
1986   *Prophecy in Cross-Cultural Perspective*. Atlanta: Scholars Press.
1988   "The End of Prophecy: No players without a program." *JSOT*
                42:103–15.
1989   *Channels of Prophecy: The Social Dynamics of Prophetic Activity*.
                Minneapolis: Fortress Press.
Owsley, F. L., Jr.
1981   *Struggle for the Gulf Borderlands*. Gainesville: University Presses
                of Florida.
Paige, K. E.
1983   "Virginity Rituals and Chastity Control During Puberty:
                Cross-Cultural Patterns." In *Menarche: The Transition from Girl*

to Woman. Edited by S. Golub. Lexington, Mass.: D. C. Heath.
Pages 155–74.

Parker, S. B.
1978   "Possession, trance and prophecy in pre-exilic Israel." *VT*
28:271–85.

Parkes, P.
1987   "Livestock Symbolism and Pastoral Ideology Among the Kafirs
of the Hindu Kush." *Man* 22:637–60.

Pastner, S. L.
1971   "Camels, Sheep, and Nomad Social Organization: A Comment
on Rubel's Model." *Man* 6:285–88.

Patai, R.
1959   *Sex and Family in the Bible and the Middle East.* Garden City,
N.Y.: Doubleday.

Pattison, G.
1991   "Violence, Kingship and Cultus." *ExpT* 102,5.135–40.

Paul, S. M.
1970   *Studies in the Book of the Covenant in the Light of Cuneiform and
Biblical Law.* SVT 18; Leiden: E. J. Brill.
1979–80   "Adoption Formulae: A Study of Cuneiform and Biblical Legal
Clauses." *MAARAV* 2,2.173–85.

Paul, S. M. and W. G. Dever, eds.
1974   *Biblical Archaeology.* New York: Quadrangle/New York Times
Book Co.

Pedersen, J.
1940
[1920, 1926]   *Israel, Its Life and Culture.* London: Oxford University Press.

Peebles, C. and S. Kus.
1977   "Some Archaeological Correlates of Ranked Societies." *American
Antiquity* 42:421–48.

Pehrson, R. N.
1966   *The Social Organization of the Marri Baluch.* Edited by F. Barth.
Chicago: Aldine.

Peristiany, J. G.
1965   "Introduction." In *Honour and Shame: The Values of
Mediterranean Society.* Edited by J. G. Peristiany. London:
Weidenfeld and Nicolson. Pages 9–18.

Petersen, D. L.
1981   *The Roles of Israel's Prophets.* Sheffield: JSOT Press.
1987   "Introduction: Ways of thinking about Israel's prophets." In
Prophecy in Israel: Search for an Identity. Edited by D. Petersen.
Philadelphia: Fortress Press. Pages 1–21.
1988   "Rethinking the End of Prophecy." *Wunschet Jerusalem Frieden.*
Edited by M. Augustin and K. D. Schunk. Frankfurt: P. Lang.
Pages 37–64.

Pfuhl, E. H.
1980   *The Deviance Process.* New York: Van Nostrand Reinhold Co., Inc.

Phillips, A.
1970   *Ancient Israel's Criminal Law: A New Approach to the Decalogue.*
Oxford: Oxford University Press.
1975   "*NEBALAH*—A Term for Serious Disorderly and Unruly
Conduct." *VT* 25:237–42.
1984   "The Laws of Slavery: Exodus 21:2–11." *JSOT* 30:51–66.

Phillips, D.
1964   "Rejection of the Mentally Ill: The Influence of Behavior and Sex." *ASR* 29:679–87.

Pilch, J. J.
1981a   "Biblical Leprosy and Body Symbolism." *BTB* 15:108–13.
1981b   "Healing in Mark: A Social Science Analysis." *BTB* 15:142–50.
1991   " 'Visiting Strangers' and 'Resident Aliens.' " *TBT* 29:357–61.

Pitt-Rivers, J.
1965   "Honour and Social Status." In *Honour and Shame: The Values of Mediterranean Society*. Edited by J. G. Peristiany. London: Weidenfeld and Nicolson. Pages 19–78.
1968   "The Stranger, the Guest, and the Hostile Host." In *Contributions to Mediterranean Sociology*. Edited by J. G. Peristiany. Paris: Mouton. Pages 13–30.
1975   "The Kith and the Kin." In *The Character of Kinship*. Edited by J. Goody. Cambridge: Cambridge University Press. Pages 89–105.
1977   *The Fate of Shechem*. Cambridge: Cambridge University Press.

Polanyi, K.
1977   *The Livelihood of Man*. Edited by H. W. Pearson. New York: Academic Press.

Pomeroy, S. B.
1976   *Goddesses, Whores, Wives and Slaves: Women in Classical Antiquity*. New York: Schocken.

Pope, M. H.
1965   *Job*. Garden City, N.Y.: Doubleday.

Porter, J. R.
1967   *The Extended Family in the Old Testament*. London: Edutext Publications.
1982   "The Origins of Prophecy in Israel." In *Israel's Prophetic Tradition: Essays in honour of Peter R. Ackroyd*. Edited by R. Coggins, A. Phillips, and M. Knibb. Cambridge: Cambridge University Press. Pages 12–31.

Pospisil, L.
1974   *Anthropology of Law: A Comparative Theory*. New Haven, Conn.: HRAF Press.

Postgate, J. N.
1969   *Neo-Assyrian Royal Grants and Decrees*. Rome: Pontifical Biblical Institute.
1975   "Some Old Babylonian Shepherds and Their Flocks (with a contribution by S. Payne)." *JSS* 20:1–21.

Potash, B.
1986   "Widows in Africa: An Introduction." In *Widows in African Societies: Choices and Constraints*. Edited by B. Potash. Stanford: Stanford University Press. Pages 1–43.

Potts, D.
1983   "Salt of the Earth: The Role of a Non-Pastoral Resource in a Pastoral Economy." *Oriens Antiquus* 22:205–15.

Prag, K.
1974   "The Intermediate Early Bronze-Middle Bronze Age: An Interpretation of the Evidence from Transjordan, Syria and Lebanon." *Levant* 6:69–116.
1985   "Ancient and Modern Pastoral Migration in the Levant." *Levant* 17:81–88.

Price, J. L., Jr.
1985   "Widow." *Harper's Dictionary of the Bible*. San Francisco: Harper
               & Row. Pages 1132–33.
Priest, J.
1980   "Huldah's Oracle." *VT* 30:366–68.
Pritchard, J.
1969   *Ancient Near Eastern Texts Relating to the Old Testament*. 3d ed.
               Princeton, N.J.: Princeton University Press.
Radcliffe-Brown, A. R.
1948   *The Andaman Islanders*. Glencoe, Ill.: Free Press.
1952   *Structure and Function in Primitive Society: Essays and Addresses*.
               New York: Free Press.
Radcliffe-Brown, A. R. and C. D. Forde, eds.
1950   *African Systems of Kinship and Marriage*. London: Oxford
               University Press.
Radday, J. T.
1990   "Humour in Names." In *On Humour and the Comic in the Hebrew
               Bible*. Edited by J. T. Radday and A. Brenner. Sheffield: Almond
               Press. Pages 59–97.
Rahner, K. and H. Vorgrimler.
1965   *Theological Dictionary*. New York: Herder and Herder.
Rainey, A. F.
1966   *A Social Structure of Ugarit*. Jerusalem: Mosad Byali.
1971   "Woman in Public Life." *Encyclopaedia Judaica*. Vol. 16.
               Jerusalem: Keter Publishing House. Page 626.
Raswan, C. R.
1929   "From Tent to Tent Among the Bedouins." *Asia* 29:570–80.
Redfield, R.
1956   "How Human Society Operates." In *Man, Culture, and Society*.
               Edited by H. L. Shapiro. New York: Oxford University Press.
               Pages 345–68.
Reif, S. C.
1971   "What Enraged Phinehas?—A Study of Numbers 25:8." *JBL*
               90:200–206.
Relandus, H.
1716   *Palaestina ex monumentis veteribus illustrata*.
Rendsburg, G. A.
1990   "The Internal Consistency and Historical Reliability of the
               Biblical Genealogies" *VT* 40:184–206.
Renfrew, C.
1972   "Beyond a Subsistence Economy: The Evolution of Social Organi-
               zation in Prehistoric Europe." In *Reconstructing Complex Societies*.
               Edited by C. B. Moore. Cambridge, Mass.: ASOR. Pages 64–85.
1976   *Before Civilization*. New York: Penguin Books.
1982   "Socio-Economic Change in Ranked Societies." In *Ranking,
               Resource and Exchange: Aspects of Early European Society*. Edited
               by C. Renfrew and S. Shennan. Cambridge: Cambridge
               University Press. Pages 1–12.
Retzinger, S. M.
1991   *Violent Emotions: Shame and Rage in Marital Quarrels*. Newbury
               Park, Calif.: Sage Publications.
Reventlow, H. G.
1963   *Liturgie und prophetisches Ich bei Jeremia*. Gütersloh: Gütersloher
               Verlagshaus Gerd Mohn.

Reviv, H.
    1989   *The Elders in Ancient Israel*. Jerusalem: Magnes Press.
Richardson, S. A. and A. F. Guttmacher, eds.
    1967   *Childbearing: Its Social and Psychological Aspects*. Baltimore, Md.:
                      Williams and Wilkins.
Richter, W.
    1966   *Recht und Ethos. Versuch einer Ortung des weisheitlichen
                      Mahnspruches*. SANT 15. Munich: Kaiser.
Ridderbos, J.
    1985   *Isaiah*. Translated by J. Vriend. Grand Rapids, Mich.: Regency
                      Reference Library.
Ridout, G.
    1974   "The Rape of Tamar: A Rhetorical Analysis of 2 Sam 13:1–22."
                      In *Rhetorical Criticism*. Edited by J. Jackson and M. Kessler.
                      Pittsburgh: Pickwick. Pages 75–84.
Ringgren, H.
    1982   "Prophecy in the Ancient Near East." In *Israel's Prophetic
                      Tradition: Essays in honour of Peter R. Ackroyd*. Edited by R.
                      Coggins, A. Phillips, and M. Knibb. Cambridge: Cambridge
                      University Press. Pages 1–11.
Roaf, M.
    1990   *Cultural Atlas of Mesopotamia and the Ancient Near East*. New
                      York: Facts on File.
Roberts, J. and D. Van Lier.
    1984   "Which Positions for the Second Stage?" *Childbirth Educator*
                      3:33–41.
Roberts, J. J. M.
    1980   "The Hand of Yahweh." *VT* 21:244–51.
Robinson, H. W.
    1971   *Corporate Personality in Ancient Israel*. Philadelphia: Fortress
                      Press.
Rofe, A.
    1982   "The Acts of Nahash According to 4QSam^a." *IEJ* 32:129–33.
Rogers, S. C.
    1975   "Female Forms of Power and the Myth of Male Dominance: A
                      model of female/male interaction in peasant society. *AmEth*
                      2:727–56.
    1978   "Women's Place: A critical review of anthropological theory."
                      Comparative Studies in Society and History 20:123–62.
Rogerson, J. W.
    1970   "The Hebrew Conception of Corporate Personality: A
                      Reconsideration." *JTS* 21:1–16.
    1980   "Sacrifice in the Old Testament." In *Sacrifice*. Edited by M. F. C.
                      Bourdillon. London: Academic Press. Pages 45–59.
    1984   *Anthropology and the Old Testament*. Sheffield: Almond Press.
    1989   "Anthropology and the Old Testament." In *The World of Ancient
                      Israel*. Edited by R. E. Clements. Cambridge: Cambridge
                      University Press. Pages 17–37.
Rogerson, J. W. and P. Davies.
    1989   *The Old Testament World*. Englewood Cliffs, N.J.: Prentice-Hall.
Rolfe, B.
    1979   "Introduction." In *Mimes on Miming: Writing on the Art of Mime*.
                      Edited by B. Rolfe. Los Angeles: Panjandrum.

Rosaldo, M. Z.
1974   "Women, Culture, and Society: A Theoretical Overview." In
            Women, Culture, and Society. Edited by M. Z. Rosaldo and L.
            Lamphere. Stanford: Stanford University Press. Pages 17–42.

Rosen, L.
1989   *The Anthropology of Justice: Law as Culture in Islamic Society.*
            Cambridge: Cambridge University Press.

Rosenberg, J.
1986   *King and Kin, Political Allegory in the Hebrew Bible.* Bloomington:
            Indiana University Press.

Rosenfield, S.
1982   "Sex Roles and Societal Reactions to Mental Illness: The
            Labeling of 'Deviant' Deviance." *Journal of Health and Social
            Behavior* 23:18–24.

Ross, J.
1962   "The Prophet as Yahweh's Messenger." In *Israel's Prophetic
            Heritage.* Edited by B. W. Anderson and W. Harrelson. New
            York: Harper and Brothers. Pages 98–107.

Roth, M. T.
1989   "Marriage and Matrimonial Prestations in First Millennium B.
            C. Babylonia." In *Women's Earliest Records: From Ancient Egypt
            and Western Asia.* Edited by B. S. Lesko. Atlanta: Scholars Press.
            Pages 245–55.

Rowe, J. H.
1965   "The Renaissance Foundations of Anthropology." *AA* 67:1–20.

Rowley, H. H.
1952   "The Nature of Old Testament Prophecy in the Light of Recent
            Study." In *The Servant of the Lord and Other Essays on the Old
            Testament.* London: Lutterworth Press. Pages 91–128.

1985 [1965] "The Marriage of Ruth." In *The Servant of the Lord and Other
            Essays on the Old Testament.* Oxford: Blackwell. Pages 171–94.

Rowton, M. B.
1967   "The Topological Factor in the Hapiru Problem." *AS* 16.
            Chicago: University of Chicago Press. Pages 375–87.
1974   "Enclosed Nomadism." *JESHO* 17:1–30.
1977   "Dimorphic Structure and the Parasocial Element." *JNES*
            36:181–98.

Rubel, P.
1969   "Herd Composition and Social Structure: On Building Models of
            Nomadic Pastoral Societies." *Man* 4:268–73.

Rudolph, W.
1962   *Das Buch Ruth, Das Hohe Lied, Die Klagelieder.* KAT vol. l7, part
            1. Gütersloh: Mohn.

Safilios-Rothschild, C.
1970   *The Sociology and Social Psychology of Disability and
            Rehabilitation.* New York: Random House.

Safrai, S.
1974   "Home and Family." In *The Jewish People in the First Century.*
            Edited by S. Safari and M. Stern. 2 vols. Compendia Rerum
            Iudaicarum ad Novem Testamentum. Philadelphia: Fortress
            Press.

Saggs, H. W. F.
1962   *The Greatness That Was Babylon.* New York: New American
            Library.

Sahlins, M. D.
1967   "Segmentary Lineage: An Organization of Predatory
              Expansion." In *Comparative Political Systems: Studies in the
              Politics of Pre-Industrial Societies*. Edited by R. Cohen and J.
              Middleton. Garden City, N.Y.: The Natural History Press. Pages
              89–119.
1968   *Tribesmen*. Englewood Cliffs, N.J.: Prentice-Hall.
Sakenfeld, K. D.
1988   "Zelophehad's Daughters." In *Perspectives on the Hebrew Bible*.
              Edited by J. L. Crenshaw. Macon, Ga.: Mercer University Press.
              Pages 37–47.
Salmon, J. M.
1968   *Judicial Authority in Early Israel: An Historical Investigation of Old
              Testament Institutions*. Ph.D. dissertation, Princeton University.
              Ann Arbor, Mich.: University Microfilms, Inc.
Salzman, P. C.
1971   "Movement and Resource Extraction Among Pastoral Nomads:
              The Case of the Shah Nawazi Baluch." *AQ* 44:185–97.
1979   "Inequality and Oppression in Nomadic Society." In *Pastoral
              Production and Society*. Cambridge: Cambridge University Press.
              Pages 429–46.
Salzman, P. C., ed.
1980   "Introduction: Processes of Sedentarization as Adaptation and
              Response." In *When Nomads Settle: Processes of Sedentarization as
              Adaptation and Response*. New York: Praeger. Pages 1–19.
Sarbin, T. and V. Allen.
1985   "Role Theory." In *The Handbook of Social Pyschology*. 3d ed.
              Edited by G. Linzey and E. Aronson. New York: Random House.
Sarna, N. M.
1966   *Understanding Genesis*. New York: Schocken.
1989   *The JPS Torah Commentary· Genesis*, Philadelphia: Jewish
              Publication Society.
Sasson, J. M.
1969   *The Military Establishments at Mari*. Rome: PBI.
1977   "Treatment of Criminals at Mari" *JESHO* 20: 90–113.
1979   *Ruth, a Commentary*. Baltimore, Md.: Johns Hopkins University
              Press.
1987   "Queries and Comments." *BAR* 13,2:12–15, 60.
1989   *Ruth: A New Translation with a Philological Commentary and
              Formalist-folklorist Interpretation*. Sheffield: JSOT Press.
Schafer-Lichtenberger, C.
1983   *Stadt und Eidgenossenschaft im Alten Testament*. Berlin: Walter de
              Gruyter.
Schapera, I.
1985 [1955]   "The Sin of Cain." *JRAI* 85:33–43. Reprinted in *Anthropological
              Approaches to the Old Testament*. Edited by B. Lang. Philadelphia:
              Fortress Press. Pages 26–42.
Schatz, W.
1972   *Genesis 14: Eine Untersuchung*. Bern: Herbert Lang.
Scheff, T. J.
1966   *Being Mentally Ill: A Sociological Theory*. Chicago: Aldine.
1990   *Microsociology: Discourse, Emotion and Social Structure*. Chicago:
              University of Chicago Press.

Scheff, T. J. and S. M. Retzinger.
1991   *Emotions and Violence: Shame and Rage in Destructive Conflicts.*
                Lexington, Mass.: Lexington Books.
Schlegel, A.
1991   "Status, Property, and the Value of Virginity." *AmEth*
                18,4:719–34.
Schley, D. G.
1989   *Shiloh: A Biblical City in Tradition and History.* Sheffield: JSOT
                Press.
Schmitt, H. C.
1972   *Elisa: Traditiongeschichtliche Untersuchungen zur vorklassischen*
                nord-israelitischen Prophetic. Gütersloh: Gerd Mohn.
1977   "Prophetie und Tradition." *ZTK* 74:255–72.
Schmitt, J. J.
1983   "The Gender of Ancient Israel." *JSOT* 26:115–25.
1985   "The Motherhood of God and Zion as Mother." *RB*:557–69.
1991   "The Land is Mine." *BTB* 29:336–40.
1992   "Virgin." *ABD* 6:853–54.
1993   "The Virgin of Israel: Referent and Use of the Phrase in Amos
                and Jeremiah." *CBQ* 55.
Schneider, J.
1971   "Of Vigilance and Virgins: Honor, Shame and Access to
                Resources in Mediterranean Societies." *Ethnology* 10:1–24.
1987   "The Anthropology of Cloth." *ARA* 16:409–48.
Schunk, K.-D.
1963   *Benjamin. Untersuchungen zur Entstehung und Geschichte eines*
                israelitischen Stammes. Berlin: A. Töpelmann.
Schur, E. M.
1971   *Labeling Deviant Behavior: Its Sociological Implications.* New York:
                Harper & Row.
1974   "The Concept of Secondary Deviation: Its Theoretical
                Significance and Empirical Elusiveness." (Unpublished).
1983   *Labeling Women Deviant: Gender, Stigma, and Social Control.*
                Philadelphia: Temple University Press.
Schwally, F.
1901   *Der heilige Krieg im altern Israel.* Leipzig: Deiterich.
Schwartz, B. J.
1986   "A Literary Study of the Slave-Girl Pericope: Leviticus
                19:20–22." *SH* 31:241–55.
Scott, B. B.
1989   "You Can't Keep a Good Woman Down." In *Hear Then the*
                Parable: A Commentary on the Parables of Jesus. Minneapolis:
                Fortress Press. Pages 175–87.
Seeden H. and M. Kaddour.
1984   "Space, Structures and Land in Shams ed-Din Tannira on the
                Euphrates: An Ethnoarchaeological Perspective." In *Land*
                Tenure and Social Transformation in the Middle East. Edited by T.
                Khalidi. Beirut: American University in Beirut. Pages 495–526.
Seibert, I.
1974   "Women as Mirrored in the Tables of the Law." In *Women in the*
                Ancient Near East. New York: A. Schram. Pages 11–23.
Selvidge, M. J.
1984   "Mark 5:25–34 and Lev 15:19–20: A reaction to purity
                regulations." *JBL* 103:619–23.

Service, E. R.
1962   *Primitive Social Organization, An Evolutionary Perspective*. New
            York: Random House.
1975   *Origins of the State and Civilization*. New York: Norton.
1978   "Classical and Modern Theories of the Origins of Government."
            In *Origins of the State*. New York: Norton. Pages 21–34.
Severin, T.
1973   *Vanishing Primitive Man*. New York: McGraw-Hill.
Shapiro, H. L., ed.
1956   *Man, Culture, and Society*. New York: Oxford University Press.
Sherratt, A.
1981   "Plough and Pastoralism: Aspects of the Secondary Products
            Revolution." In *Pattern of the Past: Studies in Honour of David
            Clarke*. Edited by I. Hodder et al. Cambridge: Cambridge
            University Press. Pages 261–305.
Shoup, J.
1990   "Middle Eastern Sheep Pastoralism and the Hima System." In
            *The World of Pastoralism: Herding Systems in Comparative
            Perspective*. Edited by J. G. Galaty and D. L. Johnson. London:
            Guilford Press. Pages 195–215.
Shyte, M. K.
1978   *The Status of Women in Pre-industrial Societies*. Princeton:
            Princeton University Press.
Sigonius, C.
1583   *De re publica Hebraeorum libri septem*.
Sikes, E. E.
1914 [1974] *The Anthropology of the Greeks*. London: David Nutt. Pages
            69–89. Reprinted as "The Ancient Greeks Do Not Recognize
            'Race' and, Indeed, Deny It." In *Frontiers of Anthropology*. Edited
            by A. Montagu. New York: G. P. Putnam's Sons. Pages 7–18.
Simon, U.
1976   "I Kings 13: A Prophetic Sign—Denial and Persistence." *HUCA*
            47:81–117.
1988   "A Balanced Story: The stern prophet and the kind witch."
            Prooftexts 8:159–71.
Smith, H. P.
1929   *The Books of Samuel*. New York: Charles Scribner's Sons.
Smith, M. S.
1990   *The Early History of God: Yahweh and the Other Deities in Ancient
            Israel*. San Francisco: Harper & Row.
Smith, R. H.
1965   "Abram and Melchizedek (Gen. 14:18-20)." *ZAW* 77: 129–53.
Smith, R. T.
1980   "Societal Reaction and Physical Disability: Contrasting
            Perspectives." In *The Labeling of Deviance: Evaluating a
            Perspective*. 2d ed. Edited by W. R. Gove. Beverly Hills: Sage
            Publications. Pages 227–36.
Smith, W. R.
1969 [1889] *Lectures on the Religion of the Semites*. 3d ed. New York: KTAV.
1903   *Kinship and Marriage in Early Arabia*. 2d ed. London: Black.
Snaith, N. H.
1967   *Leviticus and Numbers*. London: Nelson.
Soggin, J. A.
1981   *Judges*. Philadelphia: Westminster Press.

1982   "Compulsory Labor under David and Solomon." In *Studies in the
                Period of David and Solomon.* Edited by T. Ishida. Winona Lake,
                Ind.: Eisenbrauns. Pages 259–67.
1984   *A History of Israel, From the Beginnings to the Bar Kochba Revolt,
                A.D. 135.* London: SCM.

Sorre, M.
1950   *Les fondements de la Géographie Humaine.* Paris: A. Colin.
Spalinger, A. J.
1978   "A Canaanite Ritual Found in Egyptian Military Reliefs." *Journal
                of the Society for the Study of Egyptian Antiquities* 7:47–60.

Speiser, E. A.
1956   "Coming and Going at the City Gate." *BASOR* 144:20–23.
1964   *Genesis.* Garden City, N.Y.: Doubleday.
Spina, F. A.
1983   "Israelites as *gērîm*, 'Sojourner,' in Social and Historical
                Context." In *The Word of the Lord Shall Go Forth.* Edited by C. L.
                Myers and M. O'Connor. Winona Lake, Ind.: Eisenbrauns. Pages
                321–35.

Spooner, B.
1973   *The Cultural Ecology of Pastoral Nomads.* Reading, Mass.:
                Addison-Wesley.

Stager, L. E.
1982   "The Archaeology of the East Slope of Jerusalem and the
                Terraces of the Kidron." *JNES* 41:11–21.
1985   "The Archaeology of the Family in Ancient Israel." *BASOR*
                260:1–35.
1986   "Archaeology, Ecology, and Social History: Background Themes
                to the Song of Deborah." In *Congress Volume, Jerusalem.* Edited
                by J. A. Emerton. *VTSuppl.* 40; Leiden: E. J. Brill. Pages 229–32.

Stager, L. E. and S. R. Wolff.
1984   "Child Sacrifice at Carthage—Religious Rite or Population
                Control?" *BAR* 10,1:30–51.

Steinberg, N.
1989   "The Genealogical Framework of the Family Stories in Genesis."
                Semeia 46:41–50.

Steinmetz, D.
1991   *From Father to Son: Kinship, Conflict, and Continuity in Genesis.*
                Louisville: Westminster/John Knox Press.

Steponaitis, V.
1978   "Locational Theory and Complex Chiefdoms: A Mississippian
                Example." In *Mississippian Settlement Patterns.* Edited by B.
                Smith. New York: Academic Press. Pages 417–53.

Stiebing, W.
1989   *Out of the Desert? Archaeology and the Conquest Narratives.*
                Buffalo, N.Y.: Prometheus.

Stoebe, H. J.
1973   *Das erste Buch Samuelis.* Gütersloh: Gerd Mohn.
Strange, J.
1985   "The Idea of Afterlife in Ancient Israel: Some Remarks on the
                Iconography in Solomon's Temple." *PEQ* 117:35–40.
1987   "The Transition from the Bronze Age to the Iron Age in the
                Eastern Mediterranean." *SJOT* 1:1–19.

Stuhlmueller, C.
1986   "Prophet, Who Are You?" In *The Biblical Heritage in Modern
                Catholic Scholarship*. Edited by J. Collins and J. Crossan.
                Wilmington, Del.: M. Glazier. Pages 58–84.
Sundberg, A. C., Jr.
1964   *The Old Testament of the Early Church*. Cambridge, Mass.:
                Harvard University Press.
Swidler, W.
1972   "Some Demographic Facets Regulating the Formation of Flocks
                and Camps Among the Brahui of Baluchistan." In *Perspectives
                on Nomadism*. Edited by W. Irons and N. Dyson-Hudson. Leiden:
                E. J. Brill. Pages 69–75.
1973   "Adaptive Processes Regulating Nomad-Sedentary Interaction in
                the Middle East." In *The Desert and the Sown: Nomads in a Wider
                Society*. Edited by C. Nelson. Berkeley: University of California
                Press. Pages 23–41.
Szasz, T. S.
1970   *Ideology and Insanity*. Garden City, N.Y.: Doubleday.
Tadmor, H.
1962   "The Southern Border of Aram." *IEJ* 12:114–22.
Talmon, S.
1980   "The Biblical Idea of Statehood." In *The Bible World: Essays in
                honor of Cyrus H. Gordon*. Edited by G. Rendsburg et al.; New
                York: KTAV. Pages 239–48.
Tambiah, S. J.
1990   *Magic, Science, Religion and the Scope of Rationality*. New York:
                Cambridge University Press.
Tapp, A. M.
1989   "An Ideology of Expendability: Virgin Daughter Sacrifice." In
                *Anti-Covenant: Counter-Reading Women's Lives in the Hebrew
                Bible*. Edited by M. Bal. Sheffield: Almond Press. Pages 157–74.
Tapper, N.
1981   "Direct Exchange and Brideprice: Alternative Forms in a
                Complex Marriage System." *Man* 16:387–407.
Tapper, R. L.
1979   "The Organization of Nomadic Communities in Pastoral
                Societies of the Middle East." In *Pastoral Production and Society*.
                Cambridge: Cambridge University Press. Pages 43–65.
Teubal, S. J.
1984   *Sarah the Priestess: The first matriarch of Genesis*. Athens, Ohio:
                Swallow Press.
Thompson, D. and T. Thompson
1968   "Some Legal Problems in the Book of Ruth." *VT* 18:79–99.
Thompson, J. A.
1980   *The Book of Jeremiah*. Grand Rapids, Mich.: Eerdmans.
1986   *Handbook of Life in Bible Times*. Downers Grove: InterVarsity
                Press.
Thompson, S.
1955–58   *Motif Index of Folk-Literature: A Classification of Narrative
                Elements in Folktales, Ballads, Myths, Fables, Mediaeval Romances,
                Exempla, Fabliaux, Jestbooks, and Local Legends*. 6 vols.
                Bloomington: University of Indiana Press.

Thompson, T. L.
    1978   "Historical Notes on Israel's Conquest of Palestine: A Peasant's
                      Rebellion?" *JSOT* 7:20–27.
Thornton, T. C. G.
    1963   "Charismatic Kingship in Israel and Judah." *JTS* 14:3–11.
Thurston, B. B.
    1985   "The Widows as the 'Altar of God.' " *SBL Seminar Papers*
                      24:279–89.
Tigay, J.
    1982   *The Evolution of the Gilgamesh Epic*. Philadelphia: University of
                      Pennsylvania Press.
Towler, J. and J. Bramall.
    1986   *Midwives in History and Society*. London: Croom Helm.
Trible, P.
    1978   *God and the Rhetoric of Sexuality*. Philadelphia: Fortress Press.
    1984   *Texts of Terror*. Philadelphia: Fortress Press.
    1985   "The Other Woman: A Literary and Theological Study of the
                      Hagar Narratives." In *Understanding the Word: Essays in Honour
                      of Bernard W. Anderson*. Edited by J. T. Butler et al. Sheffield:
                      JSOT Press. Pages 221–46.
Tsevat, M.
    1961   "Studies in the Book of Samuel." *HUCA* 32:191–216.
Tsukimoto, A.
    1989   "Emar and the Old Testament—Preliminary Remarks." *Japanese
                      Biblical Institute Annual* 15:3–24.
Turkowski, L.
    1969   "Peasant Agriculture in the Judean Hills." *PEQ* 101:101–12.
Turnbam, T. J.
    1987   "Male and Female Slaves in the Sabbath Year Laws of Exodus
                      21:1–11." *SBL Seminar Papers* 26:545–49.
Turner, V. W.
    1969   *The Ritual Process: Structure and Anti-Structure*. New York:
                      Aldine.
Tyler, S. A.
    1987   *The Unspeakable: Discoure, Dialogue, and Rhetoric in the
                      Postmodern World*. Madison: University of Wisconsin Press.
Tylor, E. B.
    1891   *Primitive Culture: Researches into the Development of Mythology,
                      Philosophy, Religion, Language, Art and Custom*. 2 vols. London:
                      Murray.
Ursinus, J. H.
    1663   *Arboretum Biblicum*.
Ussishkin, D.
    1976   "Royal Judean Storage Jars and Private Seal Impressions."
                      BASOR 223:1–14.
Valeri, V.
    1985   *Kingship and Sacrifice*. Chicago: University of Chicago Press.
van Baal, J.
    1975   *Reciprocity and the Position of Women*. Amsterdam: Van Gorcum.
van der Ploeg, J.
    1950   "Les chefs du people d'Israël et leurs noms." *RB* 57:40–61.
    1972   *Slavery in the Old Testament. VTSup* 22. Leiden: E. J. Brill.

van Dijk-Hemmes, F.
1989   "Tamar and the Limits of Patriarchy: Between Rape and
               Seduction." In *Anti-Covenant: Counter-Reading Women's Lives in
               the Hebrew Bible*. Edited by M. Bal. Sheffield: Almond Press.
               Pages 135–56.
Vanel, A.
1974   "Tab'el en Is. VII 6 et le roi Tubail de Tyr." *VTSup* 26:17–24.
van Gennep, A.
1960   *Rites of Passage*. Chicago: University of Chicago Press.
1974   "Arnold Van Gennep On The Rites of Passage." In *Frontiers of
               Anthropology*. Edited by A. Montagu. New York: G. P. Putnam's
               Sons. Pages 315–19.
van Leeuwen, R. C.
1990   "The Sage in the Prophetic Literature." In *The Sage in Israel and
               the Ancient Near East*. Edited by John G. Gammie and Leo G.
               Perdue. Winona Lake, Ind.: Eisenbrauns. Pages 295–306.
van Nieuwenhuijze, C. A. O.
1971   *Sociology of the Middle East: A Stocktaking and Interpretation*.
               Leiden: E. J. Brill.
Vannoy, J. R.
1977   *Covenant Renewal at Gilgal: A Study of 1 Sam 11:14–12:25*. Cherry
               Hill, N.J.: Mack Publishing Co.
van Selms, A.
1957   "The Origin of the Title 'The King's Friend.' " *JNES* 16:118–23.
van Seters, J.
1987   "Love and Death in the Court of David." In *Love and Death in the
               Ancient Near East*. Edited by J. H. Marks & R. M. Good. Guilford,
               Conn.: Four Quarters. Pages 121–24.
van Wyk, W. C., ed.
1981   "The Fable of Jotham in its Ancient Near Eastern Setting." In
               Studies in Wisdom Literature. OTS 15 & 16:89–95.
Vawter, B.
1977   *On Genesis: A New Reading*. Garden City, N.Y.: Doubleday.
1986   "Yahweh: Lord of the Heavens and the Earth." *CBQ* 48:461–67.
Viberg, A.
1992   *Symbols of Law: A Contextual Analysis of Legal Symbolic Acts in
               the Old Testament*. Stockholm: Almqvist & Wiksell.
Vikander-Edelman, D.
1986   *The Rise of the Israelite State Under Saul*. Ph.D. dissertation,
               University of Chicago Press.
Viviano, P. A.
1989   "Genesis." In *The Collegeville Bible Commentary*. Edited by D.
               Bergant and R. J. Karris. Collegeville, Minn.: Liturgical Press.
               Pages 35–78.
Vogt, E.
1972   "Jesaja und die drohende Eroberung Palästinas durch
               Tiglath-Pilizer." *FB* 2:249–55.
Von Rad, G.
1961 [1972]   *Genesis, a Commentary*. Rev. ed. Philadelphia: Westminster Press.
1962   *Old Testament Theology*. Translated by D. M. G. Stalker. New
               York: Harper & Row.
1991   *Holy War in Ancient Israel*. Translated by M. J. Dawn. Grand
               Rapids, Mich.: Eerdmans.

Waldbaum, J. C.
  1978   *From Bronze to Iron: The Transition from the Bronze Age to the
                    Iron Age in the Eastern Mediterranean.* Goteborg: Paul Astroms
                    Forlag.
Waldman, N. M.
  1989   "The Imagery of Clothing, Covering, and Over-powering."
                    JANES 19:161–70.
Wallace, A. F. C.
  1972   *The Death and Rebirth of the Seneca.* New York: Vintage.
Ward, J. M.
  1976   "Faith, faithfulness, OT." *IDB.* 2:329–32.
  1988   "The Eclipse of the Prophet in Contemporary Prophetic Studies."
                    USQR 42:97–104.
Watson, P. J.
  1980   "The Theory and Practice of Ethnoarchaeology with Special
                    Reference to the Near East." *Paleorient* 6:55–64.
Webb, B. G.
  1987   *The Book of Judges, An Integrated Reading.* Sheffield: JSOT Press.
Weber, M.
  1952 [1920]   *Ancient Judaism.* Translated and edited by Hans H. Gerth and
                    Don Martindale. New York: Free Press.
Wegner, J. R.
  1992   "*Attah Konanta Mesharim*: God and King in the Theocratic
                    Jurisprudence of Ancient Israel." *Jewish Law Association Studies*
                    6:157–78.
Weinfeld, M.
  1970   "The Covenant of Grant in the Old Testament and the Ancient
                    Near East." *JAOS* 90:184–203.
  1972   *Deuteronomy and the Deuteronomic School.* Oxford: Clarendon
                    Press.
  1977   "Judge and Officer in the Ancient Near East." *IOS* 7:65–88.
  1986   "The Protest Against Imperialism in Ancient Israelite
                    Prophecy." In *Origins and Diversity of Axial Age Civilization.*
                    Edited by S. Eisenstadt. Albany: State University of New York
                    Press. Pages 169–82.
Weippert, M.
  1971   *The Settlement of the Israelite Tribes in Palestine.* London: SCM.
Weir, S.
  1976   *The Bedouin.* London: World of Islam Festival Publishing
                    Company, Ltd.
Weiser, A.
  1962   *The Psalms.* Philadelphia: Westminster Press.
Wellhausen, J.
  1973   *Prolegomena to the History of Ancient Israel.* Gloucester, Mass.:
                    Peter Smith.
Wemple, S. F.
  1981   *Women in Frankish Society: Marriage and the cloister, 500 to 900.*
                    Philadelphia: University of Pennsylvania Press.
Wenham, G. J.
  1987   *Genesis 1–15.* Waco: Word Books.
Wertz R. W. and D. C. Wertz.
  1977   *Lying-In: A History of Childbirth in America.* New York: Free Press.
Westbrook, R.
  1990   "Adultery in Ancient Near Eastern Law." *RB* 97:542–80.

1991 [1977]   "The Laws of the Biblical Levirate." In *Property and the Family in Biblical Law*. Reprint. Sheffield: JSOT Press. Pages 69–89 [RIDA 24. Pages 65–87].

Westermann, C.
1967   *Basic Forms of Prophetic Speech*. Translated H. C. White. Philadelphia: Westminster.
1984   *Genesis 1–11*. Minneapolis, Minn.: Augsburg Press.

Whedbee, J. W.
1971   *Isaiah and Wisdom*. Nashville: Abingdon Press.

Whitelam, K. W.
1986   "The Symbols of Power: Aspects of Royal Propaganda in the United Monarchy." *BA* 49:166–73.
1989   "Israelite Kingship, The Royal Ideology and its Opponents." In *The World of Ancient Israel: Sociological, Anthropological and Political Perspectives: Essays by Members of the Society for Old Testament Study*. Edited by R. E. Clements. Cambridge [England]/New York: Cambridge University Press. Pages 119–39.

Whybray, R. N.
1990   "The Sage in the Israelite Court." In *The Sage in Israel and the Ancient Near East*. Edited by John G. Gammie and Leo G. Perdue. Winona Lake, Ind.: Eisenbrauns. Pages 133–39.

Whyte, M. K.
1978   *Status of Women in Preindustrial Societies*. Princeton: Princeton University Press.

Wicker, K. O.
1975   "First-Century Marriage Ethics: A Comparative Study of the Household Codes and Plutarch's Conjugal Precepts." In *No Famine in the Land: Studies in Honor of John L. Mc- Kenzie*. Edited by J. W. Flanagan and A. W. Robinson. Missoula, Mont.: Scholars Press. Pages 141–53.

Wifall, W.
1974   "Breath of His Nostrils: Gen 2:7b." *CBQ* 36:237–40.

Wikan, U.
1984   "Shame and Honour: A Contestable Pair." *Man* 19:635–52.

Wilcoxen, J. A.
1977   "The Political Background of Jeremiah's Temple Sermon." In *Scripture in History and Theology*. Edited by A. L. Merrill and T. W. Overholt. Pittsburgh: Pickwick Press. Pages 151–66.

Wilhelm, G.
1970   *Untersuchungen zum Hurro-Akkadischen von Nuzi*. AOAT 9. Kevelaer: Neukirchen-Vluyn.
1978   "Zur Rolle des Grossgrundbesitzes in der Hurritischen Gesellschaft." *RHA* 36:205–13.

Wilkinson, J.
1977   "Leprosy and Leviticus: The Problem of Description and Identification." *SJT* 30:153–69.

Willeson, F.
1954   "Die Eselsohne von Sichem als Bundesgenossen." *VT* 4:216–17.

Williams, G. R.
1985   "Frustrated Expectations in Isaiah V 1–7: A Literary Interpretation." *VT* 35:459–65.

Williams, J. G.
1982   *Women Recounted: Narrative Thinking and the God of Israel*. Sheffield: Almond Press.

Willis, J. T.
1971   "An Anti-Elide Narrative Tradition from a Prophetic Circle at
                the Ramah Sanctuary." *JBL* 90:288–308.
1977   "The Genre of Isaiah 5:1–7." *JBL* 96:337–62.
1978   "The Meaning of Isaiah 7:14 and Its Application in Matthew
                1:23." *RQ* 21:1–18.
Wilson, A. E.
1935   *King Panto, the story of pantomime*. New York: E.P. Dutton.
Wilson, R. R.
1975   "The Old Testament Genealogies in Recent Eastern Research."
                JBL 94:169–89.
1977   *Genealogy and History in the Biblical World*. New Haven: Yale
                University Press.
1979a   "Anthropology and the Study of the Old Testament." *USQR*
                34:175–81.
1979b   "Prophecy and Ecstasy: A re-examination." *JBL* 98:321–37.
1979c   "Between 'Azel' and 'Azel': Interpreting the Biblical
                Genealogies." *BA* 42:11–22.
1980   *Prophecy and Society in Ancient Israel*. Philadelphia: Fortress
                Press.
1983   "Enforcing the Covenant: The Mechanisms of Judicial Authority
                in Early Israel." In *The Quest for the Kingdom of God: Studies in
                Honor of George E. Mendenhall*. Edited by H. B. Huffmon et al.
                Winona Lake, Ind.: Eisenbrauns. Pages 59–75.
Wilson, R. W.
1985   "The Family." In *Harper's Bible Dictionary*. San Francisco:
                Harper & Row. Pages 302–3.
Williams, J. G.
1982   *Women Recounted, Narrative Thinking and the God of Israel*.
                Sheffield: Almond Press.
Wolf, E. R.
1966   "Kinship, Friendship and Patron-Client Relations." In *The Social
                Anthropology of Complex Societies*. Edited by M. Banton. London:
                Tavistock Publications. Pages 1–22.
Wolff, H. W.
1972   "A Solution to the Immanuel Prophecy in Isaiah 7:14–8:22." *JBL*
                91:449–56.
1974   *Anthropology of the Old Testament*. Philadelphia: Fortress Press.
1974   *Hosea*. Philadelphia: Fortress Press.
1981   *Micah the Prophet*. Translated by R. D. Gehrke. Philadelphia:
                Fortress Press.
1986   "Prophets and Institutions in the Old Testament." *Currents in
                Theology and Mission* 13:5–12.
Wright, D. P.
1984   *The Disposal of Impurity in the Priestly Writings of the Bible with
                Reference to Similar Phenomena in Hittite and Mesopotamian
                Cultures*. Ph.D. dissertation, University of California-Berkeley.
1990   Personal Communication, July 6.
Wright, D. P. and R. N. Jones
1992   "Leprosy." *ABD* 4:277–82.
Wright, H. T.
1984   "Prestate Political Formations." In *On the Evolution of Complex
                Societies: Essays in Honor of Harry Hoijer*. Edited by W. Sanders
                et al. Malibu, Calif.: Undena. Pages 41–77.

Wright, R. A.
1989   *Establishing Hospitality in the Old Testament: Testing the Tool of Linguistic Pragmatics.* Ph.D. dissertation, Yale University.

Yadin, Y.
1961   "The Four-Fold Division of Judah." *BASOR* 163:6–12.
1963   *The Art of Warfare in Biblical Lands in the Light of Archaeological Discovery.* London: Weidenfeld and Nicolson.
1971   "The Life and Trials of Babatha's Archives." In *Bar-Kokhba: The Rediscovery of the Legendary Hero of the Second Revolt Against Rome.* New York: Random House. Pages 222–53.

Yanagisako, S. J.
1979   "Family and Household: The Analysis of Domestic Groups." *ARA* 8:161–205.

Yedid, H.
1984   "Crise et regression du systeme pastoral de bedouin nomade des Hauts Pateaux du Nord-Est de la ville de Hama (Syrie)." In *Nomades et sedentaires: Perspectives ethnoarchéologiques.* Edited by O. Aurenche. Paris: Editions Recherche sur les civilisations. Pages 19–50.

Yee, G. A.
1981   "A Form-Critical Study of Isaiah 5:1–7 as a Song and a Juridical Parable." *CBQ* 43:30–40.

Zagarell, A.
1986   "Trade, Women, Class, and Society in Ancient Western Asia." *CA* 27:415–30.

Zajonc, R. B.
1968   "Cognitive Theories in Social Psychology." In *The Handbook of Social Psychology.* 2d ed. Edited by G. Lindzey and E. Aronson. Reading, Mass.: Addison-Wesley. Pages 320–411.

Zakovitch, Y.
1981   "Sisseras Tod." *ZAW* 93:364–74.

Zeid, A. M. A.
1966   "Honour and Shame Among the Bedouin of Egypt." In *Honour and Shame: The Values of Mediterranean Society.* Edited by J. G. Peristiany. London: Weidenfeld and Nicolson. Pages 245–59.
1968   "The Changing World of the Nomads." In *Contributions to Mediterranean Society.* Edited by J. G. Peristiany. Paris: Mouton. Pages 279–88.

Zertal, A.
1986   *The Israelite Settlement in the Hill Country of Manasseh.* Ph.D. thesis, Tel Aviv University (Hebrew).

Zevit, Z.
1976   "The Egla Ritual of Deuteronomy 21:1–9." *JBL* 95:377–90.

Zias, J.
1989   "Lust and Leprosy: Confusion or Correlation?" *BASOR* 275:27–31.

Zimmerli, W.
1985   "The 'Land' in the Pre-Exilic and Early Post-Exilic Prophets." In *Understanding the Word.* Edited by J. Butler, E. Conrad and B. Ollenburger. Sheffield: JSOT Press. Pages 247–62.

Zohary, M.
1982   *Vegetation of Israel and Adjacent Areas.* Wiesbaden: Dr. Ludwig Reichert Verlag.

Index of Literary and Social Scientific Terms

Index of Modern Authors

Index of Ancient Sources